PLAYS OF THE YEAR

Volume 12

1954-1955

PLAYS OF THE YEAR

CHOSEN BY

J. C. TREWIN

THE LONG SUNSET
R. C. Sherriff

SOUTH
Julien Green

UNCERTAIN JOY
Charlotte Hastings

SAILOR, BEWARE!
Philip King and Falkland Cary

THE SHADOW OF DOUBT
Norman King

VOLUME 12

1954-1955

London ELEK *New York*

14 *Great James Street, London W.C.*1.
Printed in Great Britain by Page Bros. (Norwich) Ltd.

CONTENTS

FOR WENDY

Naturally

INTRODUCTION

I

Under the old night's nodding hood
The sea-folk breaking down the wood
Like a high tide from the sea.

CHESTERTON

The first play in this, our twelfth, volume is THE LONG SUNSET *by* R. C. *Sherriff, author of* Journey's End. *Those last few words are inevitable: Sherriff has to go through life trailing the glory of his famous war play, record of the doomed soldiers before St. Quentin in March* 1918. *But he has done much besides; no doubt he feels that it is unfair always for* Journey's End *to be dragged in to the detriment of its successors.*

I mention it here because THE LONG SUNSET *shows again Sherriff's way of bringing us (unconsciously, I imagine) to journey's end, to the butt and seamark of the utmost sail. He is a dramatist of finality. It is rare, in a Sherriff play, that a leading character is left in mid-career: the phrase "journey's end" is never far from our lips. There are, let us remember, the soldiers of* 1918. *There is Napoleon, dying eagle, tethered to the rock of St. Helena, to the house of Longwood (Jeanne de Casalis collaborated in this chronicle). There is the little play of* Miss Mabel. *(What will happen to the dear woman—dear yet in spite of what has chanced?) And there is* The White Carnation, *with the earthbound ghost finally released. Now, in* THE LAST SUNSET, *we know, as Julian and Serena move toward the woods, that their bright day is done, that hard frost binds the land Rome has quitted: "Age-encamped oblivion Tenteth every light that shone." Only the Christian altar glimmers.*

Here we are at the end of an era: the close of the Roman occupation of Britain early in the fifth century, in what Sir Mortimer Wheeler has called "the age of crépuscule *and quicksand." It is the autumn of A.D.* 410 *in the distant province of the Roman Empire. Alaric has sacked the City; the Empire has crumbled at its heart, and, after four-and-a-half centuries under the wings of the eagle, Britain must seek a new life. For a moment the sun is down, and there is strange work beneath the cold embers of the sky: strange work in a Britain now to be a cockpit for small and sanguinary wars.*

This slipping into the dark, this gap in time, this sudden chaos in the ordered land between Vectis and the Wall, has haunted Sherriff's mind as it haunted Kipling's. Phrases flicker in the memory, "When Rome was rotten-ripe to her fall" and "After the sack of the City, when Rome was sunk to a name." The sack of the City; it is an unbelievable catastrophe, the shattering of an empire across which a man could have toiled twenty miles a day for a full year, safe under the writ of Rome.

The play, then, is shadowed by the death of what once was great. It is also lighted for us by the knowledge that a greater empire stirs to its birth, that we can call to Arthur, uncompromising Cornish soldier of fortune, "Regions Caesar never knew, thy posterity shall sway." The piece is fixed powerfully in the imagination. We are on three levels: Rome that was, the Roman province that is ceasing to be, and the Britain that will rise. Sherriff has never been a blaring, obstrusive dramatist, a man given to rantipole exhibitionism. His play is the more persuasive because it is civilised. It does not shout. If we listen between the lines we can catch in the mind's ear the failing trumpets of Rome*, the dwindling tramp of the legions, and—borne up through the stillness—the march of another army.*

Julian's celebration of the Roman *Empire is the best speech Sherriff has written for the stage. Elsewhere it is colloquial dialogue that can smoulder like touchwood, as in Arthur's remembrance of the star-sown sky of Cornwall and what he read into it. With any other dramatist, Arthur would be the night's romantic torch. Not so with Sherriff. His Arthur is an uncompromising leader of mercenaries, a most un-*Tennysonian *(and maybe more plausible) battler who comes to train the forces of the* Roman *merchants of* Richborough*. He is fiercely practical, tossing aside legend, seeking only to resist the invader by sea or land. "If you want to impress a man," he says in effect, "always talk to him with your back to the sunset; it makes you look bigger." Arthur does stand for a moment with his back to the sunset, but he goes from us into legend, into the night that Sherriff does not pierce: one that, in our history, is oddly like the dark patch, the "coal-sack", in the Milky Way. The most sympathetic personages are the* Roman *merchant Julian—liberal pagan converted at the last by his Christian wife—and the wife herself, rightly named Serena: they, too, pass quietly into the dark.*

To call the end sentimental is singularly maladroit. The pair represent, in our imagination, the end of Rome*. The light on the Christian altar behind them is the gleam that one day must widen and shine across Britain. It is piercing, this end of a world: the more affecting in the theatre because Sherriff writes without any hollow pomp.* Rome *has been for Julian, and for so many in the sundered island, a symbol of certainty. It has gone. Britain must find her own path to daybreak, the new life, the new God. Journey's end for Julian and his house, not for the land that bred him and will breed the new knights of Arthur. Meanwhile, the sun has gone, and we remember Chesterton's lines:*

When Caesar's sun fell out of the sky
And whoso hearkened right
Could only hear the plunging
Of the nations in the night.

The play, which was acted first on sound-radio in the Home Service of the B.B.C., was done movingly under Bernard Hepton's direction at the opening of the Birmingham Repertory Theatre season of 1955-56 *Even people frightened by the past, bent upon keeping resolutely in the present (with an occasional wan glance towards the future), should feel the impact of* THE LONG SUNSET.

II

Julien Green prefaces SOUTH *very simply.* " '*The purification of a dangerous passion by a violent liberation.*' *Such is Aristotle's definition of tragedy and I don't think I can give a better* résumé *of the play.*" *Like* THE LONG SUNSET, *it was acted first upon sound-radio—a medium that remains more exciting than television. In the spring of* 1955 SOUTH *reached the Arts Theatre Club during the middle of the newspaper strike. It lost a great deal of publicity. Further, the Lord Chamberlain had refused it a licence for performance in a public theatre.* SOUTH, *therefore, has stayed oddly in shadow, though many playgoers who saw it at the Arts are fervid admirers.*

The producer, Peter Hall, whose work did a lot for his dramatist, said that SOUTH (Sud *in the original*) *was a play about* "*extremes: North versus South, white man against coloured man, the old world of Europe in contrast to the new world of America, the difficulty that the sexually normal have in understanding the sexually abnormal.*" *Mr. Hall was at pains to point out that although the Lord Chamberlain had refused to grant a licence for public performance,* SOUTH *was* "*not primarily about homosexuality: this topic is only a thread in Green's tapestry.*"

Very well. The play, I think, ought to speak for itself. It is the tale of what a critic called the "doomed love" of a young officer (finely acted at the Arts by Denholm Elliott). Here I will merely set the background. It is the spring of 1861. *We are told the exact day of the month, April* 11, *a Sunday. Why is the author particularising! What does it matter to the people gathered on this torrid Sunday in the plantation house of Bonaventure in South Carolina: to the young lieutenant with the Polish name and the bitter smile, to the plantation owner who appears to carry the world's weight, to his niece from the North, or to his daughter Angelina? It should mean much. It was on this day that General Beauregard, commanding the Provisional Forces of the Confederate States, sent a message to Major Robert Anderson, commander of Fort Sumter garrison on the island in Charleston harbour, requesting the fort's evacuation. Anderson wrote a reply: "It is a demand with which I regret that my sense of honour, and of my obligations to my Government, prevent my compliance." At twenty minutes past four in the early dawn of April* 12, 1861*—the precise moment when the play ends—Edmund Ruffin, a white-haired Virginian farmer* 67 *years of age, loosed the first Confederate cannon-ball towards Fort Sumter, and the Civil War was on. It would not end until Ulysses Grant met Robert E. Lee in a house on the edge of the village of Appomatox upon Sunday, April* 9, 1865.

As an amateur of the Civil War, I wished with all my heart—though irrelevantly, I am sure—that the cast could have included the name of Beauregard. He lives for me in that short prose passage from the opening of Book Two of Stephen Vincent Benét's John Brown's Body *as he watches the United States garrison march from Sumter at the end of a brief siege, thirty-six hours of bombardment: "Beauregard,* beau sabreur, *hussar-sword with the gilded hilt, the gilded metal of the guard twisted into lovelocks and roses, vain as Murat, dashing as Murat, Pierre Gustave Toutant Beauregard is a pose of conquering courtesy under a palmetto-banner."*

There is no need, I suppose to summon Beauregard's ghost for he is outside the picture of SOUTH. He is over thirty miles from the plantation of Bonaventure—just one of the figures of the historical background. Besides Beauregard one thinks of the gallant commander of Sumter, Major Anderson, who bore away the burnt and shot-riddled flag he had defended and which he asked to have wrapped round him in the grave. The young lieutenant who wanders around the plantation house is one of Anderson's men. He should have been at Sumter. Instead, in the last second of the play, the first cannon-shot of the Civil War is fired, as it were, over his dead body. "Go, bid the soldiers shoot." They are shooting many miles away, but up in Bonaventure the windows are rattling and the veranda doors are flying open as the report of the Charleston cannon—dulled by distance—is heard in the daybreak, and in the drawing-room where the body lies.

When you read this drama of complex personal relationships, it is well, I think to remember the events beyond it, the Civil War's swelling anvil of thunder-cloud.

III

The ingenious UNCERTAIN JOY also appeared during the newspaper strike. It began its life at the Royal Court Theatre on March 31, 1955 (the night after SOUTH at the Arts) and was transferred later to the Duchess. There is thunder, too, a milder variety, above the household invented by Charlotte Hastings: everything here moves into a fair day and a happy ending. Most reasonably: we should have been bitter if the dramatist (who wrote Bonaventure**—no connection with Julien Green) had allowed anything to dull the portrait of the night's dominant child. He is a problem-child with one of the most appalling fathers in stage history, and he is cared for by a schoolmaster who understands him, and by the schoolmaster's wife, a novelist less receptive than her husband. Before the end he has almost (and unwillingly)*

**Bonaventure* was published in *Plays of the Year*, Volume 3.

cleft his guardians' house and wrecked their marriage. We are sure that the jealousy cannot last: I refer you to the text for what occurs.

Roger Livesey and Ursula Jeans were the foster-parents at the Court Theatre. A boy, Michael Brooke, played the child without any professional glossiness, a change from most Infant Phenomena. He said, a the time, that he did not want to be an actor all his days. Maybe in years to come, as Brooke, R. N., *or Brooke, Q. C., he will drop occasionally into a theatre and view the business with a knowing eye. At the première of* UNCERTAIN JOY *he seemed to be the perfect leading juvenile—in my sense of the word, not the theatre's. If ever a piece was child's play, this is it.*

IV

In the middle of Priestley's endearing London novel Angel Pavement, *we reach the party scene at* 17 *Chaucer Row, N.*16; *"'Come along, dad,' cried Mrs. Smeeth, pouring out the Rich Ruby Port for the ladies, 'Buck up. Join in the fun!' She had herself a rich ruby look, for what with eating and drinking and shouting and laughing and singing, her face was crimson and almost steaming." As I said at the time, this resembles SAILOR, BEWARE! The authors prefer to call it a comedy; it has in it most of the jests, familiar to farce, that have drawn laughter like a cork popped from a bottle. Always there will be in the mind the memory of that night at the Strand with its rich ruby look, a night when the stage was crimson and almost steaming. Mrs. Smeeth, dear soul, would have enjoyed herself immensely.*

As I say, Philip King and Falkland Cary have used almost everything—except, perhaps, kippers—that has been a sure laugh in the theatre. I would not have been surprised if the action had stopped now and then, and someone had come forward to say, more or less in the terms of the late Syd Walker, "And what would you *do now, chums!"*

Peggy Mount, who governs the play, reached London from the Worthing Repertory (where SAILOR, BEWARE! began) as an actress unknown to the West End. A day or so later she had her name in lights outside the Strand Theatre. She is abundantly a flame-thrower as Emma Hornett, agreeably named, who has for long dragooned her suffering family—domineered over it so much that the young sailor, her potential son-in-law, decides, on the morning of his wedding to Shirley Hornett, not to appear in church. In its broad generous way the farce sweeps along its audience; Miss Mount has the swirling breadth required. Wildly unlike Mrs. Smeeth, she is, nevertheless, "crimson and almost steaming." It takes the Royal Navy itself to defeat her.

V

Norman King's THE SHADOW OF DOUBT was good enough to keep its first-night audience tense with expectancy on one of the sultriest evenings of a sultry summer. It is a strung-wire drama about a nuclear physicist who has served a sentence for treason, a patently honest man who should not be under the gaze of M.I.5. Between them John Clements and Norman King did get us to believe in the man's powers. That, in itself, needs to be put on record. Think of all the hollow shams, all the turnip-lanterns that playwrights put up to us, crying as they do so: "Watch! A genius!" I can vouch for the tautness of the play in the theatre. Here now is the text.

J. C. TREWIN

Hampstead,
October, 1955.

I am grateful to The Illustrated London News *and to* The Birmingham Post *for permission to quote passages.*

THE LONG SUNSET

A Play in Three Acts

by

R. C. SHERRIFF

During the long Roman occupation of Britain, the southern part of the Island became for the first time a pleasant place to live in. Woodlands were cleared and marshes drained. New lands were cultivated and many Roman families settled in the Island, building for themselves fine country houses.

But these people lived under the protection of Roman Legions quartered in the Island. Beyond the military frontiers were natives hungering for the loot which the Roman province offered.

When final disaster came to the Empire, Britain was deserted by the Legions and the Roman population found itself totally unprepared to meet the invaders who came from every side. They were an unorganized, beleaguered community clinging to the relics of a civilisation far above the people who came to destroy them.

With the going of the Legions, Britain faded out of history for over 150 years. When the light returned the homes of the Roman settlers were deserted and a new people occupied their land.

Nothing is known about the way in which these Romans faced the end.

The Long Sunset was first broadcast in the Home Service of the British Broadcasting Corporation on April 23, 1955. The Birmingham Repertory Theatre presented it for the first time on the stage upon August 30, 1955, with the following cast:

MARCUS	*Michael Robbins*
LUGAR	*Eric Jones*
SERENA	*Nancie Jackson*
PAULA	*Doreen Aris*
JULIAN	*Kenneth Mackintosh*
OTHO	*Alan Rowe*
PORTIUS	*Redmond Phillips*
LUCIAN	*Ronald Hines*
ARTHUR	*Geoffrey Taylor*
GAWAINE	*Oliver Neville*

The play directed by Bernard Hepton

The setting designed by Finlay James

*

SERVING MAN: The master's not here at present, sir. I'll tell the mistress.

[*He gives a little bow and leaves the room.*

The visitor is a big, gaunt man in his fifties: dirty, travel-stained and exhausted. His clothes are old and roughly patched, his armour tarnished, his grey beard and hair tangled and neglected. Around one arm is an old, soiled bandage. He is a harsh, incongruous figure in this pleasant, peaceful room.

While the serving man is present, he stands erect and commanding, as becomes a Roman Officer in the presence of a native servant. But when the man has gone, his weakness overcomes him. He sinks into a chair and seeks to recover himself before his hostess comes.

Presently Serena enters, and the soldier rises to meet her.

Serena is an attractive, graceful woman in early middle age. She wears the simple dress of a Roman lady in her country home.]

SERENA: Marcus!—it's wonderful to see you again!—it's ages!
MARCUS: Yes. It's a long time.

[*She takes his hands, happy to see an old friend again.*]

SERENA: But why didn't you send word that you were coming? Julian would have been here to meet you.
MARCUS (*anxiously*): Is Julian away?
SERENA: No, he's out on the farm. They're getting the harvest in, but he'll be delighted to see you. We haven't had a real visitor—oh, for years.

MARCUS: Last time I stayed here, you had a crowd.

SERENA: We always did. Everybody came in to see us on their way to London, but nowadays the people they send here from Rome are terrible. The last one was a seedy little tax-collector who said we owed for seven years. Julian made him drunk and gave him a rabbit and the poor little man went away as happy as a king and fell in the river and got drowned. Julian just said: "That's Rome today." It's hopeless. (*She sees the bandage on his arm.*) What have *you* been doing to yourself?

MARCUS (*explaining it away*): It's nothing. Fooling about in camp the other night. . . .

SERENA (*examining the bandage*): It isn't a proper bandage at all. I'll get you a clean one.

MARCUS: Don't you worry. I'll see the doctor in the fort this evening.

SERENA (*surprised*): But you're going to stay with us?

MARCUS: I wish I could. But I'm sailing tonight. I've brought some men down from the north who are leaving Britain. I just had time to come over and see you.

SERENA: You'll be coming back?

MARCUS: Oh, yes. I hope so.

[*There is a slight silence. Marcus is making a gallant endeavour to conceal his anxiety and weakness, but Serena vaguely senses something wrong. She has been shocked by his untidy appearance and haggard face, but as a tactful hostess pretends not to have noticed.*

Serena's daughter, Paula, comes in from the terrace: a nice looking girl of nineteen, dressed like her mother in simple country clothes. She is carrying two baskets which she puts down by the wall.]

PAULA: They're wonderful blackberries this year,

mother . . . masses of them. . . . (*She sees Marcus.*) Oh, I'm sorry. . .

SERENA: Here's an old friend, Paula. (*To Marcus.*) You remember Paula, Marcus?

MARCUS: Last time I was here you were *this* high! (*Paula is perplexed and confused.*) Don't you remember?

PAULA: Why, of course!—Have you come to take Otho with you?

MARCUS: Otho?

SERENA (*laughing*): Now don't tell me you've forgotten Otho!—If you still think he's a little boy you'll get the surprise of your life. He's enormous now.

PAULA: You promised to take him to York when he was old enough, and train him to be an officer!

SERENA: He's eighteen this autumn and he's set his heart on being a soldier. Julian's hoping you'll take care of him.

MARCUS: Yes, of course I remember Otho

[*Marcus is very tired. He tries to be interested in Otho, but it is difficult.*]

SERENA. Paula, dear, he's hurt his arm. Will you bring the dressings out of the cupboard in my bedroom?—and a bowl of water. And tell Lugar to bring some wine.

PAULA: Yes.

[*She goes out.*]

MARCUS: She's a charming girl.

SERENA: I'd like her to meet more people, but there's nobody round here, and Canterbury is almost empty now . . . no society or parties or anything. But we enjoy the country life. Now, sit down and let me get this horrible bandage off.

MARCUS: There's no need to bother.
SERENA: Come on. Let me have a look at it.

[*Marcus sits down. Serena draws up a stool and begins to untie the bandage.*]

SERENA: Now tell me all the news—the *real* news. We get nothing but ridiculous rumours here. They were saying the other day that the Emperor Honorius had been murdered.
MARCUS: It's the first I've heard of it.
SERENA: They ought to punish people for talking like that. A little man who comes round mending pots and pans told the servants the other day that the Goths had captured Rome!—I wonder they don't say the crocodiles have captured Egypt. (*Pause.*) Things aren't really as bad as people make out, are they?
MARCUS (*on his guard*): We don't hear very much ourselves, up there in the north.
SERENA: We've given up the business in Canterbury for the time being. We had to. Most of our best wine came from Spain—but they've had so much trouble over there and the vineyards were ruined. As for Italy, we hadn't had any wine for years. It came by sea, and the pirates used to sink the ships.
MARCUS: So you decided to be farmers?
SERENA: Until things get right again. It was a wrench for Julian to close the offices in Canterbury. It was such an old family business, you know. One of the oldest in Britain. But he's done wonderfully well with the farm.

[*Paula returns with a bowl of water and the bandages.*]

SERENA: Put it down here, Paula.

[*Paula puts the bowl down beside Serena. The bandage is now off and Serena examines the wound.*]

MARCUS: It's practically healed.
SERENA: It hasn't. It's quite deep. It's lucky I took these horrible rags off it. (*She begins to bathe the wound.*)
PAULA: How did you do it?
MARCUS: Oh, just playing about. (*He doesn't want to talk about it, and changes the subject.*) So you help on the farm?
PAULA: Yes. We're preserving the fruit this week. You mustn't look at my hands. It's blackberries.

[*The little bearded servant comes in with a flagon of wine and a goblet.*]

SERENA: You'll have some wine?
MARCUS (*gratefully*): Thank you.

[*The little man pours the wine for Marcus, puts down the tray and goes out.*]

MARCUS: He's new since I was here last?
SERENA: Oh no. We've had him for years. Julian bought him in Canterbury for sixpence. It was during that panic when the Irish landed in Wales. A lot of people left Britain and sold their servants for anything they could get. Julian wanted a little man who was small enough to creep about under the floors and clean the flues, but he was so good that we put him in charge of all the indoor servants. He's a Caledonian—captured with his people when he was a little boy. All our servants are Caledonians now.

[*Voices are heard outside. Paula looks out on to the terrace.*]

PAULA: Here's father and Otho.

[*Julian and his son Otho are seen coming up the steps on to the terrace.*]

JULIAN (*to Otho, as they approach*): If you take a dozen men tomorrow you can clear that field by sunset.

[*Julian and Otho come into the room. Julian is a vigorous man in his fifties: a big, jovial man with the good-natured, easy-going tolerance of a well-born Roman: secure in his estate and master of his own small but prosperous world.*

If he is inclined to be self-satisfied and rather pleased with himself, he has good reason in the success he has made of his farm.

Otho is a good-looking boy of seventeen.

Both wear the practical, workaday clothing of country life: brown woollen tunics and breeches with leather strappings to the knees.

Julian carries a long, stout walking staff. Otho has a brace of rabbits which he dumps on top of the altar.]

SERENA: Here's Marcus come to see us, Julian.

[*Marcus rises to greet his old friend. Julian, taken by surprise, is less observant than his wife. He does not notice his friend's exhaustion and comes forward to shake his hands—delighted to see him again.*]

JULIAN: Marcus!—this is wonderful!—but why didn't you let us know you were coming?—(*He sees the wounded arm*)—and what have you been doing to yourself?

MARCUS: It's nothing . . . playing about in camp the other day.

JULIAN: I thought one of my young bulls had been at you!

MARCUS: You're looking well, Julian.

JULIAN: Farming. That's what does it. It's too late to show you round tonight, but tomorrow we'll make a day of it. How long are you staying?

MARCUS: I must go before it's dark. We're sailing tonight.

JULIAN: Oh, but that's ridiculous. You *must* stay!

MARCUS: So this is Otho?

JULIAN (*proudly*): What d'you think of him? He'll make a fine young Centurion by the time you've put him through it.

OTHO: I'm eighteen next month, sir. You said when I was eighteen?

JULIAN: Will you be coming back soon?

MARCUS: Yes. I hope so.

OTHO: Could you give me a letter, sir?—to the Legion Commander at York?—I could go there at once and start my training.

JULIAN: He won't leave you alone till you've taken him!

OTHO: I'd like to serve in a cavalry regiment if there's any chance.

JULIAN: Pity you can't stay a few days to see what we're doing here. I reckon this is one of the best farms in Britain now. Has Serena told you we've closed down the old wine business?

MARCUS: Yes.

JULIAN: We've always kept this old place for holidays, but when I looked round and saw what a hopeless mess these fools had got the Empire into, I made up my mind to build my own little empire on this land of mine and be damned to the lot of them. When Rome was young, every man was a farmer. It's time we got back the old pioneering spirit again.

SERENA: We're self-supporting now. We don't have to depend on anybody for anything.

JULIAN: We've got our own corn and cattle and vegetables. . . . . .

SERENA: We spin our own yarn and make our own clothes.

JULIAN: We tan our own leather for shoes and harness. The only thing we can't produce for ourselves is coal for the winter and iron for farming tools. But there's a man near Dover who mines coal and there's plenty of iron in the weald. We exchange our surplus corn for coal and iron, and there we are. (*He walks to the windows*) Of course we're lucky here, living close to the fort with a good sound garrison inside it. They say these Saxon raiders are a nuisance farther up the coast. But they never come near Richborough. They run like rabbits at the sight of a Roman helmet.

SERENA: Of course, it's quiet in the winter. We used to go to the theatre in Canterbury quite a lot, but that's closed now.

JULIAN: Still, we pass the time when it's too dark to work outside. Look what Serena's been up to.

[*He goes to the alcove and draws aside the curtain, revealing the little Christian shrine with a small lamp burning on the altar.*]

SERENA: Leave it alone, Julian. (*To Marcus.*) He's always making fun of it.

JULIAN: I never make fun of it, darling. I think it's charming. (*To Marcus.*) Have you got many Christians in the army nowadays?

MARCUS: A few. Not many.

JULIAN: There used to be a lot until the Government began to encourage it. Then it went out. Christians don't want to be encouraged: they like being persecuted. That's why I persecute Serena. She loves it.

PAULA: I'm a Christian now.

JULIAN: It's all right for women. Otho and I stick to old Sylvanus. He's a man's god. (*He goes to the altar by the terrace door.*) Otho, I've told you before not to leave rabbits on the altar. (*He takes them off and throws them out on the terrace.*)

OTHO: You left your boots on it the other night.

JULIAN: That's a different thing altogether.

OTHO: You might call rabbits an offering, but Sylvanus doesn't want your boots.

JULIAN (*by the altar*): Good old Sylvanus. We forget sometimes, but you never let us down. You never let the spring run dry. (*To Marcus.*) The natives used to worship the spirit of the spring that rises in the woods over there, but we took him over and made him into a Roman. He's been our family god for 300 years. In dry summers when everybody round here cries for water, Sylvanus goes on feeding our little river and keeping the meadows green. (*To Serena.*) That's more than you can say for that Christ of yours.

[*Serena smiles patiently and shakes her head. She is accustomed to her husband's little jokes about her faith. She finishes the bandage on Marcus's wounded arm.*]

SERENA: There you are. That's all right.

MARCUS: Thank you, Serena.

SERENA: I'd keep this on for quite a week. Don't touch it. (*She gets up.*)

[*There is a silence. Serena glances from Marcus to her husband.*]

SERENA: Now you two want to have a yarn about old times, don't you?—Come along, Paula. We must finish bottling that honey before supper.

[*Paula gathers up the old bandages. Serena picks up the bowl.*]

PAULA (*to Marcus*): I'll see you before you go?
MARCUS: Yes, Paula.
PAULA: Would you like some fruit to take with you?
MARCUS: I would very much.
PAULA: I'll pack a basket. We've got some wonderful apples this year.
OTHO: If I walk down to the fort with you, sir—could you show me round?—I'd love to see it.
MARCUS: Another time, Otho. I'm afraid it's too late now.
OTHO: Will you write that letter for me?
MARCUS: It's best to wait. Till I come back.
SERENA: Come along, Otho. You've got plenty of time to be a soldier. (*To Marcus.*) Are you sure you won't stay to supper?
MARCUS: I wish I could. I'm afraid not.
SERENA: Call out when you're going

[*She leaves the room with Otho and Paula, who takes the blackberries with her. Otho takes the rabbits.*

The two men are alone.]

JULIAN: Well, you old villain. It's wonderful to see you again. You look as if you've had some hard marching. Would you like a bath?
MARCUS: It's all right, thanks.
JULIAN: Plenty of hot water. (*Marcus shakes his head.*) More wine?

[*As Julian pours the wine, he notices for the first time how tired and worn his old friend looks.*]

JULIAN: You know, Marcus, you're getting too old for the army. You ought to retire and join us here. It's fascinating, running a good farm, wonderful feeling of freedom and independence In the old days, if there was a revolution in Africa or a usurper in Spain, I'd worry my head off in case it affected the wine market. Nowadays they can murder half a dozen Emperors a year, and it makes no difference to me. My corn grows just as tall.

MARCUS: How long is it since you had any news, Julian?

JULIAN: Oh, good heavens . . . it's ages since we had any real news. Rumours all over the place, but we don't listen to them any longer. Too much work to do.

MARCUS: I didn't realise that you'd cut yourself away from the world like this.

JULIAN: I suppose things are muddling on in the same old way?

MARCUS: Until the spring this year. Then suddenly, everything happened at once. Huns, Vandals, Moors, Goths—heaven knows who else. The whole lot of them came at us together. The frontiers all round the Empire caved in like a rotten ship. Africa's gone: the Germans are across the Rhine: Spain and Gaul are in chaos.

JULIAN (*soothingly*): Well, it's happened before. In my grandfather's time they said Rome was finished, but things got right again. We run into a bad patch, now and then—but there's always some good man who turns up at the last moment. These savages, they can't destroy Rome. They swarm into some province like a plague of flies: they sack a town—

fight each other for the spoils and destroy themselves. There's no need to worry, Marcus. Rome always gets her own back and wins the last battle.

MARCUS: Yes. It's happened so often that we didn't worry any longer. Even when the Goths invaded Italy this spring we sat back as usual and waited for a great man to come along and drive them out again. But this time there wasn't one. No leader. The Emperor and his hangers-on ran for their lives. Alaric marched through Italy without a fight and broke down the gates of Rome and sacked the city.

JULIAN (*subdued*): We heard a rumour about that. It's true, is it?

MARCUS: It was bound to happen one day. But I never thought it would be in our time.

[*There is a silence. Julian is shaken, but more contemptuous than concerned. It gives him an opportunity to harp on his own pet theme.*]

JULIAN: Well, it only goes to prove what I've been saying for years. We've got to stand on our own legs in this Island, Marcus. There's no need for us to be dragged down with the rest of the Empire if we organise these British people and train them to fight for their homes. We'll have to keep the Legions here until we can defend ourselves: but if we build our own fleet and a few more forts along the coast, then nobody on earth can touch us.

MARCUS: It might have been possible. But it's too late now.

JULIAN: Why should it be?

MARCUS (*he hesitates*): It's not a pleasant thing to tell an old friend in his own home on a peaceful summer evening like this. But the Roman Legions have given up this Island, Julian. It isn't a part of the Empire any longer. The whole Army's gone, and taken the fleet with it.

JULIAN (*incredulous*): What d'you mean?

MARCUS: After the sack of Rome, the Commanders in Britain took matters into their own hands. They were ambitious men: too big for this small Island. They saw the Empire lying in the gutter, waiting to be picked up by anyone with the strength to take it. There were four good Legions here. They persuaded them to march on Rome. I was in charge of a small outpost in the north when orders came to bring the men back. I thought it was simply a routine relief, then gradually I discovered that we had been the last troops in Northern Britain. The news was out by then. Rome was finished. Rome had gone. The Welsh tribes came pouring down from the mountains. The Scots came flooding across the Wall and the Saxons came sailing in. Every night we saw the whole sky behind us alight with burning villages and towns. London was full of refugees scrambling for places on the remaining ships. Romans were offering bags of gold to squeeze a woman or a child into the corner of a fishing boat. We had to cross the Thames before we could sleep in peace again. We got to Richborough this afternoon. Those men of mine in the fort down there are the last Roman soldiers left in Britain. When we sail tonight, it'll be the end. (*Pause.*) But I didn't come here this evening to talk about that, Julian. I came because I've got a chance to help you. There are ships to spare down there in the harbour; room for you and your family. If you load a wagon with the things you need and come down before midnight, I'll be there to meet you and we'll travel together as far as Boulogne.

JULIAN: But my dear fellow! . . . how *could* we go?—Where could we go to?

MARCUS: Haven't you any friends over there?
JULIAN: But you say the whole Empire is in chaos?—it'll be worse over there than it is here!
MARCUS: Not in the same way, Julian. These Goths and Germans, they're not savages: they come to settle, not to murder. The new people and the old settle down together peacefully, but the men who're swarming into this island—they're not human beings—they're animals. I know, because I've seen them and fought them. You can't stay here, Julian. You've got to come away.
JULIAN: But this is my home, Marcus. We've been in Britain for generations. I've no friends over there. We'd be foreigners in a strange country—sleeping under haystacks—begging for food. We couldn't do it, even if it was as bad as you think. But I'm sure it isn't.

[*Paula comes in with a basket covered with a cloth.*]

PAULA: There's something of everything here: apples, pears, plums, apricots. . . .
MARCUS: That's good of you, Paula. Thank you. (*He has risen.*)
PAULA: Are you leaving now?
MARCUS: Presently.
PAULA: You'll stay with us when you come back?
MARCUS: Yes.
PAULA: Then I'll say goodbye for the present.
MARCUS: Goodbye, Paula.

[*Paula goes away.*]

JULIAN: You've had a rough time, Marcus. Naturally things seem hopeless, but there are thousands of Roman settlers in this Island like me:—thousands of British-born Roman boys like Otho who'll fight much better than those half-hearted foreigners who made up the Legions here. It's a shock to hear what's happened, naturally—but in the long run it'll be a blessing in disguise . . . once we've organised ourselves and built up an army of good native Britons. It's no good asking you to stay and help us?

MARCUS: I would, gladly. But I'm still a soldier of the Empire: I'm still bound by my oath. (*Pause.*) You talk of organising and leading these British people, but are you sure that we Romans have done enough for them in the past to make them want to follow us now?

JULIAN: Heavens above!—we've done everything for them!

MARCUS: So long as we were masters of the world and kept a big army here, they looked up to us and respected us. But I'm wondering what they're going to think now—when they find out that the Legions have gone and we're not masters of the world any longer?

JULIAN: They can't run the country themselves. They know quite well that if we Romans don't do it, they'll go under to the Saxons.

MARCUS: They may prefer the Saxons.

JULIAN: That's ridiculous.

MARCUS: Defeated people think in strange ways. We came here as conquerors four hundred years ago and we've remained as conquerors ever since. They may prefer the Saxons for a change.

JULIAN: Then you think we're finished?

MARCUS: No. I don't say that. If you can persuade these British to work with you as partners and stop thinking of them as slaves. . . But it's going to take time to raise a native army. If I were you I'd begin with some kind of local defence. What are your neighbours like?—Are they any good?

JULIAN: There's only Lucian—he's an old man full of rheumatism—and Portius: his family were shipbuilders in the old days. We three are the only big landowners round here. We might raise 500 men between us.

MARCUS: They'll need to be trained as soldiers.

JULIAN: I'd do that myself, but it's years since I was in the army. Lucian can hardly walk and Portius wouldn't be any good. We'd need an experienced man. I wish you could do it.

MARCUS: I met a man in Winchester last year. Interesting fellow. When those Welsh tribes began making trouble, he raised a small private army of his own and helped the Romans in the Severn valley to organise themselves. Did a very good job, they say.

JULIAN: Do you think he'd come and help us here?

MARCUS: He might.

JULIAN: Would we have to pay him?

MARCUS: Naturally. He's not likely to come for nothing.

JULIAN: If he brought his army with him, it'd cost a fortune.

MARCUS: It's not an army. They're just a band of adventurers. Couple of hundred of them, I suppose.

JULIAN: What sort of a fellow is he?

MARCUS: I wouldn't call him a gentleman, but I don't think you need a gentleman at the moment. He's a thick set fellow with red hair. Probably got some of the old West country native blood in him. He calls himself Arthur. I think you'd get on with him all right because he talks in the same way as you do about making Britain strong and independent. (*He rises to go.*) Why don't you see those two friends of yours and send him some kind of proposition? He may not come. There are plenty of people who'd give a lot for his help today. (*Pause.*) You're sure you won't come with me?

JULIAN: I'll speak to Serena. But I'm certain she'd rather stay here than be without a home in a strange country.

MARCUS: Well, if you do decide, then I'll be down there waiting for you till midnight. Shall I say goodbye to her?

[*Julian goes to the door of the dining-room.*]

JULIAN: Marcus is going now, Serena.

[*Serena comes in. She also carries a small gift for the departing guest, something done up in a parcel.*]

SERENA: I've packed you some cold chicken. I'm sure the food on the ship won't be any good.

MARCUS: Thank you, Serena.

[*She pushes it into the basket on top of Paula's fruit.*]

SERENA: I'll get one of the men to carry this down for you.

MARCUS: I can take it. (*He picks up the basket.*)

SERENA: It doesn't look right—a Roman officer carrying a basket.

MARCUS: Oh, we do lots of funny things these days.

SERENA: Take care of that arm of yours. If it begins to ache, have it dressed again.

MARCUS: I will.

SERENA: Well, goodbye, Marcus. We'll be seeing you again soon?

MARCUS: I hope so.

SERENA (*at the terrace door*): Go this way. Across the terrace and through the garden. You'll be able to see my roses before it's dark.

MARCUS: Yes. I'd like to. Well, goodbye, Julian.
JULIAN: Goodbye, old friend.

[*Marcus goes out, across the terrace and down the steps. He looks back and waves goodbye from the terrace door, then he goes across the garden.*]

SERENA: Poor Marcus. He looks ill. I hope he'll be all right. His hand was trembling when I dressed his arm.

[*It is almost dark now. Lugar, the serving man, comes in with a taper and lights the lamps around the walls. Serena is standing by the terrace door, looking out across the downs towards the distant fort.*]

LUGAR (*to Serena*): Shall I close the door, madam?
SERENA: No. Leave it for a while, Lugar. It's a lovely night.

[*Lugar goes out.*]

SERENA: They're late with the lamps in the lighthouse this evening. I've never seen it dark like that before.
JULIAN: I don't expect they'll trouble about them tonight.
SERENA: Why?

[*Julian is silent. Serena is disturbed: vaguely sensing something wrong.*]

SERENA: What is it, Julian? There's something very strange going on down there in the fort. I was out in the garden just now and I could hear the soldiers shouting and singing. They were making a horrible noise . . . as if they were drunk.

JULIAN: They probably *are* drunk.
SERENA: But why?
JULIAN (*hesitant*): I'm afraid something rather bad has happened, Serena. The Roman Army has left Britain. Those drunk men down there are the last to go. They're sailing tonight.
SERENA: But that's absurd. Why *should* they?
JULIAN: It's one of these mad things that happen nowadays. There's nothing we can do about it.
SERENA: But what's going to happen here?
JULIAN: We've got to look after ourselves.
SERENA: But how can we?—without an army?
JULIAN: We shall make a new army. Britons this time. They'll be a lot better than these Germans and Spaniards and Dalmatians that have packed up and gone.
SERENA: Is Marcus going with them?
JULIAN: He had to. He wanted us to go with him on his ship to Gaul.
SERENA: But what on earth would we do in Gaul?
JULIAN: He thinks it would be safer there than it will be here.
SERENA: But what's the good of being safe if you haven't got a home?
JULIAN: You'd rather stay here and see it through?
SERENA: Well, of course! (*Pause.*) Wouldn't *you*, Julian?
JULIAN: *I* would. Yes.

[*There is a silence.*]

SERENA: It's hard to think of being here without the Roman Army. Does it mean that we're not part of the Empire any longer?
JULIAN: In a way. But you mustn't worry, Serena. Everything's going to be all right. Marcus told me

of a good fellow who might come along and train our own men for us. I'll see Lucian and Portius in the morning and we'll send somebody to bring him here.

SERENA: Shall we have dinner at the same time to-night?

JULIAN: We'll do everything at the same time. (*Pause.*) Is Otho in his room?

SERENA: I think so.

JULIAN: I'd like to speak to him.

[*She turns to go.*]

JULIAN: For the time being, Serena—it'll be best to stay in the house after dark.

SERENA (*surprised*). But my dear!—surely . . . our own garden?

JULIAN: I'd rather you didn't. For the present. (*Pause.*) Tell Otho to come here.

[*Serena leaves the room. Julian wanders restlessly to the windows. It is quite dark now. He closes the doors and bolts them. Presently Otho comes in.*]

OTHO: Has Marcus gone?

JULIAN: Yes.

[*There is a silence. Julian finds it difficult to talk to his son.*]

There's something I've got to tell you, Otho. . . . (*He hesitates.*) You know things haven't been going too well for Rome. Things began to break up rather badly last year. Rebellions, revolutions, all over the place. We've had them before, but it was worse this time. That rumour we heard about Rome being captured—it's true. It was captured.

OTHO: Well, if it's like that, then it's no good me

hanging about here until Marcus comes back. If you wrote me a letter to the Commander of the Sixth Legion and said I was your son, that would be enough, wouldn't it?—I could take the letter to York and get on with my training at once. I could leave tomorrow.

JULIAN: I was going to tell you about that, Otho. The Sixth Legion isn't in York any longer

[*Otho stares blankly at his father. Julian blunders on—trying to explain.*]

It's left Britain. The Commanders have taken the whole Army on some crazy march to Rome.

OTHO: You mean they're going to recapture Rome? Is that where Marcus was going?

JULIAN: Marcus is an officer of the Legion. He had to obey orders.

OTHO: But that's wonderful!—to march through Gaul and Italy and recapture Rome!—and Marcus wanted me to stay here till he comes back!

JULIAN: You're not trained, Otho.

OTHO: But he promised to train me!—I'll be his servant: I'll clean his armour and groom his horse: I'll do anything to be with an army in the field on a wonderful campaign like this. I'll go down to the fort and see him now. . . .

[*He turns to leave: excited and happy.*]

JULIAN: It isn't what you think, Otho. This isn't a glorious march of the Imperial Army to save the Empire. It's a sordid scramble for what's left on a dead body. It's happened before. Time and again. It's the thing that's torn Rome to pieces and thrown it in the gutter. In two hundred years we've had

79 Emperors, and 72 of them were murdered. That's a nice record, isn't it? These men will never get to Rome. Half way across Gaul they'll meet another army on its way to grab what it can get. They'll fight each other and wipe each other out. Two more armies lost and another swarm of savages pour across the Rhine. I don't want you to have any part in this madness, Otho. Your place is here—in this Island—where we're going to keep our reason and commonsense.

OTHO: You're not saying this because it's true. You're saying it for yourself, aren't you?

JULIAN: It *is* true

OTHO: You're saying it because I'm more use to you digging cabbages and planting onions. Ever since I was a boy you've told me how proud you were to be an officer in the Sixth Legion. What shall I have to be proud of when I'm your age?

JULIAN: A great deal more. If we can save this Island.

OTHO: How can you save this Island if you don't save Rome? I don't care what you say!—I'm going! —I'll get my things and go down to Marcus at the fort.

[*He turns angrily to the door.*]

JULIAN: You're not going, Otho I'm not going to have you wasted on a thing like this. Marcus won't take you without my authority, and I'm not going to give it to you.

OTHO: If your father had done this to you . . . if a wonderful chance had come, and he had stopped you because he wanted you to feed the pigs? . . . what would you have thought of *him*?

JULIAN: We've never misunderstood one another, Otho. Above all, I don't want it to happen now.

You've got to try and understand how things really are. Since the day you were born, since the day *I* was born—everything that's happened took us a step nearer to this final breakdown.

OTHO: Ever since I was a boy you've talked about "The glories of Rome"—what a wonderful thing it was to be a Roman!—Why did you talk like that if it wasn't true?

JULIAN: If I was wrong, then I'm sorry. But do you think I wanted you to grow up in an atmosphere of dishonour and defeat and disgrace?—When I was telling you of the great days of Rome I was praying to the gods that the great days would return before you were a man. I gambled on it and lost. I don't blame you for being angry. I only want you to understand that I did what I thought was right. But there's one thing I've always said that's still true today. It's still a splendid thing to be a Roman.

OTHO: Splendid to be a Roman when there's no Rome?

JULIAN: To be at the beginning of a new adventure. Isn't that a splendid thing?

OTHO: Skinning rabbits—feeding pigs?—if you'd let me go with Marcus I'd have been out there to-night on one of those ships—on the way to Rome. You take away the chance I've wanted all my life to save yourself the cost of a new slave. Does *that* make you proud of being a Roman?

[*He is nearly crying. He turns away and goes out of the room. Julian stands unhappily alone. He wanders over to the old altar to Sylvanus.*]

JULIAN: Well, Sylvanus. I've never asked much of you beyond keeping the spring going and the meadows green. I don't know whether you're any good at anything else, but do what you can,

[*He glances round, rather guiltily, to be sure that he is alone, then draws back the curtain that conceals Serena's little Christian altar, and looks in.*]

My wife and daughter think a great deal of you. Serena tells me that you can perform miracles. Well, you've got your chance now.

[*He looks through the windows towards the distant fort with its unlit beacon, then goes away to get ready for dinner.*]

Curtain

ACT TWO

Scene 1

A week later. The terrace door stands open. It is a fine, clear day.

Julian is alone. He is now dressed to receive visitors, and makes an impressive figure in his white tunic and toga. He is preparing the room for a meeting, pulling up chairs and couches to form a wide semi-circle.

He takes up a scroll of paper, examines it and spreads it out on the table for use at the coming meeting.

Presently Portius comes up the terrace steps and into the room. He is a tubby little man with a red face: dressed, like Julian, in ceremonial attire. He glances anxiously around, relieved to find that he has arrived in time.

JULIAN: Hullo, Portius.
PORTIUS (*out of breath*): They've come then?
JULIAN: They're up at Lucian's house now.
PORTIUS (*hopefully*): How many of them?
JULIAN: Just Arthur and one of his officers, that's all. (*He looks at the distressed Portius.*) What's the matter? You look worried?
PORTIUS: I am worried. A whole crowd of my slaves have gone. Disappeared in the night. Without a word. They'll starve in a few weeks and serve them right. The whole country's swarming with escaped slaves.

[*There is the sound of horses. Julian goes on to the terrace, then returns to the room.*]

JULIAN: Well. A lot depends on this meeting, Portius. (*He glances at the distressed Portius.*) It won't do any good to let him think we've lost our nerve.

PORTIUS: You can depend on me for *one* thing. *I'm* not going to give in to him. I've heard a good deal about this fellow Arthur since we met last week. When he helped those Romans in the Severn Valley, he put in an enormous bill for expenses—practically ruined them.

JULIAN: But he saved them, didn't he?

PORTIUS: He saved them, but he left them practically without their boots. He's not going to do that to us. We've got to stand up to him.

JULIAN: I don't think that'll be necessary. If he's got any sense he'll realise that we can do as much for him as he can for us.

[*The door is opened, and Lucian comes in with two strangers. The elder of the two is Arthur, a man in his thirties. He is not a prepossessing figure: thick set, with a shock of sandy hair and a broad freckled face with a deep scar on the cheek. He wears a tunic of chain mail and shabby, ill-fitting clothes that look like the cast-off uniform of a* Roman *officer. A massive sword is thrust in a broad leather belt, on the other side a dagger. He looks like a bandit. The younger man (Gawaine his nephew) is not much over twenty, tall and handsome in a bold flamboyant way. His clothes are as shabby as those of his uncle, but there is gaudy colour in them: a scarlet cloak and a royal blue tunic under silver chain mail. He carries a plumed helmet that also may have come from a* Roman *officer. His attitude through the meeting is one of amused, rather bored tolerance. Julian is taken aback by their barbaric appearance. The contrast between their outlandish dress and the fine white tunics and togas of the* Roman *aristocrats is almost ludicrous. Lucian is a tall, bent old man of more than seventy. But he has a quiet dignity, and looks like a Senator of the great Augustan days as he hobbles painfully forward to make the introductions.*]

LUCIAN (*to Arthur*): This is my good friend Julianus Licinius Severus . . . and this is Portius Flavius Albinus.
ARTHUR: This is my nephew Gawaine.

[*There is an awkward silence.*]

JULIAN: Did you have a good journey?
ARTHUR: No better than I expected.
PORTIUS (*trying to build up the conversation*): Wonderful weather for the time of year.
ARTHUR: Wonderful. (*He goes to the windows.*) Wind from the north-east, isn't it?
PORTIUS: Yes. It's cold, of course. But it always brings a dry spell for the harvest.
ARTHUR: If that's all it brings you'll be lucky.

[*There is another silence which Arthur breaks abruptly.*]

ARTHUR: Well, gentlemen. You're in a mess, aren't you?
PORTIUS (*sharply*): I wouldn't say that. We're not beaten yet by a long way. And we don't intend to be. Not if *we* can help it.
ARTHUR: You mean you don't intend to be—not if *I* can help it?

[*Lucian tries to steer the conversation on to more constructive lines.*]

LUCIAN (*to Julian*): I think you might explain what you had in mind, Julian (*To Arthur.*) Julian held strong views about the administration of this Island. Some of us considered him a revolutionary, but this disaster . . . I think it proves him entirely right.
JULIAN: Well, I simply believed that Britain should

be run by the Romans who've made their homes here, and not by a crowd of officials who just came for what they could get. I stood for an all-British army instead of foreigners. I wasn't thinking of a complete break from Rome, but we should have taken a strong line and governed Britain for the benefit of the people who lived here.

ARTHUR: If you believed in that, then why didn't you do something while you had the time?

JULIAN: I'm not trying to make excuses. We hoped for the best and let things slide. But despite what's happened I still think we've got the time.

ARTHUR: If you've got the time, then how do you propose to employ it?

JULIAN: When I say we've got time, I don't mean there's any to spare. If there was, then the first thing would be a strong central government to organise the defence of the Island in a big way, but that's impossible at the moment because the men most fitted to lead are scattered all over Britain with no chance of getting together.

ARTHUR: Who do you mean by the men most fitted to lead?

LUCIAN: The responsibility falls on men like us: brought up to organise and manage large estates. It's our duty to give a lead to the whole people in a time of emergency.

JULIAN: We must begin by organising strong centres of local resistance: self-supporting and proof against attack.

ARTHUR: You three gentlemen propose to be the first centre of resistance?

LUCIAN: Does that sound absurd to you?

ARTHUR: No. Not at all. It's very sensible.

JULIAN: If you'll look at this map I think you'll understand what we have in mind. . .

[*He goes to the map on the table. Arthur and Gawaine follow him and study the details as Julian explains.*]

You see, our three properties stand together in a good position for defence. Along the north we're protected by the River Stour: to the south we've got the marshes: over here my own land joins the sea coast with a steep cliff along its whole front. You might say we're on a miniature island.

LUCIAN: We're only exposed along the western side where my own land meets the open downs.

JULIAN: That could be protected with a ditch and palisade. Inside these boundaries we farm a thousand acres of land. We've had a good harvest. If we pool our resources we could support a small army. I think we could make ourselves impregnable against any sort of attack.

LUCIAN: If we set an example here, then other groups of Romans might do the same thing. We could establish a network of strong points right across the Island. When that's done we can set about the business of electing a new Government.

ARTHUR: What part do you propose I play in all this?

LUCIAN: You have your own small army . . . at present, I think, about two hundred men?

ARTHUR: One hundred and eighty-seven to be exact. And three boys.

LUCIAN: And that, so far as I know, is the only effective army at present in existence to defend Britain. With all respect to your men, it's not a pleasant thought.

ARTHUR: It's not much to shout about, is it?

LUCIAN: It may well be the beginnings of a fine British Army.

JULIAN: If you were to bring your own men here and set up your standard, then I guarantee you'll have a thousand men by the spring—twenty thousand when word gets round that a stand is being made to save Britain.

ARTHUR: You're paying me a great compliment.

JULIAN: We're not thinking in terms of compliments. We're all in the same boat and we sink or swim together. You and your little army can't hold this Island if the rest of us sit back and do nothing. We'll do all we can to provide food and equipment if you train and organise the men.

ARTHUR: I would be Commander-in-chief and you would be the Senators?

LUCIAN: In the way that Rome began a thousand years ago. A few farmers joined together for their own protection. They made a miniature kingdom that grew until it embraced the world. Perhaps that's how it will begin again: three farmers and a soldier, working together in the only remaining corner of the old Empire that has the will to hold its own. But we're asking you to accept a great responsibility. No doubt you would like to consider it and discuss it privately?

ARTHUR: If you like.

[Lucian rises, and goes towards the door with Julian. Portius lingers to put in a word.]

PORTIUS: We shall need a new fleet to fight these Saxons, besides an army. The Legions took every ship away.

ARTHUR (*with mock interest*): Oh yes. I was forgetting that.

PORTIUS: My family were ship-builders in the old days. On my land I've some of the finest oak trees in Britain. We could build down there in the old harbour below the fort.

ARTHUR: Excellent.

LUCIAN: You may ask yourself whether the other big Roman landowners in the Island will support you. I know a great many of them and I think I can say that the whole Roman community in Britain is waiting—and praying for a leader. I hope we've found in you the man we need.

ARTHUR: Well, that's nice of you.

JULIAN: We shall be at your service when you've had your talk.

ARTHUR: Right.

[Julian holds open the door for Lucian, and the old man, leaning heavily on his stick, limps out. Portius follows, and Arthur and Gawaine are alone. Arthur wanders to the terrace door and looks out across the downs.]

ARTHUR: These poor fish. Poor dead fish. Dead for years, and they talk as if they've just been born.

GAWAINE: You needn't waste your pity on them. They've had a good time. Plenty to eat and drink: hot baths and feather beds. They're poor fish now, but they were comfortable fish until the tide went out and left them rotting on the beach. Were they serious about all this?—about starting a new Rome?

ARTHUR: Oh yes. You could see that.

GAWAINE: You're to set up your standard here and rally the poor old British to fight for them. Funny we never thought about a standard. We'll have to get one and do things in style.

ARTHUR: At least they've got the pluck to stand their ground. Most of them went scuttling away like rats off a sinking ship.

GAWAINE: You'll be crazy if you waste your time here.

ARTHUR: I'm interested in this part of the Island.

We may not have a chance of seeing it again for a good many years.

GAWAINE: In a few months it'll be a death trap.

ARTHUR: It will be. But I've got to have supplies to see us through the winter and these men are rich.

GAWAINE: You can pick supplies up anywhere.

ARTHUR: You saw the country between here and Winchester. Deserted farms. Corn rotting in the fields: men throwing their land away and shutting themselves up in the towns. There'll be a famine next spring.

GAWAINE: Give me a dozen good fellows and I'll find enough to keep us going for a year.

ARTHUR: You know what I've taught my men. We work for what we need. We don't loot and we don't rob. If we start that game, we're finished.

GAWAINE: Well, you do what you think. But if you stay here you can say goodbye to all your grand schemes. You take my advice and start back to Winchester before it's dark.

[*The door opens and Paula comes in with a tray of wine and silver cups.*]

PAULA: We thought you'd like some wine.

[*Gawaine swings round in surprise. In her simple dress he takes her for a slave, but he has an eye for a pretty girl and she interests him.*]

GAWAINE: Well!—and who do *you* belong to?

PAULA (*not understanding*): Who do I *belong* to?—my family, I suppose. This house.

GAWAINE: You're pretty.

[*He puts his hand under her chin, raises her head and admires her.*]

GAWAINE: What are you?—German?—Greek?

[*Paula is puzzled. She has never met anybody like Gawaine before.*]

PAULA: I'm a Roman, like my parents. My mother thought you would like a cup of wine.
GAWAINE (*aghast*): You're . . . you're not the daughter of. . . ?
ARTHUR: If you had any sense you'd stop making a fool of yourself.
GAWAINE (*full of shame and apology*): I'm very sorry. In that simple dress I. . . .
PAULA: You thought I was a servant?
GAWAINE: Well, all the Roman girls I've seen, they . . . they dress up and paint their faces and give themselves airs . . . I've . . . I've never met one like you before.
ARTHUR: If you want some wine, then take it and don't blather.
PAULA (*to Gawaine*): I don't mind you thinking I'm a servant, because I am. We all work here. We all serve one another.
GAWAINE: You're very nice.

[*He takes some wine, and Paula goes to Arthur with the tray.*]

ARTHUR (*helping himself*): Don't you have lots of servants in the house?
PAULA: We used to in the old days. But things got difficult and father made them do more useful work on the farm. You're Arthur?
ARTHUR: That's right.
PAULA: We've heard so much about you.
ARTHUR: You have?—Who from?

PAULA: Oh, men who come here from other parts of the Island to do special work. They bring the news. You did wonderful things to save the people when the Irish raiders came. They say you've got a magic sword.

ARTHUR: Yes. Here it is.

[*He slaps the broad sword against his thigh.*]

PAULA: You were the only man who could pull it out of a great block of stone?

ARTHUR: That's it.

PAULA: When you carry it in battle, the enemy run away?

GAWAINE: Like rabbits.

PAULA: And now you've come to help us?

ARTHUR: If I can.

PAULA: We're very grateful to you. I don't understand everything that's happened, but it's serious, isn't it?

ARTHUR: It's not going to be easy.

PAULA: Father doesn't want you to see that he's worried, but he is. We all want to help. My brother's longing to be one of your men, but he says he couldn't ask you in case you didn't want him.

ARTHUR: You've got a brother, have you?

PAULA: He's nearly eighteen. Quite big and strong.

ARTHUR: Well, you tell him not to be afraid of asking.

PAULA: And if there's anything I can do?—We make our own clothes from our own sheeps' wool. (*She glances at his threadbare tunic.*) Could I make you a warm riding cloak for the winter?

ARTHUR: That'll be fine.

GAWAINE: You couldn't manage one for me too, could you?

PAULA: I'll try.

[*There is a silence. She prepares to go.*]

ARTHUR: Well—if you'll tell your father and the others to come in, will you?

PAULA: Yes. And I'm so glad you're going to help us. We shall sleep well tonight with you here with that wonderful sword.

[*She gives him a smile and goes away.*]

GAWAINE: Well, she's really something, isn't she?

ARTHUR: Fancy that yarn about this sword getting right across Britain!

GAWAINE: She's a wonderful girl—lovely.

ARTHUR: Well, you definitely think we ought to go tonight?

GAWAINE: Oh no. I don't think so.

ARTHUR: But if you think it's a death trap? . . .

GAWAINE: *I* don't mind a death trap if you don't. After all, we can't let these old fellows down after raising their hopes.

[*Julian returns with Portius and Lucian. They are very anxious, but try hard to appear cool and unconcerned.*]

ARTHUR: Well, gentlemen. We'll do what we can to help you.

[*There is an almost audible sigh of relief from the* Romans.]

LUCIAN: I don't think you'll have cause to regret it.

ARTHUR: I'll write a letter to my second-in-command and your steward can take it this afternoon. I'll have fifty of my men sent here at once. The others will remain at my Headquarters in Winchester.

PORTIUS (*anxiously*): But you'll transfer your Headquarters here?

ARTHUR: That I can't say for the present. For the time being I can only do for you what I did for the Romans in the Severn Valley. I'll help to organise your defences and train the men you can put at my disposal. What sort of men have you got?

JULIAN: From me, a hundred good fellows—all working on my farm.

ARTHUR: What are they?

JULIAN: Caledonians, tough little men.

ARTHUR: Slaves?

JULIAN (*nodding*): Most of them were born and bred on this farm.

LUCIAN: You can count on me for two hundred men of fighting age.

PORTIUS: I'm afraid most of mine are rather old: excellent craftsmen, but hardly fighting men. I *did* have more, but . . . I can manage about twenty able-bodied fellows.

ARTHUR: We'll say three hundred between you—with a dozen or so boys for look-outs and messengers. Now then . . . let's have a look at this map. . . .

[*He goes to the map on the table.*]

These boundaries: how long are they?

LUCIAN: About eight miles all round—but there are two miles of river and three of marsh.

JULIAN: And a mile of cliff.

ARTHUR: Get every man you can spare on to cutting strong stakes for a palisade across these unprotected downs. When my men arrive, we'll organise gangs to dig a ditch. You fill the ditch with brambles and thorns and you'll be all right.

PORTIUS: If these Saxons *do* attack, then your men are pretty good, aren't they?

ARTHUR: They can deal with most things. But it's

going to be a hard job and they don't work for nothing.

[*The Romans stiffen up as the question of the cost approaches.*]

PORTIUS: Naturally, we . . . we quite understand they must be paid. I think all three of us have taken care of our money. Personally, when things got bad, I took the precaution of burying my fortune of gold in a secret place and my friends have done the same.

ARTHUR (*laughing*): Gold?—that wouldn't be worth the bags you put it in. You can't eat gold, you can't wear it to keep the cold out or make swords and daggers with it. A mountain of gold wouldn't keep one Saxon out today.

PORTIUS (*offended*): At the moment, possibly. But its value *will* come back when things get straight again.

ARTHUR: We'll forget about gold and get down to business. I understand you were all trading in a big way. (*To Lucian.*) You were a woollen merchant? . . . (*To Julian.*) and you were a wine dealer? (*To Portius.*) and I think you were in the timber trade? . . .

PORTIUS: Yes, but we've all had to close our businesses, in these bad times.

ARTHUR: But you're careful men. When you closed your warehouses in Canterbury I'm sure you laid by ample stocks on these country estates of yours?

LUCIAN: Naturally, we did what we could in that way.

PORTIUS: We had to keep a reserve for when we start again.

ARTHUR: Then I'll tell you what I shall need. (*To Lucian.*) From you I suggest two hundred suits of woollen clothing, with woollen underwear and stockings to see my men through the winter months ahead. (*To Portius.*) From you I shall need twelve strong timber wagons for transport in my future campaigns. (*To Julian.*) From you, I think, fifty jars of good wine. The big jars, you know. Those would be the individual payments. Collectively you would supply five tons of corn, twenty bullocks and a hundred sheep.

PORTIUS (*breathlessly*): But my dear sir!—that's . . . that's an *impossible* price!

ARTHUR: If you don't think your homes and lives worth paying for—then that's your affair, not mine.

JULIAN: Personally I'll give all I have, gladly—if it goes towards the defence of this Island as a whole. I was thinking of something rather more than a business deal to hire a soldier to dig a ditch round three Romans.

ARTHUR: It *will* be something more. You admit yourselves that this small army of mine is the only thing that stands between you Romans and complete disaster. If they starve, then you're finished. I've got to keep them alive and strong enough to be the leaders of this great army you're praying for. That's what your provisions will do this winter and I'm ready to pay you in full by working for them. If I wanted to I could bring fifty armed men here next week and take the stuff. I could take everything you've got and you couldn't raise a finger. But I don't do things that way.

LUCIAN: We hoped you would make this your permanent Headquarters.

ARTHUR: That I can't say. We're all groping in the twilight. It may get darker. It probably will. I can only promise what I know that I can do. In return for those stores and equipment I promise to put this land of yours into a good state of defence and train your own men to defend it. Beyond that I'd be a fool and a rogue to promise what I may not be able to do.

[*There is a silence.*]

I'm not going to force you into anything. If you prefer not to pay, and look after yourselves, then that's all the same to me. But I must know at once because I can't waste time.

[*Lucian glances at his two friends and accepts their silence as a reluctant agreement.*]

LUCIAN: Well, we're in your hands. We must accept the best you can do for us. Naturally we would have preferred an arrangement like the one we had in mind. We can only hope that it'll lead to that in the end.
ARTHUR: All right You'd better get the lamps in that lighthouse going again this evening. You don't want to advertise to every pirate on the sea that the fort's deserted.
JULIAN: I was down at the fort with my son this morning. There's any amount of old swords and helmets that the Army left behind.
ARTHUR: Collect everything you can and get it cleaned up. You'll need all the weapons you can lay hands on. (*He prepares to go.*) Now I'll get that letter written to my second-in-command at Winchester.
JULIAN: If you'd care to use my library? . . . I've got writing materials and everything that's necessary.
ARTHUR: Good. Have you got somebody who can write?
JULIAN: I'll do that for you myself.

[*Arthur and Gawaine leave the room with Julian. Lucian and Portius are alone.*]

PORTIUS: I told you it'd be like this! The man's a bare-faced robber.

LUCIAN: I think he's honest.

PORTIUS: D'you call it honest to strip us of everything we've got? It's humiliating . . . this half-breed—whatever he is—dictating terms to Romans!

LUCIAN: We've only ourselves to blame, Portius. We've had years of warning and we did nothing. We found it pleasanter to live in a fool's paradise, but it's an expensive place to live in.

Curtain

Scene 2

Six weeks later. A grey October morning.

Serena is standing at the terrace door, looking across the downs towards the fort from which comes a distant, confused hubbub of cheering and shouted orders. A column of black smoke is rising from behind the cliffs.

Presently Gawaine comes up the terrace steps: hot, dishevelled and triumphant. He carries his sword.

SERENA (*anxiously*): What's happening?

GAWAINE: It's happened. It's all over. Best fight I've had for years. We've never had one like that before—right down on the beach.

SERENA: Were they men trying to land?

GAWAINE: Yes. My goodness, I've got a thirst! (*He goes to a tray of wine on a side table.*) Can I help myself?

SERENA: Have they gone now?

GAWAINE (*pouring himself some wine*): Those that got away did. We killed twelve of them. (*He takes a long drink and smacks his lips.*) Ah!—I needed that. Great stuff, this wine of yours.

SERENA (*horrified*): You *killed* them?

GAWAINE: Well, what d'you think?—They didn't come to play games with us. Arthur timed the whole thing beautifully. We were having breakfast when one of the look-out boys came running in to say there were seven ships out there in the distance. Arthur got everybody under cover. He wanted to catch them by surprise. I went off to fetch your husband. . . .

SERENA: He's all right?

GAWAINE: Oh, *he's* all right. He was in great form

SERENA: And Otho?

GAWAINE: He's all right too. From out there on those ships the Saxons couldn't have seen a thing, but we had a hundred men hidden away behind the rocks. They sailed up and down for a bit, spying out the land, then the first two ships came straight in, right up the beach. There must have been about twenty men on each. They'd come to stay all right because they began unloading stacks of stuff. Then Arthur gave the word and out we came, yelling our heads off. You never saw anything like it. Those little Caledonians of yours went fighting mad: like a pack of devils. The other ships didn't attempt to land. The men aboard stood shouting to the ones on the beach to swim for it, and off they went, with those Caledonians after them, strangling them and dragging them down. Funniest thing you ever saw. Arthur wanted some prisoners but your fellows wouldn't have it. They drowned all the ones they could catch, then swam back and started cutting up the dead ones on the beach. Arthur stopped that. He doesn't like that sort of thing. But he let them break the ships up and pile the bodies on it and have a bonfire. They're probably eating them by now. A nice piece of roast Saxon is something new to those boys.

[*He laughs Serena turns away, horrified.*]

GAWAINE (*gently*): Don't you worry. Your two men are all right. Otho was terrific. He sailed in with that Roman sword of his slashing out right and left. He nearly cut *my* head off. It's no good arguing with those people. You've got to teach them. That's what we're here for.

SERENA: It sounds horrible.

GAWAINE: Well, it's all over now. You won't see *them* again for a bit.

[*There is a silence. There is something else that Gawaine wants to say, but he is hesitant and rather shy about it.*]

I'm sorry this happened today because I'd made up my mind to see you about something else this morning. Something quite different. (*Pause.*) Has this thing upset you too much?—I'll do it some other time if you like.

SERENA: What was it?

[*Gawaine hesitates. He finds it difficult.*]

GAWAINE: I've been meaning to say it for a long while, but . . . you know how I feel about Paula, don't you? (*Serena turns away. It is something she has expected.*) Would you rather not talk about it now?

SERENA: If you want to, Gawaine. It's all right.

GAWAINE: She's fond of me. I'm sure of that. (*He blunders on.*) I know you people are particular about these things, but I'm really quite all right because my father was a Roman General. I haven't got anything to prove it but I know my mother wouldn't have made it up. He was a real high-class Roman

SERENA: Naturally I've known for a long time that Paula's fond of you, Gawaine. I want her to be happy and I'm sure you would do your best to make her happy—but would you be able to, do you think?—you see, it's really the question of a home, isn't it?

GAWAINE: Oh, she'd have that all right. When the Roman Governor cleared out of Winchester we took his house: a fine big place. Lots of our men are married, and when we're away like this, the women all live together and Arthur's wife takes care of them. She's very nice and Paula would like her.

SERENA: Paula's a Christian. Did you know that?

GAWAINE: Oh yes. Guinevere's a Christian, too. . . . Arthur's wife. She runs a school for the children. She's more educated than Arthur. He doesn't bother much about anything but the fighting, but Guinevere thinks a lot about what's *going* to happen when the fighting's over. She wants better people than the ones we've got today. So if *we* had children, they'd be all right.

SERENA: In the old days a girl was betrothed for a long time to the son of people that one knew. I'm not saying that against you, Gawaine. Times have changed. All I want is for Paula to be happy and well cared for. In these difficult days a man has to be very strong and good to do that.

GAWAINE: Do you like me well enough to let me try?

SERENA: I wouldn't stand in your way, Gawaine. If Paula agrees, then I think my husband would.

GAWAINE (*delighted*): That's fine!

SERENA (*at the windows*): He's coming now. I'll talk to him later and let you know.
GAWAINE: Could I come in this evening?
SERENA: If you want to.

[*Julian comes up the terrace steps and into the room. He is dressed in his country clothes, but now wears a breastplate, and a sword buckled to a leather belt. He looks very tired: rather dazed by his experience at the beach.*]

JULIAN: Well, Gawaine?—You all right?
GAWAINE (*heartily*): Yes, rather!—*I'm* all right. Great show, wasn't it?
JULIAN: Yes.
GAWAINE: Not much doubt who won *that* battle!
JULIAN: No.

[*There is a silence. Gawaine realises that he is in the way.*]

GAWAINE: Well, I'll be off. There'll be some clearing up to do down there. See you later!

[*He goes away in high spirits.*]

SERENA: Oh, Julian . . . I'm so glad you're all right. . . . I didn't realise what was happening. . . .
JULIAN: It's all over now. It was nothing much.

[*He sits down. He tries to make light of things but Serena sees how exhausted and distressed he is.*]

SERENA: Sit down, dear, and have a rest. Take those heavy boots off.
JULIAN (*with a sigh*): It's funny to fight a battle and come back to one's own armchair and slippers.
SERENA: It was terribly sudden, wasn't it?

JULIAN: Arthur doesn't say much. . . . I think he was expecting it, but I wish he could have done it in a different way.

SERENA: What else could he have done?

JULIAN: I don't think those fellows really wanted to fight. There were women and children in the other ships. . . . Just a few families looking for somewhere to settle. Their own land is very poor, you know.

SERENA: What were they like?

JULIAN: Big, lazy-looking men with yellow hair and light eyes. Not bad looking. They fought well, but all the time I had a feeling they didn't want to. They didn't seem to understand why our men were so violent. There was something rather pathetic about the stuff they landed before we attacked them . . . neat little baskets of food, a box of children's toys, and some funny little dark green trees done up in sacking.

SERENA: What did they want trees for?

JULIAN: To plant, I suppose. To make this country look like home.

SERENA: It must have been horrible.

JULIAN: It didn't seem like that. It wasn't real. There we were—all mixed up—scrambling and slipping on the seaweed, shouting and screaming—and all the time I was thinking to myself: "This is the place where I taught Otho to swim when he was a little boy." I could see the ledge of rock where we used to have our picnics—where you and I used to lie in the shade on a summer afternoon and watch Otho and Paula hunting for baby crabs in the pools when the tide was out. That was all I was thinking. They didn't seem to be my arms that were swinging this sword around or my voice that was shouting.

SERENA: Gawaine says Otho fought well.

JULIAN: Yes. I was proud of Otho. I'm glad Arthur was there to see him fight. Arthur despises us, you know.

SERENA: Oh no, I don't think so.

JULIAN: He does. He thinks we Romans are soft—pampered—finished. When I saw Otho there, fighting like a young lion, I felt like shouting at Arthur: "There's a pure bred Roman for you!—he's as good as any of you and better!"

SERENA: Gawaine told me what those little Caledonians of ours did.

JULIAN: That was different. Otho fought like a man. The Saxons fought like men, too—but those little dark creatures fought like animals. It frightened me a bit, Serena. I couldn't believe they were the same nice little men who used to go about their farm work so quietly and obediently. Their faces seemed to go black and horrible. Now they've tasted blood, I . . . (*He checks himself.*) . . . but don't let's talk about it.

SERENA: You must go and lie down and have a rest before lunch.

JULIAN: And after lunch I've got to go out and pick the rest of the apples. It doesn't make sense, does it?—Nothing makes sense nowadays. (*He sips his wine.*) What was Gawaine doing here?

SERENA: It's what we both expected, Julian. It was about Paula.

JULIAN: What did you say?

SERENA: What *could* I say?—He's quite a nice boy. . . . He says his father was a Roman General.

JULIAN: They're a funny lot—these men of Arthur's. Sitting round their fires at night they ridicule Rome for hours on end, but if you tell any of them that they're a bit above the others, they take you aside and explain it's because their fathers were Roman Generals.

SERENA: Don't you like Gawaine?

JULIAN: I don't mind him. He's young and strong and he's got courage. Those are the only things that are going to matter in the next few years.

SERENA: He told me how they lived in Winchester. I think I'd be happier for Paula to be there. . . .

[*Arthur and Otho come in. Arthur is calm: his mind seems to be on other things, but Otho is jubilant. He now wears the full armour of a Roman officer: helmet, breast-plate and tunic, no doubt salvaged from remnants left in the fort. His own short sword is in his belt, but he carries a long Saxon sword that he has taken as a trophy. There is a wound on his cheek, and his hands are bleeding. He goes straight to his mother and holds out the captured sword with mock ceremony*]

OTHO: That's for you, mother. Spoils of war!—captured it myself.

[*Serena takes the sword, but is more concerned with Otho's wounds.*]

SERENA: Otho . . . my dear! . . . they didn't tell me you were hurt.

OTHO (*touching his bleeding cheek*): This?—It's nothing much. My helmet stopped the worst of it.

SERENA: But your hands. . . .

OTHO: They'll be all right. Funny, I never noticed anything until it was over. Have they told you all about it?—it was terrific.

SERENA. Yes. They told me. But you must let me dress these wounds for you.

OTHO (*disappointed*): But aren't you glad, mother?—We gave them a tremendous beating.

SERENA: Of course I'm glad: but this cut, it might have blinded you.
OTHO (*laughing*): The way you fuss! (*To Arthur.*) Are you talking to the men this afternoon, sir?
ARTHUR: Yes. There's a lot of things I want to tell them.
OTHO: Where will it be?
ARTHUR: On the cliffs. At sunset. If you want to impress your men, always talk to them at sunset. with your back to the sun. It makes you look bigger.
OTHO (*very impressed*): I'll remember that, sir. (*To Serena.*) Now, mother—it's your turn to have some fun—with all those bits of wool and bandages.

[*Serena and Otho go out together. Julian pours Arthur some wine and takes it to him.*]

ARTHUR: Thanks. (*He drinks, then glances at Julian with a sly smile.*) Well, that flanking attack of yours was really something.
JULIAN: Was it all right?
ARTHUR: Perfect. Couldn't have been better.
JULIAN: It was the only way I could get there—down that cliff path.
ARTHUR: It might be a good idea to get those big catapult affairs out of the fort and rig them up on the cliff. You could fire big stuff with them.
JULIAN: They're not much good. I used to watch the legions practising. They couldn't hit a cow at fifty yards.
ARTHUR: They'd make a big splash. You could frighten people off with them.
JULIAN: Julius Caesar wrote a very good account of his first fight on the beach against the Britons. I've got a copy in my library. I'll read it to you one day if you like.

[*Arthur doesn't answer. He is lost in his own thoughts.*]

JULIAN: I'm afraid those men of mine got out of hand this morning.
ARTHUR: I'm going to talk to them about that. It's a good thing this happened before I went.
JULIAN: You won't be leaving us yet, will you?
ARTHUR: In about ten days. I've done what I promised: trained them, organised them. Built you a defence line
JULIAN: I know. But I did hope . . . perhaps you'd make your Headquarters here.
ARTHUR: I'd like to, but it's no good. I've got to think of the other side of the Island as well as this. From Winchester I can be anywhere in a few days I can knock hell out of anybody who tries to push in, no matter where they come from: north, south, east or west. But stuck away down here in this corner . . . you see what I mean?
JULIAN. Yes. I do see that.
ARTHUR: Still, I'm sorry to go. I've enjoyed working with you here.
JULIAN: You don't really think much of us, do you?
ARTHUR: I like you personally. I like your family. But one family doesn't alter what I think of Rome.
JULIAN: Why do you hate everything that's Roman?
ARTHUR: Well, I suppose I'm the same as any other human being. I don't like a thing when it's dead. It's the same with animals. Gulls don't like dead fish: snakes don't like dead rabbits. Something tells them to leave dead things alone.
JULIAN: Everything that's Roman isn't dead. We go on talking the Roman language: the people go on living.
ARTHUR: If you cut a chicken's head off it runs round in a circle before it dies. That's what the Romans are

doing. They look in front of them when they talk, but there's something dead in their blood that makes their brains look backwards. All they want is to bring the old, dead, moth-eaten Rome back to life again. You might as well try to make one of those dead crabs on the beach get up and run back to the sea.

JULIAN: None of us want to bring back the Rome that we've had for these last hundred years.

ARTHUR: There's no other Rome.

JULIAN: There *was* another Rome: magnificent beyond the understanding of this world of ours today.

[*He goes to a table and picks up a little ornament, a little ivory figure a few inches high.*]

This little thing. It isn't valuable: just a souvenir. There were men in the heart of Africa who used to hunt elephants and take their tusks and carve these little ivory figures out of them. They loaded them on horses and took the road that the legions built across the desert to the valley of the Nile. They followed the road to the Pyramids and across the sands of Arabia and over the Jordan to Palmyra and Antioch: then over the mountains of Asia to the Black Sea and a thousand miles along the Danube: Over the Alps and down the Rhine. They crossed the sea and landed at this harbour of ours down there by the fort. One of them came here and sold this little statue and went on until one evening he sold the last of them to the soldiers in a lonely hill station away up in the heart of Scotland a year after he left his home in Africa. Can you imagine what that meant?—to cross the Roman Empire from one corner to the other a man would have to travel twenty miles a day for a full year.

ARTHUR: Well, I suppose it helped to keep him warm.

JULIAN: Every night of that year he slept securely in some little wayside inn with the Roman symbol of welcome on its door. He paid a Roman coin to people who spoke the Roman tongue and obeyed the Roman law. Every day of the year he passed through peaceful olive groves and vineyards and fields of corn and grazing cattle. He carried no weapon to defend himself. He had no need of it. He passed great convoys carrying oil from Spain to light the lamps of Rome, and marble from Tuscany for palaces in Gaul. He'd pass the time of day with merchants bringing silk from India and amber from the Baltic: rugs from Persia for homes in Germany and glass from Syria for windows that looked out across these British downs. And do you know how that miracle began?—a few small farmers in Etruria got together to protect themselves against some people who were trying to take their land away from them. No more than perhaps a hundred men to start with. Less than the men you've got under your command today.

ARTHUR: What's all this to do with me?

JULIAN: That depends on you. You've got a tremendous opportunity. You've made a great name for yourself in this Island. There's no one else, so far as I know. You've got it in your power to give these people the same kind of security and happiness that Rome gave to the world. But you won't do it if you begin by despising and destroying the memory of Rome.

ARTHUR: You're like all the rest of them. If you speak fine words you think you can make the sun and the moon go backwards. These farmers you talk about who started Rome. There were big Empires in the world before them, but d'you suppose they said to themselves "we must remember those dead Empires and do what they did?" You bet they didn't! They cared no more for those dead Empires than I do for Rome. *They* started with nothing and *I'm* starting with nothing: no memories, no history, no examples to follow or promises to keep—It acts like magic when I say to a man: "The only thing we've got is the future and the only thing the Romans have got is the past." The things we're going to do are new things with life in them, not old worn out things that people have done before.

JULIAN: What are the new things you're going to do? —to keep a few savages out of this Island? That's not a new thing. It's the oldest thing on earth. You talk about having no history? The day you were born your little boat was pushed out on a great river of history that'll take you with it until you die. You can pull this way or that, but you'll never reach the shore and find another river because there's only one.

ARTHUR: I wasn't born on any river. When I was a boy I lived in a village of little huts on the moors in Cornwall, and I used to go out when it was dark and sit with an old man who took care of the sheep. One night he told me about the great light that lay behind the curtain that came across the sky when the sun went down—and how all those thousands of little holes were made by famous warriors who cut their way through on the night they died. There are clusters in places where a whole army of warriors who fell together climbed through together, and here and there you'll see a solitary gleam of light where one great warrior climbed through alone. There's a place in the western sky: a big dark place without a single sword cut in it. On the night before I lead my men into battle, I take them out into the fields and point to that dark place and tell them it's been kept for us to cut our own way through together on the night of our last fight. That's all I tell them and that's all they need.

JULIAN: And that's all you want to do?—to climb through a hole in the sky?

ARTHUR: Isn't it something to win the power and the glory of it? It's a long time since a new gleam of light shone through up there. Maybe those farmers of yours went through on the night they died. Since then your people gave up trying, and that's why your Empire's gone.

[*There is a silence. Julian gets up with a sigh. He is stiff from his exertions on the beach and very tired.*]

JULIAN: Well, there's still some of this good old Roman wine left. Will you have a drop more?

ARTHUR: Yes. I don't mind.

[*Julian takes the jug and refills Arthur's cup.*]

ARTHUR: I will say that for them, they did know the way to make wine. (*He drinks.*) What about this boy of yours?—Has he told you that he wants to come with me?—(*Pause.*) I won't take him unless you agree.

JULIAN: If I knew what you were fighting for, then I'd know better what to say.

ARTHUR: I've told you what I'm fighting for.

JULIAN: For the honour of crawling through a crack in the sky on the night you're killed?—For my son I'm thinking in terms of life—not death. He's only just eighteen, you know. (*Pause.*) If I let him go with you, will you do one thing in return?

ARTHUR (*on his guard*): Depends what it is.

JULIAN: There are lots of these British-born Roman

boys like Otho. This Island's their home. They've never been touched by the rotten things that destroyed the Empire. Will you be generous and give them a chance?—make it known that you want them, and let them work together, and fight together as a separate unit under your command?

ARTHUR: You mean my other men aren't good enough for them?

JULIAN: I mean that if you treat them in the right way they'll give you something that these other men of yours can never give.

ARTHUR: They'll follow me to the ends of the earth and die for me. What more do I need than that?

JULIAN: They'll follow *you* and die for *you*, but not for the things you stand for. If you're going to save this Island you'll need more than a crowd of men who follow you like sheep because they think you've got a magic sword. If you're merely fighting for your own glory, then that's enough, but if you're fighting for something bigger, then you need some young men who can go with you all the way.

ARTHUR: In other words, I need Romans?

JULIAN: Not because they're Romans.

ARTHUR: You tell me they can give me something, but you don't say what it is?

JULIAN: If I did, then you'd laugh at me and say I'm using fine words again. They *are* fine words, but you don't hear very much of them today. Ideals: loyalty: devotion to great purposes that make a man stand by his leader in defeat as well as victory. They're bred in these Roman boys through generations of service to the Empire. The Empire's dead, but the fire to serve still burns in them because they're young. Why do you throw away a precious thing like that when you can so easily make your purpose theirs?

ARTHUR: What are my other men going to say if I bring in a bunch of Romans?

JULIAN: Forget the word "Romans". That's the least important thing. All the great leaders of the past gathered young men like these around them and made them their knights. You said just now that you're going to talk to the men this evening with your back to the sunset because it makes you look bigger. When you've finished, turn round and see how much bigger your destiny looks with the sun behind it.

ARTHUR: Destiny?—What does *that* fine word amount to?

JULIAN: You'll find out: if you think quietly about it until it's dark.

[There is a silence. Arthur doesn't quite know what to make of Julian.]

ARTHUR: When we were walking round the sentry posts on the cliffs the other night, you said that the sun takes longer to set over Britain than it does down south over Rome.

JULIAN: It takes longer to rise, too.

ARTHUR: What exactly did you mean when you said that?

JULIAN: Only that it's in the nature of men to do their best and deepest thinking when the sun's going down. That's why we're lucky to live in this northern Island. We think more slowly. All our ideas come from the south, you know, but we take them and let them mellow and deepen in these long sunsets of ours. There used to be an old saying that children born in the sunset were the ones who came to greatness. I'd like to think that Arthur's knights were born in the sunset of an Island that once belonged to Rome. (*Serena returns.*) Well?—Have you patched him up?

SERENA: As best I can. He doesn't seem to realise how easily that wound could have blinded him. (*To Arthur.*) He's going with you, isn't he?—when you leave?

ARTHUR: What about both of you coming as well?

SERENA (*surprised*): I don't think we could possibly do that.

ARTHUR: There's lots of ways you could help my wife. She's full of ideas, but she needs somebody like you to talk to and help her. I want a good man, too: somebody that understands farming in a big way. There's going to be a famine in this Island if we don't get the farms working again. I'd do the fighting and you'd take the land and get stuff growing like it does here. Instead of these thousand acres you could have a hundred thousand with all the men you need, and make a real thing of it.

SERENA: I don't see how we *could* leave here. You see, nearly all our servants are Caledonians. They're wonderful people, but they depend on us for everything.

JULIAN: It isn't only that. There's poor old Lucian: he's getting on for eighty. He can hardly walk. He wouldn't leave his home.

SERENA: And Portius and his wife. She's an invalid and he's really not much good. When this happened we all agreed to stay together and help one another. And when you've gone, Julian's the only one who can take charge.

ARTHUR: Well, if you feel like that . . . there's no more to say.

SERENA: Are you going soon?

ARTHUR: In about ten days. We'll travel with the next full moon.

SERENA: You don't mean that *nobody* ought to stay here?—that everybody ought to leave?

ARTHUR: I didn't mean that. You'll be all right.
SERENA: It's only for the winter, isn't it?—In the spring you'll be back with a big army and garrison the forts along the coast again?
ARTHUR: Yes. That's what I plan to do.

[*He picks up his helmet, goes out across the terrace and down the steps.*]

SERENA (*watching him go*): He's a strange man. (*Pause.*) Why do you think he asked us to go with him?—He must have known that we couldn't leave here?
JULIAN: I suppose, with Otho and Paula going—he thought it was the right thing to do.

[*He looks out of the windows towards the cliffs. The smoke from the burning ships has nearly died away.*]

JULIAN: If you feel you'd like to go, Serena. . . . I'd miss you, naturally—but I'd manage all right.
SERENA (*surprised*). But you wouldn't *want* me to go, would you?
JULIAN: I wouldn't want you to stay on my account. I've got to be here in any case, but if you'd rather be with the children. . . .
SERENA: Would *you* go?—if it were possible?

[*Julian hesitates.*]

JULIAN: I don't see that we can ever leave here from now on, Serena. It used to be our home but today it's our world. You can leave your home and go on living, but if you leave your world, you become a ghost, and that's what we should be if we went to Winchester with Arthur. Does it make you unhappy to think of it in that way?

SERENA: No. It's what I've felt, ever since the night we stood out there on the terrace and watched the last of the Roman Army sail out of the harbour. You said it was the end of an old world and the beginning of a new one, but I don't think either of us really believed that we should *belong* to the new one.

JULIAN: When big changes come suddenly like this, it's as if a curtain comes down to separate the young from the old. Otho and Paula on one side: you and I on the other.

SERENA: But can people live like that?—when their own world dies and leaves them—out of reach of the one that's coming?

JULIAN: We couldn't if we'd chased after what was left of the old world by sailing to Gaul with Marcus or gone groping after the new one with Arthur.

SERENA: But can we hold out here when Arthur's gone?—I'm not afraid to know the truth, Julian.

JULIAN: Of course we can hold out. We've built ourselves a fortress here with a well trained army to hold it. There's nothing to worry about, Serena, we can feed ourselves off our land and support ourselves in everything. We were lucky to make a little world of our own before the crash came. It may be a small world, but it's healthier than the one that's gone and I shouldn't be surprised if it isn't better than the one that's coming.

Curtain

ACT THREE

Scene 1

The day of departure. There is snow on the downs beneath a dark November sky.

Some bales of luggage are stacked beside the terrace door, and as the scene opens, Lugar, the serving man, comes in with two more strapped bundles which he puts down beside the others.

He is going out again when he sees Arthur coming up the terrace steps. He turns to let him in, closing the door after him to keep out the cold air.

Arthur is dressed in a heavy riding cloak and woollen cap.

ARTHUR: Is your master here?
LUGAR: He's waiting for you, sir.
ARTHUR: You better get that stuff loaded up.

[*Lugar bows and leaves the room. Presently Julian comes in.*]

JULIAN (*looking out at the snow*): Well? Is this weather going to affect you?
ARTHUR: It'll be all right. These worn out roads: I'd rather travel on snow than mud. The convoy got off at dawn.
JULIAN: Yes. I saw them go.
ARTHUR: We shall catch up with them in Canterbury by midday. If we're lucky we'll be in Rochester for the night. Then keep along the river valley. (*Pause.*) I said goodbye to Lucian last night. He talks about getting up and doing his share of duty—but he'll freeze to death, hobbling round with that lame leg.

JULIAN: His steward is a good man. I'll make him my second-in-command.
ARTHUR: In weather like this when you can't work the land, get the men out on field manoeuvres. Send some across the borders and let them spring a surprise attack. Keep them busy.

[*Lugar comes in with a tray containing a jug, glasses and a dish of cakes. He puts it on the table, then opens the terrace door and begins to carry out the bales of luggage.*]

ARTHUR (*to Lugar*): There's a couple of my men with the horses out there to help you load up.

[*Lugar proceeds with his task. When all the luggage is on the terrace he closes the door and begins to carry the bales down the steps and away to where the horses are waiting. Arthur goes over to the big jug on the tray and looks into it curiously. It is steaming.*]

ARTHUR: What have you got here?
JULIAN. Mulled wine.
ARTHUR: Mulled?—What's that?
JULIAN: Oh, just wine with ginger and nutmeg in it, heated up with a red-hot iron. It's what you want for a journey on a day like this.

[*Serena comes in with Paula and Otho, who are clad in warm cloaks and hoods. The boy and girl are full of high spirits and excitement over the coming journey, and Serena is making a valiant attempt to respond.*]

SERENA: These children!—they'd forget everything if you didn't run after them the whole time!
OTHO: She's made me put on so much I can hardly walk!

ARTHUR: You'll need it

PAULA: When I got up this morning and saw the snow, I knew that it was a good omen. I love riding in the snow.

[*Gawaine comes up the terrace steps. Paula sees him.*]

Here's Gawaine.

[*She runs to the door and opens it for him. Gawaine is clad in a heavy grey cloak like Arthur's. He comes in and gives Paula a boisterous embrace.*]

GAWAINE: This cloak!—it's wonderful!

PAULA (*happily*): Is it comfortable?

GAWAINE: Makes me feel like an Emperor.

[*Julian has been pouring the mulled wine. He hands it round.*]

JULIAN: Now then, you travellers—here's something for the journey!

GAWAINE (*drinking*): This is wonderful! We'll get to Rochester all right on this stuff!

SERENA (*to Arthur*): You'll never get to Rochester to-day, will you?

ARTHUR: If the snow keeps firm. It's a good road from Canterbury.

SERENA: It's over thirty miles.

ARTHUR: There's a full moon. We may not be there till midnight but it's the only place to stay.

GAWAINE: If we don't get there it doesn't matter. We've got two wagons rigged up for sleeping in.

SERENA: You'll be frozen, sleeping in wagons in this weather.

GAWAINE: Not in *our* wagons. It's an idea we got

last winter, up in the Welsh hills. You light a brazier underneath and you're as warm as toast.

SERENA (*startled*): A brazier?—underneath the wagons? It sounds terribly dangerous.

GAWAINE: There's an iron sheet over it. You can always get out if you smell burning.

ARTHUR (*raising his wine to Julian*): Well, here's to you and this little fortress of yours. Keep the lamps in the beacon going. We shall look for them when we come back one summer night.

JULIAN (*to Arthur*): Here's to the future King of Britain. Is that saying too much?

ARTHUR: It may be. But there's no harm in saying it.

JULIAN: We shall be thinking of you this winter.

ARTHUR. We shan't forget you down here.

[*Lugar has come up the steps on to the terrace He enters the room and stands by the door.*]

(*to Lugar.*) Ready?

LUGAR: All ready, sir.

ARTHUR: Well, we must go. (*He turns to Serena and takes her hand.*) Goodbye.

SERENA: Until the summer. It's not a long time. In two months the evenings will be getting light again. After then, we shan't worry.

ARTHUR: The first men I can spare I'll send back here to garrison the fort. You won't recognise this Island by the time we've done with it. (*To Julian.*) Goodbye and good luck. Keep your men together and you'll be all right.

[*Gawaine joins in the final leave-taking and goes with Arthur. Paula and Otho are left alone for a moment with their parents.*]

PAULA: Goodbye, mother.

SERENA: Goodbye, darling. Take care of yourself.
PAULA: I'll write as soon as I can.
SERENA: We'll send you letters every month.
PAULA. And you'll come and stay with us?
SERENA: Of course we shall. Everything's going to be all right.

[*They embrace. Paula turns to say goodbye to her father.*]

OTHO (*to Serena*): Goodbye, mother. And thanks for so many things.
SERENA: Goodbye, dear. I'll keep your room as it is for when you come back. You won't be far away. In the summer it's no distance at all from Winchester.
OTHO: On a good horse it's two days, that's all.

[*They go together to the terrace door.*]

SERENA: The lunch is in the little basket in the green cloth.
OTHO: Don't you worry. We shan't forget the lunch!

[*He stops by the altar to Sylvanus and gives it an affectionate pat of farewell.*]

Goodbye, Sylvanus, old chap. Behave yourself!

[*Julian and Serena stand by the terrace door as Otho and Paula hurry down the steps and away to join Arthur and Gawaine by the horses. They remain by the door for a little while, then wave, and call a final goodbye. Then they return to the room and Julian closes the door.*]

JULIAN: Well, there it is.
SERENA: I was dreading this, Julian—but it wasn't

so bad in the end. It's been such a rush I hardly had time to think. I can't believe they've really gone.

JULIAN (*by the window*): I don't think there'll be any more snow. They'll make good going on this.

SERENA: I hope they get to Rochester tonight. I hate the idea of them sleeping in wagons with fires burning underneath.

JULIAN: It sounds rather a good scheme. We'll put one under our bed one night and see what happens.

[*There is a silence. Both are feeling the sudden emptiness, now that their children have gone.*]

SERENA: It'll be strange for a while, without them.

JULIAN: We'll pass the time all right. The other day when I was helping Otho clear out that box of his, we found the old draught-board. D'you remember? —We used to play every night at one time. We'll get it out and have a winter tournament. Three games every night after supper.

SERENA: I've almost forgotten how to play.

JULIAN: You'll pick it up again.

SERENA: Are you going round to see the men on guard this morning?

JULIAN: Yes. Quite soon. Lucian's steward will be my second-in-command now. We shall take duty in turns: twenty-four hours on, twenty-four off.

SERENA: Does that mean you'll be out the whole night?—every other night?

JULIAN: Oh no. We've got good fellows in charge of all the sentry posts. It simply means going round once every evening after dark.

[*Serena is restless.*]

SERENA: Well, it's going to be a long day. It's only

breakfast time—and we seem to have been up for hours.

JULIAN: You didn't get much sleep last night. Have an early lunch and then turn in for a bit.

SERENA: I don't feel I want to lie down and do nothing. After lunch, why not put on our snow boots and go for a walk along the cliffs?

JULIAN: That's a good idea. I'll take you round and show you how we've got the place protected.

SERENA: We can watch the sun go down across the bay, and by the time we get back it'll be time for supper. You used to read aloud after supper in the old days.

JULIAN: I tell you what we *will* do! I've always been meaning to start that History of Britain I used to talk about. With Otho and Paula running round there was never a quiet moment, but what about you and me doing it together now?

SERENA: I wouldn't be any good at that.

JULIAN: Why not?—We've got all those family letters in the library. They go back for years. Nobody's written a good history of Britain. Every night we'll draw the curtains and settle down. We'll hardly notice the dark evenings at all.

SERENA: All right, then. We'll start after supper tonight.

[*She has been collecting the glasses together on the tray. She picks it up to take it out.*]

JULIAN: That was a wonderful hot drink you made.

SERENA: I'm afraid it was the last of the ginger and the nutmeg.

JULIAN: Really?

SERENA: I always kept a little in reserve for some special occasion. I never thought it would be for anything like this.

JULIAN: Oh, well . . . it might have been a lot worse. Otho might have gone on that crazy march to Rome. Then it *would* have been goodbye. (*He goes to the sideboard and collects some papers together.*) I've got to make out these duty rolls this morning. Then we'll have an early lunch and away we go along the cliffs. (*He sits at the table and prepares to work.*) You might tell Lugar to come in, will you?
SERENA: Poor Lugar. He's going to miss the children. He was almost crying when he was packing their things last night. I never realised how fond he was of them.

[*She goes out. Julian begins to work at the table. Presently Lugar, the serving man, comes in.*]

JULIAN: There are one or two things I want to tell you, Lugar. Now that Arthur and his men have gone, I shall be in charge of the defences with Lucian's steward as my second-in-command. Every other night I shall be on duty. That means I must go out—quite late, sometimes. With Master Otho and Miss Paula away, my wife may be lonely here.
LUGAR: You would like more servants sleeping in the house?
JULIAN: How many are sleeping in at present?
LUGAR: Only three women and myself, sir. That is the cook and her daughter and Mistress Serena's maid.
JULIAN: That's all right. But I want three good men to patrol the gardens of the house on the nights when I'm out on duty.
LUGAR: Very good, sir.
JULAIN: There are lots of these wandering vagabonds in the country now. On a dark night they might possibly get through somewhere. I don't think it's likely, but we must be prepared for these things.

LUGAR: I'll arrange everything, sir.

JULIAN: Are the people in good spirits?—quite happy?

LUGAR: I think so, sir.

JULIAN: How do they feel about Arthur and his men leaving us?—Does it trouble them?

LUGAR: They say nothing, sir.

JULIAN: What does that mean?

LUGAR: They were fond of Arthur, sir. But not of his men.

JULIAN: Yes. I know that. (*Pause.*) You understand your position as my chief servant?

LUGAR: Yes, sir.

JULIAN: You're in closer touch with the people than I am. I expect you to report to me everything I should know.

LUGAR: I understand, sir.

JULIAN: Have you anything to report now?

LUGAR: Nothing, sir.

JULIAN: Are you sure of that?

LUGAR: What should there be to report, sir?

JULIAN: Who were the two men who came over the downs last night—just after sunset?—Two small, dark men who came up to the ramparts and talked for a long time with our men at the sentry post near the quarry.

LUGAR (*hesitating*): I know nothing of that, sir.

JULIAN: The sentries at that post were your own people—Caledonians. One of them was your own son. You saw your son this morning?

LUGAR: He comes to see me at my room, sir. Every morning.

JULIAN: Did he tell you of these two men on the downs last night?

LUGAR: You must be mistaken, sir. I know nothing of two men on the downs.

JULIAN: I'm not mistaken, Lugar. It was reported to me by the men who went out last night to bring the cattle in when the snow began to fall. They saw the two strangers standing there, talking to our sentries on the rampart.

LUGAR: They may have been our own men, sir. They sometimes cross the rampart to snare the rabbits in the far bank.

JULIAN: But they went away again and disappeared in the woods.

LUGAR: I know nothing of it, sir.

JULIAN: You've nothing to tell me?

LUGAR: Nothing, sir. The men who went for the cattle must have been mistaken.

JULIAN: Very well. (*Pause.*) You understand that I still trust you to tell me everything?

LUGAR: Yes, sir.

JULIAN: You'll find the old draught-board in Master Otho's room. You might bring it in here later on.

LUGAR: Very good, sir.

[*Julian nods dismissal to his servant. Lugar goes away. Julian returns to his papers and tries to work. But he is troubled, and cannot concentrate.*]

Curtain

Scene 2

Evening on the same day.

The room is empty until Julian and Serena come up the steps and let themselves in by the terrace door. They are returning from their afternoon walk. They knock the snow off their boots before they come in.

SERENA: That was wonderful. We must have walked ten miles.

JULIAN: Not quite that—about five.

SERENA (*happily*): It's one thing nobody can take away from us: the cliffs and the sea and the downs. Standing out there just now, looking across the bay, I forgot for a minute that anything had ever happened. We were back in the old days again. I can't think why we gave up going for these long walks in the afternoon.

JULIAN: Tomorrow we'll go along by the river, another day the downs, then the cliffs—and the sea shore: we'll plan a different walk for every day of the week. Mind you—in the spring, when the farm gets busy, we'll have to cut them short.

SERENA: It's all right in the spring. I can work in the garden while you're out on the farm. It's only these winter days when it's dark so early. If you stay indoors, you think of all the frightful things that might be going on outside until you're almost afraid to look out of the window. But this afternoon—it was wonderful to see all those sentry posts along the cliffs with the log fires blazing—and the men singing those queer little Caledonian songs of theirs. I felt as if we were on a great strong ship.

JULIAN: One of these night when it's fine I'll take you up to the top of the hill to see the fires burning in a great circle round the boundaries: you'll feel better still when you see those fires and know there are men on guard beside them all night. At six o'clock this evening Lucian's men take over, and ours go back to the village to their own beds and a day on the farm. It's a funny life. One day farmers, next day soldiers.

SERENA: At six o'clock this evening *you* come off duty?

JULIAN: At six o'clock, Lucian's steward takes over and I'm free until tomorrow night. So after supper we'll settle down and write Chapter One of the History.

SERENA: Where shall we start?—with the ancient Britons?—before the Romans came?

JULIAN: I don't know much about those days. We'll begin with the landing of Julius Caesar and finish up with Arthur. That'll keep us busy till the summer.

[*He goes to the terrace door to draw the curtains and looks out in surprise.*]

Here's Portius coming.

SERENA (*annoyed*): Oh, I don't want to see him to-night—he'll go on for hours about his wife's neuralgia.

JULIAN: He's in charge of stores and supplies now. He's probably got some new scheme.

SERENA: He won't want to stay to supper, will he?

JULIAN: Oh no. His wife doesn't allow him out after dark. You go along and have a rest before dinner.

[*Serena leaves the room. Julian opens the terrace door and goes out to wait for Portius, waving to him as he approaches. Twilight is coming, and while Julian is outside, Lugar the serving man comes in with a taper and lights the lamps in the wall brackets. He draws the window curtains, but seeing Julian outside, he leaves the curtains undrawn across the terrace door. He goes out of the room and presently Portius comes up the terrace steps.*]

(*Cheerfully.*) Hullo there!—come along in. Don't often see *you* at this time in the evening!

[*Portius doesn't answer. He is pale and subdued.*]

JULIAN: What's the matter?—What's happened?
PORTIUS: Lucian's dead. He's been murdered.

[*He fumbles for a chair and sits down. He looks like a dead man himself, ghastly in the flicker of the oil lamps.*]

PORTIUS: My wife and I were going to have supper with him. There were no servants to meet us when we arrived. The door was open but no one answered when we knocked. I went in, through the hall and the dining-room and the long corridor. Nothing was disturbed: it was just deserted. I went to Lucian's private room. He was sitting in his chair beside the bed—murdered. Over by the window his steward was lying across a couch—dead too. Outside in the stables I found an old man . . . Lucian's personal servant. He'd escaped and hidden, and he told me what had happened. London's been taken by an army of escaped slaves. They call themselves the army of liberation. They say the leader is an African Negro. He sent out orders for all slaves to murder their masters and join him.
JULIAN: Why should they murder their masters?
PORTIUS: A symbol of freedom, that's all Those who refused to carry out their orders were to be branded as traitors and outlaws.
JULIAN: When did this happen?
PORTIUS: This afternoon. Some of the men went to the big house. They told Lucian their orders and asked him to forgive them for what they had come to do. They were fond of Lucian. They had no wish to do it, but they murdered him out of fear of what might happen to their wives and children if they disobeyed their orders. When his steward tried to save him they killed him too.
JULIAN: Have they gone?

PORTIUS: Men, women and children—they've all gone. They took the road for London with everything they could carry. Very quiet and orderly they were. They must have passed within a hundred yards of my house, but I heard nothing. Lucian's people were always quiet and well behaved.

JULIAN: What about your own?

PORTIUS: They chose another way. They followed Arthur's men when they left at dawn this morning. I wasn't surprised. They were British. I had a feeling that they would go with Arthur.

JULIAN: Are you alone up there now?—you and your wife?

PORTIUS: There are four old men, old ship builders. They were not slaves.

JULIAN: Well, it's not going to be easy for us, Portius. But we must re-organise things as best we can. You and your wife had better come and stay with us here. Bring those old servants with you. I'd come this evening if I were you. In the morning you can send over for any personal things you need.

PORTIUS: That's really what I came to tell you, Julian. We're leaving here tonight. It's impossible to stay.

JULIAN: How *can* you leave?

PORTIUS: I must think of my wife. You can imagine her state of mind after what happened at Lucian's house this afternoon.

JULIAN: But you can't get away from here. Where could you go to?

PORTIUS: There's something I've always had in mind if a thing like this happened. I've always kept that old boat of mine that we used to go fishing and sailing in. It's a good seaworthy craft. There's a small cabin for my wife and these old men of ours can handle it quite well. It's down in the shipyard by the harbour. They're getting it ready now and we're sailing at the turn of the tide this evening. . . .

JULIAN: Where to?

PORTIUS: We shall make along the coast to Porchester: then across to the Isle of Wight where my brother lives. I'd ask you and Serena to come with us, but. . . .

JULIAN: That's all right.

PORTIUS: I don't want you to feel I'm letting you down, Julian, but I've got to think of my wife . . . in her state of health she'd lose her reason if she stayed here.

JULIAN: I think you'd be safer with us, but that's your own affair.

PORTIUS: It's not safety we're thinking of. My wife and I . . . we're not such children as to think there's safety for any of us in this world of ours today. It's moving about: doing something: going somewhere, no matter where it is. That house up there in the woods: we loved it in the old days because it was quiet and secluded—but now this awful waiting in the silence and the darkness, it's. . . .

JULIAN: Yes. I know. It's very difficult. (*Pause.*) Well, you better be getting along before it's dark, hadn't you?

PORTIUS: If we thought we could be of any use we'd gladly stay—but you're better off without us . . . with your own men. Have you heard what happened on the coast north of here last night? There was an appalling raid. These Saxons. They landed and burnt Reculver to the ground. It's Arthur's fault. That man was a curse and a menace to us all.

JULIAN: Why should it be his fault?

PORTIUS: You know quite well. The way he attacked those people who tried to land here the other day. They would have been friendly enough if we had treated them as friends. But Arthur chose to attack them and murder them and drive them away with murder in their blood—and they came back last night to murder.

JULIAN: Well, it's nice to talk to somebody who's cheerful and reassuring, Portius.

PORTIUS: There's no need for *you* to worry. These Caledonians of yours enjoy fighting. I'm thinking of those poor defenceless people in the fishing villages. Arthur didn't care what happened to *them* after he'd gone. Or us, for that matter. Lucian wouldn't have been murdered if it hadn't been for Arthur. It was Arthur's men who treated Lucian's servants like animals and drove them to join this army of slaves in London.

JULIAN: Arthur did the best he could. I don't blame him for anything. You'd better get along and see to that boat of yours. I shall have a lot of work to do this evening.

PORTIUS: May I say goodbye to Serena?

JULIAN: No. I don't think so. She's resting. (*Pause.*) Well, I hope you have a good journey. You'll need plenty of blankets.

PORTIUS: Well—goodnight, and good luck We shall meet again in happier days.

JULIAN: We may. Goodnight.

[*He watches Portius as he goes away. Then he returns and closes the door. The full moon is coming up over the downs. He picks up a small hand bell and rings for his servant. He waits, but Lugar does not come. He rings again. Presently Lugar enters.*]

JULIAN: I expect you've heard what's happened, Lugar. We shall be alone here now: you and your people, my wife and I. It's not going to be easy for us, but we can defend ourselves. Our men will have to stay on duty tonight, now that the others have gone. I want you to go round and tell the commanders of each post to stand by until I come to see them myself. Arrange for the women and boys in the village to take food up to them. All right, Lugar. You better start now. There's a good moon up. You won't need a lantern.

[*There is a silence. Lugar does not go.*]

Is there something you want to say?
LUGAR. There is something, sir.
JULIAN: Well?—What is it?
LUGAR: We have to go, sir. We have orders to leave here and join our people in the north.
JULIAN: Your orders come from me, Lugar.
LUGAR: I'm sorry, sir. We have no choice.
JULIAN: I told you this morning that I trusted you, Lugar. I still trust you, and I trust all your people. Tell me what's happened and I'll see what I can do.
LUGAR: When the Roman Legions gave up the Great Wall, sir—our people broke down the gates and came through. They left the poor mountain country and took the good land below the wall. They have their own kingdom now and their own king who has ordered all his people still in servitude to return home.
JULIAN: But this *is* your home, Lugar. More than half your people were born here. You're not in servitude. I've never treated you as slaves.
LUGAR: We *are* slaves, sir. We're happy here, but we still belong to the north. When we were called back, we knew that we must go.
JULIAN: Who brought you these orders?—the men who came across the downs last night?
LUGAR: Those men and others, sir. For some weeks they've been coming to our people in the night.
JULIAN: Do you realise what this means, Lugar?

LUGAR: We understand what it means to you, sir. We're very sorry.

JULIAN: I'm thinking of you as well. Do you know how far it is to the north? Some of your people are old. Do you think they can travel 400 miles at this time of the year?

LUGAR: We shall help those who're old, sir. Travelling is never hard when one is going home.

JULIAN: Are you all agreed on this?—they all want to go?

LUGAR: We have no choice, sir. Those who disobey the order to return will be branded as traitors and outlaws.

JULIAN: What other orders were you given?

LUGAR: We were ordered to kill you before we go, sir. But not to rob you.

JULIAN: Why not rob me as well?

LUGAR: Our king doesn't want his people to be robbers. But they can't be free so long as their masters are alive.

JULIAN: I see. Well?—when are you going to kill me?

LUGAR: We have no wish to kill you, sir.

JULIAN: If you've orders to do it—won't you be in trouble if you don't?

LUGAR: If it were known, sir, then we *should* be in trouble. But we are all agreed to say that we *did* kill you. If we say it with one voice, it will be believed.

JULIAN: Do you think if I spoke to your people and asked them to stay with me until the spring? . . .

LUGAR: That would be impossible, sir. There are spies in the woods—watching us—waiting to see that we obey. If we fail now, then we shall never be allowed to return: we shall be enemies of our own people.

JULIAN: When are you going?
LUGAR: In the morning, sir. The sentries will remain at their posts until it is light Then we must go.
JULIAN: Very well. You can take three of the wagons for the older people, sufficient food for a month's journey, a few cattle and sheep. I shan't need them.
LUGAR: We've orders not to rob you, sir.
JULIAN: Oh, well, you must work it out the best way you can. If those old people of yours are to see their native land again, then you'll have to have some means of carrying them. (*Pause.*) You realise of course that your mistress and I will be entirely alone?
LUGAR: I realise that, sir. It grieves me very much. You've been very kind to me. For my own part I would gladly stay. But I have to think of my children.
JULIAN: Yes. We all have to do that.
LUGAR: It may be hard for them if it were known that their father was an outlaw.
JULIAN: I'm not blaming you, Lugar. I understand.
LUGAR: There's one other thing, sir. I wouldn't be happy in years to come if I were to leave you to-morrow as an escaped slave. If you will allow me, I would like to buy my freedom.

[*He fumbles in his tunic and pulls out a little bag of money.*]

JULIAN: That's all right, Lugar. You needn't worry.
LUGAR: It's something I've always looked forward to, sir. I hope you won't deny me the privilege? You paid sixpence for me in Canterbury thirty years ago, sir?
JULIAN: You were worth a great deal more than that.

LUGAR: I'm prepared to pay more, sir.
JULIAN: No. I didn't mean that. You pay your sixpence and everything'll be all right.
LUGAR: You must allow me to pay what I consider I'm worth, sir.

[*He unties the little bag and pours a stream of coins on to the table.*]

JULIAN (*surprised*): How on earth did you collect all this?
LUGAR: In the autumn, sir—when I work in the orchard. You've always permitted me to sell the windfalls.
JULIAN: I never knew they were worth that much.
LUGAR: There are forty-eight silver pennies, sir. I hoped to make it fifty, but this year Arthur's soldiers took the windfalls without paying. I hope you will accept this as the best I can afford.
JULIAN: Give me your hand, Lugar.

[*Lugar holds out his hand and Julian takes it formally in both of his and speaks the words of a slave's release from bondage.*]

JULIAN: I, Julianus Licinius Severus, Citizen of the Roman Empire, being the lawful owner of the slave Lugar, hereby grant to the said Lugar, and to his children, freedom from the bonds of servitude now and for all time.
LUGAR: I have the Cap of Freedom here, sir.

[*He gropes again in his pocket and pulls out a small red woollen cap. It is rather like the old-fashioned nightcap. Julian takes it from him and places it on his head.*]

JULIAN: Well, I think that's everything.

LUGAR: It's usual for a master to strike his slave for the last time when he grants him freedom.
JULIAN: You're a stickler for etiquette, Lugar. I've always thought it rather an unnecessary formality—but there you are.

[*He strikes Lugar lightly on both cheeks, then shakes him by the hand as one free man to another.*]

LUGAR: I've waited and prayed for this moment for many years, sir—for the honour of taking your hand as a free man.
JULIAN: There won't be any need for you to go round the sentry posts now.
LUGAR: They'll remain on duty until dawn, sir. Your dinner will be ready in half an hour.
JULIAN: What time are you going in the morning?
LUGAR: An hour after sunrise, sir. I'll see that your breakfast is served before we leave, and the fires made up. The rooms will be cleaned and lunch will be laid in the dining-room.
JULIAN: All right, Lugar. You can leave me now. We shall be ready for dinner in half an hour.

[*Lugar goes to the small table by the window and picks up a board with some little piles of wooden discs on it. He brings it over to the centre table and puts it down.*]

LUGAR: You ordered me to prepare the draught-board, sir.
JULIAN: Oh yes. The draughts. Thank you, Lugar.

[*Lugar bows and leaves the room.*]

Curtain

Scene 3

A few weeks later. A winter night.

It is pitch dark outside, but a red glow lights the sky above the distant fort, and Julian can just be seen, outlined against the glow as he stands watching from the terrace.

There is no light in the room until Serena comes in with a lamp. She puts it on the table, and the light of the lamp reveals the table laid for supper; a flagon of wine, some fruit and a dish of cakes.

Julian sees the light and comes in from the terrace.

JULIAN: How people love to burn things. We burn their ships: they come back and burn our fort. One day I suppose Arthur will come along and burn their ships again. There's a bigger blaze farther down the coast. I imagine it's Dover. By the look of it the whole town's on fire.

SERENA: We must have a lamp, Julian. We can't sit here in the dark.

JULIAN: Shall I draw the curtains?

SERENA: No please! I'd rather do without a lamp than have the curtains drawn.

JULIAN: I don't think they're going to see that small light a mile away.

SERENA: What time d'you think it is?

JULIAN: About midnight.

SERENA: It must be later.

JULIAN: That old barn owl was hooting out there just now. It always comes by here at midnight.

SERENA: It seems to have been dark for ages.

JULIAN: Well, they're the longest nights of the year now. These Saxons . . . they're good sailors. I never thought they'd face these rough seas.

SERENA: How long have we got, do you think?

JULIAN: Oh, some while yet. They'll play about round that bonfire till they're tired of it. They'll hunt round for something to eat, and when they don't find anything, I imagine they'll follow the road across the downs.

SERENA: They're bound to see this house.

JULIAN: They may not until it gets light. It's pitch dark out there. (*Pause.*) What would you like to do? Shall we stay here?

SERENA: I think I'd rather go out, wouldn't you?

JULIAN: I think that's the best thing.

SERENA: Shall we have supper before we go?

JULIAN: D'you feel like it?

SERENA: Not much. But I suppose we ought to eat something.

JULIAN: Shall we take it with us?—Have a picnic in the woods?

SERENA: That's a much better idea.

JULIAN: I was thinking about that the other morning when I was up there getting firewood. You remember the place where we used to go for picnics in the old days?

SERENA: I know the place you mean.

JULIAN: The trees have grown up a lot since then. I thought to myself, if anything like this happened, I'd rather be out there in the open than shut up down here in the house.

SERENA: I would too. I don't think they'd trouble to search the woods, do you?

JULIAN: I'm sure they wouldn't.

SERENA: I'll go along and get a warm coat and a couple of blankets.

JULIAN: I'll tie this food up in the tablecloth. We'll have a drink before we go to warm us up, and I'll take a good bottle of wine with us.

[*Serena takes a lamp from one of the wall brackets, lights it from the lamp on the table and goes out to get her coat and the blankets. Julian begins to collect the supper together. He pours out two glasses of wine and goes to the side cupboard for one of his old vintage bottles to take with them He puts it on the table and goes to the terrace door and stands for a moment watching the glow above the fort as it rises and falls with the flare and wane of the burning huts inside the walls. Turning back into the room, he pauses by the old altar to Sylvanus.*]

JULIAN: Well, Sylvanus?—is it your fault or mine? You don't care what happens to any of us, do you? Those old British people thought you were their god. We came along and tried to make you into a Roman god. Now I suppose these new people will say you belong to them, and all the time the only things you really care about are the woods and the fields, no matter who they belong to.

[*Serena comes back with her coat and the blankets. She also brings a small wicker basket.*]

SERENA: Were you asking Sylvanus to help?
JULIAN: I was telling him what an old fraud he is, that's all. He's been our family god for three hundred years and he's not even going to say goodbye.
SERENA: It's not *his* fault, Julian. You can't expect a spirit that guards a stream in a wood to understand what's happening tonight.

[*She puts the basket on the table.*]

SERENA: We might as well take the picnic basket.
JULIAN: Where did you find this? I haven't seen it for years.

SERENA: It's always been in the cupboard.

[*Julian begins to pack the supper in the basket.*]

JULIAN: No. I don't blame poor old Sylvanus. I don't see what he *could* have done about a thing like this. Or any other god for that matter. It's a bit beyond yours too, isn't it?

SERENA: He understands. He's with us here tonight.

JULIAN: It's no good *being* here if he doesn't do anything. If he wants to help, he'd better be quick about it.

SERENA: It's not now that matters. I've tried to explain so often, Julian.

JULIAN: In the old days when the gods were young they would have thrown a thunder-bolt on those fellows down there in the fort and blown them back to the place they came from. You used to tell me that *yours* could work miracles?

SERENA: Don't you think it's a miracle that he's here with us now? The old gods helped us to conquer the world, but they did nothing for us when we really needed them. That's the difference between the old gods and mine. He comes to you when you *do* need him.

JULIAN: Pity he didn't come a bit sooner. It's not much good waiting till it's all over.

SERENA: But it's *not* all over, Julian. If you go with him it's only just beginning. He can't control what those men down there may do because this isn't his world, but he can take us with him.

JULIAN: How do you *know* all this?—It's only what that old priest told you?

SERENA: It's more than that. When you said just now that we'd go up to that place in the woods, I could almost hear him saying, "I'll be up there, waiting for you."

JULIAN: For you, perhaps. Not for me.
SERENA: For you too, Julian. If you believe in him.
JULIAN: It's too late for that now.
SERENA: It's never too late.
JULIAN: That old priest took a whole morning to make you into a Christian.
SERENA: I know. But he was a very old man. I'm certain a lot of the things weren't really necessary.
JULIAN: But you've got to have a priest? There's no other way, is there?
SERENA: If we did our best, I think he would understand. He's used to people coming to him at the last moment like this.
JULIAN: D'you remember the words?
SERENA: I don't remember everything the old man said. But I'm sure it's not the words that matter.
JULIAN: Would you like to have a try? We shan't have much time. I'll do whatever you tell me.

[*Serena goes to the shrine and draws back the curtains. The small lamp is still burning on the altar.*]

SERENA: I think . . . if you come over here and stand by the altar. (*Julian does what he is told.*) You're the one that matters now, Julian. The important thing is to believe in him, and want to go with him.
JULIAN: I want to go with you. You know that.
SERENA: That's not the same thing.
JULIAN: If he doesn't let me go with you, then it doesn't matter.
SERENA: He will if you ask him.
JULIAN: You'd better do that. He'd listen to you more than he would to me.

[*Serena is anxious and uncertain but she does her best. She turns to the altar.*]

SERENA: Will you listen, Master? We haven't got a priest, but we're in great trouble. My husband wants to go with you when we leave here. He wants you to let us go together.

JULIAN: Is it all right?

SERENA: I think he would have told us in some way if it wasn't.

JULIAN: Does he refuse many people?

SERENA I don't think he's ever refused anybody who really wanted him.

JULIAN: Will you tell him it was only a bit of fun when I made jokes about him?

SERENA: He'd understand that.

JULIAN: Then that's everything, is it?

SERENA: I ought to baptize you.

JULIAN: That's a long business. That old priest was splashing about for hours.

SERENA: It needn't take long. It's quite simple really. We've got some water here.

[*She goes across the room and fills a cup from a jar on the sideboard.*]

JULIAN: That came out of Sylvanus' spring. It wouldn't be any good, would it?

SERENA: I don't think it matters where it comes from.

[*She dips her fingers in the cup and makes the sign of the cross on Julian's forehead.*]

Now you're supposed to confess your sins.

JULIAN: What am I supposed to say?

SERENA: That's really for you to decide.

[*Julian is silent for a moment.*]

JULIAN: Well—the evening I made that old tax

collector drunk and he fell in the river and got drowned. I always thought that was rather a shabby thing to do because I couldn't help being pleased he *did* fall in the river.

SERENA: And you're sorry?

JULIAN: Yes. I really am sorry.

SERENA: Then I think that's everything, Julian. Now I just have to touch your cheeks and your mouth with the water—like the old priest did to mine.

[*She dips her fingers in the cup and completes the baptism.*]

That's all.

[*She puts the cup down on the altar.*]

JULIAN: Now I'm a Christian?

SERENA: Now we shall always be together.

JULIAN: Does it mean we shall see Paula again?

SERENA: And Otho. He promised me the night before he went away.

JULIAN: I'd like to see them again, but there's a lot for them to do here before they come. Otho'll be a great soldier if he has a chance, and Paula, she may be a great lady. I'd like to have been here to see what happens in the next ten years.

SERENA: We shall know.

JULIAN: You think we shall?

SERENA: If we don't, then they'll tell us when they come.

JULIAN: Well, we'd better be getting along now.

[*He picks up the two cups of wine and gives one to Serena.*]

Have some of this before you go.

[*They drink.*]

SERENA: D'you feel happy?

JULIAN: Hungry, too. I'm going to enjoy my supper now.

SERENA: Shall we lock up before we go?

JULIAN: I don't think so. We'll take these cups. We can't drink out of the bottle.

[*He packs the cups in the basket and straps it up. He picks up Serena's cloak and helps her on with it. Then he puts on his own cloak and looks round the room.*]

I think that's everything. I'll take the basket. You take the blankets.

[*Serena puts the blankets over her arm. Julian takes the basket then blows out the lamp on the table.*]

SERENA: Leave the little lamp on the altar. We'll be able to see it from the woods.

[*They go out of the terrace door and down the steps. When they have gone, the room is dark except for the glow from the burning fort, and the gleam of the small lamp on Serena's altar.*]

Curtain

SOUTH

by

JULIAN GREEN

" The purification of a dangerous passion by a violent liberation."
Such is Aristotle's definition of tragedy, and I don't think I can give a better résumé of the following play.

J. G.

The Arts Theatre Club, London, presented *South* on March 30th, 1955, with the following cast:

REGINA	*Clare Austin*
JAN WICZIEWSKY	*Denholm Elliott*
MRS. STRONG	*Joan Young*
JEREMY	*Errol John*
ANGELINA	*Zena Walker*
EDWARD BRODERICK	*André Morell*
JIMMY	*Melvyn Hayes*
UNCLE JOHN	*John Harrison*
MR. WHITE	*Horace Sequeira*
ERIC MAC CLURE	*Lyndon Brook*
ELIZA	*Rita Stevens*
MRS. PRIOLLEAU	*Bessie Love*
MISS PRIOLLEAU	*Elaine Usher*
BARNABAS	*Buddy Pip*

The play produced by Peter Hall. The setting designed by Paul Mayo

CHARACTERS

IAN WICZIEWSKY, *aged* 24 *or* 25, *an officer*
EDWARD BRODERICK, *aged* 40, *a widower*
JIMMY, *aged* 14, *son of Edward Broderick*
MR. WHITE, *aged* 60, *Jimmy's tutor*
ERIC MAC CLURE, *aged* 20
UNCLE JOHN, *aged* 70 *or more, a coloured man*
A COLOURED CHILD
JEREMY
REGINA, *aged* 22, *Edward Broderick's niece*
MRS. STRONG, *a widow, Edward Broderick's sister*
ANGELINA, *aged* 17, *Edward Broderick's daughter*
ELIZA
MRS. PRIOLLEAU,
MISS PRIOLLEAU, *her daughter*

At the beginning of the first act, the two first verses of "Abide with Me" can be heard.

(*Wicziewsky is pronounced Veechefsky.*)

NOTE

The action takes place a few hours before the War between the States. The cannon-shot heard at the end of the last act announces the opening of hostilities between the North and South, at dawn, April 12, 1861.

The scene is laid in the drawing-room of a large plantation near Charleston, in South Carolina.

To have a correct idea of the setting, one must imagine a great mansion built on the lines of the Greek temple at Pæstum, with a pediment and very heavy columns standing flush with the ground, without bases. Two of these columns can be seen from the drawing-room, to the right and left of a large French window. Between the columns stretches a long avenue of live-oaks hung with curtains of grey Spanish moss (more exactly verdigris), which stir at the least breath of wind.

The drawing-room is furnished in the somewhat heavy style of the eighteen-fifties.

SCENE

A large drawing-room furnished in the style of 1850.

ACT ONE

Scene 1

A large drawing-room furnished in the style of 1850. *At the back of the stage, a large French window through which is visible a long avenue of live-oaks.*

As the curtain rises, Lieutenant Ian Wiczewsky stands at the right. perfectly still, a light cane in his hand, his back turned to the audience. Church singing is heard in the distance, a hymn, the words of which cannot be distinguished. A few minutes go by, then Regina runs into the room from the left and goes to the window without seeing Lieutenant Wiczewsky. She glances down the avenue as if she was looking for someone, then stands motionless and listens to the hymn, one verse of which is ending.

After a moment, she turns around as though she had sensed someone's presence and starts.

REGINA: Oh, you startled me, Lieutenant Veechefsky. I really don't know how you manage to appear so suddenly in places where no one expects to find you.
IAN: Did you expect to see me in the avenue?
REGINA: No. What makes you say that?
IAN: I might have been in the avenue.
REGINA: Allow me to tell you that it wouldn't matter to me whether you were in the avenue, or anywhere else. (*Pause.*) I wanted to see if Angelina was returning from church.
IAN: You know her very badly if you think her capable of leaving before the end of the service. She fears God and dreads her father, like a true daughter of the South. (*Pause.*) Apart from you and me, everyone is shut up this afternoon in that plank shanty

which they call a church. We are completely alone in the house.

REGINA: Do you miss not going to church on Sunday?

IAN: My sentiments on that point are of no interest. The fact remains that there's no Catholic church in the neighbourhood.

REGINA: What effect do these hymns have on you?

IAN: None.

REGINA: Try as you may, you'll never be one of us. Even I, who come from the North and who no longer believe in churches, have a weakness for those old hymns. But you, you come from somewhere else.

IAN: America is peopled by men and women who come from somewhere else.

REGINA: Yet, just the same, they end by having a family likeness. But in your case, it's not so. You remain a stranger, in spite of your uniform. (*She turns her head away as she says this sentence.*) Angelina told me that you came here when you were twelve years old, with your grandfather. Is it true?

IAN: Yes, we left Poland after the uprising of '48.

REGINA: The uprising against the Russians?

IAN: Against the Prussians. They hanged my father in the Public Square at Posen, with six other conspirators. That same night, my grandfather woke me and we ran away.

REGINA: Didn't the Prussians do anything to you?

IAN: No, nothing. They gave me a whipping after the execution, as an example, they said. That's all.

REGINA: You were whipped and you call that nothing?

IAN (*laughing softly*): That was twelve years ago. The pain has lessened considerably.

REGINA: Why did you say, a short while ago, that we were alone in the house?

IAN: Isn't it so?

REGINA: No, there are the coloured people.

IAN: Coloured people don't count. Coloured people are like so much furniture.

REGINA (*dryly*): I don't agree with you. (*Pause.*) Will you answer my question?

IAN: Why I said we were alone?

REGINA: Yes.

IAN (*turning toward her*): To give you the opportunity of talking to me.

REGINA (*with sudden irritation*): And what the dickens would I talk to you about?

IAN: You know that as well as I do.

[*The singing ceases.*]

REGINA: Is that why you were waiting here when I came in?

IAN: I wasn't waiting. I was here.

REGINA: I don't like what you say. The truth is, I never like anything you say and, in spite of myself, I listen to you. But you're mistaken if you think that I have something confidential to tell you.

IAN: I can wait.

REGINA: Upon my word, you're impertinent.

IAN: Yes, Miss Regina.

REGINA: Do you know that for the last few moments, I've been thinking with the greatest satisfaction of what you've just been telling me. Indeed, I'm delighted to know that you had a thrashing.

IAN: That's a kindly thought. Develop it.

REGINA: Very well. I see that thrashing in a new light, as a kind of part payment. You already deserved it in view of your future insolence, of your smiles, your silences, your European . . . irony. For the last three days I've been watching for this opportunity to speak my mind to you. I don't like you, Lieutenant Veechefsky.

IAN: So you see that you did have something to say to me.

REGINA: There's something about you that I dislike, although I'm at a loss to understand what it is. Oh, I know that I'm speaking too straightforwardly and that I'm laying myself open to your scoffing, to the silent derision that I can read in your eyes.

IAN: Why do you turn yours away, as you say that?

REGINA (*looking straight at him*): I'm not turning them away. I'm speaking to you as we do in my part of the world. I have none of the wiles of Southern women, to whom you pay hypocritical compliments. (*She slowly draws nearer to him.*) I was brought up very simply by people who never lied, and what I hate in you, is falsehood.

IAN: Falsehood? But why should I take the trouble to lie to you?

REGINA: To me, no, certainly not. I'm the poor relation, a little Northern chit that no one notices and who isn't even very pretty. You believe yourself to be intuitive, Lieutenant Veechefsky, but I'm as intuitive as you are and there are days when I can see you lying, from head to foot.

IAN: May I remind you that you're related to Mr. Broderick and that, in consequence, I am under your roof.

REGINA: Are you mad? This is not my home. My home is up North. I was sent here because the uncle who brought me up, failed. Mr. Broderick offered me the hospitality of his plantation, but I would never have come here, had my parents been living. I loathe the plantation. I've spent a winter on it, a snowless winter, and I long to see the snow. (*Ian moves.*) Do you know why I'm alone with you here, in this house? Because they judged it of no importance whether I went to church or not. It's always an effort for them to remember that we're of the same blood.

IAN: You too, come from somewhere else.

REGINA: Oh, but that's different. I'm an American, after all.

IAN: You spoke of the snow, a little while ago.

REGINA: Yes, I suppose you found that childish.

IAN: No. (*With a change in his voice.*) I too long to see the snow, just as you do. Sometimes, carried away by this longing, I fancy that if I pushed open the shutters, I'd see the meadow sparkling white in the sunshine and I'd shiver and laugh for joy, like a boy who feels he must run about shouting because he sniffs that marvellous ice-cold odour. . . .

REGINA: I don't want you to talk about that. Here we are, already on the threshold of summer. Already, the fiery furnace blows its breath in our faces. (*A pause.*) How long are you staying here, Lieutenant Veechefsky?

IAN: My leave expires in five days.

REGINA: Which means that you'll go Friday.

IAN: Friday at dawn. It's a three-hours ride from here to the coast.

REGINA: As a matter of fact, you'll only be here four days. Today no longer counts.

IAN: Yes, four days, if you like. Unless war breaks out before that.

REGINA: War! So you too believe there's going to be a war?

IAN: Since everyone says there'll be war, we'll end by having one. What is never mentioned, never happens.

REGINA: What will you do if there's a war?

IAN: I'll rejoin my post, Miss Regina.

REGINA: Which means that you'll remain loyal to the Government, I suppose. You won't run away into the rebels' camp?

IAN: That's a question which I will solve myself, in due time.

REGINA: How foolish of me to ask you. To whom would you be loyal? You have no roots in the country, neither North, or South.

IAN (*with a shrug*): But how is it that you remain here, considering the opinions that you've so often aired? Aren't you already in the enemy's lair?

REGINA: I've just told you that I'm here in spite of myself I cannot leave this place.

IAN: In that case, if there is war, you'll have to obey the law of the South, talk the language of the South

REGINA: Never.

IAN: Means will be found to convince you. Hell has no furies like civilians in war times. In less than six weeks you'll be turned into a good little slave-driver.

REGINA (*stamping her foot*): If I were a man you wouldn't dare insult me so.

IAN: Far be it from me to have any such intention. I merely observe that, being a Northerner, you remain in the South at a time when war seems imminent

REGINA: For the third time, I tell you that I can't go.

IAN: You could if you wanted to. Mr. Broderick would help you.

REGINA: How do you know?

IAN: He has formally assured me that he would undertake to send you to Boston within three days, if you expressed the wish to leave.

REGINA: So you've talked to him about me?

IAN: Yes.

REGINA: What business is it of yours? What does it matter to you whether I stay or whether I go?

IAN: It doesn't. I merely wish to prove to you that if you stay here, it is because you want to.
REGINA: Is that what you wanted to tell me, when you were waiting for me here?
IAN. I've already told you that I wasn't waiting for you. But you're wasting precious time in refusing to tell me what is so close to your heart.
REGINA: What is close to my heart? This is what I have close to my heart, since you insist on knowing it. I intend to stay on, and on, and on. Do you hear? (*She comes still closer to him*.)
IAN (*without moving*): And why are you staying?
REGINA: I have my reasons, Lieutenant Veechefsky.
IAN: And among all these reasons, there is only one good one, but that's the very one you'll never own to. Pride is stifling you, Regina.
REGINA: How dare you!

[*Footsteps are heard.*]

IAN: Someone is coming and you're so close to me that really, one could think . . . almost anything one pleased. You're imprudent, Miss Regina.

[*Regina springs aside violently. Mrs. Strong enters from the left, followed by a small coloured girl.*]

Scene 2

MRS. STRONG: Who's imprudent? My niece?
IAN: No doubt I'm meddling with what doesn't concern me, but I was telling Miss Regina that to remain here when the threat of war looms a little greater every day. . . .

MRS. STRONG: There won't be a war I don't wish to hear it mentioned. Child, take my hat, my sunshade, my gloves, my shawl. (*She hands these objects to the child as she mentions them.*) Close the shutters a little. Give me my fan and go. (*The child obeys. Mrs. Strong sits down in a rocking-chair—the child goes out.*) Regina, why do you stare at us like a Gorgon? Upon my word, you'd think your eyes were about to burst from their sockets and roll on the rug. Leave the room, child. . . .
REGINA: Aunt Evelyn, if. . . .
MRS. STRONG (*sits up in her armchair*): Obey.

[*Regina goes out at the left.*]

Why have you been frightening her, Lieutenant? This is the very first time I've ever heard of a soldier advising anyone to run away.
IAN: In her case, it wouldn't mean running away. She comes from the North. I'm surprised that she should still be here. She doesn't care for the South.
MRS. STRONG: Oh, for her, the South is *Uncle Tom's Cabin*, that ridiculous tale, just as she's seen it on her parents' dessert plates. Her opinions are about as interesting as those of a mosquito. Why do you wish her to go away?
IAN: I don't care particularly, but I think that if you want her to stay, she must be advised to leave.
MRS. STRONG: Ha! Ha! You know her. Stubborn as a mule. But why then do you wish her to stay?
IAN: Whether she stays or goes is no concern of mine, but in Mr. Broderick's opinion, she should be sent back to the North.
MRS. STRONG: Send her back to the North. . . . That's more easily said than done. We've had her

on our hands since she became an orphan. She has no relatives in the North, with the exception of a sanctimonious old uncle who's not capable of earning twenty dollars a week. What do you think of her?

IAN: What do I think of her?

MRS. STRONG: Why, yes. What do you think of my niece? Do you think she's pretty?

IAN: She has fine eyes. Her hair. . . .

MRS. STRONG: Ah, I expected you to mention hair, woman's crowning glory.

IAN: Her hair is also very beautiful.

MRS. STRONG: What a painter you'd make! She is now provided with eyes and hair. But perhaps that's not quite enough. What do you think of the rest of her, eh, Lieutenant?

IAN: The rest. . . . (*He hesitates.*)

MRS. STRONG: I see, the rest is silence. Mind you, I'm somewhat of your opinion, but you don't do justice to her profile which is rather fine. I know, one doesn't marry a profile. What's more, I often wonder what one *does* marry, and what makes men rave over what is termed the fair sex. For me, the fair sex happens to be the other one. How my beloved husband would have shut me up! As to my niece, I've seen so much of her that I haven't the least idea of what she looks like any more. Today, for a reason which I will give you, I'm attempting to see her through a man's eyes. Man is such a strange animal. Would you be good enough to rock my chair? Now, you know women so well and are always so courteous to them. . . . Heigh there! That's much too fast! Do you want to throw me up to the ceiling? Gently, please, gently!

IAN: I beg your pardon.

MRS. STRONG: That's better, much better. . . . Yes,

I'd like to marry off the child. She'll stay here, never fear. She'll be twenty-three at Christmas. Do you think a man could fall in love with her?

IAN (*a short pause*). Every woman has a right to hope. . . .

MRS. STRONG: Don't say another word, I understand. In spite of this pessimistic opinion, I still have high hopes that a suitable match can be found for her. Today we're expecting the visit of young Mac Clure. He came to see us once before with his father, this winter. Were you here then?

IAN: No, Ma'am.

MRS. STRONG: They came on business, they wished to sell their plantation. Unfortunately, this plantation is badly situated and the air there none too healthy. My brother refused. Since then, old Mac Clure has fallen ill and I'm afraid his son will be back today on the same errand, for they are greatly in need of money.

IAN: Mr. Broderick has spoken to me about this business.

MRS. STRONG: What you don't know, for after all, you're a stranger here . . . oh, please don't think that I wish to offend you, Lieutenant Veechefsky. (*She laughs softly.*) What makes you so attractive to women is precisely the fact that you're a foreigners. Now, now, don't deny it, women adore you. You carry them away with you to the Poland of Monsieur Chopin, and they think themselves most unhappy, most interesting, and they revel in their agony.

IAN: Ma'am. . . .

MRS. STRONG: What was I talking about?

IAN: Young Mac Clure. . . .

MRS. STRONG: That's it exactly. Young Mac Clure and his father. Let me tell you that the Mac Clures belong to a very good family. They've lived in this part of the world for the last two centuries, and their Scotch ancestors were cattle thieves which, as you must know, is quite a distinction in that country. Oh, I've dropped my fan. (*Ian picks it up and hands it to her.*) So we've invited young Mac Clure to spend a couple of days with us. It was my idea. He's twenty and he's never seen Regina who was in Florida when he came here with his father. Do you believe in miracles, Lieutenant Veechefsky? I do. We'll settle a handsome sum on the child and give her our plantation at Tomotly and a hundred slaves. To tell the truth, Tomotly is at the end of never and I'd be terrified to spend a single night there, but it's a good place to grow cotton. Make yourself agreeable to young Mac Clure.

IAN: I won't fail to.

MRS. STRONG: He's a little clumsy, even a trifle awkward in his black frock-coat, and his old-fashioned ideas about what's right and what isn't right. A real Scotch Presbyterian, a chick from Calvin's brood. Does that bother you?

IAN: Not in the least. (*Pause.*) Does he ride well?

MRS. STRONG: Hmm! I don't know. You ask such strange questions. Ah, now I come to think of it. . . . When he left the house that day with his father, I remember having watched them from the veranda, as they rode down the great avenue. Young Mac Clure sat his horse admirably. To return to his ideas that I find a trifle . . . rigid, it's not necessary to tell him that Regina does not attend church on Sunday. He can convert her later. That will provide some occupation for their deadly evenings at Tomotly.

IAN (*with irritation*): You already see them married.

MRS. STRONG: I've set my heart on it.

[*Angelina enters from the right.*]

ANGELINA: Where's Regina, Aunt Evelyn? How do you do, Lieutenant Veechefsky?

[*He bows.*]

MRS. STRONG: I don't know where Regina is, but I wish you'd tell your brother to come here to speak to me.

ANGELINA: Very well, Aunt Evelyn. (*She goes out at left.*)

MRS. STRONG: You should give my nephew a little advice, Lieutenant Veechefsky. Jimmy adores you, he'll listen to you. Teach him to hold himself straight, to speak properly, not to steal the pickles. Another thing, I don't want him to go walking by himself anywhere near the slaves' quarters. His father has told him never to go beyond the great avenue, but he has no authority over the boy. And no more has his tutor, old Mr. White.

IAN: Someone might tell me that Jimmy Broderick's education is none of my business.

MRS. STRONG: No one will say anything of the kind and if by someone, you mean my brother, I believe you're fishing for compliments, Lieutenant. You know very well what my brother thinks of you. (*She yawns.*) I don't know why I feel so weary this afternoon, perhaps it's this first hot day. And then, the sermon was unbearable. Doctor Locke dragged us through hell, to and fro, through clouds of sulphur and the fumes of his own rhetoric. I'm almost certain of having dozed once or twice.

[*Edward Broderick comes in from the right.*]

Why do you look so anxious, Edward? Would you like something to drink?

BRODERICK: No, thank you, How do you do, Lieutenant? I'm worried on account of the news.
MRS. STRONG: It's no worse than it was yesterday.
BRODERICK: It's worse to the extent that no one knows any longer what it's all about. As long as a question remains clear, there's always a chance of solving it. But when things become involved, the danger is that much more acute.
MRS. STRONG. I talked to Doctor Locke a few minutes ago. He's very optimistic.
BRODERICK: Doctor Locke is a godly man who knows nothing about worldly matters. Where is Regina? I want to speak to her.

[*Enter Jimmy.*]

JIMMY: How do you do, Lieutenant Veechefsky? Listen, can I ride with you to Tomotly, tomorrow afternoon?
IAN: Ask your father.
BRODERICK: We'll see about that later, Jimmy. Go and tell Regina that I wish to speak to her at once.

[*Jimmy goes out at left.*]

MRS. STRONG: I hope you aren't going to frighten the child.
BRODERICK: I'm going to tell her that she must leave while it's still possible.
MRS. STRONG: Are you mad? To hear you talk, one would think that the South was already invaded. No one wants war: neither President Lincoln, nor a single Southern state. What then?

[*Edward Broderick takes a newspaper from his pocket and hands it to her.*]

MRS. STRONG (*without looking at Broderick*): Well, is that all? The Federal Government refuses to withdraw its troops from South Carolina and wishes, on the contrary, to provision them. That's the usual bluster from Washington. Those people would be thunderstruck if a single shot were fired. Nevertheless, there must be someone among us with enough spirit to make them shut up.

BRODERICK: Why doesn't Regina come?

MRS. STRONG: I beg you to think over what you're about to say to her. Even if there is a war, the child's place is here. She was brought up in the North, but she can say what she likes, her blood is Southern, she'll fall into our way of thinking. I'll attend to that.

BRODERICK: You won't change her, it's too late. She's twenty-two.

[*Jimmy and Regina enter at the left.*]

JIMMY (*in a whisper, to Mrs. Strong*): Aunt Evelyn, ask Papa if I can go out tomorrow with Lieutenant Veechefsy.

BRODERICK: Leave us, Jimmy.

[*Jimmy goes out at right.*]

IAN: Do you wish me to go?

BRODERICK: Why? You are like my own son, Ian. I've never had anything to conceal from you. Sit down, Regina, I have something to say to you, but first, I want to ask you a question. Answer without hesitation or fear of hurting our feelings. You have been living at Bonaventure for a year now. Are you happy?

REGINA: Happy? No.

BRODERICK: Why?

REGINA: Simply because I don't like the South.

BRODERICK: If a conflict broke out between the North and the South, your sympathies would be with the North?

REGINA: Yes, with the North.

MRS. STRONG: Edward, I find this questioning most painful for us all.

REGINA: It's not in the least painful to me, Aunt Evelyn.

BRODERICK: Does siding with the North, Regina, mean that you wish for the victory of the Northern armies over the Southern ones?

REGINA: Please God that it won't come to that, but if there is a war, yes, I naturally hope the North will win.

BRODERICK: In that case, do you judge it reasonable for me to help you return North?

REGINA (*after a slight hesitation*): Yes, I think it would be reasonable.

MRS. STRONG: Regina, you're ungrateful.

REGINA: No, Aunt Evelyn, I'm not. I've not forgotten how much I owe you. But in spite of this, I want to go.

IAN (*angrily*): You'll look a little foolish, Miss Regina, if the war doesn't take place.

REGINA (*without looking at him*): The war won't be the cause of my leaving, Lieutenant Veechefsky.

IAN: Think it over carefully, Miss Regina.

[*Regina looks at him in astonishment.*]

BRODERICK: Regina is free to think over the matter until tomorrow if she likes. She knows we're all very fond of her. Consequently, she can change her mind, but I don't wish her to stay at Bonaventure if she's unhappy there!

IAN: Didn't you say, less than an hour ago, that you'd stay, Miss Regina?

REGINA: I've changed my mind. Anyway, it seems to me that less than an hour ago, you advised me to leave, Lieutenant Veechefsky.

IAN: I wanted then to put your decision to the proof. Remember, you'd decided to stay on, and on, and on.

BRODERICK: What am I to believe, Regina?

REGINA: Believe what I'm telling you now, Uncle Edward. I want to go, to leave this house and the South for ever.

BRODERICK (*gently*): In spite of this, I think you should withhold your answer until tomorrow. If you then decide to go, I'll accompany you myself to Charleston in the barouche. And from there, I'll take you to the railway station. I hope you aren't afraid of travelling in a train.

REGINA (*laughing*): Oh no, Uncle Edward, I came here by train. I was not in the least frightened, after the first ten minutes. One ends by becoming quite used to it.

MRS. STRONG: How lucky you are!

BRODERICK: There's something else I'd like to say to you. You'll hear us slandered in the North. The idea they have there of a Southern planter is most fantastic. Have you ever seen anyone strike a slave at Bonaventure?

REGINA: No, not at Bonaventure.

BRODERICK: I don't mean flogging—the very thought fills me with horror—I have forbidden a hand to be raised against a slave, no matter what the circumstances. You know that, don't you?

REGINA: Yes.

BRODERICK: Has a slave ever been parted from his wife, a mother from her children at Bonaventure?

REGINA: Not that I know of, Uncle Edward.

BRODERICK: Isn't it true that I freed twenty-eight slaves at Christmas and that twenty-five of them returned here because they didn't know where else to go?

REGINA: That proves you're merciful, within the limits imposed by Southern customs, but the three slaves who didn't return witness against you, and my sympathies are with them. I'll never admit that you have the right to own a single slave.

MRS. STRONG: You impertinent little hussy! You read the Bible every day and you don't know that all the patriarchs had slaves? Oh, I wish they'd take all those blacks and send them back to Africa, where they belong, or that they could be given, bag and baggage, to the virtuous Europeans who weep and wail over them, to Napoleon the Third and to Victoria. For the last thirty years we've been told that they're about to rise and butcher us all. I don't think them capable of such a thing. They're just children.

BRODERICK: Yes, children. Lost children, thrust upon our hands by Providence.

MRS. STRONG: Oh, Edward, you're so annoying when you talk about Providence. One can't hold God responsible for everything. It would be far too convenient. All the more so since He never says a word.

REGINA: Uncle Edward, will you allow me to leave the room?

BRODERICK: Yes, go, if you like, my dear.

[*Regina goes out at left.*]

(*To Mrs. Strong.*) You've shocked the child.

MRS. STRONG: I've shocked her, *I*?

BRODERICK: Yes, I know her. It was what you said about the silence of God. She believes, and I believe with her, that God speaks to every one of us. She has religious views that we should respect.

MRS STRONG: That's really a little too much. Your niece does not deign to attend church with us, but she has religious views, and if anyone shocks her, she retires like a tragedy queen. The little prig!

[*Edward Broderick moves away towards the right.*]

IAN: Can you still see Miss Regina settled at Tomotly with her hundred slaves and her abolitionist husband?

MRS. STRONG: You'll see, young man, she'll marry him yet, and they'll keep their slaves. When one has felt the pinch of poverty. . . .

IAN: But supposing she leaves?

MRS. STRONG: She won't leave, once she's seen young Mac Clure.

IAN: You told me that you believe in miracles. I'd be curious to witness this one.

[*Edward Broderick returns to the centre of the stage.*]

MRS. STRONG: What on earth's the matter with you, Edward? You aren't ill?

BRODERICK: Of course not, but I own that this conversation with Regina has pained me. I felt her so much in earnest. . . . And you, Lieutenant, what's your opinion about the burning questions that are splitting the country?

IAN: Frankly, we soldiers are less attracted by politics than are civilians. We wait for war to emerge from speeches, as is usually the case. Then our job is to defeat the enemy.

MRS. STRONG: I don't like to hear you talk so, and in such a cold and gentle voice. You'd think the first battles had already been fought.

IAN: If that were the case, Ma'am, I wouldn't be here.

MRS. STRONG: Lord, I'd like to be the older by three months. In three months, we'll know and the question will be settled one way or the other, even if we do have war. But there won't be war. (*She fidgets in her armchair.*) I feel so warm. I wonder how I'm going to struggle through the rest of the evening. Lieutenant Veechefsky, help me out of my chair. It's so stuffy here, I think I'll wait for our guests on the veranda. . . .

[*Veechefsky helps her to get up and she goes out at the right.*]

Scene 3

BRODERICK: I make no secret of it, Lieutenant, I'm most anxious.

IAN: One must keep a cool head, in times like these.

BRODERICK: I wonder how you manage to be so calm.

IAN: That's part of our profession.

BRODERICK: I know. On the battle field, a soldier mustn't shoot until he sees the whites of the enemy's eyes. But I'm not a soldier and I find it very hard to control myself and wait. To wait is horrible. (*A pause.*) I'm glad you're here. Yes, your presence is a comfort to us all, in spite of . . . do you mind if I say so? (*Veechefsky makes a gesture.*) In spite of your uniform. Oh, don't misunderstand me: it's quite normal that you should still be wearing it. We're not at war. But one of our fire-eaters might shoot at any moment and that would be enough to make this uniform that of. . . .

IAN: The enemy?

BRODERICK: Forgive me. My own tongue is astounded by the words it speaks. I'm certain that you're with us, for us.

IAN: Have you ever doubted it?

BRODERICK: No more than I would the loyalty of my own son. But I'm in anguish. . . Have you any idea of what anguish means?

IAN: No.

BRODERICK: There are times when my thoughts are in a maze. I wish I had Regina's faith. Although she says things that disturb me and sometimes make me indignant, I feel that she has faith. She leans on someone or something invisible. I pretend to. I'm not sure. She is sure.

[*A pause.*]

IAN: I have some directions to give my orderly. Do you mind if I leave you?

BRODERICK (*sadly*): Yes, go, do as you think best. (*Ian goes out. He goes towards the back of the stage.*) One ends by loathing the very walls that watch you suffer. (*He crosses the threshold of the great door at the back of the stage and pauses between the columns.*) My God, if only You could exist, even for a single minute! How gladly I would go to You!

[*At that moment Jimmy appears at the left and turns to someone invisible. Broderick moves away a little beyond the columns.*]

Scene 4

JIMMY: Come in! (*He stamps his foot.*) Come in, I tell you! Come in, you!

[*He stretches out his arm to take the hand of a small coloured boy who guides a very old blind negro, dressed in a black frock coat.*]

COLOURED BOY: I'm scared. It's forbidden.
JIMMY: It's not forbidden, if I say so. Anyway, Uncle John always has a right to come here. Papa said so.
UNCLE JOHN (*to coloured child*): Where are we, child?
JIMMY: In the big sitting-room.
UNCLE JOHN: Is there anyone here? If there's anyone here, I'm going.
JIMMY: There's nobody here. I'll go fetch Papa, Uncle John, but promise to ask him to do what I told you.
UNCLE JOHN: I promise to speak to him, Mr. Jimmy.

[*Jimmy goes out at right. The old man and the child remain standing in the middle of the room, hand in hand and motionless.*]

Child, look well at this sitting-room. Maybe you'll never see another sitting-room in all your life.
COLOURED CHILD: What's a sitting-room, Grandpa?
UNCLE JOHN: It's a room where white folks gather together to talk.
COLOURED CHILD: Can't they talk outside?
UNCLE JOHN: It's too hot for white folks outside, it's too sunny, or else it's cool, so they sit in here. White folks have got to feel good everywhere.
COLOURED CHILD: Why?
UNCLE JOHN: Just because it's so. Because the Lord gave them white skins.
COLOURED CHILD: Why didn't He give me a white skin too, Grandpa?
UNCLE JOHN: The Lord will give you far more in Heaven, my little lamb.

COLOURED CHILD: Same as white folks?
UNCLE JOHN (*after a hesitation*): I think so.
COLOURED CHILD: Grandpa, can I reach out my finger and touch the rocking-chair?
UNCLE JOHN: No, you mustn't touch a single thing in a white man's house.

[*Edward Broderick comes in by the door at the back of the stage.*]

BRODERICK: Hello, Uncle John. I hope nothing serious brings you here.
UNCLE JOHN: Are we alone in the room, Marse Edward?
BRODERICK: Yes, except for your grandson.
UNCLE JOHN (*to the coloured child*): Go wait for me in the avenue, child, and mind, be good.

[*Coloured child goes out at the left.*]

BRODERICK: Sit down, Uncle John.

[*He leads him by the hand to a sofa. He himself remains standing.*]

UNCLE JOHN: I hope I'm not disturbing you, Marse Edward. On a Sunday afternoon too. . . .
BRODERICK: You wouldn't have come if you hadn't something particular to say to me.
UNCLE JOHN: And supposing I had nothing particular to say to you, Marse Edward?
BRODERICK: I don't understand.
UNCLE JOHN: A little while ago, as I heard my little ones reading the Psalms, I was moved by the spirit to go to you. It wasn't the right time. But I didn't choose the time. I had no idea what I was going to say to you. But still, I obeyed.

BRODERICK: Obeyed?

UNCLE JOHN: The spirit bloweth where it listeth. I got up, I put on my frock coat and I came.

BRODERICK: So you sometimes hear the Lord's voice, Uncle John?

UNCLE JOHN: Yes, sometimes.

BRODERICK: Perhaps you mistake your own thoughts for His voice.

UNCLE JOHN: No, His voice doesn't have the same sound. (*Edward Broderick smiles.*) The noise our thoughts make in our head can't ever be mistaken for the voice of the Lord. The Lord's voice is not like anything else in the world and you can always recognise it.

[*A pause.*]

BRODERICK: Why are you telling me all this, Uncle John?

UNCLE JOHN: I'm scared. Something's going to happen to this house. (*A pause.*) Maybe that's what I was to tell you.

BRODERICK (*sits down*): Do you mean on account of all this talk about war? Or have you come to ask me to free a slave?

UNCLE JOHN: It wouldn't be enough to free one slave. You ought to free them all.

BRODERICK: It's easy enough to say that. Do you want to see me ruined?

UNCLE JOHN: If you don't mind my saying so, Marse Edward, I'd rather see you ruined than lost.

BRODERICK (*rising*): I've just heard one sermon, Uncle John. That's enough, even for a Sunday. I'm freeing my slaves little by little.

UNCLE JOHN: God sometimes works faster than we do. Excuse my talking so. You've been very good to me. You freed me twenty years ago, or more. You gave me a little house and a cornpatch by the roadside. We stayed on the plantation because we love you, and it's because I love you that I got up this morning when I heard the children, and came to see you. (*In a level voice and without emphasis.*) But God is going to pass in our midst, and you know what that means. Right here, in this house, God is going to pass among us.

BRODERICK: What do you mean? God is going to pass among us. . . .

UNCLE JOHN: What's there behind me, Marse Edward?

BRODERICK: Back of you? Why, the big window that leads to the veranda.

UNCLE JOHN: And right and left of me?

BRODERICK: To your left, the doors leading to the rooms. To your right, the door through which you came.

UNCLE JOHN: Then between this window and the two doors, the wrath of God will be fulfilled.

BRODERICK: Why should he punish me? What have I done?

UNCLE JOHN: He won't punish you if you haven't done anything. God is love, Marse Edward.

BRODERICK: If God is love why does he take revenge, even on the wicked?

UNCLE JOHN (*gently*): No doubt because the wicked stir the wrath of love.

BRODERICK: But how?

UNCLE JOHN (*same tone*): Through lack of love. Where there's no love, there's no religion. You can sing hymns till you're hoarse and shout Halleluiah! If you don't love your brother as yourself, and more than yourself, you're lost. (*He rises.*) Give me your hand, if you please, and lead me to the door. (*Both go toward the left.*) I still have something to say to you about your little son. He wants to go out tomorrow with the foreign lieutenant.

BRODERICK: I know. Lieutenant Veechefsky. But he isn't a foreigner.

UNCLE JOHN: He's not one of us, Marse Edward.

BRODERICK: Oh, he comes from Europe, but he's become a real American.

UNCLE JOHN (*stopping*): You're very fond of him.

BRODERICK (*quickly*): Yes, very.

UNCLE JOHN: If I were you, I wouldn't let little Jimmy go out with the foreign lieutenant.

BRODERICK: Why?

UNCLE JOHN: When little Jimmy spoke to me a little while ago, the thought came to me that the foreign lieutenant mustn't take him out.

BRODERICK: Have you heard anyone speak against Lieutenant Veechefsky?

UNCLE JOHN: Never.

BRODERICK: Has he ever spoken to you?

UNCLE JOHN: No, but once when I happened to be in the great avenue, I heard the foreign lieutenant talking to a woman. I don't know what he said, but I listened to the sound of his voice. He wasn't speaking the way men speak to women. For us blind folks, a voice means almost everything. I don't like his voice, Marse Edward. It's a cruel voice.

[*A pause. Regina appears left.*]

BRODERICK: He was talking to a woman, you say?

UNCLE JOHN: Yes.

BRODERICK: Do you know who the woman was, Uncle John?

UNCLE JOHN: She's just come into the room.

BRODERICK: Do you want something, my child?

REGINA: No, I was looking for Angelina.
BRODERICK: I'll lead you out, Uncle John, if you're ready.

[They go out. Once alone, Regina looks around her.]

Scene 5

She sees Lieutenant Veechefsky's cane lying forgotten on a piece of furniture, picks it up, examines it for a moment and throws it on the rug. Angelina enters from the left.

REGINA: I was looking for you, Angelina. I have something to say to you.
ANGELINA: And so have I.
REGINA: Let's go and sit down in that corner. (*They go and sit at the left, backs turned to the door at right.*) Angelina, you're the only person here that I can really trust. A moment ago, I acted on an impulse. Your father offered to let me leave Bonaventure and return North, and I accepted.
ANGELINA: You accepted? Now why?
REGINA: I really don't know why, I said yes. Your father told me to think it over, but having once said yes, I find it difficult to go back on my decision, particularly before two men.
ANGELINA: Two men?
REGINA: Yes, Lieutenant Veechefsky was there. He's always there. Anyway, I knew that I was right to say yes. When I was in my room, before your father sent for me, I had a fit of tears. (*Angelina makes a gesture.*) No, please don't question me.
ANGELINA: Regina, it's not possible. You aren't going away.

REGINA: Yes, I am. It's better so. I'll never feel at home here. Now don't cry. I've been thinking of you, Angelina. We'll meet again.

ANGELINA: But supposing there's a war?

REGINA: Then we'll see each other after the war.

ANGELINA: You'll hate me.

REGINA: Are you mad? (*She strokes her head.*) You're the only friend I have on the plantation. For the rest of the family, I'm a stranger. Very soon, if I stayed on and there was war, I'd be considered a spy. Apart from you, no one else loves me here.

ANGELINA. You're mistaken. My father . . . is very fond of you.

REGINA: Oh, he's fond of me from a sense of duty, out of Christian charity, that icy emotion. And then, I may as well tell you, since I'm going away, there's someone here who loathes me.

ANGELINA: Who can it be?

REGINA: Lieutenant Veechefsky.

ANGELINA: What an extraordinary idea! Lieutenant Veechefsky! He's so polite, so agreeable.

REGINA: You don't know him. His very smile turns me to ice. I never see him bow to me without thinking that in his heart he despises me. At home, in the North, men are blunter, but you can trust them, whereas I could never trust Lieutenant Veechefsky. I've never been able to understand the influence he has over your father.

ANGELINA: Influence, that's saying a good deal.

REGINA: Well then, the affection your father has for him.

ANGELINA: It's quite simple. Lieutenant Veechefsky's grandfather had a very large fortune that he succeeded in bringing out of Poland in 1853 or 4. Papa was on the verge of ruin, through unfortunate speculations. He applied to Count Veechefsky who knew him slightly and made him a loan which actually saved us. The old man died five years ago but his grandson is made to feel that this is his home.

REGINA: This doesn't explain why everyone should have lost their heads over him, for your father's not the only one to find him perfect. Aunt Evelyn is mad about him.

ANGELINA: That's true. Everybody adores him.

REGINA: I don't.

ANGELINA: Why, what has he done to you?

REGINA: Nothing, so far, but I never see him without feeling uneasy. Angelina: you're in love with Lieutenant Veechefsky?

ANGELINA: Me? I should think not.

REGINA: Why did you say, a moment ago, that everyone adored him? Don't you adore him too?

ANGELINA: How silly you are! That's just a way of speaking. He's so agreeable, that's it, he's too agreeable. I like men to be more . . . help me, what do I mean to say? Anyway, he's not like other men.

REGINA: Have you ever been alone with him?

ANGELINA: Yes, once or twice.

REGINA: Did he pay you any compliments?

ANGELINA: He? Never. He's very nice to me, but absent-minded, and he talks to me as if I were a little girl. Everyone treats me like a little girl here, except you.

REGINA: Can you say positively that Lieutenant Veechefsky has never made love to you?

ANGELINA: How strange you are! I could swear it on the Bible.

REGINA: It's useless to take an oath on the very book that forbids us to swear. Why don't you simply tell me the truth. (*A pause.*) Angelina, I'm going to talk to you as I would to a woman, not to a little girl. I'm leaving Bonaventure on account of Lieutenant Veechefsky.

ANGELINA: What! You gave other reasons, a moment ago.

REGINA: The chief reason is that I don't want to see this man again.

ANGELINA: You hate him to that extent?

REGINA (*after a hesitation*): Yes. At any rate, I hate the harm he can do.

ANGELINA: That's incredible. Lieutenant Veechefsky would never hurt anyone.

REGINA: That, you don't know.

ANGELINA: What about you?

REGINA: Oh, I'm certain of it. The man is an arch-deceiver.

ANGELINA: Why, Papa said only yesterday that he'd never seen anyone with such a noble expression.

REGINA: What on earth does that mean? A liar can look you straight in the eye, and no one can appear more guilty than an innocent man. I don't believe in noble expressions.

ANGELINA: I sometimes have the impression that you don't believe in anything, Regina.

REGINA: I haven't much confidence in men: "Beware of men." Christ said that. No one takes any notice of it.

ANGELINA: Why don't you go to church?

REGINA: Because my beliefs are not yours.

ANGELINA: I don't understand. You're a Christian, aren't you?

REGINA: Yes, but not quite in the way you see it. (*A pause.*) Angelina, haven't you something to tell me?

ANGELINA: Yes, but now I won't be able to, any more.

REGINA: Why?

ANGELINA: Because, since a little while, everything is different. It seems to me that we're not the same.

REGINA: That's just an idea. (*She takes her hand.*) Listen, Angelina, I'm leaving in forty-eight hours. You won't have another opportunity to confide in me.

ANGELINA: You won't make fun of me if I tell you my secret?

REGINA: When have I ever made fun of you?

ANGELINA (*with an effort*): Well, a little before Christmas, when you were in Florida with Aunt Lucy, Mr. Mac Clure and his son came to see Papa about their plantation. They wanted to sell it.

REGINA: I know.

ANGELINA: They stayed to dinner and rode away together rather late in the evening. At one moment, I was sitting in a corner of the drawing-room and everyone was talking politics, but I wasn't listening, because politics bore me, when I saw young Mac Clure leave his seat and cross the room to where I was sitting. He was dressed in black. He stood by me for an instant and he said something that I didn't understand. I saw his lips move, but it seemed to me that I had grown deaf. That frightened me and I sat there, feeling very bewildered. He came so close to me that his hand touched mine, a little above the wrist. Perhaps he expected me to say something in return, but I couldn't.

REGINA: Why?

ANGELINA: I don't know why. He stood motionless for a few seconds, then smiled and went back to his seat.

REGINA: His behaviour is as strange as yours.

[*At that moment, Lieutenant Veechefsky enters noiselessly from the right, listens a second, then seeing his cane on the rug, picks it up and stands still in the doorway, at some distance from the two girls.*]

ANGELINA: It all happened in a minute.

REGINA: What does young Mac Clure look like?

ANGELINA: You'll see him, he's considered very handsome.

REGINA: And what happened next?

ANGELINA: The next day, as I was walking on the outskirts of the plantation, a coloured child ran up to me and gave me a letter. If I didn't tell someone all this, I believe I'd die. I waited until I was alone in my room to read the letter. At first, my eyes jumped from line to line without being able to understand a word and then I noticed that I was trembling. It was a love letter. Why don't you say something?

REGINA: Well, go on. Finish your story.

ANGELINA: I took the letter and rubbed it all over my breast, my arms . . . you can't imagine how much I enjoyed doing it.

REGINA: Why didn't you tell me that you were in love, Angelina?

ANGELINA: In love? In love with young Mac Clure? Why, my dear Regina, that's not it at all. It's simply that I had asked for a sign. And the sign was given me. I want to be loved, don't you understand? No, don't tell me that God loves me, as though I were still a child of six. It annoys me. I want to be loved by men.

REGINA: Angelina, you're a wicked girl.

ANGELINA: What makes you think I'm a wicked girl? I haven't done anything wrong. I never asked young Mac Clure to write me that letter. Don't look so glum. You're the only person here to whom I can tell my secret. No one takes me seriously because I look like a little girl.

REGINA: You could confide a little in Aunt Evelyn.

ANGELINA: Are you mad? Why not in my father, while you're at it. I'd die of shame, and so would they. People of their age no longer know what love is.

REGINA: What have you done with the letter?

ANGELINA: Ah! (*She laughs.*) I ate it.

REGINA: You ate it!

ANGELINA: Yes, I did. What's so astonishing about that? We're told that Saint John the Apostle ate a book. It's far easier to eat a letter. You swallow one piece after the other, quietly as you please. But first, I rubbed my body all over with his letter.

REGINA: So you've just told me. I don't care for your story, Angelina.

ANGELINA: That's because you're evil-minded, like all persons of your age.

REGINA: A person of my age! I'm twenty-two!

ANGELINA: Just so. You're five years older than I.

REGINA: Listen, Angelina, you're very flippant. I'm afraid that through thoughtlessness you may commit some error, an error that might be dangerous to you.

ANGELINA: Oh please don't say embarrassing things. I feel that you're about to talk to me about my soul, and when people talk to me about my soul, I have the impression that I'm stark naked.

REGINA: But someone must talk to you. . . .

ANGELINA: You're just like Mammy. She says: "If no one talks to you about your soul, you'll go to hell, Miss Angelina (*She mimicks her.*) and it's very easy to get to hell, but once you're there, you've got to stay." She annoys me. I said to her the other day: "You talk about hell as though you'd been there." "I haven't been there," she answered, "but I know what it's like because the preacher told me." "And what about the devil," I asked, "what is he like?"

Do you know what she answered? "Oh, the devil, I think he's white, from top to toe." That's not at all what we're usually told!
REGINA: Angelina, this is perhaps the last hour we'll spend together. . . .

[*With his cane, Lieutenant Veechefsky flicks a book off the table and goes out. Angelina gives a little shriek.*]

ANGELINA (*her hand on her breast*): Regina, he's heard every word! He'll tell Papa that I've been walking near the slaves' quarters.
REGINA: No, he won't, for that would mean admitting that he eavesdrops. Come along.

[*They get up to meet Jimmy and his tutor, Mr. White, who enter at the right.*]

What's the matter, Mr. White? You seem so upset!
MR. WHITE: Nothing's the matter, Miss Regina. I'm looking for Mr. Broderick.
ANGELINA: I hope you haven't heard any bad news.
MR. WHITE: No, Miss Angelina, but I wish to speak to your father.
ANGELINA: I saw him a moment ago in the great avenue with Uncle John.
MR. WHITE: Thank you, Miss Angelina, I'll go to meet him.

[*Angelina and Regina go out at right.*]

(*To Jimmy.*) You stay here, Jimmy, until I've found your father, then I'll leave you alone with him. You must tell him yourself what has happened.

[*Jimmy sticks his hands in his pockets and looks out of the window.*]

Do you hear?
JIMMY: Yes.
MR. WHITE: Don't you budge until your father returns.
JIMMY: And what shall I do in the meantime?
MR. WHITE: You can think over your sins, my boy.

[*Jimmy shrugs his shoulders. Mr. White goes out at right. Jimmy looks out of the door at the back of the stage. In the distance a negress is heard singing "Way down upon the Swanee Ribber". In a moment, Jimmy advances between the columns and signals to someone. A few seconds go by, then Lieutenant Veechefsky comes in by the door at the back of the stage.*]

IAN: What do you want, Jimmy?
JIMMY: I've done something silly. Just now, I told Sam to polish my saddle and he answered that he'd other things to attend to. So I slapped his face so hard that he almost fell down.
IAN: I see. And what then?
JIMMY: You approve?
IAN: I have nothing to say on the subject. Why did you tell me?
JIMMY: Because unfortunately, Mr. White saw the whole thing from the window of his room and he wants me to tell Papa about it myself, to confess it, if you like.
IAN: Well?
JIMMY: Well, if you said a few words to him, to Papa, you could smooth things over.
IAN (*he hesitates*): Listen, Jimmy, does anyone here ever mention me to you?
JIMMY: Mention you? I don't know. My father is devoted to you.
IAN: Good. And what about the others?

JIMMY: The others?
IAN: Yes. Your cousin Regina, for instance.
JIMMY: Regina never speaks to me, and I never speak to Regina.
IAN: Why?
JIMMY: Because she's from the North.
IAN: I'd rather like to know what she thinks of me. I want you to ask her tonight, but she mustn't know that I. . . .
JIMMY: I refuse to speak to Regina.
IAN: In that case. . . .

[*At that moment Edward Broderick comes in. He enters from the left, advances to the centre of the stage and looks at the place where Uncle John sat.*]

JIMMY (*after a pause*): What's the matter, Papa?
BRODERICK: Nothing, I was thinking. I happened to be thinking about you two. Jimmy, you asked me to let you go out with Lieutenant Veechefsky. (*To Lieutenant Veechefsky.*) You would give me great pleasure in accepting my son's company.

[*Veechefsky bows.*]

JIMMY: Thank you, Papa.
BRODERICK: Lieutenant, I'm happy to see you. I have something to say to you that I'd rather my sister didn't hear.
JIMMY (*very quickly*): Would you like me to leave the room, Papa?
BRODERICK: No, no, you can stay. It's a good thing you should know. (*To Lieutenant Veechefsky.*) A moment ago, I went a little way with old Uncle John. He had just paid me a visit to inform me that he'd had visions, forebodings or some such things.

Returning, I met a horseman with a letter for you. I told him to give it to me, and he did when he found out that I was the master of the plantation. Here it is. (*He takes a letter from his pocket and hands it to Veechefsky.*) I'm afraid your leave has been curtailed and that this means that very serious events are about to happen.

IAN (*glancing at the note*): Yes, my leave has been curtailed. I must leave Bonaventure at dawn, but there's nothing extraordinary about that. I must admit that it was a trifle . . . irregular. Our major shuts his eyes to that sort of thing but Washington has sent a general on a tour of inspection, the kind of general that wears his spurs out on an office floor.

BRODERICK: So you're leaving?

IAN: For a soldier, an order is an order.

BRODERICK: Need I remind you how particularly situated we are? Bonaventure is thirty-seven miles from Charleston. Exactly in front of Charleston harbour are an island and a fort, Fort Sumter, occupied at present by United-States' troops that Washington has decided to provision instead of withdrawing them as General Beauregard demanded. We're all of us more or less related in the South, and I know General Beauregard. He's a fire-eater, like so many of us. If he takes this decision of the North as a challenge, he won't hestitate long to fire on the United-States' troops.

IAN: And what if he doesn't take it as a challenge?

BRODERICK: Then the discussion with President Lincoln continues and there's still a chance for peace.

IAN: Let's wait and see.

BRODERICK: Lieutenant, I'm afraid you won't be given much time to wait. Don't misunderstand me. If something happens, it will be tomorrow, it will be tonight. It may be that in a few hours the cannon's roar will shatter the silence of Bonaventure. Then you'll be in one camp, or in the other. (*With an effort.*) I ask you to remain with us.

IAN: My mind's made up.

[*Regina enters and remains motionless. Edward Broderick does not see her, but Veechefsky looks her straight in the eye.*]

BRODERICK: Well?

IAN: I'll let you know in due time.

BRODERICK (*sees Regina*): What do you want, Regina?

REGINA: Aunt Evelyn has gone to her room. She'd like to speak to you.

BRODERICK: I'll come in a moment. (*To Veechefsky.*) I have every confidence in you. To me, you're like a son, my own son. My son wouldn't make a mistake.

[*Mr. White enters from left and goes up to Edward Broderick.*]

MR. WHITE: Did your son speak to you, Mr. Broderick?

BRODERICK: My son? I don't understand, Mr. White.

MR. WHITE: I see that he's told you nothing.

BRODERICK: If you want to complain of him, Mr. White, I'd rather put off our conversation till later. I have a good many worries, as it is.

MR. WHITE: I'm sorry, sir, but this is a serious offence, and one that you should know of at once.

BRODERICK: What have you to say, Jimmy?

JIMMY: I refuse to speak.

MR. WHITE: Then I will.

JIMMY: I'd rather it were Lieutenant Veechefsky. I've told him the whole story.

IAN: Jimmy slapped a disobedient negro.

BRODERICK: You dared to raise a hand against a negro?

JIMMY: Yes. I told him to polish my saddle and he refused.

MR. WHITE: He said he'd do it later.

BRODERICK. Didn't you know that I've forbidden anyone to touch a negro, or even to reprove him without my permission? (*Flying into a rage, suddenly*). Here we are, within an ace of war, for which our slaves are the alleged excuse, and you choose this moment to strike one! If I didn't control myself, I'd strike you until the blood streamed from your face. It's pride, it's your mother's pride that speaks in you, but I'll break your pride, I'll bring you to your knees. (*To Veechefsky.*) Lieutenant Veechefsky, take him to the house behind the silo and punish him as you think fit.

IAN: Isn't it his tutor's place to punish him?

MR. WHITE: I've never raised a finger against the child and I won't do it now.

BRODERICK: (*beside himself*): No one has ever raised a finger against him. That's what he lacks. The old-fashioned upbringing had some good. For the second time, I ask you to take him away and to thrash him in such a way that his howls can be heard even in the negroes' cabins. I want them to know. . . .

REGINA: Uncle Edward. . . .

BRODERICK: Leave me alone, Regina. .

[*Veechefsky goes away with Jimmy at right. Mr. White goes out at left.*]

REGINA: Uncle Edward, listen to me.

BRODERICK (*throwing himself on the sofa*): I don't want to listen to anyone.

REGINA (*cries out suddenly*): Lieutenant Veechefsky must not touch your son.

BRODERICK (*rising*): You don't know what you're talking about.
REGINA: If you only knew what kind of man he was, you'd turn him out of Bonaventure.

[*Edward Broderick goes out at right. Regina throws herself down on her knees in front of the sofa and buries her head in her arms. After a few seconds, Angelina enters from left and runs to* Regina.]

ANGELINA: Regina, what's happened? I heard Papa talking very loudly, and you too.
REGINA (*rising brusquely*): What's happened! At this very moment the foreign lieutenant that your father has been weak enough to welcome to his house is beating his son as a planter beats a slave. . . .
ANGELINA: Why, what's the matter with you?
REGINA: Because Jimmy did something wrong, your father is doing something worse. He's having the child thrashed by the brute you all adore. (*She seizes Angelina by the wrist.*) To your knees, Angelina, and ask God to spare you.
ANGELINA: Regina, you're mad.
REGINA: You none of you seem to know what you're doing. That man is a monster and all of you are blind, blind!
ANGELINA: I can hardly believe my ears Is this you, who, only a moment ago were talking to me so reasonably, and now you're raving! To get into such a state because a disobedient boy gets a caning. . . .
REGINA: I beseech you to run to the sile and prevent him from touching your brother.
ANGELINA· Why don't you go yourself?
REGINA: He won't listen to me. I've already told you that he loathes me. (*Stamping her foot.*) Why don't you obey, you stubborn girl! I order you to go.

ANGELINA: I certainly won't. You're ridiculous.
REGINA: Angelina, there are some things that I can't tell you. (*She throws herself down on the sofa.*) I seem to feel in my flesh every one of the blows given to Jimmy. That man's brutality is horrible! (*She cries out.*) Can't you see that he's a fiend!

[*Angelina draws back a few steps.*]

ANGELINA: Regina, you frighten me. I'll run to the silo.
REGINA (*rises and takes Angelina's hand*): Listen, Angelina: I love Lieutenant Veechefsky to distraction. That's why I wanted to run away from Bonaventure. I love this man, and at the same time, something in me hates him. He's taken all peace, all joy of living from me. He is waiting for my lips to tell him that I love him, so as to turn me into a slave, but I won't say a word. I'll run away from the plantation because all he has for me is contempt. He alone is enough to make me hate the whole South. . . .
ANGELINA: But he doesn't come from the South.
REGINA: He has all of its arrogance. I've tried to stand up to him, I've told him that he came from over there, from Europe, but what does the South consist of but exiled aristocrats? The very pride that will be your ruin I can feel in the least gesture of a man that I adore because I'm vile.
ANGELINA (*moves away from* Regina): Don't say such things!

[*The sound of footsteps at left.*]

Someone is coming, let's run. . . .

[*They go through a door at left. An instant later appears*

on the threshold, at left, a young man dressed in black. He stands motionless. Almost at the same time, Veechefsky enters at right and stops short on seeing the stranger. The two men look at each other. Neither one moves. It grows darker.]

Curtain

ACT TWO

Scene 1

Same scenery as in Act. I.—There is no interval of time between the first and second acts. The young man in black removes his hat and comes forward a step. Veechefsky remains motionless and seems dumbfounded.

YOUNG MAN IN BLACK: Allow me to introduce myself: Eric Mac Clure.

IAN (*advances and holds out his hand to Mac Clure*): Excuse me. I didn't expect . . . Lieutenant Veechefsky.

MAC CLURE: Mr. Broderick talked about you a great deal to me, Lieutenant Veechefsky. You must find it strange that I didn't come in through the front door in the veranda but to tell the truth, I hoped to meet a servant who'd announce me to Mr. Broderick. (*A pause.*) May I ask why you're looking at me so closely?

IAN: Were you alone when you came in?

MAC CLURE: Why . . . yes. I left my horse in the avenue and not finding anyone about, came straight to the house. Why do you ask?

IAN: I thought I saw someone behind you.

MAC CLURE: No, there was no one with me. Perhaps I wasn't expected so soon.

IAN: Oh yes, you were.

MAC CLURE: May I ask you something? I'd like to have a conversation with Mr. Broderick alone, if you don't mind.

IAN: That's very easy. (*He goes to the right and pulls a bell-rope.*) Excuse me, but it seems to me that I saw you at a ball given last year at Beaufort by the officers of the 50th Light Artillery. A few civilians had been asked.

MAC CLURE: You're mistaking me for someone else. I've never been to a ball. I don't dance.
IAN: Yet there's a startling likeness.
MAC CLURE (*coldly*): At any rate, as far as I'm concerned, I'm sure I've never seen you before.

[*A servant appears at the door, right.*]

IAN (*without taking his eyes from Mac Clure*): Tell Mr. Broderick that Mr. Eric Mac Clure wishes to speak to him in the drawing-room. (*The servant goes out.*) In spite of our never having met, I feel that I know you a little. You've been so often mentioned to me at Bonaventure, and in the most flattering terms.

[*Mac Clure bows slightly without answering.*]

Mrs. Strong, Mr. Broderick's sister. . . .
MAC CLURE: Oh, she and I have only exchanged a few words. She talked mostly to my father.
IAN: If I'm not mistaken, you're doing Mr. Broderick the pleasure of spending two days on the plantation.
MAC CLURE: Yes, Mr. Broderick did ask me to spend two days but. . . .
IAN: Unfortunately, I must leave Bonaventure at dawn.
MAC CLURE: I won't be able to stay here more than a few hours myself, at most until tomorrow morning.
BRODERICK (*enters at right*): Welcome, sir, to Bonaventure.
MAC CLURE: Thank you, sir. I'd be grateful if you could let me have a few minutes' talk with you, (*he glances at Veechefsky*) alone.
BRODERICK: Alone? Is it absolutely necessary that Lieutenant Veechefsky. . . .
MAC CLURE: He couldn't do me a greater favour at

present. (*He bows. Lieutenant Veechefsky bows and goes out at right.*) Forgive my seeming a little peremptory. Lieutenant Veechefsky is of Polish extraction, I hear.

BRODERICK: Yes.

MAC CLURE: Does he realise the significance attached to his uniform at present?

BRODERICK: Let's not draw any conclusions from the colour of a uniform before the war breaks out . . . if it does break out.

MAC CLURE: I draw no conclusions. Lieutenant Veechefsky is free to act as he pleases. Regarding the war with which we are threatened, it's not at all sure that it will take place. The North hasn't the least desire to fight.

BRODERICK: To tell the truth, I don't so much fear the North as the South and, in particular, General Beauregard.

MAC CLURE: There, you're mistaken. General Beauregard has a correct view of the situation. He won't strike the first blow unless a slur is cast on the honour of the South, and not before. Do you remember what Shakespeare said: "Rightly to be great is not to stir without great argument. . . ."

BRODERICK: . . . "But greatly to find quarrel in a straw, when honour's at the stake." The straw, in this case, is that cursed Fort Sumter. Why did God place that little island where it is?

MAC CLURE: God didn't build the fort. However, nothing will happen without His permission.

BRODERICK (*rising*): But it's God's permission that I find so terrifying! He sends us His Gospels through torrents of blood. (*Mac Clure moves.*) Let's drop the subject, if you please. My ideas on this point could only shock you.

MAC CLURE: Yes.

BRODERICK: I myself have a favour to ask of you.

[*He sits again.*]

MAC CLURE (*gently*): I didn't come here to ask a favour of you.
BRODERICK: Excuse me, I spoke too quickly. I thought that you wanted to talk to me about your plantation.
MAC CLURE: Exactly. We sold it last week.
BRODERICK: Ah! Was the transaction satisfactory?
MAC CLURE: It's impossible to keep up a plantation without slaves and God didn't wish us to have slaves.
BRODERICK: And what about you? What are you going to do?
MAC CLURE: I thought I'd tell you later on in the evening, if you'll let me wait until then.

[*The light is now so dim that the outlines of the two men are barely perceptible.*]

BRODERICK: I think I can make a guess at what you're going to tell me. Far be it from me to want to question you. (*A pause.*) As we're alone: you saw Lieutenant Veechefsky for a few moments, just now. What's your impression of him?
MAC CLURE (*hesitates*): It's difficult for me to answer. I only saw him for a minute or two. Generally speaking, I'm prepared to like all human beings. . . .
BRODERICK: Without any mental reservations concerning this young man?
MAC CLURE: A reservation? No, he was most courteous . . . almost too much so, I thought. At the same time, he seemed disturbed. He's probably more sensitive than I am to all the war rumours that have been dinned in our ears for the last two weeks.
BRODERICK: Is that all?
MAC CLURE: Why yes. I'm ready to believe all the good in the world of him.

BRODERICK (*A pause*): The reason I mention Lieutenant Veechefsky whom you scarcely know, is that I have an important one for doing so. To tell the truth I suddenly had the idea, a sort of inspiration, that you could help me.

MAC CLURE: In what way?

BRODERICK: To sum it up in a few words, I'm convinced that he's for the South, but that a last scruple of loyalty to the North keeps him in that uniform. Tomorrow morning, he must rejoin his post at Fort Sumter.

MAC CLURE: Yes, he did tell me that he was leaving at dawn.

BRODERICK: But if he goes and the war breaks out, he'll never come back. So I'd like. . . .

[*He rises and turns away slightly from Mac Clure.*]

MAC CLURE: What would you like?

BRODERICK: I'd like you to prevent him from leaving.

MAC CLURE (*also rising*): Do you want my opinion?

BRODERICK: I beg you to give it me frankly.

MAC CLURE: The man is a deserter.

BRODERICK: How dare you!

MAC CLURE: Will you calmly examine the matter with me? Major Anderson is shut up in Fort Sumter with his troops. Three days ago, he received an ultimatum from General Beauregard, threatening to shell him if he didn't withdraw from the fort. Under the circumstances, do you find it normal that he should give Lieutenant Veechefsky a leave?

BRODERICK: There's a great deal of free-and-easiness on both sides. Anyway, he returns to his post tomorrow morning.

MAC CLURE: He won't return.

BRODERICK: How do you know? What makes you so sure?

MAC CLURE: I'm quite ready to apologise if Lieutenant Veechefsky returns to Fort Sumter. Since when has he been here?

BRODERICK: Since the evening of the ultimatum.

MAC CLURE: Has he left the plantation since his arrival?

BRODERICK: No. He went as far as the silo with my son, a short while ago, but he hasn't left Bonaventure, that I know of. I'm beginning to wonder. . . .

MAC CLURE: Have no fear. Lieutenant Veechefsky won't fight for the North.

BRODERICK: Then what is he doing here, in this uniform?

MAC CLURE (*laughing*): He's doing what a lot of young Americans are doing at this moment: he is examining his conscience. It's not so easy to leave one's regiment. First of all, you need civilian clothes. It's not so pleasant to ask for them. . . .

BRODERICK (*hopefully*): Tell me: do you suppose he's going to enlist in the Southern army?

MAC CLURE: I suppose nothing.

[*A servant enters and puts a lighted lamp on a table. Edward Broderick drops into an armchair. Mac Clure remains standing. The servant goes out.*]

BRODERICK: (*under his breath*): Now I come to think of it, I don't see why he should feel obliged to fight for the South. Our quarrels are foreign to him.

MAC CLURE: If the war breaks out tomorrow, Lieutenant Veechefsky can very well put on civilian dress and remain quietly at Bonaventure—or elsewhere.

BRODERICK: To be frank, I don't like what you've just said, sir.

MAC CLURE: Would you like me to leave?

BRODERICK: No, please stay. I was wrong to ask you all those questions, but there's a doubt in my mind, and it hurts me. Everything I hear, everything I see fills me with anxiety. Something dreadful is going to happen. I'm absolutely convinced of it.

[He goes and looks out of the window and stands there motionless. The sound of carriage wheels is heard in front of house, then of voices. Almost at once, a servant enters and bows before Edward Broderick.]

[Broderick seems on the verge of saying something, but changes his mind.]

Let's go out on the porch. I think our guests have come.

[They go out.]

Scene 2

Regina enters at left and drops into an armchair. For an instant she seems dazed, completely still. A sound of laughter and conversation is heard coming from the right. Angelina comes running in from right.

ANGELINA: What are you doing here, Regina? You've scarcely time to dress for supper. Aunt Evelyn wants to know where you are. What's the matter with you? Oh, have you seen young Mac Clure? He's even better looking than I thought, but why does he always dress in black when it's so fine? . . . Hurry up, answer, what's the matter?

REGINA: I told you. . . .

ANGELINA: You must pull yourself together, my little Regina. Shall I help you?
REGINA: No, leave me alone. I'll go dress in a minute.

[*Angelina goes out. Regina remains motionless. Veechefsky comes in behind her, from left.*]

IAN (*quickly*): Miss Regina, have you seen Angelina?
REGINA (*she rises and turns around*): No. (*Suddenly.*) Lieutenant Veechefsky, I have something to say to you.
IAN (*as though he had not heard*): I want to speak to Angelina.
REGINA: I'll fetch her if you'll listen to me a moment.
IAN (*eyes turned toward the right*): What have you to say to me?
REGINA: A while ago, when we were alone in this room, you told me to speak to you.
IAN: A while ago is not now.
REGINA: You understand that I had something to tell you. Do you know what it is?
IAN: Naturally?
REGINA: Why naturally?
IAN: It was enough to look at you then. And to look at you now.
REGINA (*hiding her face in her hands*): I'm ashamed! I could die of shame right now, before you!
IAN: Go and fetch Angelina for me.
REGINA: What right have you to order me about?
IAN (*shrugging his shoulders*): Don't try to fool me, I can read you like a book. You're trembling, Regina. I have every right. I no longer need to hear what you were going to tell me.
REGINA: You were very anxious to, a little while ago.
IAN: I'm not the same as I was, a little while ago.

Since then, something happened. (*Seizing her wrist suddenly.*) All right then, tell me! Humble your pride, you haughty little piece! If that's what you're pining for. . . .

REGINA (*breaking away from him*): Let me go! I hate you!

IAN: Don't you think I know that too? Go and fetch Angelina.

REGINA: No.

[*Ian goes out left. Regina is about to follow him and stops suddenly in the middle of the room.*]

Ian!

[*Almost at the same moment, enters Edward Broderick.*]

Scene 3

BRODERICK: Regina!

REGINA: Uncle Edward!

BRODERICK: I wondered where you were. You must come with me. We're having supper in a few minutes.

REGINA: Excuse me, Uncle Edward. I'm not feeling well.

BRODERICK: What's the matter, child? You aren't ill, are you?

REGINA: I don't know. I'd like to go upstairs and lie down on my bed. (*Suddenly.*) Oh, Uncle Edward, I wish I were dead!

BRODERICK (*takes her by the shoulders*): What's that? Don't talk so, my little Regina. Is it on account of the war? Maybe there won't be a war. . . .

REGINA: No, no. It isn't on account of the war.

BRODERICK: . . . Or is it because you're leaving Bonaventure? You can stay, if you like. I've told you that before.

REGINA: I can stay. . . .

BRODERICK: The decision rests with you, child. If that's what's worrying you, we can talk it over tomorrow morning. Are you sure there isn't anything else?

REGINA: I appreciate your kindness, Uncle Edward, but you can't do anything for me.

BRODERICK (*relinquishing his grasp*): Far be it from me to wish to question you, Regina. However, it worries me to see you upset. I thought, I still think of you as being so strong-minded.

REGINA: I'll be strong enough when the time comes. Will you let me lie down on this sofa? (*Showing a sofa left.*) I'll join you all in a moment.

BRODERICK: Of course, my dear. That's the sofa where my mother used to curl up sometimes to sleep. They used to throw a shawl over her feet.

[*He squeezes Regina's hand and goes out at right. Regina snuggles down in the sofa. Angelina enters from left, in a white frock. She goes to look at herself in a large mirror and sees Regina on the sofa.*]

ANGELINA: You aren't dressed yet! What on earth are you doing? Supper will be announced in a quarter of an hour.

REGINA: I can't appear like this.

ANGELINA: Oh, it won't matter. Mrs. Priolleau's daughter is dressed for travelling. It isn't a big supper.

REGINA: I don't want to see Lieutenant Veechefsky.

ANGELINA: You're sure not to be seated next to him. If I were you, I wouldn't say a single word to him.

I'd treat him with the supreme contempt that a woman should have for any man. And then you'd see. . . . You'd see your little Polish lieutenant come fawning to you like a dog. . . .

REGINA: Hold your tongue, Angelina. You don't know what you're saying.

ANGELINA: As for me, I don't wish to be left alone one minute with young Mac Clure. He's quite capable of making love to me again. If you see him come near me, fly to the rescue! It is agreed? Oh, this supper's going to be such fun! What a pity Aunt Evelyn won't allow me to do my hair as I want!

REGINA (*rising suddenly and going toward the right*): Come, let's go, little girl.

ANGELINA: I won't be called " little girl ".

Scene 4

Enter at left, Eliza, Mrs. Strong's maid. A tall, spare women in her thirties, yellow rather than light brown, with kinky hair. She wears a big white muslin apron and a lace cap with long ribbon streamers. For some time, she stands squarely before the large mirror and stares at her reflection in silence. Then she speaks:

ELIZA: Eliza Fermor, you're a fine woman. (*She looks at herself full face, then three-quarters.*) Pale, very pale, but beautiful. (*She stretches out her hand.*) How white is . . . frightfully white! Give me your hand, Eliza, and we'll go for a turn on the lake, by the light of the moon. The two of us in the boat. . . . (*She turns this way and that, while continuing her soliloquy under her breath.*) It glides between the trees, between the tall cypresses that grow in the black water. Oh, I feel so romantic! (*She pinches her ears sharply then shakes her hands in the air, on a level with her face.*) Bright red ears, lily white hands . . . like a lady of quality!

[*Enter at left, Jeremy, a negro dressed in blue livery with big brass buttons. His hair is touched with grey.*]

JEREMY: What are you doing here, Miss Liza? If Missis sees you, she'll pull your hair for you.
ELIZA: Let me tell you, nigger, that nobody has ever pulled my hair at Bonaventure. And if Missis sees me here, I'll tell her the truth, namely that I'm straightening up the sitting room. (*She shakes up a cushion.*) Because we're receiving quality tonight.
JEREMY: Mrs. Priolleau and daughter, they're quality. Colonel Chatard too and young Mr. Mac Clure. All that's quality. But I don't know about the foreign lieutenant.
ELIZA: The foreign lieutenant's quality too. First of all, he wouldn't have been invited here if he wasn't as good as the others. We never receive anything but quality here. You don't know nothing.
JEREMY: Maybe the foreign lieutenant's foreign quality.
ELIZA: There's no such thing as foreign quality. There's just quality, pure and simple. Straighten that rocking-chair for me, nigger.
JEREMY: Yes, Miss Liza. (*He obeys.*) In the cotton fields, they say there's going to be a war.
ELIZA: Missis says she's sure there won't be. I suppose she knows better than you do.
JEREMY: Uncle John says the Lord is going to make an example. What's an example? A miracle for the black folks?
ELIZA: Uncle John is an old dodderer. There isn't going to be any war. Everything's going to stay just as it is. You hear me?

JEREMY: Yes, Miss Liza, but I'm scared. I haven't slept a wink for the last three nights. There's too many blacks talking about running away. Master doesn't know. They're scared too, just like sheep before a storm. I think if I heard a cannon-shot I'd drop dead.

ELIZA: You want to run away?

JEREMY: No, I didn't say that. And it's too difficult. But I'm scared to death. I'm not awfully brave.

ELIZA: I've been suspecting that myself for a little while. But what are you scared of, nigger? If there's a war, you won't have to fight.

JEREMY: That's so. But when all's said and done, the black man always has to foot the bill.

ELIZA: Nonsense. Go back to the pantry, Jeremy.

[*She marches up to him; he runs off towards a door at right.*]

JEREMY (*before disappearing*): You can talk like the white folks for all you're worth, Miss Liza, but you're black. When you die, you'll be buried along with the rest of us.

ELIZA: Get away with you!

[*Jeremy vanishes. Eliza returns to the mirror and smooths her hair.*]

Bury me with the black folks! Why, my hair just has a little, little wave in it, just here and there. That crazy old Jeremy. . . .

[*Angelina enters suddenly at right.*]

ANGELINA: Go away, Eliza, I wish to be alone.

ELIZA: Very well, Miss Angelina.

[*She goes out at left. Veechefsky enters from right.*]

IAN: Angelina! What's the matter?
ANGELINA: Nothing, nothing at all.
IAN: Why did you run away?
ANGELINA: I don't want to hear what they have to say, that's all.
IAN: Did they frighten you?
ANGELINA: Don't be ridiculous. I'm not afraid of anything. It's just simply that they bore me.
IAN: You must take Mrs. Priolleau's talk with a grain of salt. She seems to enjoy making bad news worse and have everyone feel uneasy. . . .
ANGELINA: I don't care a thing for Mrs. Priolleau. First of all, I'm sure that nothing's going to happen. Ever since I was a child, I've heard nothing but talk about impending calamities. All that bores me to death. And nothing happens, as you may have noticed. Nothing's happened since I was born. Can you even imagine anything happening here? We live at the end of never.
IAN: That's no reason.
ANGELINA: It seems reason enough to me. It takes an hour in the barouche to get to the nearest town. I'm glad it's that far away. . . .
IAN: So you feel a threat hanging over you?
ANGELINA: One's always threatened by something. It's enough to live in a fine house and to be, well . . . what we are, for someone to want to destroy us. The very fact that the South exists is a challenge. But you can't understand. You come from elsewhere.
IAN: I come from a country that history suppressed because its very existence was perhaps a challenge.
ANGELINA: Oh, you don't know the South. You couldn't suppress the South. If there was a war, and we were beaten, the victory of the North would be a

sort of suicide for the whole country. Because the pick of what grows on American soil, is us.

IAN: I find it very strange that, in spite of not believing in war, you should nevertheless feel the weight of something threatening.

ANGELINA: Perhaps it's just the threat of death.

IAN: At your age, to talk about death. . . .

ANGELINA: You think I'm just a little girl, who never gives death a thought.

IAN: So you sometimes think about death?

ANGELINA: Yes and no. Perhaps a little . . . Some days, when Mammy combs my hair, I say to myself: "You're combing a dead woman's hair." Just a crazy idea that flits through my mind. I don't know why. But after all, it doesn't really worry me much. Death is for other people.

IAN: But supposing there was a calamity, a real calamity?

ANGELINA: I don't know what that is.

IAN: A while ago, you said something that struck me, about the feeling of some threat hanging over us.

ANGELINA: Oh, you know, I don't always have that feeling. I usually have it as night falls.

IAN: So, for instance, this evening. . . .

ANGELINA: Stop, Lieutenant Veechefsky. You'd better go back to the porch. I don't care for this kind of conversation.

IAN: I've never taken you for a little girl and if I wanted to talk to you alone, it's because I have something important to say to you.

ANGELINA (*flattered*): To me?

IAN: Yes, certainly, to you. But first I want you to let me ask you a question. It's a very delicate one and I hesitate.

ANGELINA: I wonder what it can be.

IAN: But I must begin by confessing something that will certainly displease you very much.

ANGELINA: Well, now you've warned me. . . .

IAN: Promise you'll forgive me?

ANGELINA: Yes.

IAN: You're sure?

ANGELINA: Lieutenant Veechefsky, you're too tiresome for words.

IAN: A short time ago, when you were talking to Miss Regina, I came into the room. Do you remember?

ANGELINA: Yes. Well?

IAN: In spite of me, I heard part of what you were saying.

ANGELINA: I was certain of it! Lieutenant Veechefsky, I hate you.

IAN: You promised to forgive me.

ANGELINA: I forgive you, but I hate you. It's just as though you listened at doors, like a slave.

IAN: I wasn't listening, I couldn't help hearing. You were talking about Eric Mac Clure.

ANGELINA: That's none of your business.

IAN: If I mentioned him, Angelina, it's because I unintentionally overheard a sentence in which you told Regina about a letter he had written you.

ANGELINA: Well, after having heard that sentence you should have left the room immediately, or informed us of your presence.

IAN: And, instead of which, I stayed on until you'd finished your story.

ANGELINA: It's disgraceful.

IAN: It would be disgraceful if I'd stayed from sheer curiosity, but I had other reasons.

ANGELINA: And what are they, pray?

IAN: One should be enough for you. I won't have

that man writing you love letters. (*In a rage, suddenly.*) Do you hear?

ANGELINA: Are you mad? (*She rises.*) What right have you to speak to me in such a tone?

IAN (*rising also*): Forgive me, Angelina. I gave way to a moment of impatience. Is it true that Eric Mac Clure wrote you a love letter? Wasn't it, perhaps, one of those dreams we all have? Miss Regina seemed to think so. You see, it's hard to imagine such a serious, and you might even say, such a stern young man making love to a girl of seventeen.

ANGELINA: I have no explanations to give you. I think you're impertinent and ridiculous.

IAN: You'd judge me less harshly if you knew how deeply I'm suffering. (*A pause.*) Angelina, are you in love with Eric Mac Clure?

ANGELINA: If I were, why should it affect you?

IAN: Affect me! It goes straight to my heart. . . . (*He turns away, takes a few steps left and turns to Angelina. After a hesitation.*) . . . Because I love you.

[*Angelina goes back a step and looks long at him.*]

ANGELINA: What's the good of lying? You know very well you don't love me.

[*She turns quickly to the right and goes out. Veechefsky remains perfectly still. After a few seconds, Edward Broderick enters at right.*]

BRODERICK: I've just met Angelina. She seems upset. What's the matter.

IAN: I know nothing about it.

BRODERICK (*sitting down*): Perhaps our conversation on the porch disturbed her. Oh, I wish this night would end! There's something about the uncertainty we're in that I can't stand. It would be almost a relief to hear the guns.

IAN: Maybe we'll never hear them.

BRODERICK: You've always been more optimistic than I.

IAN: I'm not optimistic. On the contrary, I feel that there's a . . . shadow hanging over us.

BRODERICK: I've felt it for weeks.

IAN: And I, for the last hour.

BRODERICK: For the last hour! Have you heard any news?

IAN: No, none. It has nothing to do with the war. I don't know how to explain what I want to say. . . . However, I'd like to tell someone, to try to be rid of it, as you try to rid yourself of a dream by telling it. But I can't hope for anyone to understand. Everything has changed in me for the last hour.

BRODERICK: Do you imagine that I haven't felt it? You seemed so disturbed, a little while ago.

IAN: A little while ago?

BRODERICK: Yes, when young Mac Clure came into the room.

IAN: Maybe it's partly because of that. I mean that there is a kind of coincidence between the moment he came in and the time I had that sudden feeling.

[*A pause.*]

BRODERICK: Well, Ian?

IAN: When he appeared all at once in the doorway, at his left and a little behind him, I saw someone.

BRODERICK: A servant, probably.

IAN: No. A man dressed like a soldier, dressed like me, but his face was covered with a piece of black cloth, or something like a garment that had been thrown over his head.

BRODERICK: What you thought you saw in the twilight doesn't really surprise me. At that time of day in our part of the world, such illusions are quite possible.

IAN: I felt to the bottom of my soul that it was true. The man did not budge. After a few seconds, he was no longer there.

BRODERICK: Wasn't I right in saying that it was a delusion?

IAN (*as though he had not heard*): He disappeared only after I'd had time to see him. He delivered his message and then he went away.

BRODERICK: His message? Ian, what you say makes no sense.

IAN: At home, in the old country, such things have a sense. The man was my height and dressed as I am.

[*A pause.*]

BRODERICK: You stayed alone with Mac Clure for a moment.

IAN: Alone with Mac Clure. . . .

BRODERICK: At any rate, I found you both together and alone when I came in. What did you talk about? (*Ian looks at him.*) I'm sorry. No doubt he told you what he thought about what's going on, of his position towards the North and the South?

IAN: To tell the truth, I don't remember what we talked about. It's of no interest.

BRODERICK: You have a very strange expression, then.

IAN: That's quite possible. I told you why, a minute ago.

[*A pause.*]

BRODERICK: Do you still intend to leave tomorrow at dawn?

IAN: Those are my orders, sir.

BRODERICK: You can be sure that tonight, many orders of this sort will be torn up and cast to the winds. (*A pause.*) It wouldn't be dishonourable to disobey. (*A pause.*) If you have any doubts on the subject, would you like me to ask Eric Mac Clure to give us his opinion? He might even have a talk with you.

IAN: No. Forgive my speaking so openly, but I don't wish to see the man.

BRODERICK: My dear Ian, I don't understand you. In any case, you'll be obliged to see him in a few minutes.

IAN: I expressed myself badly, no doubt. I meant to say that I didn't want to see him alone.

BRODERICK: But why, Ian?

IAN: You must allow me to keep such personal sentiments to myself. I'm leaving tomorrow at dawn, as I resolved. Please Heaven that this man's path never crosses mine again on this earth.

BRODERICK: I don't want to ask any questions, Ian. But I'm twice your age. I've lived and I've been unhappy. It's not impossible that I might understand you.

[*Ian turns away and takes a few steps toward the left.*]

IAN: Do you wish to know why I don't want to find myself face to face with this man? You've asked me, I'm going to tell you: he has taken the place I wished to hold in the heart of someone who lives here.

BRODERICK: Eric Mac Clure? He's only spent a few hours in this house.

IAN: Don't you think that's time enough?

BRODERICK: I confess that I have some difficulty in understanding you. Regina was not here when he came, a little before Christmas. And then, the idea that you might be in love with Regina has something so. . . .

IAN: This has nothing to do with Regina.

BRODERICK: Then I can only suppose that you mean. . . .

IAN: Yes.

BRODERICK: My daughter? Do you mean that Angelina is in love with Eric Mac Clure?

IAN: I mean that I'm in love with your daughter Angelina, and that I have the honour of asking you for her hand.

BRODERICK: Ian. . . . What's the use of making up such a story? You're not in love with Regina, or with Angelina. And you won't save yourself by marrying my daughter. Shall I tell you who you're in love with?

IAN (*turns away so that Edward Broderick can no longer see his face*): No.

BRODERICK: After what you've just told me, how can I take your reply for anything but an admission? I can't have guessed wrong. No one escapes his fate, Ian. . . . No one escapes that fate.

IAN: You refuse me Angelina's hand?

BRODERICK: For the sake of your happiness as well as hers. . . .

IAN: You'll never see me again, Edward Broderick.

BRODERICK: I know it. (*A pause.*) You're going away at dawn tomorrow. I'll hear you go, but I won't say good-bye.

[*He appears undecided, then goes out at left. Veechefsky without looking at him, remains motionless. After a few seconds, Jimmy runs in from the left.*]

JIMMY: Lieutenant Veechefsky, aren't you coming

out on the porch? They're saying such interesting things about the war.

IAN (*without looking at him*): I'll come in a moment, Jimmy.

JIMMY: All right. Why don't you look at me?

IAN: You bear me no grudge for what happened this afternoon?

JIMMY: Why, you're joking! Of course not! But you hurt an awful lot, you know!

IAN: You're a brave boy. You didn't cry out. Neither did I, when I was your age. I made it a point of honour not to let a sound pass my lips. I have something to tell you. Shall we sit down there?

JIMMY: Sit down? I should think not. Sit down if you like. I can't.

[*They laugh.*]

IAN: Very well, we'll remain standing.

[*They are silent for a moment.*]

JIMMY: Why don't you speak, Lieutenant Veechefsky?

IAN: I was thinking. We won't go out together tomorrow, Jimmy. I must leave the plantation early.

JIMMY: When are you coming back?

IAN: I don't know. Listen, Jimmy, it's possible there may be a war and we don't know what can happen to us. I have no fears for you, but with me, it's another matter: I'm a soldier. We're going to say good-bye to each other here, like two men, but first, I have something to ask you.

JIMMY: Something to ask me?

IAN: Yes. . . . I want to ask you a question. Listen well. If someone said to you—I'm just supposing this—if someone told you that I was in love with your sister, what would you think of it?

JIMMY: You, in love with Angelina?

IAN: Yes, if someone said that to you. . . .

JIMMY: Oh, I'd find it funny. Lovers look so silly! And then, I can't imagine you in love with Angelina. I don't know why.

IAN: Will you think it over for a minute? Is it on account of Angelina? Don't you think Angelina's pretty?

JIMMY: Oh, she's not bad-looking.

IAN: Then perhaps I'm the reason that it seems funny to you?

JIMMY: I don't know. I just can't imagine such a thing. . . . You know, to me love is tomfoolery. (*A pause—Jimmy goes toward Veechefsky and takes his hand.*) But you aren't going, Lieutenant Veechefsky, not for ever?

[*Ian breaks away suddenly and goes back a step.*]

IAN: You aren't old enough to understand, and because you can't understand, I'm going to tell you a secret. My secret. Will you promise to keep it all your life?

JIMMY: Yes, I promise.

IAN (*after a pause*): This night is not like other nights. Perhaps I've never spoken to anyone as I'm speaking to you now, and you must try to remember what I say. At certain moments, freedom of will is a crushing weight, and to choose is not possible. There are days when I'd like to be one of those wretched blacks who sing so sadly in the cotton fields, or a farm hand in a Northern state. . . .

JIMMY: You're hesitating between the North and the South?

IAN: No, Jimmy, that has nothing to do with it.

JIMMY: Aunt Evelyn says that if there's a war, they'll take away the uniform you're wearing and give you another, a Southern one.

IAN: I'm in love, Jimmy, as no human being ever was before. Of course, all men say that, and each of them is right. I can't go on living any longer.

JIMMY: You can't go on living? But why?

IAN: Because the person I love can't love me.

JIMMY: How do you know?

IAN: How do I know? That's a very intelligent question. I know it because I know, that's all. A single glance was enough for me to foresee years of useless suffering.

JIMMY: Just don't think about it. Just don't see that person.

IAN: It's not so simple, Jimmy. Had that person never been born, it would have been better for both of us. You see, I don't think I'd ever fall back before the enemy, if there's a war, but tonight, I'm afraid of falling back before suffering.

JIMMY: What are you going to do?

IAN: The strangest thing I've ever done in my whole life. . . . (*he moves away a few steps and goes to the window; one has the impression that he is talking to himself*) . . . hurl myself against my fate as you hurl yourself against a stone wall.

JIMMY: What are you saying, Lieutenant Veechefsky?

IAN: Nothing. I was thinking out loud. It's far better not to know what men are thinking about, Jimmy. It's almost always sad, or shameful. I'm not ashamed, but I'm alone. I feel dreadfully alone.

JIMMY: But how can you be alone? I'm here. . . . What funny things you're saying tonight.

IAN: That's quite true, I shouldn't have spoken. One should never speak. The moment we open our lips, everything throws us back into ourselves.

JIMMY: So you're in love with Angelina? Why don't you marry her?

IAN (*shrugging his shoulders*): First of all, she'd have to be in love with me. . . .

JIMMY: So that's it!

IAN: In short, all you've understood, all you've remembered of our conversation is that I'm in love with Angelina.

JIMMY: Why . . . yes, isn't that what you meant?

IAN: Angelina . . . who knows? She might have been salvation. . . .

[*A pause.*]

JIMMY: Why don't you say something, Lieutenant Veechefsky? You aren't the same as usual. (*He comes a little closer to him.*) Won't you tell me a story? A story about your country?

IAN: A story about my country? Very well, I'll tell you one. In Poland some time around 1720, lived a boy called Ian.

JIMMY: Like you?

IAN: Yes, like me. He was my great grandfather's brother.

JIMMY: Then it's a true story?

IAN: Absolutely true. When I've told you my story, you must go to bed. Promise?

JIMMY: Papa said I could stay up until the first bell for supper.

IAN: You'll go straight up to your room? You won't hide in the staircase, as you usually do when there's company?

JIMMY: Yes, I promise.

IAN: Well, Ian was dressed like a young nobleman, he wore a fur cap, a velvet coat embroidered in silver and red leather boots. He had a palace in town and a castle in the country.

JIMMY: I wish I had some red leather boots.
IAN: Ian also had a great number of serfs, of white slaves.
JIMMY: White slaves! It would make me feel funny to order about white slaves. A slave ought to be black.
IAN: He was young and had everything in the world a man could wish for, but however, he might as well have had nothing, because he lacked happiness. He was like me. He was in love.
JIMMY: There you are again, talking about love! Is everybody in love?
IAN: He was in love to the verge of madness. When he saw that the person he adored wouldn't even look at him, he fell into a frenzy and killed his love.
JIMMY: Why?
IAN: Perhaps because he thought he'd cease being in love and suffering, at the same time.
JIMMY: Didn't they do anything to him?
IAN: No, nothing.
JIMMY: He shouldn't have killed that person who'd done nothing to him.
IAN: He couldn't help it, Jimmy. There are times when men commit the most dreadful actions without being able to help it.
JIMMY: They'd have hanged him here.
IAN: In those days, nobody would have dared to lay hands on a nobleman. But something happened which he hadn't foreseen: he went on being in love with the person he had killed.
JIMMY: Ah?
IAN: Yes, for years and years. And, one day, this is what happened: God took Ian in His great hand and, very gently, He broke him to pieces.
JIMMY: What does that mean? Very gently, He broke him to pieces?
IAN: I haven't time to explain this to you, but life will

show you how God goes about it to break a man to pieces. Sometimes it takes Him twenty, thirty years, a whole life, but time is His own and He does what He wishes.

[*A pause. A bell is heard to strike twice.*]

IAN: You heard the bell? Look at me, Jimmy. You're going upstairs and you're going to sleep. Is that a promise?
JIMMY: Yes, Lieutenant Veechefsky.
IAN: But first give me your hand and say good-bye to Lieutenant Veechefsky.
JIMMY: Good-bye, Lieutenant Veechefsky.
IAN (*grasps his hand*): Good-bye, Jimmy.

[*Jimmy goes out at left and turns around before disappearing. Veechefsky goes out at right.*]

Curtain

ACT THREE

Scene 1

Same setting as the previous acts, but the drawing-room is lit by a chandelier. Enter slowly from right, Mrs. Priolleau and her daughter, Mrs. Strong followed by Regina and Angelina, the Lieutenant Veechefsky and Mac Clure, and last Edward Broderick and old Mr. White.

MRS. PRIOLLEAU: If you want my opinion, I think we're showing very little spirit. Yes, very little indeed. Far be it from me to wish to offend anyone, but we all look as though we'd lost our last friends.

BRODERICK: You wouldn't have us dancing when war may break out at any moment now, Cousin Laura.

MRS. PRIOLLEAU: That's as it may be. I had supper three days ago on a plantation an hour from here, in other words, at the Beauchamps. Followed a ball that lasted far into the small hours. I hadn't seen anything so brilliant since the fifties. The flower of Southern youth rallied in the great gilt drawing-rooms where a toast was drunk to General Beauregard and, one after the other, to all the states that have already seceded from the Union . . . from Texas whose flag bears a single star, to Elizabeth's old Dominion, Virginia. . . .

MRS. STRONG (*in a whisper to Edward Broderick*): I told you not to give her a second julep.

MAC CLURE: I'd hate to contradict you, Ma'am, but Virginia hasn't made up her mind to secede yet, and it's an open secret that President Lincoln would like to put General Lee in command of the Northern armies.

MRS. PRIOLLEAU: Young man, those are the idle dreams of abolitionists. Virginia is all for us and the wreathed smiles of that old chimpanzee in a top hat won't change a thing. I don't suppose you're opposed to slavery?

MAC CLURE: With all my heart, Ma'am.

BRODERICK: Eric Mac Clure has freed all his slaves.

MRS. PRIOLLEAU: Monstrous! I have three hundred of them and I'd like to see the devil himself try to get them away from me.

MAC CLURE: With all due respect to you, Ma'am, allow me to tell you that if the South fights, it won't be to keep her slaves. General Lee has just freed all of his.

MRS. PRIOLLEAU: General Lee!

MRS. STRONG: Laura, why are we all standing around as though we were about to sing a hymn. . . . Sit down. Let's all sit down. I'm going to give you a cup of *café brûlot,* the kind that's served in the Vieux Carré, in New-Orleans.

[*She leads her gently to the right and sits down with her at a table in a corner. A group forms around the women. Angelina takes Regina towards the left.*]

ANGELINA: Regina, the most awful thing has happened: I'm really in love with Eric Mac Clure.

REGINA: What's awful about that? He wrote you a love letter, didn't he?

ANGELINA: Oh, a love letter. . . . Well, to begin with, he never wrote me at all.

REGINA: What! Then how about the story you told me? So you lied?

ANGELINA: I didn't lie, I really believed the story myself.

REGINA: But what you said wasn't true.

ANGELINA: Oh, you don't understand. How strange that you should be intelligent and yet not understand.

Just like a man. I'm unhappy, Regina. I don't know what to do. For a long time I've had an inkling of this and then suddenly, just now, I felt that I loved him. And he doesn't so much as look at me.

REGINA: Then don't look at him either.

ANGELINA: But he's going away tomorrow, and he's so handsome in this light. If he'd only go walking with me in the great avenue, I'd kiss him. Yes, I'd kiss him. . . . Oh! Imagine, Lieutenant Veechefsky proposed to me before supper. But I didn't believe he was sincere and I told him so, to his face.

REGINA: Lieutenant. . . .

ANGELINA: What's the matter with you? Oh, I forgot! Please forgive me.

REGINA: It's neither with you, nor with me that he's in love.

ANGELINA: Oh, you aren't going to tell me that he's in love with Miss Priolleau. (*Under her breath.*) Oh, there he is, behind us! Run away, quick!

[*She goes to the right but* Regina *remains motionless.*]

IAN (*draws near to Regina and stands a few steps behind her*): Miss Regina! (*Regina makes no reply.*) We're alone, once more, but for the last time, and now it's I that have something to say to you. (*A pause. Regina remains still.*) I've come to beg your pardon. (*A pause. Both stand motionless.*) Do you hear? I don't want to go away without begging your pardon. Time is passing, Regina. For the last few hours, I've not been the same man. I'm suffering, just as you are. There is that link between us. (*A pause.*) Will you ever forgive me? Just say yes, in a whisper and I'll be at peace. I'll go away at peace with myself. (*Regina makes no reply.*) I need only stretch out my hand to touch yours. Will you allow me to, Regina?

[*Regina, without saying a word, goes out suddenly, left. Veechefsky stands motionless for an instant and then goes towards the right.*]

MISS PRIOLLEAU: I hope our soldiers will have pretty uniforms. Those that are worn now are so severe. . . . And then, what will our flag be like, I wonder? I suppose we'll have our own flag.

MAC CLURE: Various designs have been submitted. The most popular one has a red ground with a cross of Saint Andrew in blue, spangled with white stars. One star for each state.

MISS PRIOLLEAU: Oh, I can see it already, waving over the battle fields!

MAC CLURE: You're in a awful hurry, Miss Priolleau. Have you any idea of what a battle field's like?

MISS PRIOLLEAU: Why, of course I have! Papa's library at home is full of pictures showing the chief episodes of the war against England. Not a detail missing. You can see the gunners at their posts very clearly indeed, and the cannons belching fire.

MAC CLURE: And maybe some dead and wounded soldiers too?

MISS PRIOLLEAU: Here and there, of course. There have to be some.

MAC CLURE: There will have to be a lot, if war breaks out. And what will you do then, Miss Priolleau?

MISS PRIOLLEAU: I'll shred lint, sir, to make dressings for our wounded.

MAC CLURE: Shouldn't you say for our gallant wounded? That's what they're called, in every war.

ANGELINA: I think we should talk about something else.

MRS. PRIOLLEAU: What's been said to upset you? I've never seen such long faces. You'd think really that the Lord had forsaken us and that He is not on our side.

MAC CLURE: I don't know why, but I was expecting that sentence.

MRS. PRIOLLEAU: What do you mean?

MAC CLURE: Nothing very definite, but for the last weeks, the Church keeps telling us that God is on our side.

MRS. PRIOLLEAU: Can you give that a doubt?

MAC CLURE: It's not such an easy question. We'd have to know, first of all, if God is always on the winning side—as you think we're going to win.

MRS. PRIOLLEAU: If God is with us, I really don't see how the North can win. That would be almost blasphemy, wouldn't it, Mr. White?

MR. WHITE: Since you ask my opinion, Ma'am, I'm going to quote a verse from the Bible. It's in the Book of Kings.

MRS. PRIOLLEAU: I adore the Book of Kings. Let's have your verse.

MR. WHITE: It's this: "Let not him that girdeth on his harness boast himself as he that putteth it off."

MRS. PRIOLLEAU: I really don't see the connection, Mr. White. (*She rises.*) Evelyn, you must forgive us for leaving so early, but the road is a perfect bog and we have an hour's drive ahead of us. (*Miss Priolleau rises.*) When we meet again, the face of the country will have changed. (*She kisses Mrs. Strong.*)

MRS. STRONG: I liked the country as it was.

MRS. PRIOLLEAU: You speak of it in the past. So you see that things couldn't go on as they were. Good-bye, Edward.

BRODERICK: If you must go, I'll see you to your carriage.

[*Mrs. Priolleau and her daughter take leave of everyone.*

All go out at right, except Veechefsky, Eric Mac Clure and Mr. White.]

MR. WHITE: I beg that'll you'll excuse me, gentlemen. It's earlier for you than for a man of my age. If I've understood right, you're going away tomorrow. May God keep you always.

[*He shakes hands with the two men and goes out at left.*]

MAC CLURE: Shall we join our hosts, Lieutenant?
IAN: I wish to speak to you, Eric Mac Clure.
MAC CLURE: Here? Just as you like.
IAN: What I have to say will no doubt surprise you and, however, I know only too well that I'll never be able to express my feelings. At another time perhaps, but not tonight. Everything seals my lips. The very air I breathe here seems to stifle me. This setting, these great mirrors, the trees in the avenue, all I see advises me to be silent. And I'm afraid too that, one sentence leading to another, I'll be brought to confide in you, entrapped by my own words. . . .
MAC CLURE: But you've just said that you couldn't speak.
IAN: I didn't wish to, but now, having begun to speak, I'm compelled to go ahead.
MAC CLURE: What compels you to go ahead?
IAN: You. You alone. The very way you're looking at me.
MAC CLURE: I don't know what opinion you can have of me, Lieutenant Veechefsky. I'm a plain man, used to talking plainly. If I didn't feel that you were disturbed and perhaps unhappy, I'd already have left the room, for scarcely anything you say is intelligible to me. I have the impression that all the words you use serve to hide what you're afraid of saying. Perhaps I could help you. . . .

IAN: Help me?

MAC CLURE: Yes, help you to say what you have so much to heart and that your tongue refuses to let me hear. Oh, far be it from me to force a secret from you. I have a horror of confidences and the familiarity they bring with them, but I'd be blind if I didn't realise that the man I have before me is a man . . . well, an unhappy man.

IAN: . . . Unhappy. Yes.

MAC CLURE: Do you hesitate because you come from elsewhere? You think me most unfeeling. But you and I are made of the same flesh. I have the same impulses, the same perplexities and sometimes my heart is like the kingdom divided spoken of in the Gospel.

IAN: Forgive what I'm about to say, but your austerity chills me. You are one of the righteous that we're told of sometimes, and who are never wrong. I myself have been wrong all my life. Does it seem strange to you that I should talk like this?

MAC CLURE: It seems very strange. I told you a short time ago that confidences embarrass me and the errors you may have committed are not my business. But . . . or I'm much mistaken, your conscience is troubled because, having lived in the North, you perhaps feel won over secretly to the Southern cause.

IAN: No, that has nothing to do with it.

MAC CLURE: Then what have we been talking about for the last five minutes? Well, answer!

IAN: I can say nothing to you. We are a thousand miles apart. This controversy between the North and the South is none of my business. This war is not my war. Something else is breaking my heart, something that you can't understand, and what I read in your face is the invincible ignorance of the pure in heart where the suffering of the world is concerned. You have never loved, Eric Mac Clure. Your pride has never yielded, you don't know, as I know now, that a soul can be in bondage to another soul, or the power of life and death wielded by a human face.

MAC CLURE: How do you know? If you're in love, how do you know I'm not?

IAN: You?

MAC CLURE: Why not? Answer!

IAN: Alas, what can I say?

MAC CLURE (*goes up to him and grips his wrist*): Lieutenant Veechefsky, we're to part in a little while. I'm going to enlist in the Southern army. As for you, you'll go where you please, but I'm sure we'll never see each other again. (*He drops Ian's wrist.*) For this reason and because of what you've just told me, I'm going to talk to you openly. I know perfectly well that I shall be killed.

IAN: I too shall be killed. I want to be killed.

MAC CLURE: You'll be killed if it's God will, but you may have, as I have, the conviction that the road goes no farther, that it suddenly stops short. . . . Tonight, I feel that I'll take another few steps along the road, just a few steps, but I have no regrets. Would you like to know why? You've judged me to be cold, hard, insensible, a truly righteous man, according to your view. Well, I don't know if I'm one of the righteous, but I'm certain of one thing: never have I suffered so bitterly as in this house.

IAN: In this house?

MAC CLURE: There's someone in this house that I'm in love with, and who doesn't know it.

[*A pause.*]

IAN: Why haven't you declared yourself?

MAC CLURE: It's too late. It's too late for love. War's on the threshold, and I'm going.

IAN: Why can't I die now, with those words in my ears? At least I'd leave this world with a doubt in my heart, instead of unbearable truth.

MAC CLURE: Are you afraid that we're in love with the same person?

IAN: Don't say that, it's not possible.

MAC CLURE: I don't see why.

IAN: A word would be enough to open your eyes, but that very word, which I won't speak, would seem more mysterious and more abominable to you than all the rest.

MAC CLURE: I can easily imagine you to be in love, as I'm in love myself. Love isn't a sin.

IAN: Love isn't a sin. . . .

MAC CLURE: These words seem to surprise you. It looks as though you were even more of a Puritan than I am.

IAN: I want to ask you a question. Will you allow me to?

MAC CLURE: Why, of course. I'll see if I can answer it.

IAN: You said a little while ago, that the person you love is unaware of it. Haven't you been tempted to express your sentiments?

MAC CLURE: Certainly, but I felt I shouldn't. I thought I'd told you this.

IAN: Isn't it rather because you didn't dare, because your courage failed you, that you trembled, for the first time perhaps, trembled before a human being.

MAC CLURE: No, you're mistaken. I didn't wish to inflict an unnecessary trial, to perhaps inspire love which might cause unhappiness.

IAN: Can you imagine a man lacking courage to the point of not being able to speak of his love?

MAC CLURE: Yes, one can be brave and lack that kind of courage.

IAN: Even if it kills you?

MAC CLURE: Even if it kills you. (*He goes up to Ian and takes his hand.*) Lieutenant Veechefsky, something attracts me to you that I can scarcely explain, for to tell the truth, I hardly know you. I remember that five years ago, when I was still at school, I was seized with a sudden affection for a classmate to whom I hadn't said twenty words perhaps in a whole term. We became inseparable and as we were both of us deeply religious, we exchanged prayer books. All this seems a little ridiculous now, but we weren't over fifteen and as sincere as we could be. Since then he married a girl I was in love with, but I never bore my rival a grudge. I don't know why, you remind me of him. . . . I believe that under more favourable circumstances, we might have been friends, you and I, and remained friends for many years. Don't you think so? Why don't you say something? (*He lets go Ian's hand.*) Perhaps you find me indiscreet.

IAN: Oh no.

MAC CLURE: I assure you that I'm not in the habit of offering my friendship at random.

IAN: Please believe that I . . . I appreciate it.

MAC CLURE: What's the matter? You're dreadfully pale.

IAN: Nothing's the matter.

MAC CLURE: Oh, I can see that you're moved. So am I. These last moments I'm spending with you are among the strangest I have ever lived through. It seems to me that you're helping me to bear my unhappiness. Perhaps I'm like you, I'm afraid of my love. A few steps away, in the great avenue. . . . Listen, I'm going to tell you a dream I had four months ago. I had come here with my father for the first time. We had spent the evening in this room. It was a little before Christmas. She sat there, a little apart from the others, near the window. She wasn't interested in what was being said. We were talking politics. Even then, war seemed inevitable to men capable of thought, but she didn't listen. She was alone, her cheek pressed to the wall so I could only see her profile. She was very beautiful but something in me said no. No, because war was there, no, because death was waiting. I stayed at the other end of the drawing-room. I looked at her but didn't stir. That night, when I managed to get to sleep at last, I had a dream. I dreamt that I was here, in this room, and that everything began all over again. She was over there and I here, but this time I crossed the drawing-room and went up to her.

IAN: What are you saying?

MAC CLURE: Yes, I left my seat and went up to her. She got up, very straight and her eyes on mine. I came close to her. I touched her hand, her wrist very lightly and said something to her, but I couldn't hear the sound of my own words. I told her that I loved her, I told her that she would never belong to anyone but me. She didn't answer. Perhaps she didn't hear. I went back to my seat. After a while she left the room.

IAN: And after that?

MAC CLURE: After that I tried to write to her, but I tore up letter after letter. One day I jumped on my horse and rode to the outskirts of the plantation, but something prevented me from going any farther, as though there was a ban on this house.

IAN: Why did you come back?

MAC CLURE: I was too unhappy. I wanted to see her again. I gave in.

IAN: And having seen her once more, once more you're running away from her. You might be with her now and you're here, with me.

MAC CLURE: Indeed, I believe it's my duty to run away from her, as you say, for war is at the door. And when you insisted so strongly, a moment ago, on keeping me here, I took it as a sign. . . .

IAN: What a reasonable love is yours and how curiously restrained. So easily managed . . . led here, forbidden to stray there. . . .

MAC CLURE: What right have you to question my sincerity?

IAN: I have the right because I'm twenty-five, with an experience of love that you lack. You are deluding yourself with the foolish sedateness of a boy. If you were in love with that little girl, you'd be sitting by her, good as gold, breathing sighs until the dear angel herself asked why you are so sad. . . .

MAC CLURE: You're mad!

IAN: What are you doing here, alone in this room with me, talking of love? (*He seizes his arm and pushes him in front of the mirror.*) Look at yourself! It's you that are enclosed in a ban, in a circle of horror. It surrounds your face, your shoulders, your hands. Look at that brow, innocent of all desire, those lips that no lips have ever touched because you're afraid and spread that fear around you.

MAC CLURE: Let me go! If you want to fight, we can go outside, but you're mad to pick a quarrel with me. I wish you no harm.

IAN: I'm not picking a quarrel with you, you fool! I want to kill you.

[*Edward Broderick enters at right.*]

BRODERICK: What is it? What are you doing?

IAN: What we're doing? I'm insulting this man in your presence and I'm calling him a coward. Isn't that enough?

[*He draws back a step and strikes Mac Clure's cheek. Broderick stands between them.*]

BRODERICK: If you want to fight, wait until tomorrow.
MAC CLURE: I can't wait.
IAN: I can't either. I can no more wait than a lover running to a rendez-vous. It must be tonight, under the trees.
BRODERICK: What has he done to you, Ian?
IAN: That's my business.
BRODERICK (*to Mac Clure*): Did you insult him?
MAC CLURE: Certainly not.

The women appear at right.]

MRS. STRONG: What's happening? What's the matter? You can be heard way into the avenue.
BRODERICK (*goes to them*): Leave us.
MRS. STRONG: I want to know.
BRODERICK: You can't fight without seconds.
IAN: Go fetch whom you please, but we'll fight tonight. I leave the choice of weapons to Eric Mac Clure.
BRODERICK: Ian, I beseech you to pause and reflect. You're committing a crime.
MAC CLURE: I'm quite able to defend myself, sir. Lieutenant Veechefsky is right: we can't wait. (*To Edward Broderick.*) You won't refuse me the honour of serving as my second.
IAN (*to Mac Clure*): We need another one. (*To Edward Broderick.*) Let Mr. White be fetched. Will you have lanterns sent down to the glade? That would be the best place for us. The avenue is too near the Negroes' cabins.
BRODERICK: Ian. . . .

[*Veechefsky looks him straight in the eye.*]

IAN (*to Edward Broderick*): Do as I tell you.

[*He goes out at left with Eric Mac Clure.*]

Scene 2

Same setting. All the lights are off except the lamp seen in Act II. A clock strikes three. Eliza enters at the left. She moves the cushions about and seems to be looking for something.

ELIZA: Missis and her handkerchief, Missis and her fan she's always losing everything, the crazy old fool. It's three o'clock and she isn't in bed yet. Ah! (*She has found the fan between the legs of the sofa, takes and opens it, advancing to the mirror.*) Say what you like. . . here's breeding for you. . . .

[*The coloured child seen in Act I comes running in at right.*]

What are you doing here, child, at this time of night, too? Run straight back to your cabin or I'll have your mother whip you.

COLOURED CHILD: Miss Liza!

ELIZA: Well, what is it?

COLOURED CHILD: Oh, I've been running . . . my grandpa . . . my grandpa. . . .

ELIZA: Will you speak or do you want me to tear one of your ears off?

COLOURED CHILD: Grandpa woke me up just now and told me to go speak to you. He told me that Master must be warned.

ELIZA: And what would I warn Master about, at this hour?

COLOURED CHILD: He said: "Eliza must tell Master: The Lord is going to pass in our midst and He's going to strike you, the master of the plantation. And if you don't say your prayers, you're lost."

ELIZA: Well, you little nigger, you can go straight back to the cabin and tell your grandpa that he's been having visions and if he thinks I'm going to disturb Master to tell him such nonsense, well, he'll just be having another vision, that's all.

COLOURED CHILD: He said if you didn't obey, the Lord would call you to account. That's just what he said: "The Lord will call you to account."

ELIZA: Well, you tell your old nigger of a grandpa that I don't take orders from him. Miss Eliza sends her compliments to Uncle John and begs to inform him that she doesn't take orders from him. You understand? And now, git!

[*The coloured child goes out at right. Almost at once Jeremy enters at right.*]

JEREMY: Miss 'Liza, what do you know? In the kitchen they say the two young white gentlemen are going to fight in the glade. Master told Luke and Barnabas to carry four lanterns down there.

[*Mrs Strong and Angelina enter at left.*]

MRS. STRONG: Go 'way, Jeremy. Eliza, my fan and handkerchief.

ELIZA: I haven't found the handkerchief yet, Missis.

MRS. STRONG (*taking the fan*): Go get two in my bureau. (*Eliza goes out.*) Angelina, don't you know any better than to cry before coloured people? You ought to be ashamed of yourself.

ANGELINA: I can't help it.

MRS. STRONG: A lady can always help it. What's happening is perfectly normal. Quite in Southern tradition. A duel by lantern-light. Good! I like that! With a little encouragement, I'd go watch it myself. Go and fetch Regina. I want her to stay here with us. She slyly disappeared after supper.

[*Angelina goes out at left.*]

A duel Those two handsome young men in their shirtsleeves. . . . Fire runs in our little lieutenant's veins.

[*Eliza enters from right and hands Mrs. Strong two handkerchiefs, then goes out.*]

One for Angelina, the other for the little Yankee. They're bound to bellow, the pair of them. I wonder why. Those boys will just give each other a few scratches with their swords, like a couple of angry cats, and there'll be a grand reconciliation over the punch-bowl—or over a julep. No, it's too late for juleps. They take such a time to make. It will be punch. Eliza! (*A pause, then she calls again.*) Eliza!

[*Eliza enters at right.*]

ELIZA: Missis?

MRS. STRONG: Nothing. Better not count your chickens before they're hatched. Go and fetch Angelina for me.

ELIZA: Here she is, Missis.

[*Angelina enters at left.*]

MRS. STRONG: Very well. Go, Eliza. (*Eliza goes out.*) What's the matter?

ANGELINA: Regina isn't in her room.
MRS. STRONG: Then surely she's mooning about in the avenue.
ANGELINA: Would you like me to go and see, Aunt Evelyn?
MRS. STRONG: I want you to stay right here, by me. And to begin with, sit down. Nothing fidgets me like seeing you wandering about. There, you'd better go to bed.
ANGELINA: I couldn't sleep, Aunt Evelyn. Let me stay here, just a little while. I'm afraid, all by myself.
MRS. STRONG: What of, you little fool? Of ghosts? All you have to do is say your prayers. Sit down. First, give me my biscuit-box. (*Angelina hands her the biscuit-box. Mrs. Strong opens it and gives Angelina a biscuit.*) Eat it. Nothing like a biscuit to set you to rights. I wonder when those boys will get back. (*She eats a biscuit.*) What a to-do! All that for a war that may never take place.
ANGELINA: Did they quarrel about the war?
MRS. STRONG: What else would two men quarrel about on the twelfth of April, 1861? They probably disagreed over the Southern policy. Never mind! It's been at least eighteen years since a duel has been fought at Bonaventure. It ties up with tradition.
ANGELINA: How is it you like duels if you dislike wars, Aunt Evelyn?
MRS. STRONG: What a question! Wars upset everybody. Particularly modern wars, with all the . . . up-to-date improvements we dispose of nowadays: cannons that can fire a shot every five minutes, for instance. . . . And then, you never know where a cannon-shot may drop. During the War of Independence, one fell right here: true, it was by mistake. All the same, it smashed through a door. . . . Whereas, a duel merely concerns two charming

young fools who have a good time slashing at each other in the woods.

ANGELINA: But supposing they hurt each other?

MRS. STRONG: Oh, these days, they don't do each other much harm. In the old days, it was another matter. When I was a little girl, they brought my grandfather back on a shutter, with a hole in his breast you could have thrust your fist in. But that was on account of a woman. A love affair.

ANGELINA: A love affair?

MRS. STRONG: Now, now, child, eat your biscuit. Love affairs don't concern little girls.

ANGELINA: When do you think they'll be back?

MRS. STRONG: In a quarter of an hour, at latest. Everything would have been over by now if they hadn't had such trouble in getting Mr. White out of bed. The old fellow would have nothing to do with it, at first. Edward had to beg him, shake him, help him to get into that interminable underwear of his. For shame, Angelina, you're making me talk most indelicately.

ANGELINA: How I wish everybody were back, Aunt Evelyn. It frightens me to think of them, out there with their swords.

MRS. STRONG: Frightened, child? You have nothing to fear for Lieutenant Veechefsky, nor for the other, although little Mac Clure doesn't look like a fencing master. And then, the boy's too gentle, too well-behaved. He lacks. . . fierceness.

ANGELINA: Aunt Evelyn, I don't want anything to happen to Mr. Mac Clure.

MRS. STRONG: The very idea! I'd rather something happened to him than to Lieutenant Veechefsky. We scarcely know little Mac Clure. And who is he, forsooth, to get into hot water in other people's houses? What possessed him to meddle with

Lieutenant Veechefsky? If he manages to get hurt, it'll be his own fault! Why, Angelina, are you crazy? You're crying? Where are my handkerchiefs? They were right here. . . .

ANGELINA (*sobbing*): I have one. . . .

MRS. STRONG: Then blow your nose and go up to bed. You irritate me. Go! You heard me? (*Angelina goes out at left. Mrs Strong remains alone.*) I hate to see people cry. All that emotion and sniffling because two boys are fighting. (*A pause.*) Eliza!

[*A few seconds go by, then Eliza enters at left.*]

ELIZA: Missis?

MRS. STRONG: Go see in the avenue if Miss Regina isn't walking there.

ELIZA: Miss Regina is probably in her room, Missis.

MRS. STRONG: No, she isn't. Miss Angelina went there just now. Do as I tell you.

ELIZA: Yes, Missis.

[*Eliza goes out at left. A pause.*]

MRS. STRONG: I've never been fond of solitude, but tonight it weighs heavily on me. When I was little, I used to be told: "Say your prayers. Pray to thy Father which is in secret, and thy Father which is in secret shall reward thee openly." First of all, you must have something to say to Him, to the Lord, and be sure that he hears you, but when I say my prayers, I feel as though I were talking to myself. Maybe it's very wrong to say this. I often wonder what it can be like to believe as crazy old Uncle John does. He thinks of God as a big benevolent old man who listens. He talks to him as he would to a human being: "Listen, Lord, I want you to do this for me.

Listen, Lord, do that" . . . What's so strange is that he sometimes gets what he asked for. Try as I may to go about it properly, nothing ever happens.

[*Eliza enters noiselessly from the left and stands motionless, a few steps behind Mrs. Strong.*]

I ask, but I'm almost sure that no one listens to me, as no one answers. For instance, if I ask for those boys to come back quickly and, of course, safe and sound, that's the most reasonable prayer possible, but I don't know why, I'm afraid to make it. It's probably because if they stayed too long, I'd have proof that I hadn't been heard and that there was no one. When I was little, I believed that there was someone. If only there were someone! (*A pause.*) Why doesn't Eliza come back? Eliza!

ELIZA: Missis?

[*She stands before Mrs. Strong.*]

MRS. STRONG: How long have you been in the room? I didn't hear you come in.

ELIZA: I've just come in.

MRS. STRONG: You lie. You were listening. Have you seen Miss Regina?

ELIZA: Miss Regina is in the avenue, under the trees. She said she couldn't sleep and that she wanted to stay outdoors.

MRS. STRONG: Let her do as she pleases, she's going away tomorrow.

[*Enter Barnabas, a young coloured servant. He looks terrified.*]

What is it, Barnabas?

BARNABAS: Missis. . . . Eliza, Master wants you to tell Lewis and Thomas to run to the glade.

[*Eliza goes out at left.*]

MRS. STRONG: Barnabas! (*She rises from her arm chair.*) Go! Leave the room! (*She stamps her foot and Barnabas runs out at left.*) Lord, now I'm speaking to You. You are going to listen to me. I don't want anything to have happened. If you are all-powerful, you can have it so that nothing has happened. (*She walks to the window and comes back.*) I don't want to suffer. (*She returns to the window, then goes to the table and picks up the lamp. A pause.*) Eliza!

[*Eliza enters at left.*]

ELIZA: Missis?

MRS. STRONG: Take this lamp and go up to my room with me. You can undress me, and I'm going to bed, and I'm going to sleep.

[*Eliza takes the lamp. The two women go out at right. The stage remains empty for a moment. At the end of the avenue, the first rays of dawn. After a few seconds, Mr. White enters at left, goes to the window at the back of the stage and opens it wide.*]

MR. WHITE: May God forgive them!

[*Regina enters at left and stands a few steps from Mr. White. She is extremely calm and speaks without ever raising her voice.*]

REGINA: Mr. White. . . .

MR. WHITE: What do you want, Miss Regina? You should go up to your room. You must not stay here.

REGINA: No. I know what has happened, Mr. White. I heard Barnabas talking to Eliza in front of the house. I'm not frightened.

MR. WHITE: It was the hand of God. I told them not to provoke the wrath of God, but they wouldn't listen to me. . . . The lieutenant scarcely defended himself. Perhaps a little at first, but toward the end, his face changed. You felt he was offered like a victim to the fury he had unleashed. Mac Clure was terrible. . . . He struck and struck, again and again. He was like the destroying angel. The last blow was struck at the head, the whole face. Lieutenant Veechefsky collapsed, as though he'd been felled.

REGINA: Where is he?

MR. WHITE: Mr. Broderick's orders were to have him brought here. I'm going, Miss Regina, I've done all I could. I advise you to retire.

REGINA: No, I shall stay here.

[*Mr. White goes out at right. Regina goes and stands at right, exactly where Lieutenant Veechefsky stood at the beginning of the play. She remains there motionless. After a few seconds, enter Edward Broderick and two Negroes bearing Lieutenant Veechefsky's body. His head is covered by his tunic. After them enters Mac Clure. It is still so dark that no one notices Regina's presence. The Negroes stop in the middle of the room. Edward Broderick motions to the slaves to lay the body on the floor.*]

BRODERICK: Barnabas, go to Wilmington for a clergyman and a doctor and bring them back with you.

BARNABAS: Shall I wait until daybreak, Master?

BRODERICK: No, go right now. It will be broad

daylight by the time you reach Wilmington. Leave the room. (*The slaves go. A long pause.*) I can't believe he's dead.

MAC CLURE: You know he is. You saw him.

BRODERICK: No, what I saw wasn't true. What I saw, and what is true, is the boy who stood here, in this room, an hour ago, and who talked and was alive.

MAC CLURE: He wanted to die. He wanted it with all his might. I realised it too late. He didn't even try to ward off the last blow I dealt him.

BRODERICK: You killed him.

MAC CLURE: Didn't he himself put the sword in the hand that struck him down? He made me the instrument of a will stronger than ours. We are powerless before predestination.

BRODERICK: Nevertheless, you killed him.

MAC CLURE: He knew the South. He should have known that you don't strike a Southerner, if you don't want to die. God allowed all this to happen.

BRODERICK: Don't bring God into a murder, don't make Him your accomplice. If He is the way you imagine Him, what a horrible God He is, who demands the disfigured body of a boy of twenty-five. In the bitterness of my heart, I wonder what becomes of the Gospel in your theology which reeks of blood. If Jesus were here, we'd make Him weep with shame, yes with shame before the persistent frustration of His word.

MAC CLURE: I understand your grief only too well to argue with you.

BRODERICK: You understand nothing.

MAC CLURE: War seems certain, sir. I won't wait till daylight to go. In a few hours I'll have rejoined General Beauregard's troops and enlisted.

BRODERICK: You're free to do as you please. I won't detain you.

[*Mac Clure bows and goes out at left. Edward Broderick draws close to the body stretched on the floor and lays his hand on the dead man's breast. The light grows stronger. After a time, Broderick notices Regina. Gently.*]

What are you doing here, Regina? You must go up to your room.

REGINA (*coming up to him*): No, I want to stay with him for a moment, alone. Will you allow me to remain alone with him, for a moment?
BRODERICK: He's dead, Regina.
REGINA: Life isn't cut off at one blow. The soul doesn't leave the body suddenly. I believe that he is still here, and that he hears me.
BRODERICK: Did you love him so deeply?
REGINA: Yes, I knew. I knew everything. And I've suffered too much not to be allowed the right to stay with him by myself.

[*Edward Broderick moves away from the body and goes towards the right. Before he goes out, he turn and looks at Regina.*]

You'll come back, later on?

[*Broderick shakes his head silently. He goes out. Regina remains perfectly still by the body and begins to speak, under her breath.*]

REGINA: If, as I believe, you're still here, listen to me. Ian. (*A pause.*) I won't disturb you with my tears. See, how gently I'm speaking, as a mother speaks to a sleeping child. A little while ago, when you came close to me and begged my pardon, I didn't say a word, but my heart was bursting. Do you understand, Ian? (*A pause.*) God will wipe away all tears. He said so Himself. He will wipe away your tears and mine. (*She gives a terrible cry.*) Ian, come back!

[*She crumples up by the body. At that moment, the roar of a cannon is heard in the distance; the wind springs up and the window slams.*]

Curtain

UNCERTAIN JOY

A Play in Three Acts

by

CHARLOTTE HASTINGS

" Children are certain sorrow, and uncertain joy."
Danish Proverb

Linnit & Dunfee Ltd., presented *Uncertain Joy* at The Royal Court Theatre, London on Thursday, March 31st, 1955, with the following cast:

MRS. PERRYMAN	*Jean Taylor-Smith*
BARBARY LEIGH	*Ursula Jeans*
STEPHEN LEIGH	*Roger Livesey*
ARNOLD HAMBLE, Q.C.	*Noel Howlett*
MRS. BLUNDELL	*Marda Vanne*
TOD	*Michael Brooke*
GIOVANNI DAWSON	*Richard Leech*
JULIA	*Margaret Whiting*
BIRCH	*Robert Raglan*

The play directed by Warren Jenkins

Setting by Fanny Taylor

Transferred to the *Duchess Theatre*, London, June 20th, 1955

Uncertain Joy was first presented by Linnit & Dunfee at the "Q" Theatre on October 9th, 1953, *and the cast included Stephen Murrey, Jean Kent, Tristam Rawson, Margot Lister, Peggy Hamley-Clifford, Anthony Green, Paul Whitsun-Jones, Mavis Villiers and Humphrey Morton. Directed by Stephen Murrey. Setting by Elisabeth Tapley.*

CHARACTERS

(in order of their appearance)

MRS. PERRYMAN
BARBARY LEIGH
STEPHEN LEIGH
ARNOLD HAMBLE, Q.C.
TOD
MARIA BLUNDELL
GIOVANNI DAWSON
JULIA
INSPECTOR BIRCH

SCENES

The action takes place in the Leighs' house in a Close in Grantfield, a small town about thirty miles north of London.

ACT ONE

An evening in May

ACT TWO

Scene 1. *A September evening eighteen months later.*
Scene 2. *Half an hour later.*

ACT THREE

Scene 1. *Two months later*
Scene 2. *An hour and a half later*

The quotation (page 257) from *KIM*, by Rudyard Kipling, is printed by kind permission of Mrs. Bambridge and the publishers, Messrs. Macmillan & Co. Ltd.

ACT ONE

The main room of the Leighs' house is a happy alliance of charm and practical comfort. The walls are light, decorated with a few good prints, the furniture is fine reproduction Queen Anne.

Right centre of back wall, two French windows open on to a small paved garden, with a tiny but well-kept lawn. Beyond this is a view of other houses in the Close. Just outside windows, on the right, is a small laburnum tree in full bloom, set in a green tub. Plain net curtains with outer drapes of glazed chintz cover the windows. Round the windows on shelves is a collection of Spode china.

The whole of the left wall—actors' left—is filled with built-in bookcases from floor to ceiling, crammed with books of every description. In front of these, at an angle, is a little Queen Anne desk, with telephone, a litter of papers and galley proofs, and a portable typewriter. A swing chair is pushed back below it, as if someone has risen in a hurry, Down left, below bookshelves, is a tall oak cupboard.

Centre of wall right, a coal fire burns in a marble fireplace. over which hangs a mirror. Above fireplace more low bookcases and a small table holding a radio. Before fire is a wide comfortable settee. Below it, slightly left, a low table is set with coffee cups, and a tall vase of flowers. The cloth is lace-edged, and the china Crown Derby.

Left of windows, in back wall, a small staircase mounts four steps and turns on to a little landing which leads off left out of sight. There is no banister rail, but a thick maroon coloured cord, which matches the carpet covering the whole room and the centre of the staircase.

In the corner left, between stairs and door, a corner cupboard holds more china, and on a shelf below is a glass vase filled with bright tulips and daffodils. The door to the main part of the house is right, above fireplace.

A second after the curtain rises, there is a splintering crash, a pane of the French windows shatters as something is hurled through it, and the flower vase falls off the table, taking a cup and saucer with it.

Voices are heard off right and from upstairs.

BARBARY	*(off together)*:	Perry—Perry! What's happened—what is it——?
MRS. PERRYMAN		All right—I'm coming—is someone hurt——?

[*Mrs. Perryman runs in right. She is a plump, pleasant middle-aged woman, with grey hair curled crisply all over her head. She wears a plain dark dress and frilled apron, in spite of which it is soon obvious she is no ordinary servant.*]

MRS. PERRYMAN (*as she enters*): Dear Lord bless and save us—just look at that!

[*She goes through the windows and stands looking off right as Barbary Leigh comes running down the stairs. She is in her early thirties, dark, vital, driven by a restless intensity. Her hair is caught up hastily on top of her head, and she is tying the sash of a gay bathrobe.*]

BARBARY: Is it an accident or something——?

[*She stops on the bottom step as she sees the broken china.*]

Oh, *no*!

[*She crosses centre, kneels down and picks up the fragments.*]

MRS. PERRYMAN: There he goes! You little heathen hobgoblin—if I could only get near enough, I'd knock the plain daylights out of you!

[*Stephen Leigh enters right. He is thirty-eight but already his hair is flecked with grey, and his shoulders have acquired a scholarly stoop. His sensitive intelligent face is fine drawn, his manner rather diffident, and his pleasant voice quietly pitched.*]

STEPHEN: What on earth's the matter? It sounded like the last trump——

BARBARY (*showing him the cup*): It's the last of Great Aunt Bertha's Crown Derby.

STEPHEN: But what happened?

[*Mrs. Perryman returns centre.*]

MRS. PERRYMAN (*succinctly*): It's that Tod.

[*She begins to collect the glass.*]

BARBARY: The little *beast*—just look at this room. If there's anything in modern psychology, he's certainly free of inhibitions at this particular moment.

MRS. MERRYMAN: Inhibitions poppycock! All this new fangled business about children must express themselves. (*Getting up with glass in her apron.*) I know where I'd express myself if *I* got hold of some of them.

[*She goes out right. Stephen has moved to the mantelpiece for his pipe.*]

BARBARY: The child's a horror. He's completely possessed by a spirit of destruction.

STEPHEN: All boys break windows.

BARBARY (*angrily*): It isn't only windows. There isn't a tree or a plant around that he doesn't strip to pieces sooner or later. He's got a grudge against everyone, and he's everlastingly in some kind of trouble.

[*Arnold Hamble appears outside the windows. He is a large handsome man of about sixty, with white hair, a magnificent presence, a mobile, humorous face, and a fine resonant voice.*]

ARNOLD: I say, that was a devil of a smash. Are you in trouble—— (*Pausing with a twinkle.*) Or just spring cleaning?

BARBARY (*getting up*): Oh, Arnold—come in—mind where you tread, it's all splinters. And forgive this—(*Indicating dressing gown.*) —I was just going to have a bath—we've got Lady Westbrook's dinner to-night——

ARNOLD: Oh—I heard the noise and I thought perhaps—shall I go——?

STEPHEN: No—no, stay and have a drink——

[*Arnold gingerly moves centre as Mrs. Perryman returns with a brush and pan to sweep up the rest of the glass.*]

ARNOLD: You look as though you've had burglars.

BARBARY: We've had that fiendish Tod.

ARNOLD: What—*again*?

BARBARY: Again.

[*She holds out the broken cup. He takes it from her.*]

ARNOLD: May I see?

STEPHEN (*quietly*): There *are* other children who play in the Close. I suppose you are *sure*——

BARBARY: Of course it was Tod. It always is.

[*Arnold stands delicately fitting the cup together.*]

ARNOLD: Is it possible the witness is a little—a very little—prejudiced?

BARBARY: Arnold, you're as bad as Stephen. A barrister should be on the side of law and order. Just wait till you're defending—or prosecuting—him on one of those young thug cases.

STEPHEN: Poor little devil.

[*He bends down and picks something off the rug,. Barbary straightens the books on the centre shelf.*]

BARBARY: Dirty little devil. I don't suppose he's had a bath for a month. I do wish you wouldn't encourage him in here, handling our books and covering them with grime—

[*She breaks off and looks across at Stephen.*]

BARBARY: What's that—?

STEPHEN: I'm afraid it's the evidence. Tod's little Indian mascot.

BARBARY (*exasperatedly*): Oh, *darling*—don't just stand there. Go over and see his father. He did at least pay for the last lot of damage.

STEPHEN: And Tod got a thrashing.

BARBARY: All boys get thrashings.

STEPHEN: Well, I'll go over and find Giovanni Dawson and make enquiries.

[*He pockets his pipe, crosses and puts his arm around her.*]

I'm terribly sorry about the china. One day I'll buy you a solid gold tea set, studded with rubies.

BARBARY: }
STEPHEN: } I do *not* want a solid gold——

[*She catches his eye, breaks off and suddenly they both laugh quietly together.*]

Fool!

[*She gives him a quick light kiss, and then a little push.*]

There. Now, for heaven's sake go over and talk to Dawson.

STEPHEN: Right. (*He crosses to windows and turns.*) Give poor Arnold his drink.

[*He goes off right. Barbary crosses to the corner cupboard left.*]

BARBARY: Sorry, Arnold dear—I'm a little edgy tonight. (*Bringing glasses and decanter to desk.*) You know, I've never considered myself an unnatural woman, but I do detest that child.

ARNOLD: I think this might be riveted. Would you like me to get it done?

BARBARY: I should indeed. Whiskey—sherry?

ARNOLD: Thank you. Sherry.

BARBARY: He can't be more than nine, but he's uncanny. He has no sense of time or responsibility. He doesn't even go to school if he doesn't feel like it. I met him yesterday in the town, just strolling aimlessly—and his great grey cat following. It isn't—it isn't natural.

MRS. PERRYMAN (*working round by Arnold's feet*): That Melon's natural enough, bar his outlandish name. Never seen a finer cat. Comes in here for his milk and practically says please and thank you.

BARBARY: We all know your weakness for animals, Perry. Sometimes I think you like them better than humans.

MRS. PERRYMAN (*getting up*): Most times I'm sure I do.

[*She goes out right with her brush and pan.*]

ARNOLD (*still intent on cup*): I know a little Pole in Hoxton who'd make a wonderful job of this. He feels he owes me an occasional service. I once got him two years.

[*Barbary looks up in the act of pouring out sherry.*]

BARBARY: Then what on earth does he owe you?
ARNOLD (*twinkling*): The extra five years he would have got with another counsel.
BARBARY (*laughing*): Oh!

[*She puts down the decanter, goes to pick up the glass and catches sight of the proofs on her desk. She pauses, then picks up the top sheet. Arnold glances over at her, puts the broken cup on the coffee table and crosses.*]

ARNOLD: Is that the new book? How's it going?
BARBARY (*absently*): Thanks to your invaluable advice on police procedure, we've reached the galley proofs. (*Looking up.*) I hate this stage. I know exactly how the mountain felt when it laboured and brought forth a mouse——

[*She breaks off, realising she is still holding the full glass and hands it to him, laughing.*]

Oh, how stupid of me—I'm so sorry——
ARNOLD: Well, here's to—(*Looking down at top proof.*) —" Call the Next Witness ". (*Raising glass to book-shelves.*) May it soon join that most impressive litter of best-selling mice.

BARBARY: Not a volume of quality among the lot.

[*She flicks a finger across a row of some half-dozen volumes on a lower shelf.*]

ARNOLD: Nonsense. You are one of a few writers who can produce a crime novel with style and distinction.

BARBARY: But they're still crime novels. Second rate. (*She crosses restlessly down to the fire.*) I wish I could write one—just one decent book. Something worth while—(*She says the last words almost to herself, then turns.*) Arnold, why can't I accept what I've already done—and be content. Stephen's content. (*Pausing again.*) Unfortunately.

ARNOLD: Why " unfortunately "?

BARBARY: He has such—quality. He could get a much better school than Grantley. (*Sighing.*) Sometimes I think he has no—personal ambition.

ARNOLD: Stephen has the quiet mind and civilised outlook of the classical scholar. May I put the pieces in this—thank you. . . .

[*He wraps the broken fragments in a napkin from the coffee tray.*]

BARBARY (*abruptly*): You think he's too good for me, don't you?

ARNOLD (*lighting*): What counsel thinks, is not evidence.

BARBARY: But——

ARNOLD: What he knows is another matter. And he knows he is extremely fond of two widely different people——

BARBARY: Different indeed. A quiet brilliant scholar of Balliol, and a restless writer of——

ARNOLD: —Two talented, wholly charming people. And he hates to see them at variance over a motherless small boy with a dirty face and no seat to his pants.
BARBARY: You see! Every time we come back to that wretched child. I hate it, Arnold. I resent his monopolising Stephen's time and intelligence. (*Slowing down.*) You know—I may want a great deal for myself. But I want far more for Stephen.
ARNOLD (*gently*): This dinner with Lady Westbrook tonight——

[*Barbary looks straight at him, then she turns and goes up the stairs.*]

BARBARY (*gaily*): Dear Lady Westbrook. Such poise, such diamonds, such a *wig*——

[*Arnold has followed her to the foot of the stairs. He puts his hand over hers which is resting on the banister.*]

ARNOLD: Such influence with the Governors of Wimborough School who are shortly to select a new headmaster.

[*There is a pause. He nods.*]

That's what you want for Stephen, isn't it? Wimborough.
BARBARY: Arnold, you're altogether too perceptive—

[*Mrs. Perryman enters right carrying another cup, which she takes to the table, and a square of brown paper.*]

MRS. PERRYMAN: Your bath'll be stone cold. Please yourself of course. But as you usually like to boil yourself pink——

BARBARY: All right, Perry. (*Laughing at Arnold.*) Help yourself to more sherry.

[*She runs upstairs and off left. Mrs. Perryman goes to windows with the paper and, with drawing pins from her apron pocket, starts fixing a neat patch over the broken pane.*]

MRS. PERRYMAN: I do hope Mr. Leigh's not having trouble with that Dawson. Never can trust those half-caste foreigners not to turn nasty.

ARNOLD (*pouring another drink*): I think Stephen's dealt with sufficient specimens of the genus boy to manage one small Latin gentleman.

MRS. PERRYMAN: I don't know about being Latin, but he's not the kind of person we want in the Close. That corner house has been going down ever since they turned it into flats. I wonder you like living next door. (*Darkly.*) I've heard there's all sorts of goings-on.

ARNOLD: Really? How interesting. Could you explain to my innocent mind your precise definition of " goings-on "?

MRS. PERRYMAN: Oh well, sir, you being a bachelor I suppose it's natural you shouldn't understand these things. Not that most marriages aren't one fight from beginning to end.

[*Stephen enters through windows. He takes the last couple of drawing pins from her.*]

STEPHEN: I'll finish that, shall I? I hope you've been entertaining Mr. Hamble.

ARNOLD: She has just informed me she doesn't believe in the blissful state of marriage and security.

MRS. PERRYMAN: The only time I felt secure with my husband was the day I buried him.

[*She goes out right. Both men laugh. Stephen crosses to desk for drink. Arnold sits down on the settee.*]

ARNOLD: Well, did you see Giovanni Dawson?
STEPHEN: He's out. The flat looks deserted. Arnold, that man baffles me. What exactly do you suppose he does for a living?
ARNOLD: In the absence of proof to the contrary, we must assume it to be something honest.

[*Stephen comes centre, glass in hand.*]

STEPHEN: Would you say Dawson *looks* honest?
ARNOLD: My dear Stephen, I once shook hands with a very benign and saintly old gentleman who had cut his wife into twenty-seven pieces and scattered them broadcast through the Home Counties.

[*Stephen, hardly listening, paces up right and back.*]

STEPHEN: I've tried the welfare people, several societies and the probation officer. Apparently because the child isn't starved, perverted or covered with vermin, there's no category for this case.
ARNOLD: In actual fact, there isn't any case.
STEPHEN: Then tell me how to start one.
ARNOLD (*glancing at window*): Bring an action for wilful damage, and leave the whole thing in the hands of the police.
STEPHEN: Who will fine Dawson twenty shillings and costs and that'll be the end of it.
ARNOLD: Not necessarily. We might get the boy into an approved school.
STEPHEN: For heaven's sake! Must we put Tod into a semi-criminal atmosphere before we can help him? An innocent child?

ARNOLD (*quizzically*): Innocent——?

STEPHEN: Arnold, I've known Tod for six months. He's not bad—he's lost. He's been dragged here and there all over the world for about seven years. His mind is a—a ragbag of ideas and impressions—he can swear fluently in about three different languages And yet he has some quality—a depth of intelligence——

ARNOLD (*breaking in*): What leads you to think that?

STEPHEN: I first met him in here. He'd sneaked in to the bookshelves. He was curled up reading—something he'd found in French. I discovered he has a passion for reading—and an astonishing instinct for what is good——

ARNOLD (*gently—mocking*): Don't tell me you've discovered a potential genius——

STEPHEN (*impatiently*): No, no, of course not. But Tod *has* an unusual intelligence which is trying hard to reach for something beyond his sordid background—

ARNOLD (*breaking in*): The fact remains you can't remove him from that background without his father's consent.

STEPHEN: Or by proving the father isn't fit to have him.

ARNOLD: How do you know he isn't?

STEPHEN: I only know that whenever I've spoken to him—which isn't often—I've been conscious of something—almost evil——

ARNOLD: And apart from this—er—(*Gesture.*)—whiff of brimstone, you've no definite knowledge?

STEPHEN: Nothing—except he has a British passport which describes him negatively as " salesman ".

ARNOLD: How did you manage to see that?

STEPHEN: Tod showed it to me because I didn't believe his fantastic travel stories. (*Putting glass on table.*) No—I admit it's purely my personal opinion.

ARNOLD: Then we're back where we started. No case. After all, Dawson must have some paternal instincts, or he'd simply have put the baby into a home——

[*There is a movement outside the windows right. A boy's head bobs into sight and away again. A second later, Tod runs across from right to left and crouches down behind the little tree outside the window. He takes careful aim with a catapult.*]

STEPHEN: Are you advising me to drop the matter?
ARNOLD: I shouldn't take it too seriously, Stephen. Tod's kind have a pernicious habit of survival.
STEPHEN: For what? At the moment, he hasn't one asset——
ARNOLD (*dryly, getting up*): In these days of so-called " level " education, I wouldn't entirely discount an ability to swear in three languages. (*With a sudden yelp.*) What the——?

[*Tod has taken full aim. Arnold claps his hand to his ear. Stephen turns to the window as Tod streaks off right out of sight.*]

STEPHEN: Tod—Tod! Come here——
ARNOLD (*to windows*): If I get hold of that little——
STEPHEN (*turning, laughing*): You see? It's different when it hits you personally.

[*Arnold begins to laugh too.*]

ARNOLD: Stephen, your household is altogether too unsettling for me. Also I've a red-hot brief waiting. I'm going *home.*
STEPHEN: You'll probably get another one going across the Close—

[*They go out together. Stephen still laughing, shuts the door behind them. After a second, Tod comes creeping back and peers cautiously round the edge of the curtain. He is a thin, grubby little boy, tall for nine years old, dressed in a soiled singlet, khaki shorts and sandals. His attitude is one of suspicion and distrust, except when he suddenly reveals a missing front tooth in an unexpectedly attractive gamin grin. When necessary, he can move like lightning with a curious side-ways crab-like leap. He comes into the room, suddenly darts back into the doorway, then comes forward again, keeping a wary eye on the door right. He drops on his hands and knees and begins a rapid efficient search of the carpet, feeling under the furniture with his hands. A door shuts off right. Tod leaps across the room and through the windows, out of sight. Stephen comes into the room, shuts the door and moves centre, where he pauses.*]

STEPHEN (*questioningly*): Tod——?

[*He stands for a moment in the empty room. Then he feels in his pocket and brings out the small brass image. He looks at it thoughtfully for a moment, turning it over in his hand. Then, with a quick glance at the windows, he holds it up as if admiringly, puts it down very deliberately in the centre of the coffee table, fetches a book from the table above the fireplace, returns to the settee, sits down and begins to read. After a moment, Tod cautiously returns. He puts his head round the curtain, considers Stephen for a second, then makes a peculiar hissing noise through his teeth. Stephen takes no notice. Tod tries again.*]

TOD: S-s-s. Mister. Hey—Mister.

[*Stephen looks up. Tod comes into full view.*]

STEPHEN: Hullo, Tod. Are you coming in?

TOD (*jerking his head towards door right*): Has he gone?
STEPHEN: Yes.
TOD (*cheerfully, coming centre*): Good. Thought that'd fix him. Silly old b——
STEPHEN: Tod——!

[*He gets up rather sharply. Instantly, Tod ducks, lifting his arm as if to ward off a blow.*]

TOD (*shrilly defensive*): It was my Dad said it!
STEPHEN (*quickly*): All right, Tod—all right.
TOD: My Dad said he's like bad beer. You know—all belch and no body. (*He suddenly yelps with laughter.*) He means he blows his top. (*Sobering as suddenly.*) Mister—(*He nods towards the table.*) Can I have Siva?
STEPHEN: Come here.

[*He sits on settee and picks up the image. Tod climbs on to the arm of the settee.*]

Tell me, how do you come to know about Siva?
TOD: We got him when we was in India—(*Glancing sideways at Stephen.*)—when we *were* in India. See all his arms? Some to bless and some to curse. I like the cursing ones best—I just bet they could *bash*. (*Looking up.*) You know somep'n, Mister?
STEPHEN: No, Tod. What?
TOD: When I grow up, I'm going to bash everyone—the whole *world*. Wh-e-ez!

[*With a long drawn-out, shrill sound, he dives across the room like an airplane, ending standing on his head by the settee, with his legs waving in the air.*]

STEPHEN: Tod—Tod——

[*He reaches out and slaps Tod's rear. Tod turns abruptly, right side up.*]

(*Firmly.*) Stop fooling and come here. Come on. Over here.

[*Tod climbs over the settee right end, and sits on the back with his feet on the seat.*]

Now—tell me. Just exactly why do you want to smash up the universe?

TOD: Because I hate *people*. They're all against me and I hate them—the whole lot——

[*He pauses, then puts a hand on Stephen's arm.*]

Except you, Mister. I don't hate you.

STEPHEN (*gravely*): I call that handsome. Better shake hands on it.

[*They solemnly shake hands.*]

TOD: We ought to seal that with our blood. Like I saw on the pictures. (*Suddenly excited.*) There was two fellows, see? They got to be blood brothers—they scratched their arms and the blood ran out. You should have *seen* the blood run out——

STEPHEN: All in glorious Technicolor!

TOD: You bet. Say, if we had somep'n sharp we could scratch our arms. Got any scissors——?

[*He dives for the desk. Stephen hauls him back by the slack of his pants.*]

STEPHEN: Hey, wait a minute, my lad. You're too fast and a bit too drastic. Now listen—if we're blood brothers, why did you break my window?

TOD: I didn't mean to, Mister. Honest. I was just throwing Siva. When he goes up in the air, he shines. Like the golden arrow in that book you lent me——

STEPHEN: Yes. And so——?

TOD: I reckon I threw him too far. (*Abruptly.*) Was the geezer mad?

STEPHEN (*dryly*): No one was particularly overjoyed.

TOD: I'll tell her I'm sorry. I don't mind the geezer. She feeds my cat. Here—(*He fishes a crumpled paper from the pocket of his shorts. With a magnificent gesture.*) Buy yourself another window.

STEPHEN (*gravely*): Thank you. Only it would have been better not to break it in the first place, wouldn't it—(*Pausing.*) Tod, d'you know what this is?

TOD: Sure. Money.

STEPHEN: It's a five pound note. Where did you get it?

TOD: From Giovanni—my Dad. He's got millions of 'em. Why, d'you know—right now I just bet my dad's got all the money in the world. Piles and piles and *piles*——

[*He sees Stephen's expression and backs away defensively, his voice trailing off.*]

Well—one pile anyway.

STEPHEN: Did you pinch this?

[*As Tod does not answer.*]

Tod——?

TOD (*quickly*): Don't be mad at me, Mister. I—I do like you better'n anyone——

STEPHEN (*quietly*): Thank you. But that doesn't——

TOD: That's funny, isn't it—you being a cissy schoolmaster. Say, that Miss Maddock that takes my class—you ought to see her. (*He straightens his back and pushes out his chest.) Ella est comme ceci et comme cela. (In a high mincing voice.)* Tod, de-ar, blow your nose. Tod, your *nails,* de-ar. What would your mother say? *(Sullenly.)* She knows ruddy well I never had a mother for years. I only had people. People like Rosetta.

[*He pushes Siva up and down the table, making train noises.*]

STEPHEN: Who was Rosetta?

TOD: Just someone. In Spain.

STEPHEN: Was it she who taught you that little Spanish song?

TOD: Yes. *(Singing to himself.)* "*Mi jacca galopa y corta el viento.*"

STEPHEN: Do you remember anything about your mother, Tod?

TOD: Sure. She was English—a proper lady. She made me talk right. You know somep'n? Giovanni wasn't so bad when she was around.

STEPHEN: What happened?

TOD: She went and died. *(Disgustedly.)* And we got that Greta. *C'est une vache!*

STEPHEN: And where was Greta?

TOD: In America. *(Suddenly, thrusting Siva in his pocket.)* Gosh—that's what I came to see you about. Mister—will you do me a favour? Sort of—man to man?

STEPHEN: Of course—if I can. What is it?

TOD: Will you have Melon? You know—Melon, my cat. The geezer likes him. And I reckon he's just about the best cat in the world. He eats fish—and rats and mice. And he's—very clean—he washes most—every day—*(He pauses on the edge of a sob.)*

STEPHEN *(quickly)*: Yes, all right. Mrs. Perry would

love to have Melon. But why do you want to part with him?

TOD: Because we're going away tomorrow. We're going to America.

STEPHEN: Tomorrow? Why didn't you tell me before?

TOD: Giovanni only just told me.

STEPHEN: Isn't it a bit sudden?

TOD: Oh, we always leave everywhere sudden. We don't stand on the order of our going. (*Pulling some slips from his pocket.*) See? My labels—Thomas Oliver Dawson, passenger to New York. (*Suddenly.*) Mister—you're sure about Melon?

STEPHEN: Don't you worry about him—he'll have a wonderful time. But I want you to do something in return. Tod—will you write to me?

TOD (*stowing labels in pocket*): I don't write so good. (*Earnestly.*) But I could print it clear. Would that do?

STEPHEN: Beautifully. You won't forget?

TOD: Sure, sure. Send you some foreign stamps if you like. (*Suddenly.*) Look—I know my writing's bad, but I *can* spell. Why I reckon I'm just about the best speller in my school——

STEPHEN: That's because you're always reading, Tod—you will go on reading, won't you? All the time you can——

TOD: Course. I couldn't ever not read—oh, gee—that reminds me——

[*He runs outside the window, bends down by the tree and returns with a red-covered book which he gives to Stephen.*]

TOD: I borrowed this—the other night when you were out—you didn't mind?

STEPHEN: No. I said you might. (*Pauses, ruffling pages and shaking his head.*) Oh, Tod, really! Now just how much of this did you understand?

TOD (*cheerfully*): Not a lot. But I—sort of—liked the shape of the words together——
STEPHEN (*thoughtfully, looking through book*): I—see.
TOD: *And* the *battle* pictures. Gosh—that fight between Christian and Apollyon—now that must have been really *somep'n*——

[*Stephen looks up from the book.*]

STEPHEN: Tod, would you like this? For your own?
TOD (*half incredulous*): You mean—to *keep*?
STEPHEN (*offering it*): Yes.

[*Tod slowly takes the book as if he can't believe it. He looks at Stephen, and suddenly makes a little gesture which is wholly foreign.*]

TOD. *Merci, merci, mille fois*—(*He breaks off and hands back the book.*) Please, would you write my name in it? So that *everyone* knows it's mine.
STEPHEN (*laughing*): Certainly.

[*He takes his fountain pen from his breast pocket and writes in the book. Tod hangs over the back of the settee watching.*]

TOD: It's Thomas Oli—— (*His face changes as he sees the words.*) Why, *Mister*——

[*Stephen gives him the book and sits screwing up and re-pocketing his pen, watching Tod all the time.*]

(*Reading.*) To—my friend—Thomas Oliver Dawson—from Stephen Langton Leigh—(*He looks at Stephen and for once words fail him.*) I—*Gosh!*

[*He breaks off, gives a sudden gulp and a quick swallow,*

then abruptly pulls Siva from his pocket and thrusts it into Stephen's hand.]

TOD: That's for you.
STEPHEN (*slowly*): Why, thank you, Tod.

[*They look at each other for a second, then Tod turns sharply.*]

TOD: I'll get Melon——

[*He rushes out through the windows just as Barbary, wearing a very lovely white evening dress, comes along the landing and down the stairs. Stephen snatches up the five pound note.*]

STEPHEN: Tod—you forgot this——

[*Tod puts his head round the window, breaking into rapid speech.*]

TOD (*breathlessly*): *Elle est tres jolie, mais elle me fait peur. Je viendrai quand elle sera partie*——

[*He turns, and dashes straight into the arms of Maria Blundell, who appears outside at that moment, accompanied by the barking of dogs off right. She is a large imposing woman, with a mannish hair-cut, a vast bust and a commanding manner, wearing expensive tweeds and brogues. She carries a large basket filled with papers and collecting boxes. She catches Tod and holds him firmly in one strong hand.*]

MRS. BLUNDELL: Hullo, hullo, what are you up to, you young devil——
TOD (*shrilly*): I done nuthin' to you! You lemme go——

[*He stamps viciously and skilfully on her feet, one after the other. With a shout of pain, she relaxes her grip, he twists away and disappears out of sight.*]

(*Off right.*) Yah!

[*The dog barking redoubles. Rubbing first one foot and then the other, Mrs. Blundell shouts after them. With a little grimace at Stephen, Barbary goes to her desk and sits down. Stephen, putting the note and Siva hastily in his pocket, crosses to window.*]

MRS. BLUNDELL: Warrior—Darby! Here, here! Back—leave the boy alone. (*Whistling.*) Back, I tell you! (*Turning.*) Evenin', you two. Just taking the boys for their walk. (*Turning again.*) Warrior, Warrior! Off those flower beds, sir! (*Looking at broken window.*) The Dawson boy, I suppose. Y'know, something ought to be *done* about him.
STEPHEN (*politely, as he moves to fireplace*): What do you suggest?

[*Mrs. Blundell comes to settee with her basket.*]

MRS. BLUNDELL: If he tries any nonsense with me, he'll find himself in the hands of the police. (*Sorting out the boxes.*) Not that I think that'd do much good.
STEPHEN: You haven't a very high opinion of our present penal system?
MRS. BLUNDELL: Not these days. Too much pampering—psychiatrists and wet nurses. (*Thrusting a box at Stephen.*) Dumb Friends League—your box returned. Receipts on the back. Try and do better next time. (*Putting other boxes back in bag.*) No, the whole country's gone soft if you ask me.
STEPHEN (*putting box on mantelpiece*): Oh, I don't

know. There have been a *few* reforms in the past hundred years.

MRS. BLUNDELL: I've been on the bench myself for a considerable time, and I can't say I've noticed much change for the better. As for the modern youth—the only word is scandalous. Don't you find that, Mr. Leigh?

STEPHEN: They live in rather a difficult age, don't you think?

MRS. BLUNDELL: No excuse for slackness. I brought my three sons up the hard way, and I've never regretted it. What's more, they haven't either. (*Turning.*) Finished your new book, Mrs. Leigh?

BARBARY: Very nearly, thank you.

MRS. BLUNDELL: I enjoyed your last one. Can't remember the title though. Something—about a stain?

BARBARY: "Out Damned Spot." (*Sweetly.*) Shakespeare, you know.

MRS. BLUNDELL: Writing a book has always seemed to me a very comfortable way of earning one's living—just sitting down, putting your thoughts on paper.

BARBARY (*glancing at Stephen*): Yes.

MRS. BLUNDELL: I've often thought I'd write a book myself. When I heard about your success—I'm being perfectly frank—I said "If she can do *it*, I can do it." It's just getting the time.

BARBARY: Yes, of course. It *is* the time.

MRS. BLUNDELL: The Colonel always said I should write. You write a very good letter, my dear, he used to say. A very good letter indeed. And personally, I always think a person who can write a really good letter is halfway there, don't you?

BARBARY: Undoubtedly.

[*There is another outburst of barking off.*]

MRS. BLUNDELL: I must rush, the chaps are getting impatient. Good evening to you. (*Moving to windows.*) Warrior, down sir! (*Off right.*) Leave those tulips *alone*!

[*She strides off right, out of sight, accompanied by more whistling and a rapidly diminishing barking. Stephen mops his forehead. Barbary folds her hands and casts up her eyes.*]

BARBARY (*piously*): Dear heaven, please make me a good woman that I may meet Maria Blundell without wanting to crown her!

STEPHEN: Amen to that! (*He crosses to desk, laughing.*) Behold the famous novelist, seated peacefully and placidly at her desk, watching a masterpiece flow from her pen. (*He gives her a light kiss.*) Coffee as usual, before we go?

BARBARY (*putting on her spectacles*): Yes. (*Looking up.*) Stephen, what did Tod say just now? When he jabbered all that French?

[*Stephen takes the spectacles off her nose and cleans them on a handkerchief from his breast pocket. It is a familiar little action, almost unconscious, and does not interrupt their dialogue.*]

STEPHEN: He said you're very pretty, but you frighten him. He'll come back when you've gone.

BARBARY: Very diplomatic. What did he want here, anyway?

STEPHEN: To pay for the window and ask Perry to adopt Melon.

BARBARY: Adopt the cat? Why?

STEPHEN: Because they're going to America. To-morrow.

BARBARY: Stephen, really? It isn't a joke——?

STEPHEN: Apparently not. He's bringing the cat down presently. I—*did* promise him—you don't mind?

BARBARY: Not if Perry doesn't. And they're actually going? What a blessed relief!

STEPHEN: Barbary——

BARBARY (*looking down at her papers*): I've just thought of something in these wretched proofs. (*Turning.*) Here, give me those—— (*She takes her spectacles from him.*) Thank you, I'll correct it now. (*Looking up.*) Darling, *do* see if coffee's ready, or you won't have time to change.

STEPHEN (*laughing*): Good.

[*He crosses right. Barbary looks up, half exasperated.*]

BARBARY: Oh, *Stephen*——!

[*He goes out, still laughing. She turns back to her desk, frowning over the proofs. Tod appears outside the windows and stands watching her. After a second, she shivers as if feeling a draught, and puts her hand to the back of her chair. She exclaims impatiently, puts down the proofs, gets up and crosses to the stairs. She pauses as she sees Tod. He stands his ground, rubbing one foot against the other ankle.*]

What do you want?

[*He does not answer.*]

BARBARY: Well, what is it? What do you want?

TOD: I want to speak to Mister.

BARBARY: You can't. He's busy. (*Looking at him distastefully.*) You can't come in here just when you like. Go along. Do you hear? Go away.

[*Tod looks at her, scowling, his lower lip thrust out. Barbary suddenly pulls the French windows to, making him step back. She shuts them firmly in his face and turns the key. Then she goes up the stairs and off left. After a second, Tod rattles the doors savagely. Then he deliberately puts his doubled fist through the brown paper patch, reaches in and turns the key. He opens the windows, walks triumphantly into the room and stands looking up the stairs.*]

TOD (*to himself*): *Sacré crapaud—sale vache*——

[*He goes to the desk, inspects it, sweeps two books to the floor, then grabs up the galley proofs, looks at them, then back to the stairs, then rips the proofs viciously across, flings them on the floor, stamps on them, and rushes out through the windows, just as Barbary returns downstairs carrying a light wrap over her arm.*]

BARBARY (*calling*): Stephen, have you——

[*She pauses on the staircase, seeing the damage, then runs to her desk, flings the wrap over the chair and frantically collects the scattered papers. She is shaking with rage.*]

My God, I'll kill him—(*Almost sobbing with fury.*)—the little savage! Stephen, Stephen——!

[*Stephen hurries in right carrying a silver coffee pot.*]

STEPHEN: Barbary——

[*He hastily puts the coffee pot on the table and goes back to her.*]

BARBARY (*getting up*): Look—*look* what he did—all my proofs—(*Thrusting the bundle at him.*)—all that work—

hours of it—midnight last night and the night before —look at it—*look at it*!

[*She is practically hysterical as he catches hold of her.*]

STEPHEN : Barbary, please—stop it! Control yourself—He didn't realise what he was doing—how could he know——?
BARBARY : Why did you let him come in here?—he isn't civilised—I'll tear him apart——

[*She breaks away to the mantelpiece.*]

Don't make excuses for him. I can't *stand* it!

[*She grips the mantelpiece and leans on it, fighting for self-control. Stephen looks at her, then he gathers up the proofs, glances at them and puts them on the desk. He crosses back and stands behind her, putting an arm round her. There is a tiny pause.*]

STEPHEN (*gently*): Hullo—you.
BARBARY (*shakily*): Hullo—Professor.

[*She lightly kisses his hand on her shoulder.*]

I think—the devil has retreated.
STEPHEN (*quietly*): Good. It—isn't so bad, you know. He had only time to make one tear across. I'll help you paste them up.
BARBARY (*wiping her eyes*): But the wanton *wickedness*. Just because I sent him away. I hope we never see the little monster again.

[*Stephen goes to the table.*]

STEPHEN: I don't suppose we shall. (*Pouring coffee.*)

Come and sit down and drink this. You've had a pretty trying day.

[*They sit down side by side. He pulls out his handkerchief.*]

STEPHEN: And here—you've made your eye-black into a sort of striped effect. Smart, I grant you, but a bit unconventional for tonight's very formal " do ".

[*While they are talking, he gently removes the smudged make-up from her eyes.*]

BARBARY: Stephen, I do want you to be a great success tonight.
STEPHEN (*laughing*): Is that why you're bullying me into a dinner jacket?
BARBARY: I don't manage it often, do I? No—I mean—try and be impressive with Lady Westbrook.
STEPHEN (*replacing his handkerchief*): With the most civilised intentions, I can never see that woman as anything but a large whale. I think it's the grey chiffon dresses and the little folded-up eyes.
BARBARY: Darling, to please me——

[*He gets up to pour out his own coffee.*]

STEPHEN (*lightly*): Let's do one of those highly intellectual unintelligible modern things on her. (*Standing centre cup in hand.*) Now how would it go—— (*Dramatically, improvising.*) " Deep in the drowned dead iridescent waters—deep and dead are her grey corrugant eyelids——"
BARBARY (*exasperated*): Stephen, won't you be serious——
STEPHEN (*sitting on settee*): Not about the headmastership of Wimborough.

[*There is a little pause. He drinks his coffee.*]

BARBARY (*slowly*): I hoped—you'd been thinking it over. Wimborough's famous.

[*He finishes his coffee and puts the cup on the table.*]

STEPHEN: I don't want to be headmaster of any school. Especially Wimborough. The job's entirely administrative. I like *teaching*.
BARBARY: But you're brilliant——
STEPHEN (*gently mocking at her*): I *know*, darling. Positively scintillating.
BARBARY: You're wasted at Grantley.
STEPHEN: I don't feel a bit wasted. Grantley may not be spectacular or fashionable. But it's a good school —I feel I can do a good job there. And I do—like being with the boys.
BARBARY (*breaking in abruptly*): Would it have made any difference if we'd had children of our own?

[*There is another pause.*]

STEPHEN (*quietly*): I thought we'd agreed not to mention that again?
BARBARY (*slowly*): Yes. Only—sometimes I can't help wondering.
STEPHEN: Bradley says we're two normal healthy people. There's no reason why we shouldn't have normal healthy children. We just don't, that's all. (*Putting his arm round her.*) Does it have to be such a tremendous issue?

[*She does not answer.*]

Darling, don't let this get out of proportion. We still have a good marriage, haven't we?

BARBARY: It isn't complete. Why can't I complete it for you, instead of writing stupid books which are read and forgotten in half an hour?
STEPHEN: You've a creative brain and the intelligence to use it. And I promise you, my darling— (*Smiling.*)—I promise you across my heart, that I love you as much—if not more, than ever.
BARBARY (*smiling*): That goes for me, too.
STEPHEN (*getting up*): Good. Now stop all this silly self-reproach. And stop seeing me as a reincarnation of Arnold of Rugby. Instead of what I am—a dull classics master—whose only ambition is to write a sober text book on the *De Senectute* of Cicero.
BARBARY: I happen to have been in love with that dull classics master for eight years. Tonight, I shan't take my eyes off him throughout dinner, and poor Lady Westbrook will have a very dull evening.
STEPHEN (*gaily*): She's going to have the evening of her life. I shall probably charm her completely out of her grey chiffon. (*Darkly.*) Then we really shall *know*.
BARBARY: Know what?
STEPHEN (*dramatically*): Whether or no, she *is* a whale.

[*Barbary gets up, laughing.*]

BARBARY: If your boys could hear their professor now they would be positively ribald.
STEPHEN: Then I should punish them severely.

[*He meets Barbary centre. With a sudden complete change of voice and mood, he takes her close into his arms, looking down at her.*]

Do you know what I should do? (*Quietly.*) I should

make them write out one thousand times—Professor Leigh adores his wife——

[*He bends his head to kiss her. There is a sudden high shrill screaming off. Tod comes charging through the windows, completely out of control, in a state of blind, terrible hysteria. He rushes to Stephen, clutching at him frantically.*]

TOD: Mister, Mister, come quick! *Please* come quick——

STEPHEN: Tod, what is it——?

TOD (*pulling at Stephen*): He's drowning Melon—Giovanni's drowning Melon——

BARBARY: Drowning——

[*Mrs. Perryman hurries in right.*]

MRS. PERRYMAN: What on earth——

TOD (*dragging Stephen to window*): Somebody *come*! (*Agonisedly.*) He's drowning Melon—he's struggling in the water—I tell you Giovanni's drowning Melon.

MRS. PERRYMAN: My God—keep the boy there——

[*She rushes out through the windows and off right. Tod, still crying frantically, tries to pull Stephen after her.*]

TOD: Let me go too—let me go—I got to go too——

[*Stephen holds him tightly.*]

STEPHEN: All right, Tod—all right. Mrs. Perry's gone. She'll deal with it. Tod—listen to me—Tod——

[*Tod goes limp in his arms, sobbing heartbrokenly.*]

TOD: He was my own cat—mine——

STEPHEN: Leave it to Mrs. Perry. Hold on to me—that's better.

[*He brings Tod down centre, holding him close and trying to soothe him. Barbary goes to the table and hurriedly pours out a cup of black coffee. She turns to Tod.*]

BARBARY: S-hush, there's a good boy. Look, drink this. Come along, drink this——
TOD: Go away—go away!
BARBARY (*kneeling beside him*): Just try and drink some——
TOD: I don't want it—go to hell!

[*He sweeps the cup aside. Barbary catches it, but the dark liquid cascades down the skirt of her dress. She gets up angrily.*]

BARBARY: Damn!
STEPHEN: He couldn't help it, Barbary—he's distracted—I'm so sorry. Tod—come over here——

[*He takes Tod to the settee and sits down, still holding him tightly. Barbary puts the cup on the table and dabs at her ruined skirt with a napkin. Tod still sobs bitterly.*]

Take it easy now—easy——

[*Mrs. Perryman comes back through the windows, carrying a bundle rolled in her apron, and crosses right. She jerks her head at Tod as she passes.*]

MRS. PERRYMAN: Don't let him see.

[*Stephen quickly pulls Tod's head against him.*]

(*At door left.*) And better take him upstairs. Dawson's coming over.

[*She goes out right. Tod pulls away from Stephen and looks up at him.*]

TOD (*blankly*): He isn't *dead*——? Melon isn't *dead*?

[*Stephen doesn't answer. Tod breaks away. He hurls himself on the hearthrug, beating on the ground with his fists.*]

No! No! *No!*

[*Stephen goes on his knees beside him.*]

STEPHEN: Tod—please, Tod——
TOD: I want to be dead too! I want to be dead too!
STEPHEN: I know, I know. Suppose you come upstairs—Tod—try and listen to me——

[*Giovanni Dawson enters angrily through the windows. He is a tall, strongly built man in his forties, lithe now, but promising to run to fat. There is a suggestion of Latin blood in his quick dark eyes, black hair and full too-red mouth. He speaks perfect English, but his gestures occasionally betray him. He wears grey flannels, tightly belted at the hips, a cream silk shirt rolled to the elbows, and a flamboyant tie.*]

DAWSON (*coming centre*): What the hell is all this——?

[*Tod leaps from the rug and hurls himself on Dawson, screaming and battering with both fists.*]

TOD: You killed Melon—God damn and blast you—you swine——

[*Enter Mrs. Perryman.*]

DAWSON (*viciously*): Quiet——!

[*With a hard blow on the side of the head, he sends Tod reeling back against Stephen. Tod screams. Everyone speaks at once.*]

BARBARY } : Stephen—get him away——
MRS. PERRYMAN } : You vicious brute——
STEPHEN (*above them all*): *Please!*

[*There is a pause.*]

DAWSON: I'm sorry, Mr. Leigh—but——
STEPHEN: Just a moment, Dawson. Perry, take Tod upstairs.

[*Mrs. Perryman crosses. Tod clings to Stephen.*]

TOD (*wildly*): I won't go!
DAWSON: You'll come here——
STEPHEN: Leave the boy alone, Dawson.
DAWSON (*angrily*): Whose kid is he——
STEPHEN (*quietly*). Tod, go with Mrs. Perry.

[*Mrs. Perryman puts her arm round Tod and takes him to the stairs, motioning to Barbary to follow. Dawson makes a grab at Tod.*]

DAWSON: You damn well come with me——
TOD (*frantically*): I won't—I won't——

[*He breaks free and runs up the stairs, Barbary and Mrs. Perryman following.*]

I'll kill him. When I'm big enough, I'll *kill* him!

[*He goes screaming, upstairs, and out of sight.*]

MRS. PERRYMAN } : Tod—wait—Tod——
BARBARY } : Stop him screaming——

[*They go off along the landing and a door bangs, abruptly shutting off the screams. Dawson stands at the foot of the stairs, looking up. Stephen, obviously shaken, turns down to the mantelpiece for his pipe.*]

DAWSON: What *is* this?
STEPHEN (*without turning*): Dawson, sit down.

[*Dawson swings round on the bottom stair. He eyes Stephen calculatingly across the room.*]

I'd like a word with you. (*Indicating a chair by table.*) May as well discuss it comfortably.

[*Dawson pauses, then he comes centre. He is quiet, but it is obvious his anger is only just under control.*]

DAWSON: Now look, Mr. Leigh, I like to be civil. But don't you think you're being a bit high-handed?
STEPHEN (*filling his pipe*): Don't you realise you've just done a very brutal and unimaginative thing?
DAWSON: What—a tap on the head? Tod's had worse than that and lived through it.
STEPHEN: I mean—his cat.

[*Dawson drops into the chair centre and shouts with laughter.*]

DAWSON: Good God—is that all this three-ring circus is about? We're sailing tomorrow. I had to get rid of the brute somehow.
STEPHEN: In a way that will haunt a child like Tod for years.
DAWSON: You got any kids?
STEPHEN: Of my own? No.
DAWSON: I thought not. Easy to see you don't know

much about 'em. Tod'll have forgotten this by tomorrow. Alley cats are ten a penny. He can have a dozen cats in America if he wants them. I'm easy.

STEPHEN (*lighting his pipe*): Are you?

DAWSON: Too true I am. Otherwise I'd have stopped all this nonsense before.

STEPHEN: What nonsense?

DAWSON: Letting Tod slip over here every minute my back's turned.

STEPHEN: Why should you object?

DAWSON: Because he's getting big ideas, that's why. Mr. Leigh doesn't like this—Mr. Leigh wouldn't do that. And he talks too much—exaggerates. He's probably given you a completely wrong impression.

STEPHEN: He gives me the impression that basically he's extremely unhappy.

DAWSON: Don't you take him seriously. He gets worked up—makes scenes. He's like his grandmother, all spit and passion. (*He brings out a cigarette and flicks on a lighter.*) There's only one way to deal with a hysterical kid and that's to knock it out of him—hard. (*He lights his cigarette.*)

STEPHEN: I would not have believed anyone could be so blatantly ignorant as to——

[*Dawson jerks upright.*]

DAWSON: Ignorant, is it? Now look here, Mr. Leigh—if you think you can talk to me like that—just because you happen to be educated——

STEPHEN: It has nothing to do with education. If you've not the bare intelligence to see Tod's a very unhappy child who needs careful handling——

DAWSON: He's a vicious little brute who wants mastering.

[*He breaks off, blowing a cloud of smoke, and eyeing Stephen again. Suddenly his attitude changes. He sits on the arm of the settee, leaning forward and speaking almost placatingly. He has a considerable amount of coarse charm, and he uses it.*]

You know, Mr. Leigh, I do think you've got me wrong. Tod's not so badly off as you imagine. And there's two sides of this. He's not altogether an easy set-up for me. For instance, did you ever wonder why I keep him tagging after me all over the place?

STEPHEN: I should be very interested to know.

DAWSON: Time and time again I've boarded him in schools. Good schools too, when I could afford it. And what does he do? He runs away.

STEPHEN: So——?

DAWSON: So he's fetched back. And then what does he do?

STEPHEN: He runs away again.

DAWSON: Exactly. Once he even bites the warden. And temper——! I'm telling you. Half a ton of explosive with a split second flashpoint. Why—look at him just now——

[*Mrs. Perryman comes down the stairs and crosses right.*]

MRS. PERRYMAN: The child's demented. Violently sick. What he needs is a doctor. (*She goes to the door.*)

STEPHEN: I'll ring Bradley, if necessary.

[*Mrs. Perryman goes out right. Dawson's attempt at conciliation vanishes.*]

DAWSON: You'll do nothing of the kind. I've told you—he's playing up purposely. And I've had about enough of this. I'm the boy's father, aren't I?

STEPHEN (*quietly*): Unfortunately.

DAWSON: Then just remember that and——

[*Mrs. Perryman hurries back left carrying a bowl and a towel over her arm.*]

Hey you——! Bring that kid down right away. I'm not chewing the rag any longer.

[*Mrs. Perryman does not even pause.*]

MRS. PERRYMAN (*briskly*): If you speak to me like that, young man, you'll have nothing left to chew with

[*She whisks up the stairs and off left. Dawson returns centre to Stephen.*]

DAWSON: Mr. Leigh, let's not have any more unpleasantness. Will you just fetch that old—that—lady help back and tell her we're going——

STEPHEN: Tod's not fit to be moved tonight. I doubt if he will be any fitter in the morning.

DAWSON: And what d'you suggest I do when I leave? Put him out with the empty milk bottles?

STEPHEN: Haven't you any feeling at all? That child's sick with misery——

DAWSON: Sick with misery! Temper—that's all it is—temper. What do you understand about children? You haven't even managed to have any of your own.

[*Stephen looks down at his pipe. There is the briefest pause before he answers.*]

STEPHEN (*quietly*): My job—is children.

DAWSON: Other people's. And Tod isn't one of them. (*Beginning to lose control again.*) Now—will you go and fetch him down. Or shall I do it myself?

STEPHEN: I'm afraid you'll have to wait till the morning.

[*Dawson blows up.*]

DAWSON: The hell I will! Calmly telling me what to do!—And there's another thing—you needn't think I don't know about your whispering campaign——

STEPHEN: If you've heard——

DAWSON: Oh, I've heard all right. I get around. Trying to blacken me with the local busybodies—saying you don't think I'm fit to control Tod——

STEPHEN (*breaking in*): I think you're not fit to be his father.

[*Dawson stops dead He exhales a long stream of smoke. Very deliberately he crushes out his cigarette in a saucer on the table. His expression is not pretty.*]

DAWSON (*quietly*): I ought to knock you right through that wall.

STEPHEN: That will be assault, and I shall call the police.

DAWSON: Suppose I beat you to it? Suppose I call them and demand you give up my kid?

STEPHEN: By all means call the police, Dawson. I shall refuse to give up Tod, and any doctor will support me that he shouldn't be moved tonight. You'll get him, of course—eventually. But it will all take time, and——

DAWSON: You listen to me——

STEPHEN: —And it's highly probable you won't be able to sail for America tomorrow.

[*Dawson pauses.*]

(*Quietly.*) I may be wrong, but I've a feeling this

American trip is important to you. Somehow, I don't think you'd like it postponed.

DAWSON: What exactly do you want?

STEPHEN: To make you a proposition.

DAWSON (*briefly*): Let's hear it.

STEPHEN: I don't think you're very receptive at the moment. (*He crosses to the desk.*) Suppose you go home, cool down, and allow me to come across and explain in about twenty minutes?

[*He pours a drink, comes back and offers it to Dawson.*]

DAWSON (*explosively*): Well, my God——!

STEPHEN: Be sensible, Dawson. Hear what I've got to say. You can always refuse.

DAWSON (*slowly*): Yes. Yes, I can. (*Taking the glass.*) Bit of a slippery customer, aren't you? Believe in keeping your temper. Well, sometimes it works and sometimes it doesn't. (*Nodding.*) All right, Mr. Leigh. (*He gulps the drink.*) Twenty minutes.

[*He puts the glass on the table, goes to the windows and turns.*]

And this proposition of yours——

[*He makes an expressive gesture with the flat of his hand.*]

It better be good.

[*He goes out through the windows. Stephen goes to the telephone on the desk and dials a number. While he is waiting he takes out his handkerchief and passes it over his forehead and upper lip.*]

STEPHEN: Arnold——? I want to talk to you—

urgently. May I come over? Yes—now. What? I'm afraid that will have to wait. Thanks very much. Yes—right away.

[*Barbary, wearing a different evening dress, comes hurrying down the stairs.*]

BARBARY: He's much calmer. Perry's coping wonderfully—oh, Stephen—quickly—get changed! We ought to be starting—— (*She goes to glance in the mirror over the fireplace.*)
STEPHEN: Barbary, can you wait? It's important——
BARBARY (*turning*): But darling—we're late. Not now. What's so important now?
STEPHEN: It's about Tod.

[*He turns to face her across the room.*]

I want to adopt him. Legally.

Curtain

ACT TWO

Scene 1

Autumn, about eighteen months later. The room is unchanged. Outside the windows it is a sunny evening. The laburnum tree has been replaced by a small mountain ash, gay with berries, and a bright creeper has been trained round the doorway.

Barbary's desk is covered with newspapers, magazines, and a pile of novels in bright dust jackets. There are flowers everywhere, chrysanthemums, dahlias; and a little florist's spray in a cellophane wrapper.

Arnold and Mrs. Perryman are standing by the desk. He is looking through a newspaper and she is reading a magazine.

MRS. PERRYMAN: I certainly shouldn't be disappointed if it was me. Listen to this. (*Reading.*) " Miss Leigh's light and amusing detective yarns have kept us entertained for many years. In her latest book ' Carry Me Back ' she proves that she can be grave as well as gay and still remain entertaining." (*Glancing at cover.*) *Girlhood's Companion.*

ARNOLD: I fancy she is more likely to be influenced by the learned gentleman in the *Sunday Times.* " Miss Barbary Leigh is a classic example of the clown who yearns to play Hamlet. In her new book, ' Carry Me Back ', three hundred and twenty pages of turgid misgivings, encircling a non-existent plot and a completely unintelligent set of characters, are no welcome substitute for her usual style of work which, if not exactly enriching our literature, at least pleasantly passes an idle hour." (*Putting down paper.*)

Whoever wrote that last sentence should be strangled with it.

MRS. PERRYMAN: Oh well, she's had her way. Now perhaps she can go back to the old stuff.

ARNOLD: That may not be so easy. (*Glancing at his watch.*) Just how much longer are they going to be?

MRS. PERRYMAN: She said she'd catch the five fifteen. You never know what time *he'll* get in——

[*Tod appears suddenly on the stairs, wearing a formidable pair of boxing gloves.*]

TOD (*striking an attitude*): Put 'em up!

[*Arnold and Mrs. Perryman turn. Eighteen months with the Leighs have made an appreciable difference to Tod. His rough speech has gone; he is clean, his hair trim and glossy, and he is neatly dressed in a striped T-shirt and flannels. His manner is bright, he has lost much of the old sullen suspicion, though his movements are still quick and highly-strung.*]

ARNOLD: What's this? Assault and battery? (*Firmly.*) Six months without option!

MRS. PERRYMAN: That's right. You put the fear of the law into him Those gloves! He'd eat his dinner in them if he could.

TOD (*dancing on the landing*): *Gee*-zer! *Gee*-zer!

MRS. PERRYMAN: That's enough, my lad—or I'll cut down your supper. And remember—Mr. Hamble's not so young as you are. No half larks with those gloves.

[*She goes out right. Tod comes shadow boxing down the stairs.*]

ARNOLD: Now I wonder what precisely is—half a lark?

TOD: It's one of her rot sayings. She's got millions.
ARNOLD: I say! Where did you get those magnificent weapons of pugilistic attack and defence?
TOD: Aren't they super-colossal? Mister gave them to me—I'm learning properly. Look out—put up your guard, seconds out—wheez, wham!

[*He smacks Arnold smartly just above the belt. Arnold doubles up and yelps. Tod dances round him, shouting with delight.*]

I'm the Wonder Boy—I'm Billy the Kid—I'm the Golden Smasher—put 'em up!

[*Stephen, wearing his gown but no hat, enters through the windows, catching Tod from the rear.*]

STEPHEN: Hey—what're you up to—slaughtering my best friend!
TOD (*joyfully*): Mister—Hullo, Mister——
STEPHEN (*sparring with him*): I'll Mister you—come on—where's that right?

[*He spars round the room with Tod, both shouting at once. Arnold retreats up a couple of stairs in mock terror.*]

STEPHEN : Watch out—you're too excited, mind your footwork—come on, you smasher —I'll jolly well show you——
TOD : You can't get me—I'm the Champ—I'm the tops—I've won the belt and fifty million smackers——

[*Stephen trips and falls, tangled in his gown. Tod throws himself on him, flailing his arms and pretending to beat Stephen. He shouts with delight and Stephen yells back at him.*]

STEPHEN: Stop it—get off my chest! You're killing me—you weigh a ton! *Get off me!*

[*Barbary, in outdoor clothes and laden with parcels, enters right.*]

BARBARY: Well——!

[*There is dead silence. Tod gets off Stephen and moves down left, suddenly subdued. Stephen, panting and laughing, props himself on his elbows.*]

STEPHEN: Hullo, darling. Welcome to the peace conference. (*He gets up, brushing himself down.*)
BARBARY: It sounded like a full scale murder. I heard you right across the Close. Hullo, Arnold (*Pausing.*) Oh, Stephen—you've done it again!
STEPHEN (*blankly*): Done what?
BARBARY: Cycled home in your gown.
STEPHEN (*realising*): Oh, Lord—sorry. Here, Tod—(*He strips off the gown and tosses it to Tod.*) I was talking to Odiham about some exam papers and I forgot.

[*He sits down on the settee and unlaces his shoes. Tod takes the gown to the cupboard left and hangs it on the door. He goes back to Stephen with a pair of slippers. Arnold takes some of Barbary's parcels to the desk.*]

BARBARY: Thank you, Arnold. Have you been dragged across to referee?
ARNOLD: I merely called in with the peaceful suggestion that you come over for a drink tonight.
BARBARY: I'd love to. How about you, Stephen?

[*Tod has squatted down beside Stephen and is speaking to him. Stephen looks up rather absently.*]

STEPHEN: Mm? Oh, yes, fine. (*Back to Tod.*) And did you sneak the pump off my bicycle?
TOD: I *borrowed* it—for an experiment.

[*He goes on talking. Barbary turns to Arnold. For a moment they all talk together.*]

ARNOLD: What *have* you been up to? Buying the Metropolis?
BARBARY: Celebrating recklessly. Look at my idiotic hat—no—it's on my head—how does it strike you?
TOD: Mister, I got that other skate. It's wonderful what you can do with two skates. D'you know you can make different *noises*?

[*Barbary breaks off. Tod's excited voice has topped them all.*]

If you go bending down—see—it's *just* like an engine. (*shouting*) who-oo-whoo!
BARBARY (*cutting in*): Tod, you'd better get bathed and do your homework.

[*Tod turns, still on his knees. He looks straight at her. He speaks with perfect courtesy but unmistakable rebuke.*]

TOD (*coldly*): I was talking to Mister.

[*Stephen taps him sharply with a slipper.*]

STEPHEN (*quickly*): Here—steady. You mustn't speak to Mrs. Leigh like that.
TOD (*turning to him*): I'm sorry.
STEPHEN: Thank you. (*Prompting.*) And——?

[*Tod eyes him for a moment, his lip jutting out in the old manner. Then he gets up and turns to Barbary.*]

TOD (*quietly*): I—beg your pardon.
STEPHEN: Right. Now go and put my bike away, will you? I think the back tyre needs a go with the pump. There's some books in the basket—you might bring them in. Go on—hop it. I'll be up later.

[*Tod goes out through the windows. Stephen looks at Barbary for a second, then gets up and goes to the fireplace. Barbary turns to Arnold.*]

BARBARY: Thank you for the flowers, Arnold. You're a dear. (*Taking off her hat.*] And what do you really think of the book?

[*Stephen, with an air of apprehension, half turns.*]

ARNOLD: Do you really want to know?
BARBARY (*wryly*): When anyone says that, I sense what's coming. Yes. I really want to know.
ARNOLD: I don't think you've written a best seller. I don't think you'll make much money. But the book will be read by a few people who will appreciate that you've approached your subject with intelligence and sincerity.

[*Stephen relaxes and takes his pipe from the mantelpiece.*]

BARBARY: Thank you, Arnold. I wish you were a critic. You know how to combine honesty with courtesy.

[*She puts her hat on the desk and pauses, picking up the little nosegay in the cellophane case.*]

Hullo—where did these come from? Oh, there's a note. (*She tears open the envelope, saying over her shoulder.*) Excuse me——

[*She begins to read, then picks up her spectacles and continues. Arnold moves down to Stephen.*]

ARNOLD: Mr. Leigh, you have a brilliant wife. (*Laughing.*) You know, of course, that I fully intend to be her second husband.

STEPHEN: Don't risk it. In twelve months you'll have beaten her to death with a copy of the *Judge's Rules.*

BARBARY (*suddenly*): Listen—just listen to this.

[*She sits down in her desk chair, reading the note in her hand.*]

" Dear Mrs. Leigh. Everyone is sending you flowers because you wrote the book. I thought you would like me to send you some too. Here they are. With —with—"(*Looking close at the note.*)—there's an enormous blot—"with compliments and best wishes I am yours faithfully, Thomas Oliver Dawson." (*Looking up.*) In brackets—" Tod ". (*She takes off her glasses.*) And what do you think of that?

STEPHEN: Well, good for him.

BARBARY: Wait. (*Replaces glasses.*) There's a p.s. (*Reading.*) " I read the book—the copy you gave Mister—I don't think it's good writing. If you think I don't know good writing, there's some in ' Kim '— page ninety. I have marked the place. (*Turning the note over.*) P.P.s. I have marked it in soft pencil. It will rub out." (*Looking up again.*) Well——!

[*Arnold turns away to hide a smile.*]

STEPHEN: *Kim*—but of course. India—he's been there. He knows. (*To bookshelves.*) Now, let's see— where—(*He comes back centre with a small red book.*) —what page?

BARBARY (*shortly*): Ninety. Give me that.

[*She takes the book sharply from him, finds the page and runs her finger down the print. She begins to read, at first quickly, then her voice changes.*]

"By this time the sun was driving broad golden spokes through the lower branches of the mango trees; the parakeets and doves were coming home in their hundreds. (*She murmurs a few lines inaudibly. Aloud.*) Swiftly the light gathered itself together, painted for an instant the faces and the cart-wheels and the bullocks' horns as red as blood. Then the night fell, changing the touch of the air, drawing a low, even haze, like a gossamer veil of blue, across the face of the country, and bringing out, keen and distinct, the smell of wood-smoke and cattle and the good scent of wheaten cakes cooked on ashes."

[*She closes the book, puts it on the desk, and removes her spectacles.*]

(*Quietly.*) At least he paid me the compliment of setting a high standard.

STEPHEN (*bubbling*): It's marvellous—d'you hear that, Arnold? A child of his age to have such an instinct for good literature——

BARBARY (*crisply*): I hate to remind you—but in advanced circles of literary thought, the late Mr. Kipling is not altogether considered a master.

STEPHEN. Oh, rubbish—— (*He turns suddenly, sees her face and pauses.*) Why, Barbary——

[*She turns away. He crosses, puts his hands on her shoulders and swings her round to face him. He is half laughing, half serious.*]

Darling—where's your sense of humour?

BARBARY: Sense of humour! I could kill him——

STEPHEN: But just because——

BARBARY (*flaming*). Because he's right. Damn it—do you think I don't know? Of course he's right. And how do you suppose I like it?

STEPHEN: Barbary——

BARBARY (*sweeping on*): I work like a black for a year, trying to do something good—really good—and when it fails a little bit of an urchin bobs up from nowhere and puts me in my place.

[*She stops, picks up her bag and takes out a handkerchief.*]

I'm *sorry*, Arnold. An awful exhibition——

[*She dabs her eyes. Arnold comes forward.*]

ARNOLD: As a matter of fact, it gives me the very opportunity I want.

BARBARY: What on earth do you mean?

ARNOLD: I asked you over tonight for a drink. I really want a discussion. Perhaps we could consider the preliminaries now. This situation touches right on the subject. (*Looking from one to the other*) I mean—Wednesday—of course.

STEPHEN: You mean—the case.

ARNOLD: Yes. You know—you can still wait——

STEPHEN: We've waited long enough. I did think *you* might be able to cut through these exasperating legal delays.

BARBARY (*quickly*) Stephen, you can't blame Arnold. The adoption papers were sent out to Dawson quickly enough. We weren't to know he'd moved on. And you can't get a signature if there's no one to sign. That alone wasted six months.

STEPHEN: But surely there won't be another adjournment?

ARNOLD: I think the Court will be quite satisfied that every attempt has been made to trace Dawson. What I want you two to realise is this. Once those papers are signed on Wednesday Tod is yours as legally and morally as if he had actually been born to Barbary.

STEPHEN: Then what *is* the difficulty?

ARNOLD: My dear children, don't treat me like a village idiot—and a blind one at that. The difficulties I foresee are not legal ones. (*He looks at them in turn again.*) Answer me truthfully. Do you two still want to go through with this?

STEPHEN: Don't be ridiculous.

ARNOLD (*quietly*): Barbary——?

[*Barbary pauses. She looks down at her handkerchief.*]

STEPHEN: Barbary—for heaven's sake! Tod's lived here for eighteen months. Do you suggest we go to the judge and say, "We've changed our minds—take him away?"

ARNOLD: I would suggest—in all fairness—that these eighteen months haven't been easy.

STEPHEN: One couldn't expect otherwise.

BARBARY: What I didn't expect was that Tod would take an unreasonable—and apparently unalterable—dislike to me.

STEPHEN (*slowly*): I hadn't realised you felt like this.

BARBARY (*getting up*): Let's face it. I agreed—I don't deny it was against my will but I agreed—that we should adopt Tod. (*Crossing to fire.*) I was prepared to tolerate him—even in time to be fond of him. But from the first he's seemed to set himself against me in every way.

STEPHEN: We knew we had to cope with a difficult

child. A background like his can't be overcome in a matter of months.

BARBARY: But I have *tried*. For a person like me, I've been patient to the point of martyrdom. And he now tolerates *me* with a—a chilly politeness. It's a little wearing.

STEPHEN: Just a phase. It will pass suddenly.

ARNOLD: How long since you had any real trouble?

STEPHEN: Four or five months. The last major battle was about staying away from school.

BARBARY: Pretending he'd been there, and coming home with a graphic and completely untrue account of the day's happenings.

STEPHEN: Well, that's over.

BARBARY: Not the lies.

STEPHEN: Oh, yes. He sometimes exaggerates a bit but——

ARNOLD (*breaking in*): Even now he could be placed in the care of the authorities, pending some trace of Dawson——

STEPHEN: No—never. (*Looking over at her.*) Barbary, you couldn't seriously ask me——

ARNOLD: I must impress this upon you. The final moment of signing is a solemn one. The judge will ask you—both of you—if you are in—and mark this —in complete agreement.

[*There is another pause.*]

I should like to quote to you a little Danish proverb. "Children are certain sorrow—and uncertain joy." (*Very quietly.*) I think the decision rests with Barbary.

[*Barbary looks at Stephen across the room, a long steady look. He looks back at her. They are both tense. Suddenly she holds out her hand. He crosses and takes it.*]

BARBARY. I'll never desert the Professor. (*To Arnold.*) This is ridiculous. Go away—both of you. I want to write a letter before dinner.
ARNOLD: Right. (*Crossing to door right.*) I'll expect you about nine——
STEPHEN (*following him*)· Better say a quarter past—I have to glance through——

[*They go out, talking. Barbary stands thinking for a moment, then goes to her desk, sits down, slides a sheet of paper into the machine and begins to type. Tod returns through the windows, still wearing his boxing gloves and carrying two books. He is whistling happily and shrilly through his teeth till he sees Barbary, then he stops. She does not look up and he tries to pass behind her to the bookshelves. There is not much room, he catches her chair, jerking her forward. She looks up, with an impatient little exclamation.*]

TOD: Sorry!

[*She resumes her typing*]

May I put these over there, please? They're Mister's.
BARBARY: Yes, of course.

[*She shifts her chair slightly to let him pass. He puts the books on the shelf and moves to the stairs. She swings her chair round and takes off her spectacles.*]

Tod——

[*He turns politely.*]

Thank you for your note. I gather you didn't—care—for the book.

TOD (*simply*): I think it stinks.
BARBARY: Oh
TOD (*quickly*): I shouldn't have said that. Mister wouldn't like it.
BARBARY: I don't particularly like it, either.
TOD: Then I apologise.

[*Barbary looks at him, torn between anger and laughter.*]

BARBARY: Thank you.

[*There is an awkward pause. He stands thumping his gloved hands together.*]

TOD (*at last*): I guess I'd—better go and have my bath.
BARBARY (*gravely*): I guess you'd better.

[*He turns to the stairs again.*]

Tod——

[*He comes back obediently beside her.*]

Tod—(*Pausing.*) I suppose you couldn't tell me just *why* you don't like me?
TOD (*frankly*): I don't know. I do try to.
BARBARY: I do want you to be happy. You know that, don't you?

[*He nods.*]

Wouldn't it be much better if we were friends?

[*He nods.*]

(*Battling on.*) I don't think I've ever been deliberately

unkind to you. I may have told you off now and then, but we all have to be told off. And I do want you to be happy.

TOD (*looking straight at her*): Do you?

BARBARY: If I didn't want you to be happy, why would I have you here?

TOD: To please Mister.

[*Brought up short, Barbary looks at him. Then her careful control snaps in one sharp, irritated burst.*]

BARBARY: Oh—must you call him by that ridiculous name? Couldn't you say Stephen—or even Steve? You don't call me Missus.

TOD (*politely*): I could if you like.

[*She looks at him sharply, but he is perfectly serious. She turns back to her desk.*]

BARBARY: I think we'll leave it as it is for the moment. Go along now.

[*He goes upstairs. She glances up again.*]

Oh, Tod—thank you very much for the flowers. It was a nice thought.

TOD: It wasn't my idea. It was Mister's.

[*He runs off left along the landing. Then he returns, hanging over the banister rope.*]

I say——

[*She looks up.*]

I did *pay* for them.

[*He runs off left and out of sight. Barbary rubs her hand fretfully across her forehead. Then she reaches for an envelope and touches the red book. She picks it up, turns a page, then puts on her spectacles and begins to read with absorbed attention. Mrs. Perryman enters right with the coffee tray.*]

MRS. PERRYMAN: You were back late tonight. (*Accusingly.*) And where's that special cheese I asked you to bring?
BARBARY (*looking up*): Oh, Perry—I *am* sorry! I completely forgot.
MRS. PERRYMAN: Forgot! And I even wrote it down for you.
BARBARY: I know—there was a rather dreary discussion with the publishers and I got involved—don't scold me (*Picking up Tod's flowers.*) Put those in water for me, and tell Mr. Leigh coffee's ready.

[*Stephen strolls in right.*]

STEPHEN: I don't need telling. Anything special for dinner, Perry?
MRS. PERRYMAN: Soup, filet steak and a creme caramel.
STEPHEN (*laughing*): You're trying to murder me!
MRS. PERRYMAN (*calling upstairs*): Tod—your milk's here.

[*She goes out right. Stephen takes some exercise books from table above fire, sits down on settee, lights his pipe and throughout the next scene, makes corrections in the books. Barbary seals an envelope with a thump, takes off spectacles, stretches luxuriously and gets up.*]

BARBARY: Oh, it's nice to be home.

[*She goes to hearthrug, steps out of her shoes and pours out the coffee.*]

Your cup, Professor Leigh. And I hope it follows the correct formula. As black as night, as hot as hell, as sweet as love.

[*Stephen takes his cup, laughing.*]

STEPHEN: Has it ever struck you that so many enjoyable things are *hot*? Hot coffee, hot baths, hot sunshine——

BARBARY (*curling up beside him*): Hot music. And red-hot mommas.

STEPHEN: Oh, no!

[*They both laugh, drinking their coffee companionably together.*]

BARBARY: Do you know, for eight years this has been the happiest part of my day?

STEPHEN (*smiling at her*): And mine. (*Scribbling in the book on his knee.*) Thank you for backing me up about the adoption just now. I do know things have been difficult.

BARBARY: He's doing quite well at the Grammar School, isn't he? Catching up on his work?

STEPHEN: Thanks to his knowledge of languages. Naturally, in that respect he's ahead of much older boys.

[*Tod, in pyjamas and dressing gown, appears on the landing.*]

Hullo, Tod. Do you want your milk?

[*He takes a glass from the tray and goes to the stairs. Tod comes down to meet him.*]

TOD: Aren't you coming up tonight?
STEPHEN: Certainly I am. We'll have our twenty minutes. What's on this evening?
TOD (*grimly*): Cube roots.
STEPHEN: Good God! All right. I'll be there later.

[*He turns centre. Tod grabs him.*]

TOD: Mister—d'you think we could go fishing again on Saturday?
STEPHEN: Saturday? Let's think. Yes, we might if I can fit it in. Tell you what—if we started out really early we could fish over Grantley Weir and be back in time for lunch.
TOD (*ecstatic*): Gosh—Mister!
BARBARY: Darling, your coffee's getting cold.
STEPHEN: Coming. (*To Tod.*) We'll talk about it when I come up. Off you go.

[*He returns to settee and sits down. Tod, carrying his glass, goes halfway up the stairs and then sits down quietly, sipping his milk and watching them.*]

BARBARY: Will Arnold keep us long tonight? Will it all be frightfully legal?
STEPHEN: I don't imagine so. Just make sure we give the right answers.

[*Barbary sees Tod on the stairs.*]

BARBARY: What is it, Tod? Do you want something?

[*He shakes his head.*]

Then start getting to bed, there's a good boy.

[*He goes off slowly left along the landing. Stephen watches him go, then he turns to Barbary.*]

STEPHEN (*slowly*) Barbary, I've been thinking. This little evening interlude of ours—

BARBARY: What about it?

STEPHEN: Don't you think Tod's old enough to sit with us for five minutes and drink his milk before he goes to bed?

BARBARY: No, Stephen—please. He's only ten. And this is *our* own interlude. We look forward to it. It's our—our *family* time.

STEPHEN: He knows that. I believe he feels left out.

BARBARY: He has a very good life. I don't feel inclined to share this part with him.

STEPHEN: Would you say that if he were—really family?

[*Barbary finishes her coffee and puts the cup on the table before replying.*]

BARBARY: Stephen, would you consider sending him to boarding school next year?

STEPHEN: Boarding school? I think it would be fatal. He's a bundle of nerves He needs home life and understanding. When he's twelve, I'd like to get him in to Grantley with me, but—(*Pausing.*)—does this mean—be frank—does this mean you want to be rid of him at home?

BARBARY: No. I only thought that if he were away from me for a time, he might outgrow his dislike——

STEPHEN: Darling, he doesn't dislike you. He's a little scared of you and that puts him on the defensive. If you'll still be patient, I'm certain, absolutely certain, that one day something quite simple will put things right between you. But it must happen naturally. It can't be forced——

[*Mrs. Perryman enters right.*]

MRS. PERRYMAN: I'm sorry to interrupt, but that Maria Blundell's called.
BARBARY: Oh, Perry, not *now*. Tell her we're frightfully sorry, but——
MRS. PERRYMAN: She says it's important. I think it must be. She's got that purple hat on.

[*Stephen gets up, laughing.*]

STEPHEN: Better bring her in, then.

[*Mrs. Perryman goes out right.*]

We'll cut her short. (*Calling.*) And Perry—? Bring another cup, will you?

[*Barbary gets up and steps back into her shoes.*]

BARBARY: This means a rushed dinner. She's probably consumed by a burning zeal about something and wants a subscription
STEPHEN: Then I hope the price of peace is not prohibitive.

[*Mrs. Perryman enters left with Mrs. Blundell, who is wearing her usual tweeds and a fashionable hat.*]

Good evening, Mrs. Blundell.
MRS. BLUNDELL: Good evening.
STEPHEN: Do come in and sit down.
BARBARY: Will you have some coffee? Perry's gone for another cup.
MRS. BLUNDELL (*raising her eyebrows*): Coffee? Before dinner?
STEPHEN (*apologetically*): It's a silly little personal habit of ours—I'm sorry. Perhaps you'd prefer a whisky and soda

[*He starts to cross left. Mrs. Blundell raises a massive hand, and sits on settee.*]

MRS. BLUNDELL: Thank you, no. I have no objection to coffee as coffee. It just seemed a peculiar time.

[*Mrs. Perryman enters right with another cup and saucer. Stephen takes it and puts it on the table.*]

BARBARY: Thank you, Perry. Black or white, Mrs. Blundell?

MRS. BLUNDELL: White, please. I never drink black coffee unless I make it myself. Very few people in this country know how to make coffee. The Colonel always used to say I was one of them. Now your coffee, my dear, he used to say, your coffee definitely has a bite to it.

MRS. PERRYMAN (*as she goes through doorway right*): I bet it had.

[*She exits. Barbary turns quickly to Mrs. Blundell.*]

BARBARY: Sugar, Mrs. Blundell?

MRS. BLUNDELL: No, thank you. (*Tasting coffee.*) H'm. Perhaps I will.

[*She sugars her coffee, stirs it, drinks and puts down her cup. She looks round at them. Barbary on the settee, Stephen on the hearthrug.*]

Well, I'd like to say I'm sorry about this. But I think you're two intelligent people, so I've come straight to you, rather than to the police.

BARBARY: Police?

MRS. BLUNDELL: It concerns Tod.

STEPHEN: What concerns Tod?

MRS. BLUNDELL: You remember the Italian glass basket I brought back from Florence last year?
BARBARY: Yes, indeed. All that lovely coloured glass fruit.
MRS. BLUNDELL: I went out yesterday at midday. When I returned at two o'clock someone had broken into my house and wrecked my drawing room in a most senseless manner. Nothing of any real value was taken—some Indian daggers, the Colonel's case of butterflies, and the glass basket. Obviously not the work of an adult mind.
STEPHEN: You're not suggesting——
MRS. BLUNDELL: I'm not suggesting anything. I'm dealing with facts.

[*She drinks some more coffee. Stephen and Barbary exchange glances.*]

I made enquiries, and sure enough, Brocken's boy, Eddie, had been seen hanging round at lunch time. He has a bad reputation. I had him up before the Bench last year.
STEPHEN (*quietly*): So——?
MRS. BLUNDELL: I went to his father and we tackled the boy together. After a little questioning, he broke down and admitted everything.
STEPHEN: If he admitted everything, why do you come to us?
MRS. BLUNDELL: Because he said he had an accomplice. In his own words—gleaned, I should imagine, from a comprehensive study of American films and literature—"Me and my buddy made a big bust and knocked 'em off clean."

[*She breaks off, looking severely at Stephen who has involuntarily chuckled.*]

STEPHEN (*gravely*): I beg your pardon.

MRS. BLUNDELL: I'm sorry to say he—er—*ratted*, I believe is the term, on that buddy. (*Looking at them.*) It was Tod.

STEPHEN: I don't believe it.

MRS. BLUNDELL: As it happens we may be able to prove it.

STEPHEN: Well——?

MRS. BLUNDELL: I recovered everything from Brocken except the lid of the glass basket. Eddie says Tod took a fancy to it. He put it into a box he has—which looks like a book.

[*Barbary and Stephen look at each other. Then Stephen knocks out his pipe and puts it into his pocket.*]

STEPHEN: Mrs. Blundell, I'm grateful to you for coming straight to me. Will you let me handle this now?

[*Without waiting for an answer he goes to the foot of the stairs and calls up.*]

STEPHEN: Tod? Tod, will you come down here a moment?

[*He returns to the fireplace, standing with his back to it.*]

MRS. BLUNDELL: I hardly think Tod will break down and confess. Wouldn't it be better to look for the box?

[*Tod, pulling on his dressing gown, comes running joyfully on to the landing, and halfway down the stairs.*]

TOD: Did you want me, Mister? Did you——?

[*He stops, looking across at them. There is a pause.*]

(*Polite but subdued.*) Good evening, Mrs. Blundell.
MRS. BLUNDELL (*grimly*): Good evening.
STEPHEN: Tod, you know that box of yours that looks like a book?

[*All the bright eagerness dies out of Tod's face.*]

TOD (*quietly*): Yes, Mister.
STEPHEN: I want you to bring it down to me.
TOD: Now——?
STEPHEN: Yes, please.

[*Tod looks from one to the other, then he turns and goes up and off left, trailing his girdle behind him.*]

MRS. BLUNDELL: Very touching. And quite obviously, that box will be empty.
STEPHEN: Mrs. Blundell, I'm hoping to prove to you that Tod isn't just an ordinary dishonest boy. If he did take your basket, I'm convinced he had a reason.
MRS. BLUNDELL: A reason——?
STEPHEN: Oh, an unsound one, no doubt. But nevertheless, a reason. That's why he'll bring down that box with the contents intact. He'll have that much common sense.
MRS. BLUNDELL: If this is child psychology, Mr. Leigh, I think you're extremely foolish. No boy could resist such an opportunity to—to——
BARBARY (*wryly*): To dispose of the evidence?
MRS. BLUNDELL: Exactly. I'm sorry for you both. I think you're going to be sadly disappointed.

[*Tod comes down the stairs carrying a large box shaped like a book. He crosses to Stephen.*]

STEPHEN. Thank you, Tod. Put it down on the floor, will you—just there.

[*Tod puts the box down by the table.*]

Now, will you take everything out and put it on the table? (*To Barbary, indicating tray.*) Would you mind, darling—?

[*Barbary gets up and moves the coffee tray from the table to the one above the fireplace. She returns to stand right above settee. Tod opens the box and puts various articles on the table, a book, a fountain pen, a belt with a snake clasp, and finally, lifting it out with extreme care, his tongue between his teeth, the lid of the basket covered with its gay, glass fruit. He stands back centre, his hands twisted together in front of him. He does not take his eyes off Stephen.*]

Thank you, Tod.

MRS. BLUNDELL: You little thief.

STEPHEN (*ignoring her*): Did Eddie Brocken give you this?

MRS. BLUNDELL: You're putting words into the boy's mouth——

BARBARY: Please, Mrs. Blundell——

STEPHEN: Did Eddie Brocken give you this?

TOD: No.

STEPHEN: Did you take it—and the other things—from Mrs. Blundell's house?

TOD: Yes.

STEPHEN: How did you get in?

TOD: Ed forced the lock. With my penknife.

STEPHEN: Why did you do it?

[*A pause. Tod still looks at Stephen. Then suddenly he turns and bolts for the stairs.*]

Tod.

[*Tod stops dead with his back to them.*]

Come here.

[*Tod returns slowly centre. Stephen takes his pipe and begins to fill it. He does not look at Tod.*]

Right over here—to me.

[*Tod crosses and stands in front of him.*]

If we were alone together, would you tell me exactly why you did this?

TOD: Yes, Mister.

STEPHEN: But if we were alone, people might think we were making up a good story. Can you understand that?

[*Tod shifts from one foot to the other, twisting his girdle. He glances at Mrs. Blundell, then back to Stephen.*]

TOD (*slowly*): It was yesterday—lunch time. I went to the library on my way home, to get that book you told me about—the one about cats in Egypt. You know—how they were like gods and people had them embalmed——

STEPHEN: Yes.

TOD: She—Mrs. Blundell—was up by the desk. She didn't see me. She was asking for Mrs. Leigh's new book. She was talking to the librarian, that Miss Fowler, who always has a dewdrop on her nose.

STEPHEN: Yes.

TOD: She said, " How strange an intelligent couple like the Leighs should take on that—that revolting little boy. They'll be sorry in the end."

MRS. BLUNDELL: Well, if one can't pass a casual remark——

STEPHEN (*quietly*): Go on, Tod.
TOD (*suddenly eloquent*): Mister—I was mad—I was all hot. Honest, I wanted to bash someone. I came outside and I saw Ed Brocken. I *had* to tell someone. I told Ed. He said—— (*He stops short.*) Must I?
STEPHEN: Yes, please.

[*Tod hesitates, looks at Mrs. Blundell, then at Stephen and breaks into rapid speech.*]

TOD: *Je vais vous le dire en français et vous pourrez le lui répèter en anglais—ça ne semblera pas si mal venant de vous——*
MRS. BLUNDELL: Young man, I had better warn you I have fluent French, average German, a little Italian, and a fair smattering of Hindustani.
STEPHEN (*intent on his pipe*): Better be good plain English then, hadn't it, Tod?

[*Tod braces his shoulders. He takes a deep breath.*]

TOD: He said, "I got it in for the old bitch, too. Let's do her."

[*There is a grisly silence. For a moment no one moves or speaks.*]

STEPHEN (*quietly, at last*): I see. Thank you for explaining. Now go up to bed. I'll see you presently.
TOD: Yes, Mister.

[*He goes quietly centre. Suddenly he stops, going tense. He turns on Stephen, his eyes blazing.*]

She damn well shouldn't have said it!
STEPHEN: Tod!

[There is a silent battle of wills between them for a moment. Tod gives way. He returns to table, and takes up the glass basket.]

TOD (*to Mrs. Blundell*): It isn't hurt at all. I wouldn't have broken it. But it isn't very bright, you know. If you washed it clean with soapy water and polished it with a little bit of leather, all those fruits would shine like they were jewels.

[He places it carefully on her lap, and goes quietly up the stairs and out left. There is another pause, again broken by Stephen.]

STEPHEN (*quietly*): Will you—have a little more coffee?

MRS. BLUNDELL: Well—really! The boy—— (*To Barbary.*) No, no more, thank you—the boy is quite unrepentant

STEPHEN: He thinks he had justification for what he did. You know, it was rather an unfortunate thing to say.

MRS. BLUNDELL: In the circumstances, I consider it fair comment.

BARBARY: Perhaps. It's a pity he overheard.

MRS. BLUNDELL: Yes, it is. I am very sorry about that. But I would remind you that he did break into my house, and he did steal.

STEPHEN: Not out of ordinary malice or because he's a thief by nature. He wanted to hit back at you because you hurt him. His—his reasons and values were mixed——

MRS. BLUNDELL: What does a child of that age know about reasons and values? All he needs to understand is the plain difference between right and wrong.

STEPHEN: Very well. What do you want me to do?

MRS. BLUNDELL: In the ordinary way, I should go

straight to the police. In view of your position as a senior master at Grantley, and also the fact that the adoption case comes up so soon—it wouldn't be advisable to bring the boys into court.

STEPHEN (*quickly*): It would be disastrous. I do hope you won't——

MRS. BLUNDELL: I'm not a hard woman, Mr. Leigh. I've had three boys of my own. I don't want to make unnecessary trouble. I've agreed with Fred Brocken that if he gives his son a thorough thrashing, I'll let the matter drop. But—what's fair for one boy is fair for the other.

BARBARY: Hardly——

MRS. BLUNDELL: Definitely. (*To Stephen.*) Mr. Leigh, if you will agree to give Tod, here and now, a sound and proper thrashing, then as far as I'm concerned, we'll say no more about it.

[*Stephen has struck a match. He pauses, looks at her, blows out the match, throws it into the fire and puts his pipe on the mantelpiece.*]

STEPHEN (*quietly*): I'm sorry. It's out of the question.

MRS. BLUNDELL: Good heavens, why not? Tod's been thrashed before.

STEPHEN: Not by me.

MRS. BLUNDELL: Then it will be all the more effective.

STEPHEN: No—it's not quite so simple as that. (*Pausing.*) When we took Tod, eighteen months ago, he'd been clouted and kicked into a tough, violent little boy, resentful and suspicious of everything and everybody. I've had to work, slowly and painfully—God knows how painfully—with infinite patience, to give him a basis of respect for me—and Barbary.

[*Tod's head appears round the corner of the stairs, then bobs back out of sight.*]

MRS. BLUNDELL: Well——?

STEPHEN: Can't you see? If I do as you ask, all that bitterness and resentment will return—against me. And all our work will be destroyed.

MRS. BLUNDELL: You're being far too tense about this, Mr. Leigh. No normal boy resents a thrashing. If the Colonel were alive he'd deal with the matter in twenty minutes—and both boys would think twice before being in trouble again.

STEPHEN: If you'll leave it to me, I promise you I'll punish Tod severely—in a way he'll understand——

MRS. BLUNDELL: The only argument the Brocken boy understands is his father's belt.

STEPHEN (*stung*): Tod isn't a lout like Eddie Brocken. He has a highly sensitive imagination——

MRS. BLUNDELL: Rubbish. I brought up my three sons without any nonsense about sensitive imagination. And two of them are doing extremely well in the higher Civil Service.

STEPHEN: But you can't apply the same methods to all children. Any psychologist will tell you——

MRS. BLUNDELL: Psychology is a modern excuse for lack of self-restraint. I've no use for it. (*Pausing*) Surely, Mr. Leigh—do you never thrash boys at Grantley?

STEPHEN: When necessary, most certainly I do. Let us have this quite clear, Mrs. Blundell. I am not campaigning against corporal punishment. In the last eighteen months I've often been tempted—sorely tempted—to give Tod the hiding of his life, but——

MRS. BLUNDELL: I'm giving you the chance to do that now—and keep him out of court.

STEPHEN: Mrs. Blundell. (*Slowly.*) Please don't force me into this.

MRS. BLUNDELL: Frankly, I don't think you've any alternative. I've offered what I consider a perfectly reasonable solution—and if I may say so, a very lenient one. If you won't accept, I shall be obliged to take the matter to the police. (*Getting up.*) Good night, both of you.

BARBARY: Mrs. Blundell—just a moment. I think I see a way. Would you—would you mind waiting in the dining room while I speak to Stephen?

MRS. BLUNDELL: Very well, my dear. I don't want to be unreasonable. But mind—no compromise.

BARBARY: Thank you. (*She goes to the door right and calls.*) Perry! (*To Mrs. Blundell.*) Perry will show you.

[*She ushers Mrs. Blundell out, shuts the door and turns to look over at Stephen. He slowly sits on the settee.*]

(*Quietly.*) The damn woman's perfectly right, you know.

STEPHEN: I'm afraid she is. (*Looking up.*) I couldn't do it, Barbary. All his confidence in me will be destroyed.

BARBARY: Now why? You maintain he's exceptionally intelligent. Couldn't you go to him and explain that he's forced you into this position—that he's given her the right to insist on a thrashing, and he has to put up with it, and not feel resentful against you?

STEPHEN: My dear girl—he's ten years old. Do you expect him to work out that piece of adult reasoning?

BARBARY: Tell him he's let you down in the worst possible way. He's committed a criminal offence—yes, I know you think he had provocation. So do I. But he's taken the law into his own hands and you can't—you simply can't—condone it.

STEPHEN I don't. I know he has to be punished. But not in this way. I dare not risk losing his respect.

BARBARY: If he goes to court, you risk losing him. For good.

[*He looks at her.*]

You *do* realise *that*?

STEPHEN (*moving to the mantelpiece*): Yes. (*Suddenly.*) Confound the woman! Why can't she keep her gossiping mouth shut! First she creates the trouble, then she comes in here like some—some sanctimonious female Chadband—calmly telling me how to handle my own child. (*He breaks off, looking at her.*) But he *is*, Barbary. Just like my own child.

BARBARY (*gently*): I know, darling. But at this particular moment you can't afford to be sentimental.

[*He turns down to the fireplace. She waits a second longer, then holds out her hand.*]

Come on, Professor. Into battle.

[*He turns, looks at her, takes her hand for a second, then abruptly lets it go, crosses to the door right and opens it for her to pass through. They go out together, shutting the door behind them. Tod peers out from the end of the landing left. He bobs back, then comes cautiously down the stairs. He wears his long flannels and a blue blazer with a mackintosh belted over them, and carries a little case. He goes to the table, puts down the case, glances quickly at the door, then goes to the bookshelves, stands on a chair and finds a book on the upper shelves. He returns centre to table and puts the book in his case, then sees the other articles on the table, takes up the belt and the pen, puts them in the case, shuts it and turns centre to the windows. He pauses, then returns to the table, picks up the catapult and stuffs it into his pocket. He starts towards the window again. Mrs. Perryman enters right. Tod makes a frantic leap up the stairs and out of sight. She collects the coffee cups on to the tray, shakes up the cushions on the settee, goes to the window, shuts them, draws the top bolt and pulls the curtains across. She then returns for the tray and goes out with it right. Tod comes quietly back down the stairs again. He puts down his little case, goes to the windows, tugs back the curtains and tries to open the windows. He realises the bolt is drawn, tries to reach it and cannot. He picks up his case, returns to re-arrange the curtains, crosses to door right, opens it and peers out, listening. Voices are heard, he shuts the door quickly, rushes back to the windows, makes a last ineffective effort to reach the bolt, turns, looks desperately from side to side, then dashes down left to the big cupboard and shuts himself in just as Barbary and Stephen enter right. Stephen carries a light malacca cane under his arm. He turns to speak to Mrs. Blundell outside the door. Barbary crosses down to the settee.*]

MRS. BLUNDELL (*off*): If Tod is a normal boy, he won't bear any grudge. After all, right is *right* and we *must*——

STEPHEN: I will see you in a moment, Mrs. Blundell. (*Closing door and turning.*) Barbary, you wait here.

BARBARY: Yes, of course.

[*Stephen goes up the stairs. Speaking without pausing or turning.*]

STEPHEN (*quietly*): This is just about the bloodiest evening of my life.

Curtain

Scene Two

About half an hour later. Arnold is standing by the desk, speaking into the telephone. The French windows are wide open, the curtains drawn back to show a vista of garden and moonlight.

ARNOLD: —Blue blazer and shorts underneath. Nothing very conspicuous. Yes. We'll cover this end as far as the station. No, I don't think there's any need for panic yet. What? Yes, we thought about buses, but they aren't so frequent this time of night. Good. Yes—you've got this number. Thanks very much, Station-master.

[*He puts down the telephone. Barbary and Mrs. Perryman come down the stairs.*]

BARBARY: He must have got out of his window on to the garage roof—he's done it before.
ARNOLD: What do you think he had in that case?
MRS. PERRYMAN: As far as we can tell, pyjamas and his boxing gloves and a few oddments. He meant to stay away. Are you going to try the B.B.C.?
ARNOLD (*smiling*): I hardly think it's of national importance just yet. Don't worry. He can't get any distance in such a short time.

[*Stephen enters through windows.*]

STEPHEN: Mrs. Blundell's taken the car up to the crossroads and I've been down the side lane as far as Whitewood Avenue. There's no sign of him.
ARNOLD: He hasn't been seen at the station—although if as you say he's practically no money——

STEPHEN: But Arnold, where would he *go*? There's no one round here——

[*The door bell rings off right. Stephen and Mrs. Perryman start forward.*]

MRS. PERRYMAN: I'll go—it might be him——

[*She goes out right. Arnold stops Stephen as he is following her.*]

ARNOLD: He'd hardly return in state through the front door, do you think? I'm certain he's only hiding somewhere to give you a scare.

STEPHEN: He wouldn't do that. He might bolt in a state of nerves——

[*Mrs. Perryman, looking very flustered, hurries in right.*]

MRS. PERRYMAN: Mr. Leigh——

[*Giovanni Dawson pushes past her into the room.*]

DAWSON: Don't worry about announcing. I think they'll remember me.

[*He moves centre taking off his smart soft hat and smiling maliciously. He has thickened and coarsened, but also obviously prospered. He is very well dressed in an expensive double breasted suit and overcoat, but the over-large signet ring and red carnation in his button-hole spoil the effect.*]

STEPHEN: Dawson——

DAWSON: How do you do, Mr. Leigh? Nice to see so many old friends all at once. May I add another lady to the party—just to even things up?

[*Without waiting for an answer he goes back to door right.*]

Come in, honey.

[*Julia enters right. She is a slim blonde girl, some ten years younger than Dawson, handsome in a hard way. Her black dress, small hat and fur coat are impeccable. Her voice is hard, too, but not unpleasant, and her accent beyond doubt transatlantic.*]

(*Indicating them in turn.*) Mrs. Leigh, Mr. Leigh, Mr. Hamble—the legal gentleman. (*Smiling at them gently.*) Meet Mrs. Dawson.

JULIA (*quietly*): How do you do.

BARBARY: Did you say—Mrs. Dawson?

DAWSON: That's right. Married six weeks ago in California. You sound surprised, Mrs. Leigh? Why?

BARBARY: This is rather a sudden visit after so long—

STEPHEN: Mrs. Dawson—won't you sit down?

[*He indicates the settee. She crosses to it, eyeing him appraisingly as she passes.*]

JULIA: Thank you.

[*Barbary sits in the desk chair. Arnold is right of her.*]

DAWSON: We only arrived last week. Flew over this time. First class and all the trimmings. (*Sitting on arm of settee.*) And as soon as we'd sorted ourselves out, we came straight here to see my kid. How is he?

[*There is a pause. Barbary looks at Stephen. He moves across to his favourite position in front of the fireplace.*]

STEPHEN (*quietly*): He's very well. You know, I

suppose, that we've been trying to trace you for over a year?

DAWSON: Have you, now? Too bad.

[*He brings out an ornate cigarette case and takes out a cigarette.*]

As a matter of fact, I've done very nicely since we last met. Very nicely indeed.

BARBARY: So nicely that you couldn't find time to write us for nearly eighteen months.

DAWSON: Ah now, that isn't kind, Mrs. Leigh.

[*He lights his cigarette from a lighter as ornate as his case.*]

You haven't heard the whole story. I said I'd done well, but it wasn't easy at the start. (*To Julia.*) Eh, honey?

JULIA: It certainly was not.

DAWSON: I don't mind admitting now, Mr. Leigh, that when I took that trip I was in a spot. I went out to see what I could pick up. Well, the first thing I *did* pick up was a dose of fever that put me on my back in hospital for nearly eight weeks.

STEPHEN: Didn't it occur to you to write and tell us?

DAWSON: Write what? That I was out cold, weak as a kitten, no money, no prospects? Is that anything to write home about?

ARNOLD (*breaking in*): Stephen—may I? (*To Dawson.*) I should like to remind you, Dawson, that you promised to sign certain adoption papers.

DAWSON: Did I? I don't remember any promise. Adoption papers now? Would those be the ones returned marked "Gone Away"?

STEPHEN: Why—how did you know what they were marked——

DAWSON (*pleasantly*): Because I returned them. (*Smiling.*) Personally.

STEPHEN: Dawson, why didn't you sign those papers?

DAWSON: Maybe I thought you'd changed your mind——

STEPHEN: I assure you we haven't——

[*Dawson blows a cloud of smoke. He smiles at Stephen.*]

DAWSON (*gently*): Maybe I changed mine.

STEPHEN (*hotly*): Now look here——

ARNOLD: Stephen—— (*To Dawson.*) I think you had better explain. Fully.

DAWSON: It'll be a pleasure.

[*He throws his cigarette across into the fireplace, gets up and faces Stephen.*]

(*Quietly.*) Mr. Leigh, eighteen months ago, you stood there, right where you're standing now. You stood there, so quiet and superior, with your education and your fine manners, and you talked to me as if you'd made the earth and I wasn't even the dirt you'd used for it.

STEPHEN: I asked you——

DAWSON: No. You didn't *ask*. You *decided*. You decided I wasn't fit to keep Tod. Remember what you said? "You're not fit to be his father." Because I was down then, and in a jam, I had to take it. But I'm up now, Mr. Leigh—right up. And I don't take anything from you or your kind any more.

BARBARY: Do you mean you deliberately left Tod with us——

DAWSON: You wanted him. All right. I let you have him. I didn't ask you to prepare papers and run up legal fees, did I? Well, you've had him for over a year. Thanks very much. Now—I want him back.

[*There is a pause.*]

ARNOLD: Why?
DAWSON: Because I'm his father.
ARNOLD: The sentimental point doesn't seem to have worried you unduly till now. Meantime, Mr. Leigh has taken full responsibility, morally and financially—
DAWSON: So what? Give me your account. I'll pay.

[*Barbary turns away with an exclamation of disgust. Dawson glances at her.*]

You don't believe me? I've got the cash all right. (*To Julia.*) Show 'em your ring, honey.

[*Without a change of expression Julia strips off her glove and displays the big diamond on her third finger.*]

See that? Cost me twelve hundred dollars. Show you the receipt if you like.
ARNOLD: It's not solely a question of money, Dawson. Do you realise Tod's had a new and better background? He's been sent to a good school——
DAWSON: All *right.* He can stay there. I know education's important. I can do the proper thing by Tod.
ARNOLD: You don't seem to understand. The fact that Mr. Leigh's solicitors couldn't trace you didn't stop there. The adoption has proceeded in your absence. The case comes before the court on Wednesday, and you'll have to appear. If you will arrange to be legally represented——
DAWSON: I don't need any lawyer to stand up and say Tod's my child.

ARNOLD: All the facts will be laid before the judge, and he will decide——

DAWSON: The only one who decides anything is me. And, by the way, I go to court as Tod's father. What does Mr. Leigh go as?

STEPHEN: Tod's guardian.

DAWSON: Who says you're his guardian? I haven't signed anything.

[*There is another pause.*]

STEPHEN: You agreed——

DAWSON: I signed no papers. Therefore Tod's still mine. (*To Arnold.*) Right?

STEPHEN: Dawson——

DAWSON (*to Arnold*): Right?

ARNOLD: Quite right.

DAWSON: And if he's mine, I can take him away here and now with no argument. That right too?

ARNOLD: If you take him now, the case will still be heard on Wednesday. And we shall claim the return of the boy under a proper adoption order.

DAWSON: On what grounds?

ARNOLD: On the grounds that you left him with the Leighs eighteen months ago, pending legal adoption; that there has been no communication from you during that time, amounting *ipso facto* to negligence of the child's welfare. And finally, that Mr. Leigh is a better and more responsible person to bring up a child than you.

DAWSON: It might have been like that eighteen months ago. Things are different now.

STEPHEN: How can you say that? Why, at the moment you haven't even got a proper home for Tod.

DAWSON: That's just where you're wrong. Julie and me, we've pulled off a little business deal. You know the Green Gazelle—just off the by-pass at Grantley

Cross? Took my fancy a couple of years ago. I wasn't in the money then, of course——

STEPHEN: You haven't—bought *that* place?

DAWSON: Practically. It should be all signed and sealed in time for Wednesday.

STEPHEN: It's been closed by the police—twice—

DAWSON: Not under my management. (*Shaking his head.*) No, Mr. Leigh, you've got nothing on me. (*Laughing.*) What's wrong with the Gazelle? Very high class trade. Very nice living accommodation—all separate upstairs. And let me remind you of something very important. I can not only give Tod a home. I can also provide him with a mother.

[*He looks at Julia and bursts out laughing.*]

And Julie gets a son. How's that, eh? Quick work in six weeks.

JULIA (*laughing*): Nice going, Giovanni.

STEPHEN: Oh, this is damnable——

DAWSON: What's damnable about it? Julie likes kids. I've got one—ready made and out of diapers. What more can the court want?

ARNOLD: We still have a case.

DAWSON: It's as weak as water, and you know it.

ARNOLD: It's sufficient to fight on. (*Quietly.*) My client intends to fight.

[*Dawson looks at them narrowly.*]

DAWSON (*gently*): So you want to play rough?

ARNOLD: As rough as you like. But at the end of the hearing, the judge will talk to Tod. He will probably ask Tod with whom he prefers to live——

DAWSON (*easily*): *I'll* talk to Tod. (*He looks round.*) Where is he?

[*They do not answer.*]

Yes—where is he? Why don't you bring him in? Is he still here? Has anything happened?

ARNOLD: Why prejudice your chances with the boy by dragging him out of bed and taking him away forcibly? You don't want him to dislike you——

DAWSON: He'll like me—I'll see to that——

JULIA (*suddenly*): They're right, Giovanni.

DAWSON (*turning*): What?

JULIA: I said they're right. Leave the kid here till tomorrow. You've nothing to lose by doing it legally The court must hand him over. You're his father, aren't you?

DAWSON: Just let anyone say I'm not——

[*Mrs. Blundell enters suddenly through the windows. She shuts them and closes the curtains, talking all the time.*]

MRS. BLUNDELL: I've been three miles one way and two the other. There's absolutely no sign of the boy—— (*She turns, realises and stops dead.*) Good heavens—Dawson.

[*Arnold, Stephen and Barbary have all instinctively gestured to her—too late. Dawson looks first at her and then at the others.*]

DAWSON (*quietly*). So—the boy isn't here? (*He eyes them again, and nods.*) All this fine talk about background—about dragging him away and prejudice, and you not producing him. Of course you couldn't produce him. Because he isn't here.

ARNOLD: Dawson——

DAWSON: Where is he? What have you done with him?

ARNOLD: If you will——

DAWSON: Where is he?

ARNOLD: At this immediate moment, we don't know.
DAWSON: Why?
MRS. BLUNDELL (*suddenly*): Because he is a coward.
ARNOLD: Will you please keep quiet——
MRS. BLUNDELL: Why should I? If Mr. Leigh can't control the boy, perhaps his father can. Mr. Dawson, your son has run away to escape a thrashing.
DAWSON: This is very pretty, isn't it? I'm too brutal to keep Tod with me. I thrashed him. So you take him And now you thrash him. What for? Eh? What for?
BARBARY: A perfectly fair punishment.
MRS: BLUNDELL: Tod broke into my house and stole various articles.
DAWSON: So? You've brought him up nicely, haven't you? A little gentleman—going to a good school. (*Angrily.*) He never stole when I had him. He got into trouble, he did damage, he ran away. But steal? Never.
STEPHEN: I remember returning a five pound note he stole from you
DAWSON: In the family—it doesn't count.
ARNOLD: The first thing is to find the boy. He can't be far away. Then I suggest——

[*Dawson blows up.*]

DAWSON: *You* suggest! You're not in a position to suggest anything. My God—Mr. Leigh, I came here tonight to get even with you, but I never expected a chance like this——
JULIA (*getting up*): Giovanni—please——
DAWSON (*pushing her aside*): When I think how you've all bluffed and lied, making out I was on the wrong side of the law. Cases and actions! If anything's happened to that boy, I'll bring the biggest Goddam action this town's ever heard——

ARNOLD: Dawson——

DAWSON: —When I've finished with you, the people here'll be screaming for a lynching—I'll see there isn't a school in England'll take Leigh for a master—

[*The cupboard door crashes open. Tod bursts out like a whirlwind, shouting at the top of his voice.*]

TOD: *You shut up!*

[*He brings up sharply against the table centre, white and shaking.*

STEPHEN: Tod——!

DAWSON (*easily*): Well—look who's here. How are you, son?

[*Tod turns to Arnold.*]

TOD: Was that right what I heard you say—about the judge asking me to decide?

ARNOLD: Why, yes, Tod, but——

TOD: I don't have to wait for any judge. I can say it now.

[*He turns and for a second looks full at Stephen. His lip trembles. Then he squares his shoulders.*]

(*Steadily.*) I'm going with my father.

[*Without looking at any of them, he turns and goes straight out through the window. Dawson looks at Stephen, bursts out laughing and follows.*]

Curtain.

ACT THREE

Scene 1

Two months later, about ten o'clock at night. The curtains are drawn across the windows and a bright fire burns in the grate.

Barbary, wrapped in a gay quilted dressing gown, and wearing her spectacles, is typing at the desk in the light of a shaded lamp. One other lamp by the fireplace is alight, otherwise the room is shadowed. Barbary taps for a second, then turns the page up on the rollers and reads it, rubbing her forehead fretfully. Then she gets up, crosses to the mantelpiece, finds a cigarette and a match, returns to the desk, sits down and re-reads the page. With a sudden angry exclamation, she tugs it out of the machine, crumples it viciously and flings it on the floor to join a pile of similar discarded pages.

Mrs. Perryman enters right carrying a glass of rich looking, dark yellow liquid on a small tray.

MRS. PERRYMAN: Now, now, that isn't work. Only more work for me picking it all up.
BARBARY (*getting up*): Don't pick it up then. Let it lie there till it rots. (*Crossing to fireplace.*) That's about all the whole book's fit for.

[*She stands with one hand on the mantelpiece, looking moodily down into the fire. Mrs. Perryman puts the tray on the desk and moves down right to fetch a little stool, which she brings up left centre by the settee, talking all the time.*]

MRS. PERRYMAN: You've been hunched at that silly

typewriter all day. Sit down on the settee now, and put your feet up. And you'll feel a lot better with something warm inside you.

[*She brings the glass and tray from the desk to the stool.*]

BARBARY: I wish you wouldn't fuss—— (*Turning and breaking off as she sees the glass.*) What's that?
MRS. PERRYMAN: Egg and milk——
BARBARY: Filthy insipid stuff
MRS. PERRYMAN: Not with a good strong dollop of rum in it.

[*Barbary looks at her. In spite of herself she has to laugh.*]

BARBARY (*ruefully*): Oh, Perry—I don't know what I'd do without you.
MRS. PERRYMAN: Fret yourself into rags and fringes, and bury the entire room in waste paper.

[*She breaks off as Barbary takes another cigarette from the box on the mantelpiece and prepares to light it from the half-smoked one in her hand.*]

Mrs. Leigh—not another! Three ashtrays I've emptied today already. It can't possibly help your work.
BARBARY: The damn book's got to be finished somehow.
MRS. PERRYMAN: If you go on like this, you won't produce a book. It'll be a smoked haddock.

[*Barbary throws both cigarettes into the fire and sits down on the settee. Perry hands her the glass.*]

Here——

[*Barbary waves it away.*]

Go on—drink that down. And a little commonsense with it.

[*Barbary takes the glass and drinks. Mrs. Perryman watches her for a second without speaking.*]

(*Quietly.*) Where's Mr. Leigh?
BARBARY: I don't know.
MRS. PERRYMAN: When will he be back?
BARBARY: I couldn't tell you.

[*She hands Mrs. Perryman back the glass. Mrs. Perryman goes up to the door, hesitates, then comes back to the settee.*]

MRS. PERRYMAN: Mrs. Leigh—may I speak my mind?
BARBARY: Since when have you asked permission to do that?
MRS. PERRYMAN: What's come over you and Mr. Leigh? As far as I can see, you hardly speak to each other—except about unimportant things. You're almost strangers. And he needs you badly just now. He's——

[*She pauses—then decides to say it.*]

He's fretting so after Tod.
BARBARY (*bitterly*): Tod——!
MRS. PERRYMAN (*quickly*): Now—be charitable. Tod's gone

[*Barbary controls herself. She sits looking into the fire, still speaking with bitterness.*]

BARBARY: He *hasn't* gone. He's not in the house, that's all. He's somewhere far worse. He's in Stephen's mind.

MRS. PERRYMAN: It's hit Mr. Leigh hard. I shan't forget his face when you came back from Court. He wants all the help and sympathy you can give——

BARBARY: Do you suppose I haven't tried? He won't even discuss it. It's no *use*, Perry.

[*She pauses, speaking half to herself.*]

I can't—reach him.

MRS. PERRYMAN: Humph. If that isn't a piece from one of your books, my name's not Janet Perryman

[*Stephen enters right, hatless and wearing a heavy coat. He is pulling off his driving gloves as he comes in. Barbary glances over but does not speak. Mrs. Perryman puts the glass on the table and hurries to take his hat and coat.*]

Mr. Leigh—you're late. And it's a raw night. The fire's well in—would you like a hot drink?

STEPHEN: No thanks, Perry.

[*He gives her his coat and comes centre, rubbing his hands.*]

MRS. PERRYMAN (*coaxing*): Not even a little——

STEPHEN: No, no—don't fuss. Good night.

[*She goes out right. He kneels on the rug before the fire, warming his hands. There is a pause. He does not look at Barbary.*]

You shouldn't have waited up.

BARBARY: I didn't. I've been working.

STEPHEN: Oh. Good.

[*He gets up and stands irresolute, glancing at his wrist watch.*]

Would you excuse me if I went to bed?

[*He bends down to kiss her and moves to stairs.*]

I'm very tired.
BARBARY (*quietly*): I'm not surprised. It must be quite twenty miles, there and back, to the Gazelle.
STEPHEN (*half turning*): But I said——
BARBARY: You said you were going to the school to correct papers. Why not bring them home—as you've always done? The night before last you went to John Odiham's—to return his gardening book. It's still there. On the second shelf. (*Pausing.*) I can't remember all the other reasons during six weeks.
STEPHEN: As a matter of fact, I've been over with Arnold for the past two hours.
BARBARY: So you went to the Gazelle earlier?

[*Stephen turns up to the stairs again.*]

Did you see Tod? (*Relentlessly.*) How was he?
STEPHEN: Do you mind if we don't talk about it?
BARBARY: We must sooner or later. Or something very serious will happen to the two of us.

[*Stephen returns down centre*]

STEPHEN: Barbary—why *did* he do it?
BARBARY: I don't know.
STEPHEN: Standing there, defying everyone. "I'm going back to my father." Holding out against Arnold, against the judge. No explanation, no reason. Just that—that *white* look, and the same phrase "I'm going back to my father." What happened Barbary? Where did I go wrong?
BARBARY: What's wrong with giving him a good year and starting him at a good school?

STEPHEN: I should never have allowed him to go back.

BARBARY: He went of his own free will and the judge handed him over, legally and finally. You can't set that aside.

STEPHEN (*abruptly*): Well, I'm going to try. That's what I've been discussing with Arnold.

BARBARY (*turning*): Oh, Stephen—no. Let it rest. Let it *alone*——

STEPHEN: I——

BARBARY: Dawson seems to have changed. Tod's got a good home. The probation officer saw it——

STEPHEN (*breaking in*): I've seen it, too.

[*He drives his hands deep in his pockets and turns restlessly up the room and down again.*]

BARBARY (*curiously*): So you've been there?

STEPHEN: Once, some weeks ago. I only saw the woman.

BARBARY: Mrs. Dawson? I know she seems a hard type, but——

STEPHEN: She was civil enough. She merely made it clear that once I'd satisfied myself Tod had a roof, I wasn't expected to keep calling.

BARBARY: That's only natural——

STEPHEN: It's not natural. (*Pausing.*) Barbary, I admit that all these weeks I've been trying to get hold of Tod. I've seen him three times. The first time he turned tail and ran. The second he merely said he was "very well, thank you". (*Slowly.*) Last night he passed me without a word.

BARBARY: Ungrateful little——

STEPHEN: I don't *believe* he's ungrateful. Or that he's happy. There's something very wrong somewhere, and I'm determined to sort it out. I want him back.

(*He pauses, looking down at her.*) You—you don't, do you?

[*Barbary does not answer.*]

I know you don't. (*Going to fireplace.*) I know in all fairness to you I ought to let the matter drop. You didn't want Tod. You never wanted him. But you had the strength not to try and stop me. If you'd refused in the first place——

BARBARY (*harshly*): I had no right to refuse when you hadn't a child of your own——

STEPHEN (*angrily*): Oh, for God's sake, Barbary, stop harping on that!

BARBARY (*raising her voice*): Don't *shout* at me!

[*They both stop.*]

STEPHEN (*quietly*): I'm sorry. Have you—hated it all so much?

BARBARY: I didn't hate it. (*Her control goes suddenly, she gets up.*) Hell—yes, I did! I hated the battles and the screaming scenes. I hated my work suffering because of the strain. I was trying to write one decent book. No wonder "Carry Me Back" turned out second rate.

[*She stops suddenly on a high-pitched note, and pulls herself together.*]

No—I'm being stupid. If it were in me, I could have written a masterpiece standing upside down on a pole in the Arabian desert. (*Quietly.*) The plain truth is I've been bitterly jealous for eighteen months, and it hurts my pride to admit it.

STEPHEN: It doesn't occur to you to offer me a dramatic choice between Tod and yourself?

BARBARY (*slowly*): Stephen, I would—I would like to ask you something.

STEPHEN: Yes?

BARBARY: If it were possible, by a small miracle, for us to have a child—now, would it take the place of Tod. (*Insistently.*) Would it, Stephen?

STEPHEN: Tod could never take the place of my own child, but that wouldn't mean there was no place for him.

BARBARY (*slowly*): No. I suppose I couldn't expect you to say anything else.

[*He goes abruptly to the stairs. She moves down and sits on the settee.*]

Are you blaming me because he left you? Do you think that if I'd tried harder to win his affection—he wouldn't have gone back to Dawson?

[*Stephen looks over at her. His face softens. He comes centre, and puts a hand on her shoulder.*]

STEPHEN (*gently*): Don't worry, darling. We'll work this out between us—somehow.

[*She turns to him. There is a sudden soft rapping at the window.*]

(*Turning.*) What's that——

BARBARY: Nothing—just the little tree outside——

STEPHEN: The tree's nowhere near. There's someone there—— (*He crosses centre.*)

BARBARY (*suddenly*): Stephen, don't open the window——

[*Stephen pulls the curtains aside. He opens the windows wide. Tod walks in without a word.*]

STEPHEN: Tod!
BARBARY (*desperately*): Oh, *no*!

[*Tod looks at them in a dazed way. He has no hat or coat, only grey flannels and a thin jacket with the collar turned up. He is wet and dishevelled.*]

STEPHEN: Good God—the boy's soaked. (*Hastily shutting windows and curtains.*) Tod, go to the fire—it's a bitter night.

[*Tod, walking as though in a trance, moves down centre. Barbary is right above settee. He passes her without a word and sits down, staring straight in front of him. Stephen comes down, drops on his knee beside him and takes his hands.*]

STEPHEN: What are you doing here? Tod, what's the matter? Tod. (*Looking up.*) He's shivering—he must be ill. Fetch Perry, will you? Tell her to get something hot and a warm rug——

[*Barbary crosses right, switches on the main light, opens the door and calls.*]

BARBARY: Perry, Perry——!

[*She returns centre above settee, watching as Stephen rubs Tod's hands.*]

STEPHEN: Tod, what is it? Can't you say something?

[*Mrs. Perryman hurries in right.*]

MRS. PERRYMAN: Are you all right, Mrs. Leigh? I thought—— (*Pausing.*) —Saints above, what's this?

BARBARY: Fetch a little brandy, Perry, quickly. And the thick travelling rug. It's in the hall chest.
MRS. PERRYMAN: Yes, Mrs. Leigh.

[*She goes quickly out left.*]

STEPHEN: Barbary, would you please put a log on the fire. (*To Tod.*) It's all right—don't talk if you don't want to. I think we'll get rid of this wet jacket, don't you——?

[*Tod sits quite still as Stephen removes the wet jacket and puts it down left of settee. Barbary puts a log on the fire. Mrs. Perryman returns right carrying a thick rug, which she hands to Barbary.*]

MRS. PERRYMAN: Here—(*Going up to corner cupboard.*) —I'll get the brandy.

[*She busies herself with bottle and glass. Barbary returns behind settee and helps Stephen to wrap the rug around Tod.*]

(*At cupboard.*) He must be mad to come out tonight. What's he here for?

[*She brings a small glass to Stephen.*]

STEPHEN: I don't know yet. Something must be wrong. Here, Tod, drink this. Yes, drink it—come on. That's it—gently now.

[*He supports Tod on his arm and gives him the brandy. Tod drinks and splutters. Stephen hands the glass back to Mrs. Perryman. Barbary stands behind the settee, watching.*]

That's the boy. You'll soon feel warm after that. Let's have those wet shoes off, Perry

[*Mrs. Perryman takes off his shoes and puts them on the hearth. Stephen rubs his feet.*]

MRS. PERRYMAN: He certainly can't go home tonight, unless there's anyone with him.
STEPHEN: Is anyone with you, Tod?

[*Tod looks blankly in front of him.*]

Tod—is anyone with you?

[*Tod does not answer.*]

I can't understand it——
BARBARY: Perhaps we should telephone Dawson?

[*Tod jerks upright with a little babbling sound. He grabs at Stephen.*]

STEPHEN: All right, all right. (*Holding him close.*) He's had a shock of some kind. Let him pull himself together before we ask questions.
BARBARY: Do you suppose they know he's out? Surely someone will be enquiring?
STEPHEN: Well, we'll wait till they do. Perry, will you get his bed ready? (*To Barbary.*) You don't mind, do you?

[*She looks down at Tod huddled in Stephen's arms.*]

BARBARY (*quietly*): Anything you say.
MRS. PERRYMAN: I'll go and get organised.

[*She collects Tod's jacket and the glass and goes upstairs. Stephen moves Tod gently back on the settee.*]

STEPHEN: Is that better? Feeling warmer? Good. (*Gently.*) Do you want to tell me why you've come?

[*Tod reaches out and clutches his sleeve. Stephen puts his hand over Tod's.*]

Well, then, how did you get here? On your bicycle?

[*Tod shakes his head.*]

On the bus?

[*Tod nods.*]

But the bus only comes as far as Westfield. That's nearly three miles—you haven't walked three miles——?

[*Tod does not answer.*]

Tod, what *has* frightened you like this?

[*Tod suddenly buries his face in Stephen's shoulder. Stephen holds him closely.*]

All right. All right. (*Pausing.*) I'll tell you what we'll do. We'll go upstairs to bed and Mrs. Perryman shall bring you one of her famous suppers and you can tell me in the morning.

[*He gets up, stoops and picks up Tod, still wrapped in the rug. He carries him to the stairs. Barbary follows. At the foot of the stairs he turns, speaking half over his shoulder.*]

Would you mind—not? He may talk to me if we're alone

[*He carries Tod upstairs and off left. Barbary stands looking after them. Then she comes slowly back centre and goes to the mantelpiece. The doorbell rings off right. Mrs. Perryman comes down the stairs.*]

MRS. PERRYMAN: There's a car just come up. I saw it from the window.
BARBARY (*exhaustedly*): Oh, damn!
MRS PERRYMAN: It may not be for him. Don't answer.
BARBARY: They're bound to follow him, and this is the obvious place.
MRS. PERRYMAN (*turning up*): I'll call Mr. Leigh——
BARBARY: No. I'll deal with it

[*The bell rings again.*]

Answer it, please, Perry. Whoever it is, ask them to wait and come and tell me.
MRS. PERRYMAN (*grimly*): If it *is* that Dawson, I hope I can contain myself.

[*She goes out right. Barbary adjusts her dressing gown, and smoothes her hair. Mrs. Perryman returns right.*]

It's the police! A sergeant and that inspector. You remember, the one at the court, Inspector Birch.
BARBARY: How cruel. How viciously cruel. Sending the police—why couldn't he come himself?
MRS. PERRYMAN: I haven't said he's here. Do you think we could——
BARBARY: No, no. Bring them in.

[*Mrs. Perryman goes to the door left and makes a gesture to someone outside. Inspector Birch comes past her to the centre of the room. He is a tall, soldierly man, wearing a brown overcoat and soft hat. Mrs. Perryman goes upstairs.*]

BIRCH (*pleasantly*): Good evening, Mrs. Leigh. Perhaps you don't remember me—Inspector Birch.

BARBARY: I remember you very well, Inspector. Good evening.

BIRCH: I'm sorry to make such a late call, but there's been a little trouble about Tod. Is he here?

BARBARY: Why should you think that?

BIRCH: He's not a boy who makes many friends. This really is about the only place.

BARBARY: Do you know why he's run away?

BIRCH: Before we go into that, would you tell me, please—is he here?

BARBARY: Do sit down, Inspector. (*She indicates the settee.*) Is this an official visit? Or may I offer you a drink?

BIRCH: Please don't try and evade it, Mrs. Leigh, because—— (*He pauses.*)

BARBARY: I had no intention of——

[*Birch picks up Tod's shoes from the hearth and holds them out without speaking.*]

BIRCH (*pleasantly*): I shouldn't think these would fit any of you.

BARBARY: Very well. He's here. He arrived here a few minutes ago, dazed and exhausted. We can't get a word out of him. But I suppose his father will insist he's taken straight back.

BIRCH: I shall want to talk to Tod first. (*He puts the shoes back on the hearth.*)

BARBARY: I think you'd better begin by talking to my husband.

BIRCH: Certainly, if you wish——

[*Stephen comes along the landing and down the stairs.*]

Good evening, sir.

STEPHEN: Good evening, Inspector. I can imagine what you've come for, but I don't know why the police——

BIRCH: Is Tod fit to talk?

STEPHEN: He's just talked to me. (*To Barbary.*) Get me a drink, darling, will you?

BIRCH: Mr. Leigh, has Tod told you what happened tonight?

STEPHEN: Yes. Yes, he has.

BIRCH: Was it coherent, sir? Sufficient for a statement?

STEPHEN: Coherent enough. Once he was alone with me, it came out in a few short sentences.

[*Barbary comes down with his drink. He turns to her as he takes it.*]

STEPHEN: I know now why he went back to his father. Because Dawson threatened to make trouble. You remember all that shouting about the adoption and ruining my career? Tod believed it. Do you understand, Barbary. Tod went back to that man he hated—rather than make trouble for us.

BARBARY (*quietly*): Not us. You.

BIRCH: Did Tod tell you anything else, sir?

STEPHEN: Yes.

[*He comes down centre glass in hand.*]

I'll give you a statement, Inspector, but you must realise that what I'm saying is my own picture—so to speak—of what Tod told me.

BIRCH: Of course, sir.

[*He stands, waiting, with his back to the fire. Stephen sits on the arm of the settee, looking down at the untasted drink in his hand.*]

STEPHEN: As I see it, Tod went to a film tonight. When he got home, they were all out. He was scared to go to bed; he lay down without undressing. He must have fallen asleep and some hours later woke suddenly in terror. What does a child do when he wakes in the dark like that? He runs to his mother.

[*He pauses, twisting his glass.*]

Tod hasn't a mother—he did the next best thing. He ran to Mrs. Dawson. There was a light under their bedroom door. Terrified and still only half awake, he burst in. (*Slowly.*) Dawson and his wife——

[*He pauses again.*]

Apparently Mrs. Dawson has some sense of decency. She shouted at the boy to go away. But Dawson—Dawson hit him, and said something—about " Hell, he's got to learn sometime ". And then he started laughing—and talking to Tod.

[*He pauses, speaking half to himself.*]

Deliberate and vicious corruption of a child.

[*There is another pause.*]

BIRCH (*quietly*): Mr. Leigh, is that all Tod told you—
STEPHEN: Good God—isn't it enough? He's shaking from head to foot and shocked to pieces. (*Getting up.*) And you can tell Dawson that Tod doesn't leave me again—ever. Not if I have to fight in every court in England——
BIRCH (*breaking in*): Just a moment, sir. Dawson——
STEPHEN (*angrily*): What's the matter with that man!

after a scene like that, he dares to send the police—isn't he civilised enough to come himself—to explain——

BIRCH (*interrupting*): I'm afraid Dawson isn't in a position to do much explaining, sir.

[*He looks at them for an instant.*]

(*Quietly.*) You see—he's dead.

Curtain

Scene 2

About an hour and a half later. The curtain rises on an empty stage. The doorbell rings. Barbary runs down the stairs. Arnold comes in right in outdoor clothes, followed by Mrs. Perryman. He meets Barbary centre.

BARBARY: Arnold—I'm so glad. I thought you'd never get back.

ARNOLD (*taking off his coat*): There was quite a lot to be done at the police station. These things take time. (*He gives his coat and hat to Mrs. Perryman.*) Thanks, Mrs. Perry. (*Turning to Barbary.*) Now, where is everybody?

[*Mrs. Perryman goes out right with his coat and hat.*]

BARBARY: Stephen and the Inspector are upstairs with Tod. Perry is looking after the sergeant in the kitchen. (*Suddenly.*) Arnold, what has happened?

Birch won't tell us a thing. Did you find out any more at the police station?

ARNOLD: A great deal, my dear—no, wait! One thing at a time. Nothing is to be said to anyone until I've talked to Tod. Will you bring him down? I'd rather not interview him in bed.

BARBARY: But can't you just say——

ARNOLD (*taking her hands*): Barbary, dear, you know there's nothing I wouldn't do for you and Stephen, but you must let me handle this in my own way. So make it as easy as possible. No questions. Please fetch Tod down.

[*He breaks off as Birch comes down the stairs and crosses to him. Barbary goes upstairs and off left.*]

Oh, Birch——

BIRCH: Good evening, sir.

[*Arnold brings a note from his pocket.*]

ARNOLD: I've a note for you from Chief Inspector Brampton. We've discussed it with the Chief Constable.

[*Birch reads the note.*]

This is just to clear the official conscience.

BIRCH: Right, sir. Good enough. And when's the——

ARNOLD (*quickly*): Later. When they've finished at the station. Meanwhile, I'll talk to Tod. He still refuses to tell you anything?

BIRCH: Can't get a word out of him, sir. Not a word. (*Looking at note again.*) The Chief Inspector thinks you might succeed if we fail. Well, we've certainly failed up to now. Over to you?

ARNOLD: If you wouldn't mind. Naturally you'll want to put your own questions again later. And keep Mr. and Mrs. Leigh out of the picture as much as possible.

[*He glances up the stairs and back to Birch.*]

This is going to be delicate—and difficult.
BIRCH: Very nasty business. I've a boy of my own about Tod's age.

[*Stephen comes down the stairs with Tod, followed by Barbary. Tod is wearing a dressing gown of Stephen's bundled round him, the sleeves rolled up. Arnold goes to the foot of the stairs.*]

ARNOLD: Hullo, Tod. Could you and I have a talk do you think? Let's go over by the fire.

[*He puts his arm round Tod's shoulders and takes him to the settee. Stephen follows but is checked by Birch.*]

BIRCH: Mr. Leigh——
STEPHEN: Aren't we allowed to stay——?
BIRCH: As long as you don't prompt him or try to influence his answers.

[*Stephen and Barbary stand at the foot of the stairs. Birch moves by the desk, taking out a notebook. Arnold puts Tod on the settee and folds the dressing gown round him.*]

ARNOLD: You sit here—that's right. Let's tuck this round a bit—so. Now——

[*He straightens up and stands looking down at Tod.*]

You're not a baby, and I'm not going to treat you

like one. You know Inspector Birch is a police officer, and I don't want you to be afraid of him. He's just an ordinary person, doing an ordinary job, and——

TOD (*suddenly, without expression*): Giovanni's dead.

ARNOLD: Yes. (*Gently.*) How did you know?

TOD (*nodding at Birch*): They told me.

ARNOLD: Did you know before they told you?

[*Tod looks woodenly in front of him.*]

TOD: Giovanni's dead.

ARNOLD: Would you like to tell me about it? Just between friends?

[*Tod does not answer.*]

You know, things are always much worse when you shut them up in your mind. If you told me, I'm sure it wouldn't be half so terrible as it seems now.

[*Tod looks down.*]

If you really think it's too bad to talk about, would you like to take the Inspector's notebook and write what happened in your own words?

[*Tod does not move.*]

Is there anything I could do—or explain which would make it easier?

[*Still Tod does not move.*]

(*Smiling.*) So you won't talk, eh? Just like the films.

[*He moves to the fire and stands warming his hands.*]

Tod—about your stepmother. She hasn't been too bad to you, has she? Sometimes she wouldn't let Giovanni hit you. He hit you this evening, didn't he? Hit you and said——

[*Tod puts both hands over his face. He gives a stifled sob. Stephen takes a step forward. Birch checks him. Arnold has immediately crossed to Tod and put a hand on his shoulder.*]

All right, all right—I know. That was a shock, wasn't it—a bad thing. We're not going to talk about that part any more. (*He sits down beside Tod.*) But something *else* happened, didn't it? After that. Something you're frightened to tell us. And it's very important we know. (*Pausing.*) Tod. Look at me.

[*Tod does not move. Arnold reaches out and turns him to face him.*]

Tod—I promise you there's nothing to be afraid of if you'll tell us. Will you tell us—now?

[*Tod looks at him, his underlip jutting out. Stubbornly he shakes his head.*]

So you won't tell Mr. Leigh, you won't tell the Inspector, and you won't tell me—is that it?

[*The doorbell rings. Arnold gets up.*]

Right, Inspector. Here we are.
BIRCH: Right away, sir?
ARNOLD: I think so.

[*Birch comes out right. Stephen comes quickly down beside*

Tod, and puts his arm round him. Barbary moves behind the settee.]

You see, Tod—we do know what happened. We wanted you to tell us because you might have added something we don't know already. But as you won't, we shall have to confirm it from someone else. (*He looks across at the door left.*) Come in, Mrs. Dawson.

[*Birch enters right, holding back the door. Julia Dawson comes in slowly centre She wears a dark dress, and her fur coat slung over her shoulders, and carries a large handbag. Her face is haggard, her hair in disorder, and there is a rapidly-darkening bruise across the right side of her face and jaw. Stephen gets up, staring at her. Then he hurries across, pulls out the desk chair and indicates it.*]

STEPHEN (*shocked*): Sit down, Mrs. Dawson.

[*She looks up at him with something like gratitude showing on her hard face.*]

JULIA: Thanks.

[*She sits down in the desk chair. Stephen goes to the corner cupboard.*]

ARNOLD: Mrs. Dawson, you've been extremely co-operative so far. Will you repeat the statement you made to the police earlier this evening?

JULIA: I've been thinking. Maybe I shouldn't say any more until I get a lawyer. They've got you. You can't be on both sides.

ARNOLD (*soothingly*): Why should you think you need a lawyer, Mrs. Dawson? You've not been charged with anything——

JULIA: What d'you mean? You've nothing against me.

ARNOLD. May I give you a piece of advice?

JULIA: What's it going to cost?

ARNOLD: Merely the trouble of listening.

JULIA: Well?

ARNOLD: I thought we'd made it clear you're here as a witness. Well, it isn't a good thing to be a difficult witness. It might give the impression you had something to hide.

JULIA: I've already told you the truth.

ARNOLD: Then surely you needn't mind repeating it. Believe me, Mrs. Dawson, I'm sorry to take you all through this again. I understand Dawson has been very brutal to you——

JULIA: Brutal——

[*She laughs shortly, touching a hand to her bruised face.*]

How d'you think I got this? Playing kiss-in-the-ring?

[*Stephen comes down on her right, a glass in his hand. He offers it to her without speaking. She takes it, again with the faint flicker of gratitude.*]

Thanks. You're—very kind.

[*She drinks, watching Stephen move back to Tod, who reaches out for him. He sits down and pulls Tod close.*]

Kid means a lot to you, doesn't he?

STEPHEN: He does rather.

JULIA: You wouldn't have known him earlier this evening. (*Slowly.*) Like a little mad dog.

ARNOLD: That's what we want to hear about, Mrs. Dawson. (*Gently.*) If you please.

JULIA: I don't have to go over the first part—(*Nodding at Tod.*)—not with him here?
ARNOLD: No.

[*Julia pauses a moment. Then she breaks into rapid speech.*]

JULIA: It was the way Giovanni talked to him—standing there—smiling—I couldn't bear it. (*Getting up.*) I shouted at him, "stop it—leave the boy alone." And he turned on me and knocked me down.

[*Tod gives a stifled sob. Stephen holds him close.*]

And then Tod went for Giovanni—kicking and clawing. I knew what would happen if Giovanni got hold of him—so I caught Giovanni round the legs and shouted to Tod to run. He scuttered down the stairs and through into the bar, but Giovanni broke free and was after him before he could get the front door open——

[*She looks round, then she suddenly runs halfway up the stairs.*]

Look—I ran down the stairs—like this. They were struggling at the foot of them. I tried to stop Giovanni again. And then he really turned on me. I fell on the bottom stair. He bent down. He——

[*She pauses, touching her bruised face again.*]

That's where I got this.

[*Tod buries his face in Stephen's shoulder.*]

I must have—screamed, I guess. Because that's

where Tod went mad. He screamed and spat at Giovanni. And then he grabbed up a great heavy glass ashtray off the bar—he grabbed it up in both hands—and he smashed it down on the back of Giovanni's head——

STEPHEN: I don't believe it——

BIRCH: Mr. Leigh——

JULIA (*slowly*): Giovanni fell at the bottom of the stairs. Tod ran out the door. I—I was dazed, I guess. Then I got up and went and turned Giovanni over. (*Slowly.*) I—I did what I could. I knew there wasn't anything to be done, but I called a doctor. It was—the doctor—made me call the police.

[*She goes to the desk chair and drops into it, hiding her face.*]

ARNOLD: Tod—is this correct? Exactly as it happened?

[*Tod does not move.*]

STEPHEN (*urgently*): Tod——

[*Tod slowly raises his head and looks at him.*]

TOD (*slowly*): His ring—cut her face. It got blood on it. Like when he hit Melon—before he drowned him. There was blood on Melon. I was all hot. I hit him. Then I wasn't hot any more. I was cold—like I was ice.

[*Birch slips his notebook into his pocket. He looks at Arnold, then at Stephen.*]

BIRCH (*quietly*): Better get him dressed, Mr. Leigh.

STEPHEN: Arnold—you can't take him——

ARNOLD: Just for now. I'll do my best to get him back—perhaps for tonight—but you mustn't——
TOD (*getting up*): Don't worry. I'll come quietly.

[*He goes to the stairs. Stephen hurries after him, catching his arm.*]

STEPHEN: Tod—even if you did hit him—you were defending your stepmother. It'll be all right—we'll clear it all up. Not many people need ever know.
TOD (*breaking in*): I'll know.

[*He looks round at them.*]

(*Quietly.*) All my life I'll know I killed my father.

[*He goes up the stairs with Barbary and off left. Stephen comes desperately down to Arnold.*]

STEPHEN: It's impossible—make them understand. Good God—are we to believe for one moment that Tod—*Tod*—killed Dawson——
ARNOLD: He admitted it.
STEPHEN: But it's impossible physically. He wouldn't have the strength.
BIRCH: Strength isn't the only factor, I'm afraid. There are complications like the angle of the blow and the position of the other person. Dawson was bending down—to strike his wife——

[*Barbary comes quickly down the stairs.*]

BARBARY: Stephen, go up to Tod. He's asking for you.

[*Stephen hurries up the stairs. Birch follows.*]

BIRCH: I'll come with you, sir.

[*Stephen turns to look down at him.*]

If you don't mind——

[*Stephen hurries up the stairs and off left with Birch. Barbary turns on Arnold.*]

BARBARY: Why did you bring Mrs. Dawson here?
ARNOLD: We needed Tod's personal confirmation of her story.
JULIA (*suddenly*): What can they do to him. What's the worst they can do to a little kid like that? They can't hang him——
BARBARY: Mrs. Dawson——
ARNOLD: No, no—the law isn't a machine A child will receive every consideration. He might be sent to an approved school, but we shall work like mad on the protection angle. Mrs. Dawson, you must stress to the utmost that the blow was struck in your defence.

JULIA: I'll do anything you tell me—anything!

[*Stephen comes along the landing.*]

STEPHEN: Arnold——

[*Arnold turns up to the stairs.*]

Is there any reason why I shouldn't go with Tod to the police station?
ARNOLD: There's really nothing you can do at this stage——
STEPHEN: Can they actually stop me going——
ARNOLD: No—but——

STEPHEN: Please come up and make that plain to Birch——

[*He goes off left. Arnold makes a little gesture to Barbary.*]

ARNOLD: Will you excuse me?

[*He goes upstairs and off left. Julia suddenly catches at the desk. She puts her free hand over her face. Barbary hurries to her.*]

BARBARY: Mrs. Dawson—I'm so sorry. This is dreadful for you. Come and sit down.

[*She takes her by the arm to the settee.*]

Would you like another drink?
JULIA: No, I'm all right. It's just—do you think I could have a cigarette?
BARBARY: Certainly. (*Crossing right.*) I know what I need. (*Opening door and calling.*) Perry—Perry. Will you make us some coffee, please? Hot and very strong.
MRS. PERRYMAN (*off*): Yes, Mrs. Leigh.

[*Barbary shuts the door and returns to the mantelpiece for cigarettes.*]

BARBARY: We've been most selfish—only thinking of our side. You've had a terrible time as well. After all, Dawson was your husband.
JULIA: Giovanni? He's dead. (*With sudden quiet venom.*) I hope there *is* a hell. I should hate him to miss it.
BARBARY: But you'd only been married a few months——

JULIA: It wasn't more than a few weeks when I started finding things out. He must have been just one jump ahead of the law all his life—every dirty business you can think of, and some you wouldn't even know. No. I won't exactly go into mourning for Giovanni Dawson.

BARBARY (*moved*): I *am* sorry——

JULIA: You needn't be. I'm better without him. A man who smiles pleasantly and talks sort of quiet while he's—— (*Abruptly.*) Did you know about Tod's mother.

BARBARY: We've never been able to find out anything——

JULIA: Perhaps it doesn't matter—so long after.

BARBARY (*insistently*): Tell me.

JULIA: She stuck Giovanni for four years—until she couldn't take any more. One day he came home and found her dead. When he told me—he laughed.

[*She takes the cigarette Barbary offers and looks up.*]

You're lucky, aren't you? Married to someone like Mr. Leigh.

[*Barbary lights her cigarette for her.*]

BARBARY (*quietly*): Yes. I am.

JULIA: He's swell. But you've got the strength, I can see that. Funny. You're all strung up and nervy, but you've got the strength all right. Mr. Leigh—he's kind of—gentle—and nice.

[*With sudden impulsive sympathy Barbary sits down on the settee beside her.*]

BARBARY: Things *have* turned out badly for you,

haven't they? I wonder—(*Delicately.*)—is there any way we could help? I mean—about money?

JULIA: Thanks, no.

[*She holds out her hand with the big diamond on it.*]

This should raise enough to help me through.

[*She looks at Barbary.*]

You're—very kind. I'm sorry I've been so—so sort of weak—about all this. Like getting faint just now.

BARBARY: Shock, I expect. Hardly surprising after all you've been through——

JULIA: Maybe it doesn't do to get remembering. I suddenly thought—it came over me—how his hands clutched me as he fell down the stairs.

BARBARY (*getting up*): I'm going to hurry that hot coffee.

[*She starts to cross to the door, then stops.*]

(*Abruptly.*) Mrs. Dawson—what do you mean?

[*Julia looks up.*]

JULIA: Mean——?

BARBARY: How could Dawson fall down the stairs when Tod struck him at the foot of them?

[*Julia looks blankly at Barbary for a second.*]

JULIA: Why—I——

BARBARY: Mrs. Dawson, is there something else? Something you haven't told us?

JULIA: You—you've just heard what happened. You heard it from me—you heard it from Tod——

BARBARY (*slowly*): I think I ought to tell the police what you just said.

JULIA (*slowly, suddenly wary*): What did I say? I was on the bottom step. I felt Giovanni clutch me—yes—(*Her confidence returning.*)—yes, that's right. He was bending down to hit me. Tod hit him. And—I felt him clutch at me as he fell. That's what I said. And it's the truth.

BARBARY: You twisted that very neatly. It's not what you said a moment ago——

JULIA: Maybe you thought you heard something different. But that's what I said.

[*Her nerve has returned. She brings a mirror and lipstick out of her bag.*]

BARBARY: I don't believe it. I'm sure you know something—and if it's in Tod's favour you must speak out. Mrs. Dawson, please—you must.

[*Julia looks up, lipstick in hand.*]

JULIA: I tell you there *is* nothing. You're upset about the boy and you're confused——

BARBARY (*breaking in*): You're fighting hard—I suppose I can't blame you. But it's no use. Sooner or later you'll trip up again——

JULIA: I haven't tripped. But thanks for the warning. I'll watch I don't give any more false impressions.

[*She outlines her mouth with lipstick.*]

BARBARY: That won't be very successful. Your hand's shaking too much——

[*Julia jumps up, slamming the lipstick into her bag.*]

JULIA: And I thought you were sympathetic. (*Bitterly.*) I might have known! (*Looking towards stairs.*) Why can't they finish this—you and your damn Tod——

BARBARY: Haven't you any feeling for the boy?

JULIA: They won't do anything much to him—not his age. You heard what the lawyer said. But what would they do to me if they got nasty? Before I knew where I was, I'd be in the dock——

[*She stops.*]

BARBARY (*crisply*): Why should the word dock come into your mind if you know you've done nothing to put you there?

JULIA (*swinging round on her*): I'll tell you why. I know the police. They only have to get you once. If they get you again, they check up and——

BARBARY: Have you been in the hands of the police before?

JULIA: What if I have?

BARBARY: Have you?

JULIA: Once. In Chicago.

BARBARY: We're not in America——

JULIA: It makes no difference. Police are police.

BARBARY: I can't believe it. I simply can't believe you'd let a child suffer all his life——

JULIA (*stung*): He's only a baby. In a month he'll have forgotten——

BARBARY: Forgotten? Did you hear what he said just now? "All my life I'll know I killed my father——" That knowledge would be bad enough for an adult. What will it do to a child?

JULIA (*desperately*): I tell you——

BARBARY (*driving it home*): Suppose—and it *is* only supposition—but suppose you were in some way responsible for Dawson's death——

JULIA: Listen——

BARBARY (*sweeping on relentlessly*): Do you think any jury would convict after hearing what Dawson was, and what he did to you and Tod? Can't you see—you'd have the sympathy—and with a good lawyer it would be——

JULIA (*hysterically*): Why can't you let me alone! what's it to you, anyway? You don't want Tod—you never did. He told me so himself. If they put him away, it ought to suit you fine. Why in hell are you suddenly battling to get him back?

BARBARY (*quietly*): Because my husband needs him.

[*Julia looks at her, then with a half sob, turns down to the desk chair as Stephen comes downstairs and crosses to Barbary. Birch follows, holding Tod's arm. Tod is wearing the clothes he arrived in. Arnold brings up the rear.*]

STEPHEN: They won't let me go to the police station Birch is adamant about it——

BIRCH (*gently, to Tod*): Go and put your shoes on, son.

[*Tod obediently crosses to the hearth, picks up his shoes, goes and sits on the settee and steadily and methodically puts on his shoes and ties the laces. They watch in complete silence. Barbary does not take her eyes from Julia, who stands, taut and shaking, her back half turned. At last Tod finishes, gets up, pauses, then goes up to Julia. He half puts out his hand. She turns and looks at him.*]

TOD: I'm sorry Giovanni—hurt your face. I hope it will soon be better.

[*He crosses to Birch.*]

BIRCH (*quietly*): Come along, son.

[*They move to the door.*]

BARBARY: Inspector—I think——

JULIA (*desperately*): No. No. (*She pauses.*) He—he didn't kill his father.

[*Tod runs into Stephen's arms.*]

STEPHEN: Mrs. Dawson——

JULIA: After Tod ran out, I went into the bar to get some brandy. When I came back—Giovanni was pulling himself up. He was dazed and sick. I ran and put my arm round him to help him up to the bedroom. It—wasn't easy. When we got to the top of the stairs—he seemed to remember what had happened. He started to swear at me. Then he went to hit me again, so I—I——

[*She turns to the desk chair, leaning her head on her arm.*]

(*To herself.*) Oh, my God——

BARBARY (*abruptly*): She shouldn't have tried to help him up—there was bound to be an accident——

BIRCH: Mrs. Leigh—please——

ARNOLD (*crossing centre*): Barbary—?

[*Julia lifts her head. A new expression has come into her face. She darts one swift glance at Barbary and away again.*]

BIRCH: Yes, Mrs. Dawson——?

JULIA (*slowly*): It was—like she said. An accident.

STEPHEN: Do you mean——

JULIA (*slowly*): When he tried to hit me again—he—he lost his balance. I tried to save him—the stairs are steep. I—I only just saved myself.
BIRCH: Why didn't you tell us this before?
JULIA: I was scared. I was in trouble once in America. Only for shoplifting, but I've got a record. I was scared. I know the police.

[*She pulls herself together. The old hard manner begins to come back.*]

When I saw Giovanni lying there—where Tod left him—I thought—let it alone—let it be. Why, the police——

[*She lifts her head, suddenly defiant.*]

The police might even think it wasn't an accident—that I—pushed him.
STEPHEN: And you were going to let Tod——
JULIA: I thought they couldn't do much to him—not at his age. I thought I could get away with it. And then—I don't know. Perhaps I'm soft—I suddenly knew I couldn't let a little kid——

[*She falters and stops, leaning on the desk chair for support. Mrs. Perryman enters right with coffee tray and pauses. Stephen turns to Birch.*]

STEPHEN: And Tod——?
BIRCH: If Mr. Hamble will be responsible I'll leave him with you for the moment——
STEPHEN: Put it on the table, Perry, and take Tod upstairs.

[*Mrs. Perryman puts the coffee tray on the table and moves to Tod. He protests.*]

STEPHEN (*quietly*): Go with Mrs. Perry and wait till I come.

[*Tod and Mrs. Perryman go upstairs and out left. Birch moves to Julia.*]

BIRCH: I'm sorry you didn't tell us this before, Mrs. Dawson It's just as Mr. Hamble said. It never pays to be a difficult witness.
JULIA (*abruptly*): Do you want me to come with you —now?
BIRCH: Yes, please.
BARBARY: Inspector, I—we'd like Mr. Hamble to go too. (*To Arnold.*) I think you should.
ARNOLD: Yes.

[*He looks very hard at Barbary for a moment.*]

I certainly think I should. (*Turning.*) I'll get my coat.

[*He goes out right. Birch follows him up to the door and turns.*]

BIRCH: When you're ready, Mrs. Dawson.

[*Julia turns to the desk chair for her coat. Stephen picks it up and puts it across her shoulders. She looks up at him. The faint smile touches her hard mouth again.*]

JULIA: Thanks.

[*Suddenly, she pulls the big diamond off her finger.*]

Here—give this to Tod. I think his father owes him something.

[*Stephen takes the ring. He shakes his head.*]

STEPHEN: I think Dawson owes you something, too. And so do we.

[*He replaces the ring and brings his other hand over hers in a warm clasp.*]

We're very grateful to you, Mrs. Dawson—very grateful indeed.

[*Julia looks across at Barbary. A glance of understanding passes between them.*]

JULIA: He's a nice guy. (*She nods.*) I guess I know why you battled so hard to get Tod back for him.

[*She goes out right with Birch. Barbary shuts the door and comes down to the tray to pick up the coffee pot. Stephen is looking at her with a new expression on his face.*]

STEPHEN (*suddenly*): Barbary—did you——?
BARBARY (*smiling*): Yes, Professor. (*Quietly.*) Let's have some coffee——

[*He comes quickly down and puts his hand on hers to stop her lifting the coffee pot. He takes her in his arms, looks at her for a second, then holds her closely and warmly. As he releases her, Tod comes on to the landing. He sees the coffee tray and turns to go slowly out. Stephen moves but Barbary checks him.*]

BARBARY: Wait—(*Calling.*)—Tod——

[*Tod pauses on the landing. Barbary quickly pours a cup of black coffee and goes to the foot of the stairs. He stands looking down at her. She holds out the cup.*]

There's a cup for you on the tray. Will you take this one?

[*He looks at her blankly.*]

(*Smiling.*) And give it—to Mister?

[*Tod's lip trembles. Then a smile breaks across his face. He almost falls down the stairs to take the cup from her.*]

[*Balancing it carefully in both hands, he carries it triumphantly across the room to Stephen.*]

Curtain.

SAILOR, BEWARE!

A Comedy

by

PHILIP KING

and

FALKLAND L. CARY

Jack Waller presented *Sailor, Beware!* at the Strand Theatre, London, on February 16, 1955, with the following cast:

EDIE HORNETT	*Ann Wilton*
EMMA HORNETT	*Peggy Mount*
MRS. LACK	*Mynette Morven*
HENRY HORNETT	*Cyril Smith*
ALBERT TUFNELL, A.B.	*Richard Coleman*
CARNOUSTIE BLIGH, A.B.	*James Copeland*
DAPHNE PINK	*Jean Burgess*
SHIRLEY HORNETT	*Sheila Shand Gibbs*
THE REV. OLIVER PUREFOY	*Anthony Marlowe*

Produced by Melville Gillam

Setting by Michael Eve

CHARACTERS

(in the order of their appearance)

EDIE HORNETT
EMMA HORNETT
MRS. LACK
HENRY HORNETT
ALBERT TUFNELL, A.B.
CARNOUSTIE BLIGH, A.B.
DAPHNE PINK
SHIRLEY HORNETT
THE REV. OLIVER PUREFOY

SCENE

The entire action takes place in the living-room of the Hornetts' house in a small inland town.

TIME

The present; late September.

ACT ONE

Five-fifteen p.m.

ACT TWO

Scene 1: *Nine-thirty the same evening.*
Scene 2: *The next morning—ten forty-five.*

ACT THREE

About an hour later.

ACT ONE

The scene is the living-room at the Hornetts'.

The fireplace is down right. There is a door to back kitchen up right and a window in back wall. The door to the small hall, staircase and front door is up left. The furnishings are ordinary in taste; everything about the room is spotless. The settee is of the " Put-U-up " variety.

The Hornetts are a working-class family.

When the curtain rises, the stage is empty but the wireless is playing merrily.

The front door bell rings.

Edie Hornett, a thin, nondescript spinster of fortyish rushes on from kitchen door right carrying a teapot. She hurries to door left (to answer bell) realises she has teapot in her hand, " Tut-tuts ", puts teapot on sideboard, and exits left.

After a moment, she comes back carrying a large cardboard box. She puts this on chair, flutters over it, as if she is about to open it, but doesn't; she reads the label, then taking a handkerchief from her pocket, sniffs and dabs her eyes. She then crosses up to door left and calls.

EDIE (*calling*): Emma! It's come!

[*But the wireless is playing loudly. Edie crosses to it, turns a knob (the wrong one) and loud squeaks and squawks result. Edie loses her head.*]

Oh dear!

[*She turns several knobs and the resulting noise is deafening. Edie is almost dancing in her agitation. Emma Hornett, Edie's sister-in-law, enters from left. She is a large woman of Edie's age; masterful and sharp-tongued.*]

EMMA (*as she enters*): For the Lord's sake! (*She begins adjusting knobs of wireless.*)
EDIE (*plaintively*): I was just trying to. . . .

[*But there is a loud blare of music before Emma finishes adjusting the knobs.*]

(*When music is playing softly.*) That's better!
EMMA: It's just as it was before you started your fiddlin'.
EDIE: I was just trying to turn it down a bit. You couldn't hear me calling. I wanted to let you know it's come.
EMMA: What's come?
EDIE: The wedding-cake. (*Pointing to box.*) I'd just made the tea when Co-op man rang the bell.
EMMA (*moving to box and untying string*): Where is it?
EDIE (*blinking*): Well, it'll be in the box.
EMMA (*snapping*): The tea!
EDIE: Oh! I'll bring it in. It's all ready. (*She goes off into back kitchen.*)

[*Emma with a look of dislike, switches off wireless and, having undone string of box, removes the lid. She opens out several sheets of tissue paper, then looks critically into box.*]

EMMA (*grudgingly satisfied*): H'm!

[*Edie returns with tray on which are two cups and saucers, etc.*]

EDIE (*almost throwing tray on to table*): Oh, you've. . . . Let me see! (*She peers into box rather as if peering into a grave. She then produces her handkerchief, begins to weep and move away. Through her tears.*) It's beautiful!

EMMA (*exasperated*): Oh my Lord! You startin' again?

EDIE: I can't help it, Emma. It's bringing it all back to me!

EMMA: Now then! We've had enough of that! Good heavens, it was nearly twenty years ago!

EDIE: " A few more years shall roll.
A few more seasons pass."

EMMA: Do you know what you're talking about, 'cos I don't. Come on. Let's have a cup of tea, and have it quick. There's lots to do, yet. (*She has moved to tea tray.*) H'm, that's clever, isn't it?

EDIE: What, Emma?

EMMA (*pointing to tray*): Where's the teapot?

EDIE (*fluttering*): Oh, I put it down somewhere, when the bell rang. Now where. . . ? Oh, yes. It's on the sideboard. (*She begins to move up.*)

EMMA (*alert*): On the. . . ! (*She darts up, snatches up teapot and looks at sideboard in horror.*) My Lord!

EDIE (*tremulously*): What is it, Emma?

EMMA (*furious*): Look at this! Edie 'Ornett, you haven't the brains you were born with. No more sense than to put a hot teapot down on a polished sideboard! Look at that big white ring. We'll never get it out.

EDIE: Well, you see, the bell rang. . . .

EMMA: A wedding present from my mother, this was, and never so much as a scratch on it all these years, and you have to go and. . . .

EDIE: I'll try and get it out afterwards.

EMMA: *Afterwards!* You'll try and get it out *now!* Go on! Get the furniture polish. Hurry!

[*Edie scuttles off into back kitchen. Emma moans over the mark a little longer, then brings teapot down and pours herself a cup of tea. Edie returns from back kitchen carrying a tin of polish, dropping duster as she enters.*]

EDIE (*hopefully on entering*): Here we are, Emma!

[*She hands tin to Emma.*]

EMMA (*with great exasperation as she looks at tin*): "Here we are, Emma"! And what do we put it on with? Our knickers?
EDIE: Oh!

[*She looks round for duster. Emma silently appeals to Heaven to give her patience, then drinks her tea. Edie picks up duster.*]

Here we are, Emma.
EMMA (*snatching cloth and moving up to sideboard*): You'll have to put some elbow grease into it.
EDIE: Yes, Emma. I'll just. . . . (*She pours herself a cup of tea.*)

[*Emma, meanwhile, has put some polish on sideboard and is rubbing it in with a circular movement.*]

EMMA: Come and watch. (*Edie, cup in hand, moves up.*) This is how you do it. Rub it round and round till it gets real hot and keep on rubbing, and it *might* bring it out.
EDIE (*eagerly*): Yes, Emma. (*She puts cup down on sideboard preparatory to taking up duster.*)

EMMA (*with a wail of anguish*): For Goodness sake! (*She snatches Edie's cup from sideboard.*)

EDIE: What. . . ?

EMMA: You'll have another mark in a minute! (*She inspects sideboard where cup was—there is no mark.*) I dunno! You're always moaning 'cos you never got married, but God knows what sort of a home you'd 'ave 'ad if you 'ad. (*Handing her cup.*) Here! Get this down, you, then get started. It'll take hours!

[*Edie almost pours the tea straight down her throat, chokes a little, hands cup to Emma, and begins the polishing process. Emma pours herself another cup.*]

What's the time? (*Looking at clock on mantelpiece.*) I'll never get everything done by the time they start arriving. Daphne'll be here any minute, now. Lord, I wish tomorrow was over.

EDIE (*panting as she rubs*): So do I

EMMA (*sharply*): I don't see what you're worrying about. It isn't your daughter that's getting married. (*In the same breath.*) Is it coming off?

EDIE: No.

EMMA: I know. It won't. Go on, carry on.

EDIE: It's the thought of seeing Shirley in her bridal dress. I know I won't be able to bear up. It'll take my mind back. . . .

[*Mrs. Lack's voice is heard off right.*]

MRS. LACK (*off*): Anyone at home?

EMMA (*muttering*): Oh my. . . .

[*Mrs. Lack appears in kitchen doorway. Much the same age as Emma, she takes life easily—and other folks' troubles with considerable pleasure.*]

MRS. LACK (*in doorway*): It's only me.

EDIE (*rubbing vigorously*): It's only Mrs. Lack, Emma.

MRS. LACK: That's right. It's only me. I don't want to disturb you, 'cos I know you're busy; but I thought I'd just. . . . My! Look at Edie! She isn't half going it, is she? Gettin' all polished up for tomorrow, eh, Edie? The great day, eh? (*Seeing teapot.*) Oh, you're having a cuppa, are you? I wouldn't have disturbed you if I'd known, but I thought I'd just. . . .

EMMA (*not too sweetly*): You'd better have a cup since you're here. I'll have to put some more water in. (*She exits to kitchen.*)

MRS. LACK (*as Emma goes*): No, don't bother, Emma. I didn't . . . I wasn't . . . But I thought I'd just. . . . (*But Emma has gone. Mrs. Lack moves up to Edie; then with a quick look towards kitchen door, speaks in a quiet voice.*) Got you at it, 'asn't she, Edie? She'd drive me up the wall with her everlasting polishing.

EDIE (*she is no traitress*): Well, you see. . . .

MRS. LACK (*picking up polish tin*): What does she use? (*Looking at tin.*) "Polisho". Muck!

EDIE: But. . . .

MRS. LACK: Muck, Edie; that's what that is. I wouldn't use it on the cat, let alone. . . . Still it's everyone to their taste, isn't it? You know, you'll 'ave yourself worn out if you go on like that. You won't be in a fit state for the wedding tomorrow. She oughtn't to make you work like that. . . .

EDIE: Oh, but I'm not going to the wedding, Mrs. Lack.

MRS. LACK: Not going?

EDIE (*with a whimper*): No, I'm not going.

MRS. LACK (*aghast*): Your own brother's daughter's

wedding, and you're not going! (*With a jerk of the head to the kitchen.*) *She* said you can't. . . ?

EDIE: I couldn't bring myself to go. It would bring back too many memories.

MRS. LACK (*with great understanding*): Ah, I see what you mean. How silly of me! You mean your Great Sorrow!

EDIE (*nodding vigorously as she rubs*): Ummps!

MRS. LACK: Yes, of course, it's natural you shouldn't want to go. It would be more than flesh and blood could stand, wouldn't it?

EDIE: Ummps!

MRS. LACK (*cheerfully*): Yes, of course it would. Watching Shirley standing at the altar rails, and remembering the day when you yourself. . . .

EDIE (*now completely abandoned to grief*): Don't. Don't, Mrs. Lack! I mustn't think of it.

MRS. LACK: Of course you mustn't! (*Her voice throbbing with inspiration.*) "Oh, memories that bless and burn. . . ."

EDIE (*also inspired*): "Oh, barren gain and bitter loss!" (*She rubs briskly.*)

MRS. LACK (*very practically as she points to other end of sideboard*): I should come over a bit, Edie, or you'll wear an 'ole in it.

[*Emma returns with teapot.*]

EMMA (*it might be an accusation or a statement*): Now, then. . . !

MRS. LACK: Ah! It's very kind of you, Emma. I didn't mean to . . . but I just 'appened to look over the wall . . . and I saw the door open; so I thought I'd just. . . .

EMMA: Sugar?

MRS. LACK: Two. (*Giggling.*) Well . . . I'm all ready for the bridegroom.

EMMA: What!

MRS. LACK: I mean, I've got the bedroom ready for him and his best man. I hope they'll be comfortable. I'm not used to. . . . But when you asked me if I could put them up for tonight . . . well, it was only neighbourly, wasn't it?

EMMA: Tea all right?

MRS. LACK: Yes, thanks. (*With purpose.*) I mean it would have been expensive for them if they'd had to put up at the Rose and Crown, wouldn't it?

EMMA (*rather shortly*): I shall see to it that you're paid for your inconvenience.

MRS. LACK (*quickly*): Oh no, Emma! I wouldn't dream of . . . (*Not so quickly.*) that is. . . . (*Practically.*) Of course they'd charge twelve and six each at the Rose and Crown . . . (*Hopefully.*) Anyway, we'll see when the time comes. Do you want me to give them breakfast?

EMMA: You'll 'ave to, won't you? That's the whole point of 'em coming to you.

MRS. LACK: What? To get a good breakfast?

EMMA (*very shortly*): To keep out of the way, so the bridegroom doesn't see the bride before the wedding.

EDIE (*pausing in the rubbing*): Ooh! Albert mustn't see Shirley before the wedding whatever 'appens. That'd be unlucky!

EMMA (*waving Edie's remark away*): Never you mind about who sees who—when or where. Is it coming off?

EDIE (*forcing herself to be truthful*): Not so as you'd notice.

EMMA: Well, rub harder!

EDIE: Yes, Emma. (*She rubs more vigorously.*)

MRS. LACK: Well, I hope they'll be comfortable at my place. I'll do my best for them, I'm sure.

EMMA. You needn't worry. They're both sailors, so they should be used to roughing it.

[*Mrs. Lack doesn't know how to take that.*]

It isn't *their* comfort tonight . . . it's Shirley's happiness in the future that I'm concerned about.
MRS. LACK: Yes. It must be a worry when your only daughter takes the plunge . . . wondering if she's going in at the right end, so to speak . . . a worry for you and your husband.
EMMA (*with fine scorn*): Him! A lot he worries! He never worries about anything except his blessed ferrets.
MRS. LACK (*gaily*): Oh yes! Mr. 'Ornett and his ferrets! He does think a lot of them, doesn't he?
EMMA: He thinks about 'em so much he should've married one. Nasty stinking things! They'd be out of the backyard this minute if I had my way.
EDIE: Oh, Emma, you wouldn't take Henry's ferrets away from him! Why, it'd break his heart. Always been fond of dumb creatures, he has. I remember when he was a boy he 'ad an 'edge-'og . . . and he gave it all his love. . . .
EMMA: Well, he has a daughter now, and he should give her a bit of his love. Never mind ferrets and 'edge'ogs. Hasn't bothered his head one scrap about poor Shirley's wedding, he hasn't. Left it all to me. But this I will say, and I don't care who hears me say it—are you listening, Edie?—if Shirley's marriage turns out wrong, to my dying day I'll say that 'Enry's to blame.
MRS. LACK: Now, that's interesting, Emma. What makes you say that, I wonder?
EMMA: It was 'Enry first brought this Albert Tufnell to the house, or our Shirley'd never have met him.
EDIE: It was love at first sight!

[*Emma turns and glares at her. Edie resumes rubbing vigorously.*]

MRS. LACK: What about his people?
EMMA: Yes, what about them? That's what I'd like to know. He hasn't any! He was brought up in a Sailors' Orphanage—he *says.*
MRS. LACK (*relishing this*): H'mm! Fishy, isn't it? Well, I'm sure I *hope* it will be all right. It might. You never know.
EMMA: Heaven knows I've done my best to talk to Shirley and stop her doing something she might regret for the rest of her life. The times I've said to her, " Shirley, you know what sailors are! "
MRS. LACK (*joyfully*): Yes, aren't they!
EMMA: But I might as well talk to myself for what notice she'll take.
EDIE: They love each other, Emma.
MRS. LACK: You can't set much store by that, Edie girl, can you, Emma?
EMMA: I say, and I've always said, it's the uniform that Shirley's fallen for. She'll change her tune when she sees him without it.
MRS. LACK (*with rather a naughty giggle*): Well, of course, that depends on. . . .
EMMA: He won't look so la-di-da in a suit of dungarees.
MRS. LACK (*soberly*): Oh? I see what you mean!

[*The front door is heard opening and closing.*]

EMMA: He's only got another three months to do in the Navy; then he'll have to settle down and do some real work (*All in the same breath—calling.*) That you, Henry?

[*Henry Hornett's voice is heard off.*]

HENRY (*not cheerfully*): Yes.
EMMA (*calling*): You wiped your feet?
HENRY: Yes.
EMMA: That passage is all polished up for tomorrow. I don't want you. . . .

[*Henry enters from up left. He is a smallish man of fifty. He wears a shapeless, but clean blue suit.*]

(*Looking at him disparagingly and speaking likewise.*) Oh! I suppose *you'll* want a cup of tea?
MRS. LACK: Hello, Mr. Hornett!
HENRY (*after grunting a greeting to Mrs. Lack*): *Cup* of. . . ! I want more than a cup of tea. I want my tea proper.
EMMA (*sharply*): Now then! Don't start! I told you before you went out this morning that we weren't having a meal till seven o'clock. What with Daphne arriving at six o'clock, and your precious Albert and this whoever-he's-bringing-with-him arriving at half-past. . . ! I don't run one of them "Help-Yourself" cafés I'd have you know. We'll all sit down together at seven o'clock, and that's that! Do you want a cup of tea now, or don't you?

[*Henry is removing his stiff collar.*]

HENRY: I'm not fussy.
EMMA: Well, I'm not going down on my knees to ask you.
HENRY: If there's any left in the pot I'll *have* it. If there isn't it doesn't matter. Edie, have you fed the ferrets?
EDIE: At dinner time, I did.
EMMA: Never mind about. . . .
HENRY (*overlapping—to Edie*): Did Rosie take her

dinner? How's she looking? Nothing happened yet?

EDIE: Ooh, I didn't stop to look, Henry! I was late. I had to get back to work.

HENRY: I'd better go and see.

EMMA: And what about your cup of tea?

HENRY: If you'd pour it out instead of talking about it so much. . .

EMMA: And if you'd give your mind to things that really mattered instead of. . . . (*Handing him her cup which she has refilled.*) Here! Get it down you.

[*Henry gets it down in one gulp and makes a wry face immediately afterwards.*]

Ferrets! I should have thought you could have given us a rest from them for once. Shirley's wedding-day tomorrow and all.

HENRY (*having put collar and tie over back of chair and moving towards back kitchen door*): It's her weddin'; not mine.

EMMA (*flaring*). Well, she's *your* daughter, isn't she?

HENRY (*at door*): So *you* say! (*He exits.*)

EMMA (*stunned*): Well, I. . . !

MRS. LACK (*with great "to-do"*): Oh, my goodness! Look at the time. I must be getting back. I wouldn't have come in at all really, but I thought I'd just. . . . And I've got Rita in bed, too.

EDIE: Oh dear! Is she poorly?

MRS. LACK: Oh, it's nothing. Came home from school at dinner time and said she had a headache; so I put her to bed. I think it's just excitement—being one of Shirley's bridesmaids. But I'd better be getting back in case she misses me. Well, I'll expect the boys sometime then, Emma.

EMMA: You can expect 'em at ten o'clock. I'm not

having them staying here until all hours. Shirley will want some rest tonight, and I'll see she gets it.

MRS. LACK: Yes, poor thing. She won't get much tomorrow, will she? (*With a giggle.*) Oh dear! The things I say! (*She now notices that Edie is rubbing the same place on the sideboard as before.*) Good Lord! (*With curiosity and concern.*) You all right, Edie? By the way, where *is* Shirley?

EMMA: She should be back by now. She's gone to have her hair done. She's supposed to be going to the station to meet Albert and this whoever-it-is he's bringing with him. Yes, and *she'll* want a cup of tea before she goes. (*Picking up teapot.*) I suppose I'd better. . . .

MRS. LACK (*moving slightly again*): Yes, and I suppose *I'd* better. . . .

[*Henry dashes on from kitchen almost colliding with Emma and pushing her aside.*]

HENRY (*as he does so*): Heigh-up! (*Very excited.*) Edie! Edie!

EMMA: Now what. . . ?

HENRY: Edie, warm me a drop of milk, quick, will you! It's happened. Rosie's 'ad 'em. Six of 'em.

EDIE: Six? Six eggs?

HENRY: Eg——! It's time somebody told you the facts of life! (*To Emma who is again in his way—as he dashes off again.*) Heigh-up!

EDIE: I'd better do it, hadn't I, Emma?

EMMA: Well, I'm not going to, and that's a fact. Go on if you're going.

[*Edie rushes off to back kitchen.*]

(*As Edie goes.*) And don't use this morning's milk.

There some that's just on the turn at the back of the shelf.

EDIE (*now off*): Yes, Emma.

MRS. LACK (*after a quick look after Edie*): I expect you find *her* a bit of a handful, don't you?

EMMA: Enough to drive me out of mind, she is! Always 'arping on about her Great Sorrow.

MRS. LACK: Yes, she does 'arp, doesn't she? (*Preparing to go again.*) Well, it's no use. . . . (*As she passes sideboard.*) Oh dear! Nasty mark you've got on your sideboard, haven't you? (*She is moving towards door left—stopping.*) Oh no! I'd better go the back way. Mustn't paddle on your lino, must I? (*She turns and moves to other door, talking all the time.*) Well, righto, then! I'll leave you to cope, and thanks for the cup of tea. I didn't really come in for that, you know. I 'appened to look over the wall and saw the door open, so I thought I'd just. . . . (*She has passed from view by now—off.*) 'Bye, Edie!

EDIE (*off*): 'Bye, Mrs. Lack.

MRS. LACK (*off—with great satisfaction*): H'mm! Clouding over a bit! Doesn't look too good for tomorrow, does it? Bye-bye.

[*Emma has been putting tea things on tray and giving exasperated glances towards kitchen.*]

EMMA (*as she moves up with tray*): 'As she gone? Really gone?

EDIE (*off*): Yes, Emma.

EMMA (*as she departs into kitchen*): Lord, how that woman 'arps! (*She exits right—off.*) *Now*, what are you doing?

EDIE (*off*): It's all right, Emma. It's just boiled over. I'll wipe it up.

EMMA (*off*): Oh, my Lord. . . !

[*There is a loud knocking on the front door—"Pom-diddle-om-pom. Pom. Pom."*]

(*Still off.*) Now, who'll this be?

EDIE (*off*): I'll go, Emma. (*She appears with a small pan of steaming milk in her hand.*)

EMMA (*off*): Mind what you're doing with that. . . .

[*A voice—the voice of Albert Tufnell, A.B.—is heard in the hall.*]

ALBERT (*off*): Hello, there! (*It is almost a roar.*)

EDIE (*ecstatically*): It's Albert! (*Running to kitchen door.*) Emma, it's Albert!

[*Albert Tufnell bursts into the room from door left. Albert is twenty-three, good-looking, brimming over with good health and good spirits; self-possessed, but not aggressively so. In short, Albert is the ideal sailor girls dream about. He is in his (A.B.) uniform and carries his kitbag over one shoulder and a large bag in one hand. Edie has moved to centre for his entrance.*]

ALBERT (*as he comes through the door*): Anyone at home? (*With a whoop as he sees Edie.*) Well, if it isn't Jane Russell herself!

EDIE (*bubbling with girlish giggle*): Oh, Albert!

ALBERT (*flinging his kitbag into one corner and bag into another*): Clear decks for action! (*Holding out arms.*) Come on! Into my arms!

EDIE (*writhing with delight*): Oh, Albert! Albert Tufnell! (*She is holding the pan of milk at arm's length. She backs coyly from him.*)

ALBERT: Are you coming, or do I have to fetch you? (*He moves towards her*).

EDIE (*squeaking*): Albert! Albert, stoppit, do! Mind this pan. It's hot!

ALBERT (*rubbing his hands together*): So am I! I haven't kissed a woman for three months. (*He snatches the pan from her hand and plants it on the sideboard.*) Aunt Edie, you're for it! (*He grabs her to him, plants a smacking kiss on both cheeks.*)
EDIE (*a faint voice from another world*): Oh, Albert!

[*He whirls her round, then picks her up in his arms.*]

ALBERT: Where's the bedroom?
EDIE (*kicking her legs and squeaking in a frenzy of not too outraged modesty.*) Oooh, Albert Tufnell, aren't you awful! Put me down! Do you hear? Put me down this minute!

[*Emma enters from kitchen.*]

EMMA (*stopping in doorway, looking and not liking what she sees.*) Well, I don't. . . .!
EDIE (*overlapping*): *Al-bert!* Give over. I'm going dizzy!
ALBERT: Going? I've gone!

[*With Edie still in his arms, he is about to sink into a chair on which stands the box containing the wedding cake. Emma, with a scream of anguish manages to snatch the box from under Albert, as he sits.*]

EMMA (*clutching box to her bosom*): My God!
ALBERT (*blissfully unaware of the near calamity, twirling Edie off his knee on seeing Emma and rising*): *Ma!* If it isn't Ma!
EMMA (*her thoughts still on the " might-have-been "*): Oh!
ALBERT (*advancing heartily*): How are we, Ma?
EMMA (*when he is near her, letting out another scream*): Keep away! Edie! Take this! (*Box.*) Take it while it's safe!

[*Edie takes box quickly.*]

ALBERT: That's better! Now we can get to grips. (*She manages to disentangle herself from his grip.*)

EMMA: That's enough of that! I don't hold with a lot of. . . . D'you realise what you nearly did just now?

ALBERT (*cheerfully*): No. What did I do?

EMMA: All your foolin' and jumping about! You nearly sat on your wedding cake, nearly flattened it out!

ALBERT: Blimey! Might have made it go round a bit further! Well, how are you, Ma?

EMMA: I'll feel better when you've got yourself sat down and out of harm's way. Edie, don't stand there holding that thing in your arms till it melts. Put it down—and somewhere where *he* can't get at it. And I thought you was supposed to be taking some milk out to Henry?

EDIE: Oh, the milk! Where. . . ? (*She sees pan on sideboard.*) Oooh! (*She runs to remove it but. . . .*)

[*Emma gets there first. She picks up pan and examines sideboard.*]

EMMA (*at sideboard—she can hardly speak*): You. . . Edie 'Ornett, I could kill you!

EDIE: It was an accident, Emma! Albert just came in, and. . . .

EMMA (*now fuming*): Never mind about Albert. You did this on purpose! You did it for spite!

ALBERT (*who has crossed to kitbag and is about to undo it*): Hullo-ullo-ullo! (*He moves to them.*)

EMMA (*turning on him*): And what are you "Hullo-ullo-ullo-ing" about?

ALBERT (*cheerfully*): Sounds like a bit of a squall

blowing up on the port side. Something come adrift, Ma?

EDIE: It's nothing, Albert. It's. . . .

EMMA (*very incensed*): Nothing! No, of course, it's nothing to *you*. It isn't your sideboard that's ruined, is it?

[*A sailor-hatted head comes round the door left during this, takes in the situation and withdraws. The owner of the head is Carnoustie Bligh, of whom more anon. He is unnoticed by the others.*]

No more sense than to put a hot pan. . . !

EDIE: But, Emma, I swear I didn't do it on purpose.

ALBERT: 'Course she didn't, Ma. As a matter of fact, I did it. And what have I done?

EMMA: You! So it was you, was it! Well, see what you've done. Burnt a big white mark on my sideboard.

ALBERT (*looking*): H'mm! Never mind, Ma! (*Pointing to the mark Edie had made previously.*) It matches with that one!

EMMA: Ooooh!

[*Henry comes in from right.*]

HENRY (*in the coming*): Here, Edie! Where's that milk I asked you to warm? (*Seeing Albert.*) Albert! (*He rushes to him, greets him warmly.*) When did you get here?

ALBERT (*pleased at seeing him*): How are we, Pop?

HENRY: Why didn't you let me know he'd come, Emma?

EMMA (*muttering as she goes off into kitchen*): Bad news travels fast enough! (*She exits right.*)

HENRY (*coughing to cover his embarrassment*): Well,

Albert! It's good to see you, boy! Eee! You're looking well! Plenty of sea breezes, eh?

ALBERT (*with a look towards kitchen*): You seem to get a few breezes here, one way and another.

HENRY (*coughing again*): H'mm! I wish I'd known you were here. What train did you get? Er . . . Edie . . . have we . . . er . . . we've got a drop of. . . ?.

[*Re-enter Emma with polish and rag.*]

EMMA (*as she enters*): No, we haven't!

EDIE (*fluttering—to Emma*): Let me do it, Emma.

EMMA: You've done enough damage. You just get out of my way! That's all I ask. (*She begins rubbing vigorously.*)

HENRY: But, Albert, have you come alone? I thought you were bringing your best man with you.

ALBERT: Good Lord! Carnoustie!

HENRY (*blinking*): Eh?

ALBERT: Carnoustie! I'd forgotten all about him!

HENRY: "Car——" I can't say it yet! Is that his name?

ALBERT: That's right, Pop. Carnoustie Bligh.

HENRY: Is he Russian?

EMMA: We're having no foreigners in this house. Where is he?

ALBERT: He's in the hall. (*Jerking finger towards door left.*)

EMMA: What! Paddling about on my lino that I've just polished! Albert Tufnell. . . !

[*Albert goes to door left, and stands by it, "playing" bagpipes and imitating their wails to the tune of "The Road to The Isles". He then calls out in a very bad Scots accent. . . .*]

ALBERT: Carnoustie, you Highland hopscotch, show yourself, will you!

[*Carnoustie, after a short pause, appears in the doorway. He, too, is dressed in sailor's uniform. He carries a kitbag and case. Carnousie—about the same age as Albert—has his manly beauty; but it inclines to the severe. He takes life seriously but is extremely popular with his mates, and —to his embarrassment—women are apt to fall for him. His nationality is not for one moment in doubt once he opens his mouth.*]

Pop—Ma—meet the one and only Carnoustie! The braw'est Scot that ever crossed the *borrrder*.

CARN: Ah'm pleased indeed to meet ye a'.

EMMA: How do you do, Mr. Carnoustie.

CARN (*carefully*): No' *Misterr* Carrrnoustie. Carrrnoustie is ma Chrrristian name.

HENRY: What! Bit funny, isn't it?

CARN: I fail to obsairve any humourr in it, ma'sel'!

ALBERT (*to Henry*): Go easy. He's a bit touchy on. . . .

CARN (*patiently explaining*): If it is your wish to address me in forrrmal fashion, ma name wud be Mr. Carnoustie Bligh. (*Graciously.*) But I'd be honourred if you'd just ca' me Carrrnoustie for shorrrt.

HENRY: For. . . ! Well, come on in! Put your things down. Have you been waiting all this time in the hall?

CARN (*putting down kitbag*): Ay.

EMMA: Why didn't you come in?

CARN: Because I wasna' askit.

EMMA: That's *your* fault, Albert.

ALBERT: He'll forgive me. Now, Carnoustie, that's Ma and Pop. And (*Pushing her forward.*) here's Aunt Edie for you, the pride of the harem.

EDIE (*loving it*): Ooooh, Albert!
CARN: I'm happy to meet you, Aunt Edie.
EDIE: How do you do?
HENRY: Now, Car—— er Car——?
CARN: —noustie.
HENRY: That's right. Sit you doon . . . (*then quickly.*) down. Er . . . I expect you could do with a cup of tea.
CARN (*emphatically*): I cuid!
EMMA: It isn't ready yet.
CARN (*facing facts*): In that case, I'll wait.
ALBERT: Sit down, Carnoustie boy!

[*Carnoustie sits awkwardly on settee.*]

EDIE: Shall I be laying for tea, Emma?
EMMA: You can lay; (*This to Henry.*) but no one's having their tea until seven o'clock. I've told you that once already. Go on then—lay!

[*Edie exits to kitchen.*]

HENRY (*sitting beside Carnoustie*): Are you interested in ferrets?
CARN: In wha'?
HENRY: Ferrets . . . I. . . .
CARN (*suspecting a joke*): No, I am no'. Nor in maukins nor moosies, neither.
HENRY: I *keep* ferrets.
CARN: Ma Goad! Wha' for?
HENRY: Company.
EMMA: Henry!
HENRY: Yes, Emma.
EMMA: Carnoustie doesn't want to hear about your ferrets.
HENRY: Well, I must go and see to Rosie. Make yourself at home. (*He exits right.*)

ALBERT: And now! Where's my girl? Where's the future Mrs. Albert Tufnell?

EMMA: Yes! I was beginning to wonder when you were going to condescend to ask after her. She's at the hairdresser's. She should be here any minute. Then she was going down to the station to meet you and . . . (*With a jerk of the head towards Carnoustie.*) *him*. You weren't supposed to arrive until half-past six.

ALBERT: We got ashore earlier than we expected, and there was a train just leaving ; so we. . . . How is she, Ma? Does she love me as much as she used to?

EMMA (*shortly*): She loves you as much as she's ever likely to!

ALBERT: Is she gettin' excited about tomorrow? (*Rubbing his hands and winking at Carnoustie.*) *I* am!!

EMMA (*seeing this—sharply*): Now then! That's enough of that!

ALBERT (*sobering up*): Ahem! Gone to the hairdresser's, has she?

CARN (*flatly*): Can she no' do her own hair? Ma sisterr never. . . .

ALBERT: Carnoustie, you're not in Auchtertermo-charty now; where the bonnie wee lassies put their hair up in thistle stalks. Here, come on! We'd better be getting our bags unpacked. (*He moves towards his kitbag.*)

[*Carnoustie rises.*]

EMMA: You needn't bother yourselves. You're not sleeping here.

ALBERT: Not? Then where. . . ?

EMMA: I've arranged for you both to go next door to Mrs. Lack's.

ALBERT: Oh? What's the idea, Ma?

EMMA: For one thing, I haven't room for you.

There's others coming to the wedding besides yourself. We're putting Daphne up. She'll sleep with Shirley.

ALBERT: Daphne?

EMMA: Daphne Pink, my sister's daughter, that lives at Manchester. She's going to be Shirley's chief bridesmaid. I would have thought Shirley'd have told you about her.

ALBERT: Oh—*her*! Yes, she's told me. She's a bit of all right, isn't she?

EMMA (*heavily*): She's my sister's daughter, if that's what you mean.

ALBERT (*as he moves away*): No, I didn't!

EMMA: And another reason why you're not staying here. I don't want you in the way tomorrow morning. And don't you get trying to see Shirley, either.

ALBERT: Not see her? Not see my future wife?

EMMA: Not in the morning, you won't. Not till she joins you in church. It's unlucky for the bride to see the bridegroom before the wedding, and the Lord knows things look black enough as it is without *asking* for trouble. (*She has collected her polishing things, and now marches out of the room into the kitchen.*)

[*Albert stands gazing after her. He scratches his head, puzzled. He moves down, sees Carnoustie sitting on settee, moves down to him, pats him on the shoulder then sits beside him.*]

ALBERT: Carnoustie-boy!

CARN: Ay?

ALBERT: *Have* I asked for trouble?

CARN: Ay.

ALBERT (*indignantly*): Just because I wanted to see my Shirl——

CARN: No.

ALBERT: What do you mean—" No "? You said. . . .

CARN: I dinna mean that ye were speerin' for trouble in *tha'* way. But in anitherrr.

ALBERT: What itherrr?

CARN: Yon gruesome. . . ! Yer ma-in-law!

ALBERT: You mean, she's a. . . ?

CARN (*quickly*): Ay.

ALBERT: Oh!

CARN (*after consideration*): And a bad one.

ALBERT: You could be right. (*Thinking.*) But I'm not marrying her, am I?

CARN: If ye had been, I'd strangle ye wi' ma ain hands. . . .

ALBERT: Gee!

CARN: It'd be counted a maircy-killing.

ALBERT (*a little taken aback*): M'mm . . . I can see you don't like her.

CARN: Yer fiancée must have a great deal to compensate for . . . (*With a jerk of his head.*) *yon*!

ALBERT (*brightening a little*): Oh, you'll fall for Shirl all right.

[*Front door bell. Albert rises and crosses to kitchen door.*]

Ma, there's someone at the front door. Shall I go?

EMMA (*entering from kitchen*): You stay where you are. I'll go. I don't want your big feet paddling. . . . You can be putting them . . . (*Looking at the kitbags.*) them bolsters of yours tidy. (*She exits left.*)

CARN (*in deep disgust*): " Bolsterrrs. . ."!

[*He and Albert move to kitbags.*]

DAPHNE (*off*): Aunt Emma! How are you? I thought

I was never going to get here. And how's Shirley? Isn't it all wildly exciting? Oh, have you got half-a-crown?

EMMA (*off*): I have not.

[*During this, Albert has been drawn to the door. He peeps through it, then turns in to look at Carnoustie, and gives a wolf-whistle.*]

ALBERT: Boy! Whatta peach! You're the best man; so she's yours . . . all yours!

CARN (*very gravely*): Albert, when I undertook to be your best man, did I not make it a clearr condeetion that there was to be no putting me into poseetions of embarrassment wi' young wimmin? Ye ken tha' I ha'e no time for them, and conseeder as a class they are. . . .

[*His voice has tailed away as Daphne enters left. And, indeed, there is every excuse; for Daphne is a smart, streamlined and salesmanlike piece of goods, with a charming manner and an attractive smile. Carnoustie retreats a little with praiseworthy caution—but Albert dashes to the head of the line.*]

DAPHNE (*breaking off from speaking to Emma*): Oh! I didn't know the Fleet was in. Now, which is which?

ALBERT: I'm Albert! The bridegroom. The human sacrifice! (*He takes her in his arms and kisses her.*)

[*Emma enters—to watch disapprovingly.*]

DAPHNE: You don't waste too much time, do you, Albert?

ALBERT: If you think *I'm* fast. . . ! Meet the hare—Carnoustie!

[*Albert gestures Carnoustie on. Carnoustie is staring open-mouthed at Daphne, who now " notices " him for the first time.*]

DAPHNE (*liking very much what she sees*): Oooh! How do you do?
CARN (*speaking with difficulty*): Verra . . . weel.

[*Daphne has taken a step towards Carnoustie, hopefully expecting the same treatment as she has received from Albert. But Carnoustie is not to be persuaded. He hesitates, and finally draws a little away, and speaks with a trace of apology in his voice.*]

I ha'e a slight cold in ma heid.
ALBERT (*untactfully*): You've got cold feet.
EMMA: Instead of talking nonsense, have either of you two got half-a-crown? (*To Daphne*) That was what you wanted, wasn't it?
DAPHNE: Yes; so stupid of me. I *had* to get a taxi from the station—no buses about—and I couldn't very well walk, could I?
EMMA (*looking at her high-heeled shoes*): No, you couldn't very well walk.

[*Daphne automatically hands her cases to Emma, who takes them as automatically.*]

DAPHNE: And the silly taximan had no change. . . .
ALBERT (*who has been looking in his pockets*): Half-a-crown? No! Now, Carnoustie. . . ?
CARN: Wha?
ALBERT: Half-a-croon, quick!
CARN (*putting hand faint-heartedly into pocket*): I ha'ena'. . . .
ALBERT (*cutting in*): Come on!

[*Carnoustie reluctantly produces the half-crown and holds it out to Daphne.*]

DAPHNE (*taking it*): Thanks a lot. Remind me to give it you back, won't you?
CARN (*staggered*): *Remind* you! (*Definitely.*) I *wull*!

[*Daphne hands half-crown to Emma, with an easy smile.*]

DAPHNE: Do you mind giving that to the man, Aunt Emma?

[*Emma realises that she is landed with Daphne's cases, puts them down angrily, takes half-crown, and is about to exit, before she recalls herself.*]

EMMA: Albert! (*She gives him the half-crown and nods towards door left.*)
ALBERT: O.K. (*He exits left.*)
DAPHNE (*to Carnoustie*): I didn't quite catch your name, I'm afraid.
CARN: Nae-one everr does. (*Slowly.*) Ma firrrst name is Carrr-noust-ie.
DAPHNE (*with a smile*): That's a lovely name. But it's a bit of a mouthful, isn't it?
CARN: Ma intimate frriends ha'e been known to ca' me "Carrrnie". . . .
DAPHNE (*smiling*): That's better.
CARN: . . . But I'm no' in favour o' it.
DAPHNE: Oh! (*To Emma.*) Albert's charming, isn't he, Aunt Emma? I'm sure he'll make Shirley very happy.
EMMA: *Are* you? How's your mother keeping?

[*Albert enters left.*]

DAPHNE: Oh, she's better, much better. But ever so

disappointed she couldn't come to the wedding. Aunt Emma. . . ?

EMMA: What?

DAPHNE: Would you mind. . . ? I'm just dying for a cup of tea. . . .

EMMA: Cup of. . . ! (*She marches off to the kitchen door, fuming.*)

[*As she reaches it, Edie enters with a tray of crockery.*]

DAPHNE: Aunt Edie!

EDIE: Little Daphne!

[*Edie automatically thrusts tray at Emma, who has no option but to take it, angrily. Edie kisses Daphne.*]

EDIE: My . . . but you look different!

DAPHNE: It's four years since you last saw me, Aunt Edie.

EDIE: And what a lovely little girl you were, Daphne lamb!

EMMA (*tersely—having put down tray on table*): We all change. (*She exits right.*)

EDIE: You've met Albert and Carnegie, haven't you?

DAPHNE: Oh yes. But where's Shirley and Uncle Henry?

EDIE (*getting tablecloth from drawer in sideboard*): Shirley'll be back any time now. She's having her hair done. And your Uncle's outside with his ferrets.

DAPHNE (*moving towards kitchen*): I'll go and. . . . (*She stops.*) No, I. . . . Do you think it'd be all right if I went upstairs for a wash. I'm sure I must look awful!

[*She looks at Carnoustie for the necessary denial—but Carnoustie only gulps.*]

EDIE: Of course, love! You know your way, don't you?

DAPHNE (*she is about to pick up hatbox*): Oh . . . and, Aunt Edie, I've brought you a little present. (*To Albert.*) You're not seeing yours till Shirley comes!

[*She has opened box, and takes out a little parcel, then closes lid loosely.*]

EDIE (*delighted*): Oh, Daphne, you shouldn't have bothered.

DAPHNE: It's your favourite scent, Auntie. Californian Poppy.

EDIE (*taking parcel—overwhelmed*): Oh, Daphne!

[*She is about to kiss her again, when Emma's voice is heard off right.*]

EMMA (*off*): Edie! You've forgotten the knives and forks!

EDIE (*fluttering*): I'm coming, Emma. (*To Daphne.*) I was going to . . . but perhaps, one of the boys would carry your bags up for you. . . ? (*She puts her parcel in a drawer and darts out right.*)

DAPHNE: Would one of you. . . ? (*She glances at the cases.*)

ALBERT (*to Carnoustie*): Toss you for it. Heads you, tails me. (*Spinning coin.*) Blast! Heads . . . you!

[*Carnoustie apprehensively lifts cases.*]

No, I'm damned if I'll trust you!

[*He grabs the hat-box, lifts it up, and immediately all its contents are strewn all over the floor.*]

DAPHNE (*with a little shriek*): Oh, my . . . er . . . things!

[*Albert and Carnoustie gaze at the "things"—which are mostly very delightful and intriguing articles of underwear.*]

ALBERT: Blimey! (*Holding Carnoustie back.*) Stand back, eager!
DAPHNE: Well! (*To Albert who is now on the floor, picking up garments and looking at them.*) Aren't you careless!
ALBERT: I don't know. But I'm curious. (*Holding up a transparent nightdress.*) You gettin' married, too?
CARN: Albert, wha' are ye saying, man?
ALBERT (*holding up a pair of panties*): Didn't you tell me you wanted a new pair of pants?
CARN (*looking away*): Och . . . I'm shamed. . . !
DAPHNE (*snatching pants from Albert*): Give them to me. (*A little piqued—to Carnoustie.*) There's nothing to be "shamed" about. Don't Scotch girls *wear* panties?
CARN: I wudna' know.
ALBERT: Don't you believe him, Daphne.
DAPHNE (*holding out panties for Carnoustie's inspection*): They're perfectly respectable. And *real* silk.
CARN (*turning away*): Ay. I've nae doot they'll be silk.
DAPHNE: Well, my God, what do you expect me to wear next my skin? Harris Tweed?

[*Albert is putting articles into bag during this—doing it very carefully. Daphne kneels beside him and indignantly begins to bustle the garments back into the hat-box again.*]

Thanks, Albert. (*To Carnoustie.*) Come on, give a hand.

[*Carnoustie bends reluctantly to pick up a garment on the floor near him.*]

Damn! Now I've laddered my stocking. (*She rises.*)

[*The garment Carnoustie has picked up is a pair of "falsies" He looks at them in despair. Daphne looking at the ladder draws her skirt well up above her knee.*]

ALBERT: Oh, what a shame! Can I. . . ? (*He is hopefully about to inspect the damage as:—*)

[*The door left opens, and Shirley Hornett sails into the room. Shirley is about twenty-two years of age; pretty, without Daphne's glamour. She is a pleasant-natured girl, but occasionally one sees "Emma" coming out in her.*]

SHIRLEY (*taking in what appears to be the "situation" and not not liking it*): *Well!*
ALBERT (*seeing her—jumping to his feet*): Shirl!
DAPHNE (*overlapping*): Shirley!

[*Carnoustie, still holding "falsies" in both hands unconsciously, merely stands looking at Shirley.*]

I can't get up for a minute, darling. I've laddered my stocking.
ALBERT (*overlapping*): Sweetheart! (*He puts his arms round her and kisses her; but Shirley pushes him away.*)
SHIRLEY (*rather "boity-toity"*): I'm sorry if I've interrupted something. (*Going down to Daphne.*) How are you, Daphne? (*She gives her a peck on the cheek.*) Having fun, aren't you? (*She sniffs, and turns to look at Carnoustie.*)
ALBERT (*coming down and putting his arm around her*): Oh, Shirl, it's good to see you again.
SHIRLEY (*moving away a little*): Albert, aren't you going to introduce me? (*She looks towards Carnoustie.*)
ALBERT: Of course. Shirley, this is Carnoustie—I've

told you about him in my letters. Carnoustie Bligh. Carnoustie, this is Shirley.

SHIRLEY (*rather icily, as she holds out her hand*): How do you do?

CARN (*still holding "falsies" in one hand as he shakes with the other*): I'm pleased to meet you.

SHIRLEY (*after giving him a wan smile*): It's all right, Mr. Bligh; (*With a wave of the hand to the "falsies".*) you can finish dressing! (*She crosses up to kitchen door, opens it and calls. . . .*) Mother, I'm back!

[*Carnoustie, after Shirley's taunt, glares at the "falsies", almost dancing with rage; then flings them into the hat-box, and flings himself on to the nearest chair.*]

(*Turning back to the others.*) Well, this *is* a surprise, isn't it? You weren't supposed to be arriving till half-past six. I was coming down to the station to meet you.

ALBERT: We got an earlier train.

SHIRLEY: H'mm! And how long have you been here?

ALBERT: About twenty minutes.

SHIRLEY (*with meaning*): Daphne been here all that time, too? How's Auntie Kate, Daphne?

DAPHNE (*still "fixing" ladder*): I got here five minutes ago, and Mum's very well, thank you very much. (*There is a little "bite" in her tone.*)

SHIRLEY (*to Daphne*): If I'd known *you* were here, I'd have got back sooner.

DAPHNE (*half muttering, as she dabs her stocking*): I'll bet you would.

ALBERT (*moving up to Shirley again, and putting his arms around her and kissing her again*): Oh, darling, I thought you were never coming!

SHIRLEY (*with a glance at Daphne*): You seem to have been passing the time very pleasantly!

ALBERT: Oh . . . darling. . . ! (*He goes into a huddle again.*)

SHIRLEY (*petulantly—as she breaks away*): Albert! My hair! I've just had it done. (*Straightening it.*) I want it to look *something* like tomorrow.

ALBERT: It does, Shirl. Honest, it does! Carnoustie, doesn't it look *something?*

CARN (*practically*): That's no kind of sensible question. Anything has got to look something, and. . . .

ALBERT: There you are! (*Glaring at Carnoustie.*) Even Carnoustie says it's lovely.

DAPHNE (*crossing to Shirley and handing her a parcel—which she has removed from bag*): From Mum and me to you both. With all our love and best wishes for your future happiness together.

SHIRLEY (*after a tiny pause while she struggles with her better nature—smiling*): Thank you, Daphne. (*She gives her a genuine kiss.*)

ALBERT: Thank you, Daphne. (*He is about to kiss her, but the wise Daphne grabs his hand and shakes it heartily.*)

[*Shirley's eyes are on parcel she is holding.*]

(*After a quick look towards Shirley—to Daphne, quietly.*) I see what you mean!

SHIRLEY: M'mm?

ALBERT: Nothing, darling.

SHIRLEY: Shall we open it now?

DAPHNE (*tactfully*): Wait till I'm out of the room. (*To Carnoustie.*) Do you mind? (*Indicating cases as she moves towards door left.*)

CARN (*stupidly*): No' in the least.

DAPHNE (*at door*): If you would be so good?

[*As Carnoustie still looks blank, Albert gestures to him.*

Carnoustie still looks blank. Albert gestures again. Carnoustie sees the light.]

CARN: I comprrrehend. The two o' ye want to be left alone.

[*Daphne giggles and exits left. Carnoustie prepares to follow.*]

ALBERT (*as Carnoustie goes*): Now then, Cassanova! Behave yourself!

CARN: If it were no' beneath ma deegnity I'd offerr ye the same advice. (*He exits left.*)

ALBERT (*now they are alone*): Darling!

SHIRLEY: Oh, Albert! (*They go into a big embrace.*)

[*Edie enters with knives and forks, sees the embrace and darts off.*]

ALBERT (*at last*): Happy?

SHIRLEY (*breaking away*): I don't know. I was . . . until I came in here just now and saw you . . . and Daphne . . . and that . . . that . . . disgusting Scotchman you've brought with you.

ALBERT: Disgusting? Carnoustie? What's there disgusting about him?

SHIRLEY: Standing there, holding Daphne's . . . er . . . thingummybobs in his hand as bold as brass! (*Working herself up a little.*) Yes, and you were as bad, if not worse. Heaven only knows what *you* were up to!

ALBERT: Listen, honey. . . . You've got it all wrong You see, Daphne's hat-box burst open, and . . .

SHIRLEY: But I blame Daphne as much as either of you. She's clever. She can lead any man astray.

ALBERT: She'll be *damned* clever if she leads Carnoustie.

SHIRLEY: But when I see you carrying on as you were, Albert Tufnell, it frightens me. It makes me wonder whether, perhaps, mother isn't right, after all, in what she says.

ALBERT: What does she say?

SHIRLEY: She's always rubbing it in about you being a sailor, and " you know what sailors are—a girl in every port ".

ALBERT: Shirl, you don't believe that about me, do you?

SHIRLEY (*petulantly*): Well, I've tried not to, but when I see you carrying on as you were just now . . . the day before your wedding, too . . . well, it just makes me wonder, that's all.

ALBERT: Listen, Shirley, I give you my word, we weren't doing anything wrong. Well, how *could* we, anyway, with your mother and Aunt Edie bobbing in and out?

SHIRLEY (*nattering*): I see! So, if it hadn't been for them bobbing in and out, as you call it, Heaven knows what might have happened. Is that it?

ALBERT (*patiently*): Listen, darling. . . .

SHIRLEY: It's perhaps as well I came in when I did!

ALBERT (*suddenly snapping*): P'raps it *is*. Five more minutes and we might all have been rolling stark naked on the hearth-rug!

SHIRLEY (*dissolving into tears with a slow, rising wail*): Oh, Al-bert!

ALBERT (*penitent immediately*): Sweetheart . . . I didn't mean. . . .

SHIRLEY (*weeping loudly in his arms*): *Oh . . . Al-bert. . .* !

ALBERT (*nearly weeping himself*): Honeysuckle. . . !

[*Shirley weeps louder than ever. Enter Emma, from kitchen.*]

EMMA (*as she enters*): *Now* what. . . ? (*Seeing Shirley in tears, and speaking with great satisfaction.*) Aaah! This is a *fine* kick-off, isn't it? *What* have I always said? And if he has you crying your eyes out on your wedding eve, what's he going to do when you've been married five years?

ALBERT (*desperately—as he tries to comfort Shirley*): You don't understand, Ma. It was just a little misunderstanding.

EMMA (*gloating*): Little misunderstanding, eh? There'll be lots more little misunderstandings *very* soon, if I'm any judge. Little misunderstanding about what, may I ask?

SHIRLEY (*calming down a little*): It was nothing, Mum. . . .

ALBERT (*snapping lightly at Emma*): And anyway it doesn't concern you.

EMMA (*snapping at him*): Don't you talk to me like that! Telling me my own daughter's 'appiness doesn't concern me!

ALBERT: I didn't mean. . . .

EMMA: She isn't your wife yet, remember!

SHIRLEY: Stop picking on Albert, mother.

EMMA (*to Shirley*): That's right! *You* turn on me now!

ALBERT: Listen, Ma, if you'll just leave us alone for two minutes. . . .

EMMA: You can settle your differences later if you don't mind. We've got to get the table laid. Seeing you're all here, we might as well get tea over and done with. (*Calling.*) Edie!

EDIE (*in kitchen*): Coming, Emma.

EMMA (*looking round*): Where's Daphne?

SHIRLEY: She's gone upstairs.

EMMA: And that . . . er . . . (*To Albert*) Your friend?
ALBERT: Carnoustie's gone with her.
EMMA: *What!*
ALBERT: I mean, he's taken her bags up for her.

[*Edie enters from kitchen with knives and forks. She and Emma begin laying table.*]

EMMA (*sharply*): Shirley! (*Pointing to door left.*) Up you go and look after Daphne.
SHIRLEY: But, Mum. . . .
EMMA (*quickly*): Shirley 'Ornett!
SHIRLEY (*after a long shrug of the shoulders*): O.K. (*She is moving left.*)
ALBERT (*he tries at all times to be cheerful*): Shall I be opening the parcel, Shirl? (*He picks it up.*)
SHIRLEY (*remembering*): Oh yes, do! (*She exits left.*)
EMMA (*nattering*): "Shirl"! What's the matter with "Shirley"? It's the name she was given at her baptism. (*With a snort.*) "Shirl"!!

[*Albert looks at her for a moment, but decides to say nothing. He is tussling with string on parcel.*]

What have you got there?
ALBERT: It's a wedding present from Daphne and her mother.
EMMA (*crossing to him*): Here, give it to me. I'll undo it for you.
ALBERT: It's all right, Ma, I've done it. (*He has. He removes the string.*)
EMMA (*taking the parcel from him nevertheless*): Men never were any good at undoing parcels. (*She ignores Albert, as she removes wrappings from parcel, and produces a rose bowl from the box.*) H'mm! Very nice, I'm

sure! (*She is turned away from Albert. He can only see the bowl with difficulty.*) Isn't it, Edie?

EDIE: Oh, it's beautiful! Isn't it, Albert?

ALBERT (*standing on tiptoes for a moment and looking over Emma's shoulder*): Lovely!

EMMA: We'll put it here (*Sideboard.*) until Shirley's seen it and then it can go with all the other presents. (*Handing box, paper and string to Edie.*) Here, Edie, take this out into the kitchen and tell Henry to leave his blessed ferrets and come in.

EDIE: Yes, Emma. (*She goes with alacrity.*)

EMMA (*looking at table*): Now, let me see. . . . Oh yes! (*She goes off to kitchen.*)

[*Albert stands looking after her for a moment, then he moves up to sideboard, very slowly. He looks at the rose bowl for a moment, then picks it up. He holds it in both hands and stands quite still, thinking. He then gives a big sigh and puts bowl down again. He moves down to fireplace and stands looking down into fire. Carnoustie enters from left. He does not look very happy. He wanders down to beside Albert. Albert turns and sees him.*]

ALBERT (*as he did before, pats Carnoustie on the shoulder and smiles at him—a little wanly, perhaps*): How are you, son?

[*Carnoustie tries to smile back. Henry enters from kitchen —his jacket over his arm.*]

HENRY (*cheerfully*): Hullo, there!

ALBERT (*equally cheerfully*): 'Lo, Pop!

HENRY (*taking his slippers from near fireplace; sitting, removing boots and putting slippers on—speaking a little apprehensively, perhaps?*): Everything all right?

ALBERT: Yes, thanks, Pop.

HENRY: That's right. (*To Carnoustie.*) Tea'll be in in a minute. (*To Albert.*) Gettin' nervous, Albert?
ALBERT: Nervous?
HENRY: 'Bout tomorrow.
ALBERT: I. . . . (*He changes the subject abruptly.*) How are your ferrets, Pop?
HENRY (*blinking*): Eh? (*The sudden change of subject bewilders him for a moment.*) Ferrets. . . ? Oh, they're fine, Albert. You must come and have a look at 'em after tea. I've just been cleaning 'em out.
ALBERT: Aye, I'd like to.
HENRY (*with a side-glance at him*): Well, I think I'll pop upstairs and have a wash.

[*Emma enters with more things for tea-table.*]

EMMA (*as she enters—to Henry*): Henry, I thought I told you to go up and wash.
HENRY (*with a touch of irritation*): I'm just going.
EMMA: I don't know what you want to go messin' about with them smelly things for, just before tea-time. (*Pointing.*) And them boots don't belong there. Back kitchen's the place for them. Or, better still, out in the yard.
HENRY (*as he picks up boots—to Albert*): Eee! Wait till you've got a woman chasin' you around, lad; you'll know you're born then! (*He goes off into kitchen with boots.*)
EMMA: I only hope Shirley puts her foot down right from the start. You'll take a bit of keeping in order if all I hear of sailors is true. (*She is arranging table.*)

[*Henry returns—without boots.*]

HENRY: I'll go and get my wash.
EMMA (*pointing to jacket which he has left over chair*): You'll hang that jacket in its proper place, first.

HENRY (*impatiently*): For the Lord's. . . . (*He pulls up, remembering the presence of the boys. He picks jacket up and hangs it behind kitchen door, then exits left.*)

[*Albert has not been unaware of all the foregoing. After Henry's exit he produces a packet of cigarettes, and is extracting one slowly.*]

EMMA (*seeing this*): You don't want to be lighting cigarettes now. Tea'll be in in a minute. (*She goes out into kitchen.*)

[*Albert, with no sign of irritation, replaces cigarettes and puts packet away. Almost unconsciously he whistles the first four lines of " A Life on the Ocean Wave ". Then he turns his head, looks at Carnoustie, who turns and looks at him.*]

ALBERT (*automatically—as he pats Carnoustie's knee*): How are you, son?

[*Shirley enters from left. She comes straight down to Albert, ruffles his hair affectionately, and kisses the top of his head.*]

SHIRLEY (*ill-humour gone*): Hello, darling!

[*Albert is, at once, all smiles again. Carnoustie rises from settee to make room for her.*]

No, don't move (*Slowly and smiling.*) Car-nous-tie. That's right, isn't it?

CARN: Aye.

SHIRLEY: I like it. But it takes a bit of remembering. (*Still to Carnoustie.*) I . . . I'm sorry if I was a bit snappy when I came in. I . . . er. . . .

CARN (*blushing with embarrassment*). Och! You werena'. . . .

SHIRLEY: Oh, Albert, I wish you had a lovely Scotch accent like that.

CARN (*more embarrassed*): Och . . . I. . . .

SHIRLEY (*to Carnoustie*): I don't wonder Daphne's fallen for you in such a big way.

CARN: Och, I. . . . (*Then realising what Shirley has said.*) What!!

SHIRLEY: Of course she *loves* Scotchmen.

CARN I'm no' a Scotchman.

SHIRLEY (*forgetting her manners*): Wha'!

ALBERT: Couldn't you tell he was a Cockney?

CARN: I'm a *Scots*man.

SHIRLEY: That's what I said. Anyway, she *has* fallen for you. But I warned her.

CARN: Warrrned about wha'?

SHIRLEY: You. It's the quiet ones like your sort that do the damage.

CARN: I ha'e done naeone damage in ma life.

ALBERT: Then it's high time you began.

[*Emma enters from kitchen with large teapot and water jug. Edie follows, carrying a wooden chair which she places at table.*]

EMMA (*as she enters—almost affably*): Now come on, everybody. Get sat down. Bring your chairs up. (*Crossing to door left and calling.*) Daphne! Henry! Come along. Tea's in.

[*The boys have each brought a chair to the table but are not yet seated.*]

(*Back at table which is laid for seven.*) Now, let's see. . . Albert, you sit there, (*Indicating a place; then looking at Carnoustie.*) and Car . . . (*She cannot get the name.*) will you sit next to him?

[*Daphne and Henry come in from left. Daphne has her arm linked with Henry's. Shirley has moved to place other side of Albert and is about to sit.*]

Shirley, you come here—your usual place. (*She indicates a chair a long way from Albert.*)
SHIRLEY (*protesting*): Oh, but mother, can't I. . . ?
EMMA (*tapping back of chair she indicated*): You'll have plenty of time for holding hands after tomorrow. Daphne! (*She indicates chair next to Carnoustie.*)

[*Shirley goes to her place. Daphne to hers. Carnoustie bends away from Daphne as if he feared she was going to attack him.*]

DAPHNE (*as he does so*): It's all right. I've got a slight cold in the head myself.
EMMA (*to Henry who is not yet seated*): Henry, what are you dithering about at? Sit yourself down. And you, Edie.
EDIE (*fluttering*): I was just wondering if there was anything else we wanted from the kitchen. (*She sits on wooden chair she brought in. Henry sits the other side of Daphne.*)
DAPHNE (*as he does so*): That's right, Uncle Henry, you sit by me.
SHIRLEY: Help yourself, won't you, Carnoustie? And you, Albert.

[*Edie has been pouring tea which is passed round. Emma is putting cold ham on to plates.*]

EMMA: Everybody had better help themselves. We

don't stand on ceremony here. . . . (*And in the same breath.*) Henry, you don't need that thing stuck down your throat. (*She snatches a paper serviette which Henry has tucked in his collar and puts it in his lap.*) I'm tired of telling you about that trick. Don't let me catch you doing it at the Reception tomorrow. . . . (*And in the same breath.*) Everybody 'appy?

[*They all proceed to get on with the meal.*]

DAPHNE: You're having the reception here, Shirley tells me, Aunt Emma?

EMMA: No, we're not. There's too many invited. Much better having it at Banfield's Tea Rooms. They've got a nice big place for functions.

DAPHNE: How many *are* coming, Shirley?

EMMA: Thirty, as far as we know. But there's sure to be one or two unexpecteds. There usually is.

DAPHNE: Many on your side, Albert?

ALBERT: No . . . I . . . I haven't anybody to come. Not a soul. (*Carnoustie coughs.*) Except Carnoustie, of course.

DAPHNE (*awkwardly*): Oh!

SHIRLEY: Albert's an orphan, Daphne. Aren't you, Albert?

ALBERT: That's right. An orphan of the storm.

[*Edie suddenly gives a little sniff, and quickly dabs her eyes with her handkerchief.*]

EMMA (*to her*): Good Lord! What's the matter with *you*?

EDIE: I'm sorry, Emma. It was thinking of poor Albert being an orphan of the storm and having nobody at the wedding.

ALBERT (*cheerfully*): Don't you worry about me, Aunt

Edie. I'll be all right. I'll have you there, won't I. You'll back me up.

EDIE: I . . . I . . . (*She jumps up quickly. Dabs her eyes.*) 'Scuse me! (*She darts off into the kitchen.*)

EMMA (*almost snapping at Albert*): What did you have to go and say that for?

ALBERT (*mystified*): Say what?

EMMA About her going to the wedding.

ALBERT: Well, what. . . ?

SHIRLEY: Aunt Edie isn't going, Albert.

ALBERT: Not going?

SHIRLEY: No, you see she . . . she doesn't want to. You see. . . .

EMMA (*sharply*): Never mind about that now. We don't want to go over all that again. Henry, pass Car . . . that lad . . . some more bread.

ALBERT: But why doesn't she want. . . ?

EMMA (*firmly*): I said we wouldn't talk about that now, if you don't mind. Now come on, get on with your teas. There's a lot to do tonight, yet. (*Loudly, as kitchen door opens.*) Ssssh!

[*Edie returns with jug of hot water. She has regained control now.*]

EDIE (*with just a little sniff—awkwardly*): I've brought some hot water, Emma.

EMMA: H'm! Thank you, we needed some. (*She puts water in pot.*)

[*Edie sits at table again. Meal proceeds in a rather obvious silence, which everyone would* like *to break, but no one does.*]

CARN (*at last, and practically*): Cuid I have anither cup of tea?

[*The sound of his voice makes everyone jump.*]

EMMA (*recovering*): What?
CARN (*remembering his manners*): " Please ".
EMMA: Henry, pass his cup.

[*The tension is now broken.*]

And when you've had your tea, Henry, you'd better go upstairs and have your bath; then the water will get nice and hot for me to have one before I go to bed.
HENRY: But I. . . .
EMMA (*sweeping on*): We won't all be able to have one in the morning. There won't be time. You and me'll have ours tonight. Albert, you and (*Having a shot at it.*) Carninskie will be able to have one at Mrs. Lack's, I expect.
HENRY: But listen. . . .
EMMA: Now don't start upsetting things. I've got enough on my mind. Shirley, we've got a lot to finish off tonight; you and me and Edie.
DAPHNE: Can I help, Aunt Emma?
EMMA: Yes, Daphne, you can. (*To Albert.*) And you boys'll just have to sit quiet and keep out of the way.
ALBERT: Well, as a matter of fact, we've arranged to go out, Ma.
EMMA (*disapproving at once*): What?
ALBERT: And I was going to ask Pop to come with us.
EMMA: Go out . . . where?
ALBERT: Two lads from our ship live here . . . they travelled up on the same train as us . . . and we arranged to meet 'em at eight o'clock at the White Hart.
SHIRLEY (*petulantly*): Oh, Albert!
ALBERT (*to her pleasantly*): Well, it doesn't matter,

does it? I knew you'd have a lot to do, and Ma's just said we'd have to keep out of the way.

SHIRLEY: Yes, but. . . .

EMMA: Well, of course, you'll suit yourselves, but it seems a pity to me if all you can think about the night before your wedding is drinking.

ALBERT (*still pleasantly*): It isn't the drink; but it'll be nice to see the lads.

EMMA: See the. . . ! Good Lord, it isn't an hour since you left 'em!

ALBERT: I know, but. . . . We won't be long. We'll be back by nine or half past.

HENRY: And after all, Emma, it is his last night of freedom, more or less.

ALBERT (*startled by the remark*): Eh?

HENRY: Oh, I know you've got your three months of service yet, but after that. . . !

EMMA: After that, what?

HENRY (*uncomfortably*): Well. . . .

EMMA: Anyone would think he was going to prison to hear *you* talk.

HENRY (*as before*): Well. . . .

DAPHNE: Can I have another piece of bread and butter, Aunt Emma?

EMMA (*her mind still on Henry*): Help yourself. If Albert here, has as cosy a time as *you've* had during his married life, he can consider himself lucky, and I hope he'll show Shirley a bit more appreciation than you've ever shown me.

HENRY (*wearily*): Now don't let's start on that. You've been telling me how lucky I am practically since the day we were married. Well, if it'll please you, I'll take your word for it. Edie, pass the mustard.

EMMA: Now that's enough! (*To Albert.*) So that's settled, then, you're stopping in, eh?

SHIRLEY: Of course they are, Mum. Now let's stop all this bickering, for goodness' sake.

ALBERT: But, Shirl. . . .

SHIRLEY: Now what?

ALBERT: Listen, what's the point of our staying in? *You* won't have time to be bothered with us . . . none of you.

SHIRLEY (*plaintively*): Well, it isn't my fault, is it?

ALBERT: Of course it isn't. I'm not grumbling. I realise how. . . .

SHIRLEY: If you knew how much there is to be done before tomorrow morning. . . .

ALBERT: Well, can *I* help with anything if I *do* stay?

SHIRLEY: No, Albert, they're not the kind of things you *could* do.

ALBERT (*with the slightest touch of annoyance*): Then, why not let Pop, Carnoustie and me, get out of the way while you do them?

EMMA (*really snapping now*): If Shirley says she wants you here, I should have thought that would have been enough.

ALBERT: But, Ma. . . .

EMMA: Isn't it natural she should want you here?

ALBERT: No, not if I'll be in the way.

EDIE: Emma . . . I don't want to interfere. . . .

EMMA: Then don't! (*To Albert.*) Shirley doesn't want you going out getting drunk the minute you get here.

CARN: Mrs. Hornett, I've never been drunk in ma life.

EMMA: I'm talking to Albert, Carnaskie.

SHIRLEY: I never said anything about them getting drunk, Mum. It's just that. . . .

ALBERT: That what?

SHIRLEY (*snapping*): Well, I think you ought to stay in, that's all. If Carnoustie wants to go. . . .

CARN: I must. I told the lads I'd go.

SHIRLEY (*rising and moving quickly to fireplace*): Well, Albert, I suppose you'll do what you think best, but. . . . (*She is near to tears*)

HENRY: If he has any sense he will.

EMMA: You keep quiet. You've said enough as it is. And let me tell you this. Whether Albert goes or not, *you're* not going.

DAPHNE (*who has been watching all this, but remaining tactfully out of it*): Can I have another cup of tea, Aunt Emma?

EMMA (*ignoring her—still to Henry*): There's plenty I can find here for you to do without your going out drinking. Heaven knows it's little enough interest you've taken in your daughter's wedding so far! Shirley, come and sit down, and finish your tea.

SHIRLEY: I don't want any more. I'm too upset.

ALBERT (*rising and coming to her*): Now listen, honey. . . .

SHIRLEY: I don't want to listen, Albert. I know how I feel about it, and that's that! If you want to go, go.

EMMA: That's no way to talk. It's just giving in to him.

HENRY (*to Emma*): Can't you never keep your mouth shut!

EMMA: 'Enry 'Ornett!!

ALBERT: Go and sit down, Shirl; there's a good girl.

SHIRLEY: But, Albert. . . .

ALBERT (*firmly*): Go and sit down.

[*Shirley, after a sniff, sits at table.*]

DAPHNE: Can I have another cup of tea, please, Aunt Emma?

EMMA (*picking up teapot—to Albert*): And what are *you* going to do? Have you made up your mind?

ALBERT: Yes. (*He moves to table.*) I'm going to finish my tea. (*He sits.*)

HENRY (*rising, and speaking firmly to Albert*): If you have any sense, lad, you'll do what you want to do. Don't make the mistake I did, or you won't be able to call your soul your own.

EMMA (*rising furiously—teapot in hand*): 'Enry 'Ornett. . . !

HENRY (*topping her—as he moves to door right*): I'm going out to my ferrets! (*He exits right.*)

EMMA (*putting teapot down on sideboard as she goes to door right—calling after Henry*): 'Enry 'Ornett! You'll come back here this minute, or I'll come and. . . !

EDIE (*with a scream*): *Emma!* The teapot!

EMMA (*spinning round*): What!

EDIE (*rushing to sideboard*): The sideboard. . . !!

EMMA (*almost overlapping*): Oh, my. . . !

[*She reaches sideboard at the same time as Edie. She grabs the teapot—Edie grabs also, but only gets the lid.*]

The curtain falls.

ACT TWO

Scene I

Scene: The same night.

Time: Nine-thirty.

As the curtain rises, Emma, Edie, Shirley and Daphne are discovered hovering around a large wooden box, into which they are placing the last of the wedding presents. Edie is gazing thoughtfully at a hideous china ornament which she holds at arm's length.

EMMA: Well, thank goodness that's nearly finished. You've done very well for presents, Shirley.

[*Shirley, without replying, moves disconsolately to fire-place, and looks anxiously at clock.*]

'Specially when you consider they're all from *our* side of the family! (*As Shirley does not reply.*) H'mm! (*Then turning to Edie, who is still holding ornament.*) What are you trying to do to that thing? Mesmerise it?

EDIE: I was just looking at it. I was wondering what it's supposed to be.

DAPHNE: I'd given up wondering.

EMMA: You'd better ask Florrie Lack what it is. She gave it to them. (*She takes ornament from Edie and puts it carefully into box.*) Now, is that the lot?

DAPHNE: Looks like it.

EMMA: Good! Now, Henry'll have to see this box gets safely down to Banfield's Tea Rooms first thing in the morning. They're going to set them out on a special table so everyone can see 'em. And, Edie . . . !

EDIE: Yes, Emma?

EMMA: You've made up your mind that you're not coming to the Church tomorrow, haven't you?

EDIE (*beginning to whimper*): I couldn't, Emma. I couldn't bear it. Don't ask me.

EMMA (*shortly*): I'm *not* asking you. I'm just *telling* you, as you're not coming to the Church, you'd better get yourself straight down to Banfield's as soon as you're ready and see they set the presents out nicely. See?

EDIE: Yes, Emma.

EMMA: Yes, and see the best ones are well to the front: and the further to the back that thing from Florrie Lack is, the better.

DAPHNE: You can put the rose bowl from mother and me at the back, Aunt Edie.

EDIE Oooh! I'll do no such thing. It's beautiful, isn't it, Shirley?

[*Shirley, who is near to tears, can only nod her head. Emma and Daphne look at her. She is turned away from them.*]

EMMA (*significantly nodding her head towards kitchen—to the others*): I think a cup of tea wouldn't be a bad idea. I know I'm ready for one. Edie!

EDIE: I'll make some right away.

DAPHNE: I'll come and help you, Aunt Edie.

EDIE (*innocently*): No, thank you, love. I can manage.

EMMA (*under her breath*): Fool!

EDIE (*blankly*): Eh?

[*Emma, with broad gestures, indicates that she wants to be left alone with Shirley.*]

(*Blandly.*) Oh, I see. You want us *both* to go.

EMMA (*turning her eyes heavenwards*): For the love of. . . !

DAPHNE: Come on, Aunt Edie. (*Leading her towards kitchen.*) And when we've had our tea I'm going to get you to read my cup.

EDIE: Oh, but. . . .

DAPHNE: Now, you know how good you are at it.

EDIE: Yes, but. . . . Well, you'll have to ask your Aunt Emma. You don't believe in the teacups, do you, Emma?

EMMA: A lot of tommyrot, if you ask me.

EDIE (*to Daphne as they go*): She's a "*What the stars foretell*" fan, really.

[*Daphne and Edie exit right. Emma looks across at Shirley, then moves down to her.*]

EMMA: Now, listen to me, Shirley 'Ornett. You can just stop pulling a long face.

SHIRLEY: Oh, mother, don't start on me again, please. I can't stand any more of it.

EMMA: It's no use your talking like that, my girl. "Can't stand any more of it", eh? Then, all I can say is, Lord help you; because as far as I can see your troubles haven't really started yet!

SHIRLEY: If only Albert would come back. . . ! (*She looks at clock.*)

EMMA: You should never have let him go. You should have put your foot down. I *told* you, didn't I?

SHIRLEY (*weeping*): I did put it down; but he went just the same!

EMMA: Well, you'll have to learn to put it down harder. You can't reason with men. You've just got to *train* 'em.

SHIRLEY: Oh, but. . . .

EMMA: That's what I've had to do with your father, and look at the result! He may answer back a bit now and again, same as he did tonight at tea; but he comes to heel all right. He's as happy as a lark fiddling with his ferrets, instead of wasting his money in public houses.

SHIRLEY: I wish you liked Albert a bit more, mother.

EMMA: And *I* wish I knew more about him. No parents, no relations . . . dragged up in an Orphanage; *and* a sailor into the bargain! What can he know about " home life "?

SHIRLEY: But there's nothing he wants more than to settle down.

EMMA: Well . . . so long as he *does* settle; but . . . you know what sailors are! And he hasn't done much settling down tonight, has he? Isn't in the house five minutes before he's off out drinking. (*Looking at clock.*) Yes, and look at the time! I told Florrie Lack those two would be round at her place at ten o'clock, and not a minute later. And it's well past half-past nine already.

SHIRLEY: Oh dear! And Albert said he'd be back by nine o'clock. I've got to have a talk with him before he goes to Mrs. Lack's. I mustn't see him in the morning, before the wedding, must I?

EMMA: That you mustn't. Well, I suppose I'd better send your father round to the White Hart to fetch him back. Nice start off, isn't it?

SHIRLEY: Mum. . . ?

EMMA: Yes?

SHIRLEY: I . . . I haven't said anything to Albert yet about . . . Number Twenty-Four.

EMMA: Why not?

SHIRLEY: Well, after tea, he was talking about us going over to Badcaster when we come back from our honeymoon—and having a look round for a little house, or a flat.

EMMA: You should have told him then.

SHIRLEY: I was a bit frightened to.

EMMA: What's there to be frightened about? Good Lord!

SHIRLEY: It's just that. . . . Perhaps I ought to have waited till he'd got here, and talked it over with him. . . .

[*Enter Daphne with tea things, followed by Edie.*]

DAPHNE: Here we are! Shall I pour out, Aunt Emma?

[*Mrs. Lack is heard calling off right.*]

MRS. LACK: Are you there, Emma?

EMMA: Now, what. . . ?

EDIE: It's only Mrs. Lack, Emma.

[*Mrs. Lack appears in doorway right.*]

MRS. LACK: That's right, Edie; it's only me. (*Almost cheerfully.*) And I've got bad news. Can I sit down? (*Sitting.*) We're in a nice mess now.

EMMA: Why, what's the matter?

MRS. LACK: Our Rita. (*With a show of surprise.*) Oh, were you just going to have a cuppa?

EMMA (*shortly*): Get another cup, Edie.

[*Edie exits to kitchen.*]

MRS. LACK: Oh no, Emma; I didn't . . . I wasn't. . . . Well, thank you very much.

EMMA: What about Rita?

MRS. LACK: Measles!

EMMA: What!

MRS. LACK: Measles. She's got 'em.
EMMA: Well, of all the stupid. . . !
SHIRLEY: That means she can't be a bridesmaid!
MRS. LACK: 'Fraid so, love. I mean to say, she couldn't very well, could she? You remember, Emma, I told you she stayed away from school this afternoon with a headache? Well, when I left you I went up to have a look at her in bed, and she was fast asleep, and you'd 'ave sworn there was nothing the matter with her. Then about half an hour ago I heard her calling for me. I went up to her, and—my God—you should have seen her! 'Orrid, she looked; proper 'orrid! We've got to do something about this, I says; and I went across to Nurse Smith, and she just took one look at her and "Measles", she said. Just like that. *I* said to her, "Nurse, it can't be! Rita's got to be a bridesmaid tomorrow."

[*Enter Edie with cup and saucer.*]

EDIE (*who has only heard the last sentence*): And a *lovely* bridesmaid she'll be, won't she, Shirley?
MRS. LACK (*continuing*): I said to her, "Nurse, can't you do nothing?" And she said, "Not for measles, I can't, Mrs. Lack."
EDIE (*squeaking*): Measles! Rita hasn't got the. . . !
EMMA (*snapping at her*): Quiet, you!
MRS. LACK: "Only time will cure them," she said. "Time, warmth and opening medicine. Get the doctor in the morning." So there we are!

[*As Daphne hands her a cup of tea.*]

Thank you, love. Oh . . . er . . . excuse me. . . . (*She indicates that she has not "met" Daphne.*) I was so full of my bad news, I didn't realise. . . .

EMMA (*shortly*): This is Daphne, my sister's girl.

MRS. LACK: Oh! You were going to be the *other* bridesmaid with Rita. You'll have to manage on your own now, won't you?

DAPHNE: I'll manage.

SHIRLEY: Oh dear! What will it look like—only one bridesmaid!

MRS. LACK: And Rita would have looked such a picture. She looked lovely in her dress! 'Course she wouldn't, all covered with spots, would she? (*To Emma, after a brief pause.*) Then, of course, there's the boys.

EMMA: What boys?

MRS. LACK: Why, the bridgroom and his best man.

EMMA: Well, what about them?

MRS. LACK: I won't be able to put them up for the night, now.

EMMA (*sharply*): What! Why not? There's no fear of them catching measles.

MRS. LACK: No; but you see there's Evadne. . . . (*To Daphne.*) That's Rita's sister—she's only five, bless her. (*Back to Emma.*) Well, she always sleeps with Rita; but, of course, now I'll have to put her on her own. That means she'll have to go into my spare room, and that's the room I was going to let the lads have.

EMMA: Well, this is a nice "how-do-you-do", I must say! *Now*, what are we going to do?

MRS. LACK: I'm sorry, Emma; but you see how it is, don't you?

EMMA (*shortly*): Yes. I *see*!

MRS. LACK: They'll have to go round to the Rose and Crown after all. And of course they'll have to pay there, won't they? Twelve and six a night without breakfast, I believe it is. 'Course I wasn't going to charge 'em quite as much as that!

EMMA: You. . . ! Here, give me another cup of tea, Edie, for the Lord's sake!

SHIRLEY: Oh dear, everything seems to be going wrong somehow.

MRS. LACK: May as well go wrong before as well as after, eh, Emma? Get used to it, so to speak. Er . . . where is the bridegroom, by the way? Don't tell me he hasn't arrived.

SHIRLEY: Yes, he's arrived, Mrs. Lack. He's gone down to the. . . .

EMMA (*shortly*): He's out?

MRS. LACK: Out? Where?

EMMA: Out! I expect you'll be anxious to get back to Rita?

MRS. LACK (*placidly*): Oh, no. There's no hurry. I've settled her down for the night. She'll be all right. I haven't dared tell her yet that she won't be able to go to the wedding. It'll break her heart, bless her!

EMMA: I suppose *you* won't be able to go, either.

MRS. LACK (*horrified at the suggestion*): What! *Me* not there! I'll be there all right. I was going to ask Edie, as she isn't going to the wedding, if she'd give a look in at Rita now and again.

EDIE: Oooh, but I'm going to the *reception*, Mrs. Lack. It's just the service I couldn't face. Seein' Shirley standing at the altar, and rememberin'. . . .

MRS. LACK (*rather shortly*): Oh yes. Your "Great Sorrow". We *all* know, don't we, Emma?

EMMA: Edie, if everyone's finished their tea, get the cups and sausers washed up out of the way.

EDIE: Yes, Emma. (*She puts cups and saucers on tray.*)

EMMA (*to Mrs Lack*). And don't think I'm pushing you off, but . . . we've got a lot to do yet. Thanks for bringing the bad news.

MRS. LACK: I hope you get the lads fixed up at the Rose and Crown. (*Happily.*) I doubt if you will.

SHIRLEY: Shall I slip down there now, Mum?
EMMA: You'll stay where you are. I haven't said nothing about any Rose and Crown.
SHIRLEY: But. . . .

[*Edie, who has been collecting cups and saucers, suddenly lets out a wail of anguish. She has a cup in her hand and is gazing, horrified, into it.*]

EDIE: Ooooooh!

[*The others turn to her.*]

EMMA: What the. . . !
DAPHNE: Aunt Edie, what's the matter?
MRS. LACK: Oh my!
SHIRLEY: Auntie. . . ?
(*Together.*)

EMMA (*after the chorus*): . . . Making us all jump out of our skins. What's the matter with you?
EDIE (*she points to inside of cup*): Look!

[*With enquiring noises they all crowd round*]

Do you see it?
DAPHNE: What? You mean the tea-leaves? Can you see something, Aunt Edie?
EMMA (*breaking away*): Tea-leaves! Is that all?
EDIE: I can see it as plain as daylight. Can't you see it, Mrs. Lack? Look—there. . . . (*She points.*)
MRS. LACK (*after peering*): Yes . . . I'm beginning to. . . . It looks like. . . .
EDIE: Like what? (*Dramatically.*)
MRS. LACK: Like the Mountains of Mourne rolling down to the sea.
EDIE: No. You're looking in the wrong place. Look

—there! (*Pointing again—dramatically.*) A bleeding, broken heart!

MRS. LACK (*backing—with a gasp of horror*): Lord save us!

EDIE: I wonder whose it is?

MRS. LACK: Let's hope it's yours, Edie.

EDIE (*looking*): No. It doesn't look like mine.

EMMA (*scornfully*): If it's anybody's it's mine. Mine broke years ago; but I should have thought it had bled all it was going to by now! (*To Edie.*) And now, if you've quite finished cheering us all up, perhaps you'll take those cups and saucers out of here and get 'em washed.

EDIE (*still shaken by her discovery*): Yes, Emma. (*She disappears with tray into kitchen.*)

EMMA: Her—and her. . . !

MRS. LACK: I wonder if it *was* mine! I think I'll be going.

EMMA: I should. If your bleeding heart's going to break, I should let it do it in the comfort of your own home!

[*Mrs. Lack moves towards kitchen.*]

MRS. LACK: Well, I'll say goodnight all. (*To Shirley.*) And I hope everything goes all right tomorrow, Shirley love. It'll be a very anxious time for you, I'm sure. We'll all see each other tomorrow, won't we—if we're spared?

SHIRLEY: Thank you for the wedding present, Mrs. Lack. It . . . it was just what we wanted.

MRS. LACK (*somewhat surprised*): Was it? (*As she goes—puzzled.*) Good Lord! (*She exits right.*)

EMMA: That woman is enough to. . . .

MRS. LACK (*off, in kitchen*): Got you at it, haven't they, Edie? I dunno what they'd do in this house without you. Nighty-night!

[*Emma moves up and slams kitchen door.*]

EMMA: I'll tell that woman just what I think of her one of these days.

SHIRLEY: Oh, never mind her, Mum. Hadn't I better go up to the Rose and Crown and see if they have a room?

EMMA: No, you won't. They can sleep here.

SHIRLEY: But, Mum. . . .

EMMA: *You* can do with all the spare twelve and sixpences that Albert Tufnell has got. There's no need for him to go throwing them away at la-di-da hotels.

SHIRLEY: But where are you going to put them?

EMMA: On this thing. (*She points to settee.*)

DAPHNE (*muttering*): Oh my. . . ! You mean, one at each end?

EMMA: No, I don't! Here, Shirley, give me a hand.

[*She and Shirley open up the settee so that it becomes a bed.*]

DAPHNE (*seeing this*): Oh, it's one of those things. I believe they're hell to sleep on.

EMMA (*to Shirley*): If those two don't like it they can go and sleep with your father's ferrets, for all I care. *Now*, I suppose, we've got to start finding blankets. A nice time of night to start doing *that*!

SHIRLEY: I'll help you, Mum.

EMMA: I should think you will! You might as well learn right away what it's like to be slaving your inside out while your husband's drinking himself stupid down at the pub. Come on! (*She goes off left.*)

DAPHNE (*to Shirley*): Shall I?

SHIRLEY (*with a nice smile and wink to Daphne*): No, don't bother. And don't take too much notice of mother. Her bark's worse than her bite. (*She follows Emma and exits left.*)

DAPHNE (*to herself*): But there's such a lot of it.

[*She moves to the bed and lies full length on it, thinking. Then she starts to whistle or sing* " *The Wedding March* ". *The voices of Albert and Carnoustie are heard off left, singing* " *Auld* Lang *Syne* ". *As they get near to the front door, they cease singing. The front door is heard opening, and Albert and Carnoustie can be heard* " *sshing* " *at great length. Hearing the front door open, Daphne jumps up.*]

Gosh! (*She goes quickly to door left and peeps out.*) Oh my. . . ! (*She shuts the door.*) Here! Let me get out of this! (*She exits right—very quickly.*)

[*Albert appears cautiously at door left—head around corner—he comes into the room, beckons off, and Carnoustie appears left with equal caution.*]

ALBERT (*finger to lips*): Sssssh!
CARN (*also finger to lips*). Sssssh!

[*He comes on tiptoe into the room, and he and Albert are standing together, looking round, when Henry appears in the doorway left. He is wearing Albert's sailor hat, and is sufficiently drunk to be in a* " *Don't-care-a-darn* " *mood.*]

HENRY (*singing as he enters*): " And here's a hand, ma trusty friend. . . ." (*He waves a hand about.*)
ALBERT: Ssssh! Pop! Quiet!
HENRY (*overlapping—as he grabs Carnoustie's hand and clings to him, singing*): " And gie's a hand o' thine."
CARN (*nervously*): Mr. Hornett, ye didna' ought to. . . .
HENRY (*singing him down*)· " We'll tak' a cup and drink it up. . . ." (*He stops as he realises the boys are trying to quieten him.*) Wassa matter?

CARN (*warningly*): Mrs. Hornett!
HENRY (*blinking at him*): Mrs. 'Ornett. . . ! Pah! (*And, suddenly flinging both arms out with a dramatic gesture, he bawls at the very top of his voice.*) "*For the sake of Auld Lang Syne*"!
ALBERT (*rushing at him*): Pop! (*He grabs an arm.*)

[*Carnoustie grabs the other arm.*]

HENRY (*as he frees himself—with a big gesture*): Poooh! (*He stands perfectly still for a moment, then, for no reason at all, he shouts.*) God save Ould Ireland!

[*And immediately, and with amazing agility, he begins dancing a hornpipe round the room. What the dance lacks in perfection of execution it makes up in speed. Henry is simply tearing round the room to his own vocal accompaniment.*]

ALBERT: Cor-blimey! That's done it! *Pop!* (*He is running round, trying to catch Henry.*)

[*The door right opens and Edie comes quickly into the room.*]

EDIE (*eyes popping as she speaks*): *Henry!*

[*As she is saying this, Daphne darts on quickly from door right, grabs Edie by the hand and literally yanks her off right again. As he is dancing around, Henry occasionally stretches out a hand and flicks an ornament off the mantelpiece or the sideboard, and immediately returns to the appropriate gestures required for the hornpipe. Albert in despair gives up the chase and, shuddering as an ornament crashes to the floor, crosses to Carnoustie and almost weeps on his shoulder. Henry is dancing towards the door left—he has reached the hand-over-hand movement of the dance—when it opens and . . . Emma, arms full of blankets, appears in the doorway. Henry, lost in the dance, remains in front of her, dancing. Shirley, carrying pillows, is behind Emma. Emma's mouth opens, closes, opens, closes. . . .*]

EMMA (*the roar of the Bull of Bashan is as the tinkling of fairy bells compared with Emma's*): Henry!!!

[*Albert gives a convulsive shudder as he hears Emma's voice, and his arms go round Carnoustie as if for protection. Emma's roar brings Henry to a standstill for one moment only. He looks her firmly in the eye; then, with a broad gesture and in a loud voice. . . .*]

HENRY: Split your mainbrace! (*He means " splice the mainbrace ", of course.*)

[*He recommences the hornpipe, moving round the room.*]

EMMA (*eyes blazing with rage, hurls the blankets to the floor, comes downstage, grabs Henry by the lapels, brings him to a standstill, snatches the sailor hat from his head and flings it away, as she says. . . .*): You—drunken—sot!

[*She gives Henry a vicious shove, and he collapses on to bed.*]

ALBERT (*horrified*): Ma!
CARN (*equally horrified*): Mrs. Hornett!
SHIRLEY (*as she turns and runs out of the room*): Oh-h! (*She exits left.*)

[*There is a pause. Emma turns and faces Albert.*]

EMMA (*pointing to Henry*): You did this, didn't you?
ALBERT: I. . . . (*He shrugs helplessly*).

EMMA: He would never have dared do it off his own bat. You planned it all out with him, didn't you? (*Turning and looking at Henry.*) Pretending he was out with his ferrets, when all the time he was. . . .

[*Daphne, unseen by the others, comes into doorway right, and stands watching.*]

CARN (*firmly*): Albert didna' say a worrd to yourr husband aboot comin' doon to the White Hart. Ye ha'e ma worrd for that.

EMMA: I see! It was you, was it? And what gives *you* the right, do you think, to set my husband up in defiance of me? To deliberately persuade him to sneak away behind my back and. . . ?

CARN: Is it no' possible, Mrs. Hornett, that you're underrating your husband's intelligence?

EMMA: And what do you mean by that?

CARN: What I mean is—can ye no' give your husband credit for doing the very sensible thing he did *on his own initiative*?

ALBERT (*worried*): Carnoustie!

EMMA (*flaring up*): *Sensible* thing!

CARN (*placidly*): His going out was most sensible.

EMMA (*almost shrieking*): After I'd told him not to!

CARN: That's what made it sensible.

EMMA: You. . . !

CARN: But I'll allow that his gettin' a wee bit tipsy—though natural in the circumstances—wasna' sensible. (*Looking at a smashed vase on the floor.*) It was deplorable!

EMMA: If anyone had told me that I would ever stand and listen to such downright impudence. . . !

CARN: If anyone had told me that I would ever have to stand and watch a woman treating her husband like. . . . (*Tiny pause, as his mind is called to more urgent matters—then. . . .)* Excuse me! *(To Albert.)* It's out in the yard, isn't it?

[*He moves to door right, sees Daphne, who is looking at him with eyes filled with admiration. He stops.*]

Excuse me! *(He exits right.)*

EMMA *(having recovered her breath)*: That young man leaves here as soon as the wedding's over, doesn't he? And the sooner the better. And *(To Albert.)* I can't say much for your choice of friends.

ALBERT: Listen, Ma. We're all a bit on edge tonight, so the least said the better. If you don't mind, I'll just see Shirley for a few minutes; then Carnoustie and me'll be getting off next door.

EMMA: You're not going next door.

ALBERT: Not. . . ?

EMMA: We've had to make other arrangements. You'll both have to sleep on this for the night.

ALBERT *(dismayed)*: Oh! If we'd known we could have stayed the night at Toddy's place.

EMMA: Who's Toddy? One of your drinking pals, I suppose?

ALBERT: Well . . . yes!

EMMA: Then you're safer here. But I'll tell you what you can do. You can get yourself round to Toddy's —as you call him—first thing in the morning, and stay there till it's time to go to the church. We don't want to run the risk of you and Shirley seeing each other before the wedding. And if that doesn't suit . . . well . . . you can make your *own* arrangements. There's blankets and sheets over there. *(She points to them on the floor.)* You can make the bed up yourselves, I suppose?

ALBERT: Yes, thanks.

EMMA *(going and standing in front of Henry)*: *Henry!!*

HENRY (*leaping up—and, with a wail, sitting down again*): Yes, Emma?

EMMA: Get to bed!

HENRY (*weakly*): Yes, Emma. (*Rising.*) I'll just go and look at my ferrets.

EMMA (*this is the last straw*): *You'll.* . . !

[*She takes him almost by the scruff of the neck and propels him off left.*]

HENRY (*as he is being shot through door*): Goodnight!

[*Albert stands looking at the door through which Henry and Emma have gone. He is lost in thought, and not happy thought. Daphne, after a moment, moves down towards him.*]

DAPHNE (*quietly*): Shall I give you a hand?

ALBERT (*coming to*) M'mm?

DAPHNE (*going up to blankets*): To make up the bed.

ALBERT: No, no. We can manage. Thanks all the same.

DAPHNE: It's no trouble.

ALBERT: Trouble! I seem to have caused nothing but trouble ever since I got here.

DAPHNE (*gently*): Don't you believe it, Albert. (*She is bringing the blankets down to the bed.*) You're not the cause of the trouble. You're only the excuse for it.

ALBERT: But I . . . I don't know what I've done. Oh, I know I went out when Shirl didn't want me to. Perhaps I shouldn't have done . . . I dunno. But even before that—the minute I got here, in fact—Ma was picking on me.

DAPHNE: Of course she was. (*They have automatically begun making up the bed.*) She can't help herself . . . it's just *her*.

ALBERT: But why is she like that? She must be a very unhappy woman.

DAPHNE: Don't talk nonsense. She's the happiest woman alive!

ALBERT: What!! The. . . ?

DAPHNE. Of course she is. Good Lord, you've met her sort before, haven't you? There are plenty of them about. That's how they get their happiness—making everybody's life a hell.

ALBERT (*incredulously*): You mean, she *likes* being the way she is?

DAPHNE: I should think she does. She wallows in it!

ALBERT: Good Lord! (*He is standing agape, holding end of blanket.*)

DAPHNE (*practically*): Tuck your end in. And, of course, some husbands *like* their wives that way.

ALBERT: Are you pulling my leg?

DAPHNE: I'm wondering if you're pulling mine with this " wide-eyed Winnie " act—pretending you don't know.

ALBERT (*anxiously*): I'm not. Honest, I'm not!

DAPHNE: " Join the Navy and see the World ". You must have been seeing it with your eyes shut.

ALBERT: You really mean there are husbands who *like* being treated the way Ma treats Pop?

DAPHNE: Yes, I do.

ALBERT: You're not telling me he . . . Pop's one of these. . . ?

DAPHNE: No. All Uncle Henry has ever asked out of life is . . . his fair share of peace, his bit of home comfort, and his ferrets . . . (*Tiny pause.*) . . . and all he's got is . . . his ferrets.

[*Carnoustie enters from right.*]

There don't seem to be any pillows. I'll ask Shirley where I can find some.

ALBERT: No, no. Don't bother. We can manage. (*To Carnoustie.*) Can't we, son?

DAPHNE (*laughing*): I like the way you call him "son"! (*To Carnoustie.*) You're old enough to be his grandfather, aren't you, Scottie?

CARN: No' in years, I'm no'.

DAPHNE (*trying to imitate the accent*): I didn'a mean in years. Mon! I was proud of ye; the way ye stood up to Aunt Emma just now. Ma hairt fair warmed to ye.

CARN: I'd be glad if you'd enlighten me as to what clan ye think ye belong with an accent like that! .

DAPHNE (*to Albert*): Isn't he sweet?

CARN: What for why are ye makin' up the bed? Are we no' going next door?

DAPHNE: No, you're not.

CARN (*to Daphne*): You mean we're sleeping here?

DAPHNE: *We!* Thanks for the invitation.

CARN: What!

[*Edie appears nervously at kitchen door.*]

EDIE (*looking round*): Oh! Has . . . is. . . ?

DAPHNE: Come in, Aunt Edie. The coast's clear now. "The fight is o'er, the battle *lost.*" (*To the boys.*) Poor Aunt Edie! Shut herself in the pantry; didn't you, darling?

EDIE: It was silly of me; but your Aunt Emma frightens me sometimes. Was she very cross with Henry?

DAPHNE: Well, I doubt if she's singing him to sleep with a lullaby just now.

EDIE: Oh! Has Henry gone to bed—and Emma, too?

DAPHNE: We can but hope.

EDIE: I suppose we ought to be going, too, Daphne? It'll be a . . . a long day tomorrow, won't it?

CARN (*grimly*): I've nae doot tha' every hour will be given its full value.

EDIE: Will you boys be all right on that thing? (*She points to bed settee.*)

ALBERT: We'll be fine, thanks, Aunt Edie.

EDIE: Oh, but you haven't got any pillows! I must go and. . . .

ALBERT: What you must do is stop worrying about . . . well, just stop worrying, see? (*He puts his arms round her.*)

EDIE (*suddenly bursting into tears, and burying her face on his breast*): Oh, Albert! I do want you and Shirley to be happy. You will be . . . won't you?

ALBERT (*comforting her*). 'Course we will, Aunt Edie. Once I've finished my service and we get settled down in Badcaster . . . away from . . . away from here.

[*Edie looks up at him in wonder.*]

And you must come over and see us sometimes. Promise?

EDIE (*bewildered*): But what about . . . ? Aren't you going to live at Number Twenty-Four, then?

ALBERT: Number Twenty-Four? Number Twenty-Four what . . . where?

EDIE (*still bewildered*): I thought Emma had. . . .

ALBERT (*very much on the alert*): You thought she'd what? What are you talking about, Aunt Edie?

EDIE (*distressed*): Oh dear! Now what have I done? But I thought you'd . . . I just took it for granted you'd know; that Shirley would have told you.

ALBERT (*almost impatiently*): Told me *what*?

EDIE: Albert, I . . . I'd rather not . . . I don't want to cause any more trouble.

[*Albert suddenly picks her up and puts her into the bed in sitting-up position; puts the bed-clothes round her.*]

ALBERT: You're not moving out of that bed, Aunt Edie, until you've told me what the devil you're talking about.
DAPHNE: You keep quiet, Aunt Edie, and you'll have the night of your life!! (*As she sees Carnoustie's glare of disapproval.*) Sorry I spoke!
ALBERT: Come on, Aunt Edie, out with it! (*He sits on bed by her.*)
EDIE (*sitting like a little bird in the bed*): Oh dear! Well, Albert, I . . . I can only think that Shirley was going to tell you tomorrow as a . . . a . . . (*She tries to believe this.*) wonderful surprise. You see . . . Number Twenty-Four—three doors up this street—was suddenly put up for sale, privately, about a fortnight ago it was, and . . . well . . . Emma . . . so kindly . . . as your wedding present . . . put down the deposit with the Building Society, so that you and Shirley could buy the house. . . . (*Slight pause.*) That's all.

[*Albert rises slowly. The others are watching him intently. He moves over to fireplace, slowly.*]

ALBERT (*as he goes*): That's all!

[*There is a long silence.*]

EDIE (*at last—apprehensively*): Can I get up now? (*She gets out of the bed and straightens it; then comes down to Albert.*) You won't say anything to Shirley or Emma . . . that I told you, I mean?
ALBERT: Bless you, of course I won't. (*He kisses her.*)
EDIE: Shirley's sure to tell you herself. Goodnight, Albert.
ALBERT: Sleep tight.

[*Edie gives him a little squeeze. Then, crossing to Carnoustie, she holds out her hand.*]

EDIE: Goodnight.
CARN (*unexpectedly, he kisses her*): Guid nicht!

[*Daphne has been watching this. On seeing the kiss her eyes are wide open.*]

DAPHNE: Well, of course. . . !! (*She rubs her hands together, and the look in her eyes suggests that, having seen Edie's "technique", she is going to use it, too. She is* not *unmindful of Albert's dejection; therefore she "over-plays" a little, in order to try and lighten the "darkness" —Going to Albert.*) Goodnight, Albert. (*She gives just the slightest tilt of the chin—for a kiss.*)
ALBERT (*automatically*): Goodnight, Daphne. Sleep tight. (*He kisses her.*)

[*Daphne turns, looks at Carnoustie. Then, following Edie's technique, she approaches him with hand out*]

DAPHNE: Goodnight, Scottie.

[*To her dismay, Carnoustie takes her hand—very much at arm's length, and shakes it, briefly.*]

CARN: Guid nicht!
DAPHNE (*she cannot resist it*): Well, aren't you a big lump of . . . of Scotch Broth! (*Going up to Edie who is waiting by door left.*) Come on, Aunt Edie! (*She whisks off right, taking Edie with her.*)

[*There is a pause, during which Carnoustie looks at Albert who merely stands gazing into the fire. Then Carnoustie gets his kitbag and begins to take things out of it. He eventually takes out his "best uniform" and carefully lays it out over a chair. Then, opening his suitcase, he takes out his Navy hold-all. He is about to close lid, when he notices a largish parcel wrapped in tissue paper*]

CARN (*as he takes out parcel*): Och! I'd forgotten. . . !

[*He turns, parcel in hand—it is obviously his wedding present—but Albert is still turned away. Carnoustie makes as if to give parcel to Albert, stops, looks at him, then at parcel, pauses, then puts parcel back into suitcase. He then takes off his "silk" and lanyard, picks up hold-all and crosses towards Albert.*]

(*Quietly.*) I'll away to the kitchen for a wash.
ALBERT (*turning*): What? Oh, yes, I suppose I'd better. . . . (*He begins to take off his jacket.*) I'll be out there in a minute.

[*Carnoustie exits right. Albert has removed his "silk", folded it, and put it carefully on a chair. He sits on bed for a moment thinking.*]

ALBERT (*suddenly*): Oh, what the hell!

[*He begins to struggle out of his jersey. While he is doing this, there is a light tap on the door left. Albert does not hear it. He has got the jersey over his head—covering his face—when the door left opens, and Shirley, now in her pyjamas and dressing-gown, comes nervously into the room.*]

SHIRLEY (*seeing the figure on the bed*): Oh . . . ! Is . . . is that you, Albert? (*She is trying to recognise him.*)
ALBERT (*struggling*): What? Is that you, Shirl?
SHIRLEY: Yes, Albert.
ALBERT: I'll be with you in a minute.

[*More struggling. Shirley takes a hand, and eventually Albert emerges from jersey.*]

(*Seeing Shirley.*) Hello!

SHIRLEY: Albert! (*She sits quickly on his knee and kisses him ardently. After the kiss.*) Where's Carnoustie?
ALBERT: He's out in the back kitchen, washing.
SHIRLEY (*after snuggling up to him for a while*): Did you think I wasn't coming down to see you?
ALBERT: I hoped you would.
SHIRLEY: You don't deserve it, really; not after what you did tonight.

[*Albert looks at her enquiringly.*]

Oh, Albert, *why* did you do it?
ALBERT: What?
SHIRLEY: It was bad enough *you* going out after I'd asked you not to; but to persuade Dad to follow you, and to get him *drunk* into the bargain. . . ! Albert, did you do it deliberately . . . to annoy Mum?
ALBERT (*quietly*): No . . . I didn't.
SHIRLEY: You don't like Mum very much, do you?
ALBERT: She's never given me the chance to.
SHIRLEY: Well . . she doesn't really *know* you, does she? I mean, she hasn't seen a great deal of you, has she?
ALBERT: Neither have you, for that matter
SHIRLEY: No; but . . . that's different. I love you.
ALBERT (*with a great tenderness*)· Shirl! (*He kisses her again.*)
SHIRLEY (*at last—laughing*): Now, stop it, Albert Tufnell! There'll be plenty of time for that . . . (*She smiles demurely.*) tomorrow. (*Ruffling his hair.*) Are you scared about tomorrow, Albert?
ALBERT (*after a pause*): Tomorrow? It isn't tomorrow I'm worried about.
SHIRLEY: Worried? Are you worried? What about?

Mother? (*As he doesn't reply.*) You needn't be. She isn't always like she's been tonight.

ALBERT (*eyes wide open—it almost bursts from him*): Good Lord, I should hope not! And a fat lot of consolation *that* is!!

SHIRLEY (*nettled*): Well, after all, she did have some cause, didn't she? She's got all the worry of the wedding on her mind. Then, on top of that, you had to go and get Dad drunk. . . .

ALBERT: I. . . ! Shirl, what makes you so sure I got Pop drunk? Actually, he didn't come into the room we were in until just before we left. We could tell he'd had a few—so we didn't even ask him to have *one*. We just brought him home.

SHIRLEY: You mean, he'd been drinking on his own?

ALBERT: Yes, he had.

SHIRLEY: But why? If he'd sneaked out to join you, why didn't he?

ALBERT (*quietly*): He told me why. He said he felt too ruddy miserable; he didn't want to spoil our party. So he had a few, quick—to cheer himself up.

SHIRLEY: Well, I hope you don't have to cheer yourself that way when we're married.

ALBERT: I hope *you'll* never give me cause to.

SHIRLEY: I won't, Albert. (*Coming to him and putting her arms round him.*) I won't. I promise you. And don't take too much notice of tonight. I know Mum is naturally a bit sharp-tongued; but, as I say, with the wedding as well, and . . . and she *is* losing her only child, in a way, isn't she?

ALBERT: So is Pop.

SHIRLEY: Men don't think the same way as women. And Mum's going to miss me. It isn't all honey for her here, you know; she hasn't had an easy time.

ALBERT: Hasn't she? She's got a comfortable home. . . .

SHIRLEY (*smiling*): You haven't had much . . . well, experience of home life yet, have you? So you mustn't take too much notice if she's a bit touchy. Poor Mum's got enough on her plate to make her touchy.
ALBERT: But. . . . So long as we can go our own way, Shirl, when we're married—for the first few years at any rate . . . till we've got . . . used to each other—and we'll have to do that, you know—so long as we can get away from . . . the family. . .
SHIRLEY. You mean, from Mother, don't you?
ALBERT: Well, yes—I do. (*Directly.*) And we're going to, aren't we?

[*Shirley is now very uneasy, but is trying to hide the fact.*]

SHIRLEY: But Albert, we . . . we can't go very far away, can we? I mean . . . you're going to this job you've been offered at Badcaster, and . . . Badcaster's only four miles away from here.
ALBERT (*after a longish look at her*): Those four miles will serve their purpose very nicely. . . . (*Again a pause.*) A little place, even if it's only a couple of rooms, in Badcaster. . . . Darling, don't you *see* how wonderful it will be?
SHIRLEY: But Albert. . . .

[*Carnoustie, now divested of his jersey, which he carries over his arm, enters from right.*]

CARN (*surprised at seeing Shirley*): Oh! . . . Oh! (*He goes out again.*)
ALBERT: But what, Shirl?

[*Shirley looks away from him, then rises nervously and moves away from him. Albert watches her.*]

(*He speaks slowly.*) What were you going to say?

SHIRLEY (*after a slight pause*): Say? I . . . I can't remember what it was.

ALBERT (*after a slight pause*): Then it can't have been important, can it?

SHIRLEY (*gulping*): No.

[*There is a longish, awkward pause.*]

(*At last.*) Well . . . I suppose I ought to be getting off to bed.

[*Albert rises.*]

Daphne will be asleep, almost. I don't want to disturb her. (*Trying to smile.*) And there's poor Carnoustie in the back kitchen. . . . (*Coming close to Albert.*) Goodnight, Albert . . . my darling. (*She kisses him passionately.*) Tell me you love me.

ALBERT (*holding her tightly to him*): I love you, Shirl.

SHIRLEY: Tell me you'll always love me. No matter, if. . . .

ALBERT (*after waiting for her to go on*): If what?

SHIRLEY (*in a smothered voice*): Just tell me you'll always love me.

ALBERT (*quietly*): I'll always love you.

SHIRLEY: Sure?

ALBERT: Sure.

SHIRLEY (*kissing him again*): Oh, my darling!

ALBERT (*after the kiss*). I wish you'd tell me something, Shirl. (*He says this quite lightly.*)

SHIRLEY (*with just a little start*): What?

ALBERT (*after a pause*): Whatever's in your mind.

SHIRLEY (*coming to him*): I love you, Albert Tufnell . . . and I always will. (*Giving him a short kiss.*) There!

ALBERT (*pause*): You've nothing else to tell me?
SHIRLEY (*slight pause*): Isn't that enough?
ALBERT (*pause*): I suppose it'll have to be.
SHIRLEY (*it is a whisper*): Goodnight.
ALBERT (*after the slightest pause*): Goodnight . . . my dear.

[*Shirley exits left. There is a pause, during which Albert stands lost in thought. He crosses to his kitbag and takes out his " Number One " uniform and puts it over chair. As he is beginning to do this, Carnoustie enters carrying his jersey. He watches Albert as he prepares for bed. Carnoustie is about to take off his trousers, when he pauses. . . .*]

CARN. Are we likely to have any more visitors, d'ye think?
ALBERT: Eh? I shouldn't think so. Lock the door if you're. . . .
CARN. There's no key. I've looked. (*He slips off his trousers, folds them neatly on chair.*)
ALBERT (*meanwhile crossing to his suitcase and getting hold-all*): I'll go and wash. (*He goes out right, leaving door open.*)

[*Carnoustie, who is now only in his shirt, after straightening up his things, moves to bed, tests springs, then contemplates the bed as a whole.*]

CARN (*presumably speaking to Albert*): It's a seenister-lookin' invention of the Devil, this is! (*Then calling.*) Albert!
ALBERT (*off*): Yes?
CARN: Which side do you want to sleep?
ALBERT: I'm not fussy.
CARN: You'll sleep on the left.

ALBERT (*agreeing*): O.K.
CARN: If ye sleep at a'!

[*He begins to get into the bed. He does so very gingerly. When half in, he stops and looks down, as if expecting the thing to collapse. He gets right in, lies down. As there are no pillows, his head goes down flat.*]

CARN: Oh, ma God!

[*He sits up again. Feeling his neck. . . .*]

Ah nearly broke ma bluidy neck!

[*He looks round, then gets out of bed, crosses to kitbags, picks them up and puts them on bed as pillows. He again gets into bed, lies down, and immediately sits up again, rubbing his head. He then knocks on his kitbag in several places. The bag would appear to be filled with blocks of wood. Finally, he knocks on Albert's kitbag. It is much softer. He changes the bags over, then settles down. Albert returns from kitchen and begins to prepare for bed.*]

(*His face buried in bedclothes.*) It's no' sae bad when ye get used to it.
ALBERT (*misunderstanding*): How do you know? You've never tried it.
CARN (*emerging from bedclothes and sitting up*): What the hell are ye talkin' aboot?
ALBERT: Married life, of course.
CARN: Well, I was talking aboot this bed.
ALBERT: Oh? Sorry.
CARN: Och, ye need not apologise. It's only natural that the perilous step ye're aboot to take should be uppermost in your mind. Ma God, it is!
ALBERT (*taking cigarette from packet*): H'mm! (*Then to Carnoustie.*) Have one?
CARN: Ay. Thanks. (*As Albert puts two cigarettes in*

his lips and lights them.) It's a disgustin' habit, smoking in bed. But I ha'e nae doot your wee wifie will cure ye of it. (*As Albert hands him cigarette.*) Thanks.

[*Albert now comes round to his side of the bed. Carnoustie is resting on one elbow. Albert is now only in his shirt.*]

ALBERT (*about to get into bed*): Oi!
CARN: What?
ALBERT: Move over a bit.

[*Carnoustie moves a little, and Albert gets into bed. They sit silently smoking for a moment.*]

CARN (*after the pause*): Albert. . . ?
ALBERT: Yes?
CARN (*solemnly*): I don't wish to appear presumptious, and I've no desire to interfere with your married life, but. . . .
ALBERT (*almost eagerly*): Go on!
CARN: I'd like to gi'e ye a worrd of advice.
ALBERT: Yes?
CARN (*solemnly*). Tomorrow . . . before ye set oot on your honeymoon, I think it's essential ye should. . . .
ALBERT: What?
CARN: Buy yoursel' a suit of pyjamas.
ALBERT (*not expecting this, of course*): Oh! (*Pause.*) You do?
CARN: Aye! (*Pause.*) If only for the look of the thing.
ALBERT (*after a pause*): I'll slip out in the morning and get some.
CARN: I *should*.
ALBERT: I will. (*Pause.*) Thanks for telling me.
CARN: Not at a'.

[*They smoke in silence again.*]

(*After the pause.*) Ye'll drop me a line and let me know how ye're getting on . . . on your honeymoon?

ALBERT: I will.

CARN (*slight pause*): No details, mind! . . . Just a general outline.

[*They continue smoking.*]

ALBERT (*after the pause*): I expect you'll be thinking of me.

CARN: I hope I'll keep ma imagination well under control.

[*More smoking.*]

ALBERT: Er . . . Shirley hasn't said anything.

CARN: What aboot?

ABERT: Buying that house.

CARN: Has she no'?

ALBERT: No. (*Pause.*) I wish she had.

CARN: Aye. I see wha' ye mean. It presents a problem, that does.

ALBERT: There's an awful lot of problems presented themselves, I'm thinking.

CARN (*nipping his cigarette out and putting the stub very carefully on the floor*): Ye ken the best way tae deal wi' problems, Albert?

ALBERT: No?

CARN: Sleep on 'em! (*He slides down into the bed.*)

ALBERT: P'raps it is. (*Having stubbed his cigarette he, too, slides into the bed.*)

[*There is a pause.*]

(*Only the top of his head visible.*) Carnoustie!

CARN (*likewise*): Aye?
ALBERT: The light!
CARN: Wha' aboot it?
ALBERT: It's on.
CARN: Well, put it oot!
ALBERT (*tiny pause*): The switch is on your side.

[*Carnoustie stirs and, grunting, gets out of bed, moves to the door, then discovers that the light switch is, actually, on the wall nearest Albert. He lets this register, then begins to cross to switch as:—Edie, carrying two pillows, enters left.*]

EDIE (*as she comes in*): I couldn't bear to think of you. . . .

[*She lets out a scream as her eyes fall on Carnoustie, who, with a yell, takes a flying leap at the bed and lands on top of Albert. For a second there is confusion, at the end of which Albert is on the floor on one side of the bed, Carnoustie on the other. Edie has buried her face in the pillows.*]

Very quick curtain.

Scene 2

The next morning. Carnoustie is finishing tidying himself up for the wedding when Edie enters right carrying teacup on tray. The coat of Henry's suit is hanging on the back of chair.

EDIE: I thought you'd like a cup of tea.
CARN (*only half turning*): That's unco' guid o' ye.
EDIE: To keep your strength up.
CARN: 'Tis no' ma strength that needs to be kept up but the bridegroom's.

EDIE (*giggling*): Oh, you do say such wicked things!

CARN (*who is completely guiltless of any such intention*): Wha'ever ha'e I said? (*He turns round.*)

EDIE (*candidly*): You look nicer—when you're dressed.

CARN: Thank you.

EDIE (*contemplating him*): I love a Jack Tar's uniform. It's so . . . different.

CARN: Ay. It has its little differences.

EDIE (*with a wistful sigh*): It must be wonderful to marry a sailor!

CARN: I ha'e never contemplated the thocht, ma'sel'.

EDIE: I wonder what Albert's thinking about now?

CARN: Ye need no' wonder very hard.

EDIE (*looking at him sentimentally*): Isn't there a song called "The Sailor's Wedding"?

CARN: There's ain called "The Sailor's Grave".

EDIE: Maybe that's what I was thinking of.

CARN: Maybe.

EDIE: You must excuse me I've a lot to see to in the kitchen. (*She exits right.*)

[*Carnoustie finishes dressing. Humming a lugubrious tune as he does so. Daphne, looking radiant, enters left. Carnoustie turns to gaze at her.*]

DAPHNE (*with a smile—to Carnoustie*): Will I do?

CARN (*deeply*): Ay. Ye wud.

DAPHNE (*looking at clock on mantelpiece*): Fifteen minutes to the fatal moment.

CARN: It's a fatal one, all right.

DAPHNE: Of course, you're an armoured old bachelor, aren't you?

CARN: There are chinks in ma armour.

DAPHNE: I expect you're congratulating yourself you're not in Albert's place?

CARN: I'm no' complaining o' ma ain place at the moment. (*As she is in his way near mirror, he indicates the Put-U-up.*) Will ye no' sit doon?

DAPHNE: That's the second time you've asked me to share *that* with you.

CARN (*shocked*): Och! . . . I was na' going to. . . !

DAPHNE: Come on. (*Patting seat beside her*).

CARN: I doot if there'll be time.

DAPHNE (*quickly*): Time for what?

CARN (*sternly*): For me to sit doon. Ha'e I no' to be awa' in a couple o' moments to pick up the bridegroom?

DAPHNE: Still it's wonderful what can be done in a couple of moments.

CARN (*sitting beside her*): I'm no' a quick worker.

DAPHNE: I bet you make a good job of it once you start. Have you kissed the bride, yet?

CARN: My goodness, no!

DAPHNE: You have to—after the wedding—you know. And . . . then there's the best man's privilege.

CARN: What's that?

DAPHNE: You can kiss anyone else you like.

CARN (*lured to her but pulling himself back*): I'm no' a kisser.

DAPHNE: You'll have to begin sometime. *And* with someone.

CARN (*rising*): I'd better be getting on my road.

DAPHNE: What are we going to do after the wedding, Carnoustie?

CARN (*moving centre, straightening his collar—taken aback*): Do? Who?

DAPHNE: Well . . . you and me. . . .

CARN: I hadn'a' given it ma consideration. Have we got to do something?

DAPHNE (*looking at him tentatively*): Of course, there's always the pictures.

CARN: Well now, I. . . .

DAPHNE: I've got an idea. You know, I owe you half a crown. . . . (*With a smile.*) I hadn't forgotten.

CARN: Neither had I.

DAPHNE. Well . . . *I'll* pay for your seat with that; and *you* can pay for minc.

CARN (*in admiration*): Daphne—girl, you should have been born a Scotswoman!

DAPHNE: If I had, I'd have made you pay for both of us.

CARN: But that's. . . .

[*Emma enters from left. Her hair is in a net. This apart, she is dressed for the wedding. Throughout the entire scene she gives the impression that she is fighting a losing battle against time, fate, and other malignant forces. It may be a losing battle, but it is certainly a speedy one. She carries a smartish handbag.*]

EMMA (*as she bustles in; seeing Carnoustie and Daphne*): Now then! Now then! What are you two doing?

DAPHNE: Nothing, Aunt Emma. Everything's done, isn't it?

EMMA (*going to drawer in sideboard and getting out an old black handbag, and at intervals during the following dialogue, transferring articles from it into the smart bag*): That's what *you* think! I thought you were supposed to be helping Shirley to dress?

DAPHNE: I was, but . . . well you came in and . . . took over, didn't you?

EMMA: Yes, and you can go and take over again from where I left off. You're all ready. I'm not. Now let me see. . . . (*She is busy with the bags.*)

[*Daphne moves towards door left as Edie enters right.*

Edie is dressed for the occasion, but the dress and hat would get by at a funeral without undue comment. She puts down her bag on sideboard.]

EDIE: Oh, Emma I. . . . (*Seeing Daphne's bridesmaid dress—in great admiration.*) Oooh! Daphne!

DAPHNE: Like it, Aunt Edie? (*She twirls round a bit.*)

EDIE: It's . . . it's. . . . (*Her "great sorrow" rushes into her mind, and she can only gurgle, wag her head, dab her eyes with her handkerchief and finally exit right.*)

EMMA (*seeing this*): Oh Lord! She's started! Now go on, Daphne. Up to Shirley this minute.

DAPHNE: Yes, Aunt Emma. (*She goes off left.*)

EMMA (*calling after her*): And if she wants *me*, tell her she can't have me. I'm going to the wedding as well as her. (*To Carnoustie.*) Isn't it about time *you* were getting off?

CARN: It's no' far from here to Toddy's.

EMMA: Has Albert arranged for the taxi to pick you both up at this Toddy's place?

CARN: Aye, he said he wud do that.

EMMA: And will Toddy, as you call him, be coming to the church?

CARN: Aye. I expect he'll want to see Albert going through the hoop.

EMMA: What?

CARN: I mean—getting married.

EMMA: H'm! Well, if he wants to (*Big hearted Emma.*) you can tell him he can come to the Reception afterwards. (*With sudden alarm.*) Did Albert give you the ring before he went?

CARN: Aye, he did.

EMMA: Have you got it put away safe?

CARN: I have.

EMMA: Where is it?

(*All this at terrific speed from Emma.*)

CARN: In ma pocket.
EMMA: Let me see it.

[*Carnoustie produces ring.*]

(*Taking it and peering at it.*) H'm! (*Another long look, then, calling.*) Edie!
EDIE (*off, right*): Yes, Emma?
EMMA (*calling*): Fetch me the rag I polish the brass with!
EDIE: Yes, Emma.

[*Emma breathes on the ring and rubs it on the sleeve of her coat once or twice.*]

EMMA (*after this*): I suppose it *is* gold?
EDIE (*as she enters*): Here we are, Emma! (*As she holds out the rag she sees the ring in Emma's hand. Pointing to it.*) Ooh! Is that Shirley's? (*She gulps.*)
EMMA: It is. Such as it is! (*She takes the rag; but lets Edie have a long look at the ring.*)
EDIE (*in a choking voice*): Oh, Emma, it's . . . it's . . . beauti. . . . (*Again memories are blessing and burning, and again Edie can only gurgle, wag her head, dab her eyes and rush off right.*)
EMMA (*as she polishes ring—nodding head after Edie*): Of course, she's going to have the time of her life!

[*The front door bell rings.*]

CARN: Shall I answer it, Mrs. Hornett?
EMMA (*with great resignation*): No, I'll go. (*As she puts rag and ring down and goes towards door left.*) If I get to the wedding *at all*, at this rate, I'll be lucky! (*She exits left.*)
CARN (*to himself*): And if you *don't*—everybody else

will. (*He picks up ring and looks at it—to himself as he looks at ring.*) Ma puir Albert! (*He puts ring away again.*)

EMMA (*calling—off left*): Shirley!

SHIRLEY (*from upstairs*): Yes, Mum?

EMMA (*off*). The bouquets have come. (*She re-enters, carrying a large sheaf of flowers, two posies and three small "button-holes". As she enters.*) I was beginning to think these were never coming. (*She puts them all on table and inspects them quickly.*) H'm. Not bad! (*She picks up two of the button-holes and hands them to Carnoustie.*) Here! One for Albert and one for you.

CARN: But, Mrs. Hornett. . . .

EMMA: Never mind "Mrs. Hornetting". Put yours in now. (*Snatching one from Carnoustie's hand.*) Here! I'll do it. (*As she runs her hand down the right side of his collar.*) Huh! No button-hole. . . ! I'll have to get you a pin. (*She is moving towards sideboard.*)

CARN. But, Mrs. Hornett! Albert and I canna' wear these things!

EMMA: What's the matter with them?

CARN: Nothing, but. . . .

EMMA: Then who says you can't!

CARN (*almost shouting*): Her Majesty the Queen!

EMMA: What!

CARN: It's against regulations. We'd be hanged, drawn and quartered if Her Majesty saw us wearing flowers on our uniform.

EMMA (*defeated*): H'mmm! (*Then with a sniff.*) Didn't know Albert had invited Royalty to his wedding! (*Taking button-holes from him.*) Well, that's another two three and sixes gone down the drain, as well as Rita's posy. (*She picks up posy for a moment then puts it down. Then holding up button-hole again.*) Henry had better wear one of these! Where is he?

CARN: I think he's oot wi' his ferrets!

EMMA: My Lord! His only daughter's getting married in a quarter of an hour and all he can think about is. . . . (*At the door right.*) Edie! Tell Henry I want him here.

CARN: Well, I suppose I may as well be getting off now. Where's ma hat? (*He takes it from behind door left.*) There's nothing more for me to do, is there?

EMMA: No, there isn't. Off you go! And you know what you've got to do, don't you?

CARN: Aye.

EMMA (*suddenly—rushing to table*): The ring! Where is it? Did you. . . ?

CARN (*about to go*): Aye, I did.

EMMA: Where is it?

CARN: In ma pocket.

EMMA: Let me see it.

CARN: I. . . ! (*With a sigh produces ring again.*)

EMMA: Put it away, safe. Has Albert given you some money for all the paying out you'll have to do?

CARN: Aye.

EMMA: Right! Then off you go. (*Another thought.*) Oh, and tell Albert to speak up in church. Tell him when he says "I will", I want to hear it.

CARN: Aye.

[*Daphne enters left, as Carnoustie is about to go.*]

DAPHNE: Oh! (*As they almost collide.*) Isn't it time you were going?

CARN (*muttering with much feeling*): Ma God, it is! (*He exits left.*)

DAPHNE: Shirley wants to see her bouquet, Aunt Emma.

EMMA: Can't she wait till she comes down?

DAPHNE: She says she wants to see it now.

EMMA: Here is it. Mind how you carry it! Is she nearly ready?

DAPHNE: She's getting on. (*She is holding bouquet.*)

[*Enter Edie. She is a devil for punishment.*]

EDIE: Oh, Emma, I. . . . (*Seeing bouquet in Daphne's arms.*) Oooh! Is . . . is that Shirley's. . . ? (*She gulps.*)

DAPHNE (*with justifiable apprehension*): Yes, Aunt Edie.

[*Edie "gurgles, wags, dabs" and staggers off right—punished.*]

EMMA (*looking after her*): Well, if *I'm* not in a mental home by tonight, *she* will be!

DAPHNE: Poor Aunt Edie!

EMMA: "Poor Aunt Edie", nothing! She's stark, staring, raving mad! That's all that's the matter with *her*. Go on, Daphne! Take that (*Bouquet.*) up to Shirley. Now where's Henry? I thought I told. . . .

[*The door right opens and Henry potters in—in shirt sleeves.*]

DAPHNE: Here he is!

EMMA (*turning*): There you are!

HENRY (*he is not feeling too good*): Only just.

EMMA: And what does that mean?

HENRY: I'm not feeling too good. (*Seeing Daphne with flowers.*) Them for me?

EMMA: Well, you've only got yourself to blame. If you will go out getting drunk. . . . (*She shoos Daphne off left.*)

[*Daphne exits left.*]

HENRY: Edie says you wanted me.

EMMA: Yes, I do. It's time you were ready.

HENRY: But I've got to. . . .

EMMA: You've got to do as I tell you. In case you've forgotten, you're giving your daughter away in matrimony in a few minutes' time. (*She takes Henry's coat from chair and " assists " him into it.*)

HENRY: Wouldn't you want a bit of nourishment if *you'd* just given birth to three healthy young ferrets?

EMMA: 'Enry 'Ornett. . . !

HENRY: Rosie's got to have her milk.

EMMA (*with exasperation*): Well go and give it to her quick and have done. (*She picks up one of the button-holes and stops Henry as he is about to go out right.*) Here! Wait a minute! (*She gets pin from ornament on mantel-piece and fastens button-hole in his jacket.*)

HENRY: Hey! It isn't me that's gettin' married.

EMMA (*muttering*): I wish it was—*and* to somebody else!

HENRY (*also muttering*): Same 'ere!

EMMA: H'm! Encouraging you to throw your weight about a bit, isn't it—having Albert and that Carnasty in the house? But we'll soon get you back in your place, my lad! There you are! (*She finishes putting button-hole in jacket.*) Now I'll give you two minutes to get them ferrets fed and that's all.

[*Henry moves to door right.*]

Did you get your bowler hat out, as I told you?

HENRY: Yes, It's on the bed. Do I *have* to wear it? It's dam' tight these days.

EMMA: You must be gettin' swollen headed. Lord knows what about! You'll wear it.

[*Henry exits right.*]

(*Calling after him.*) And when you come in, give yourself a brush down and wash your hands well. We don't want you arriving at church smelling of ferrets! Edie!

EDIE (*off*): Yes, Emma? (*She enters right.*)

EMMA: Are you nearly ready to get yourself off down to Banfield's?

EDIE: Yes, Emma.

EMMA: Right. Remember what I told you about the presents!

EDIE: Yes, Emma.

EMMA: Well I'm going upstairs now to finish getting myself ready (*Looking at clock on mantelpiece.*) Yes, and I've about three minutes to do it in. Fine sight I'll look! Not that it matters what *I* look like! I'm only the bride's mother.

[*Mrs. Lack is heard calling off right.*]

MRS. LACK: Are you there, Emma?

EMMA: Oh my. . . ! Get her out of here before I come down. (*She darts off left.*)

[*Mrs. Lack appears in doorway right. She is dressed for the wedding—highly coloured dress and rakish hat.*]

MRS. LACK (*as she comes into doorway*): It's only me! (*Seeing Edie.*) Oh, it's only you, Edie!

EDIE: Yes, it's only me. I thought you'd be on your way to church by now, Mrs. Lack. How's poor Rita?

MRS. LACK: Don't talk to me about poor Rita. Carrying on something awful, she is, 'cos she isn't going to the wedding. (*Sitting.*) I began to think I'd never get there myself. Doctor's only just gone. (*She is scratching her arm.*) 'Scuse me, but seeing all them spots on Rita. . . ! Emma hasn't gone yet, has she?

EDIE: She and Daphne will be off any minute now, when the taxis turn up. It's about time they were here. (*She looks out of window.*)

MRS. LACK: I'm glad they haven't gone yet. I wanted to ask Emma if she'd mind giving me a lift down to the church . . . everything throwing me so late. . . .

EDIE: You'll have to ask her, won't you?

MRS. LACK: That's what I want to do. Where is she?

EDIE: Upstairs, dressing.

MRS. LACK (*placidly*): I'll wait. I'm not in the way, am I?

EDIE. No, but . . . Emma did tell me to get you out of. . . . (*She pulls up in time.*) I like your dress, Mrs. Lack!

MRS. LACK: Do you, Edie?

EDIE: Chick, isn't it?

MRS. LACK: Glad you like it. (*Eyes on bouquets*) Oh, are these the. . . . (*As she examines them.*) Emma's splashed a bit, hasn't she? (*Picking up posies.*) These'll be the bridesmaids', won't they?

EDIE (*dabbing her eyes with handkerchief*)· Yes, that's right.

MRS. LACK: What a shame poor Rita won't be carrying one, isn't it? That Daphne won't be able to carry them both, will she? I wonder if Emma would let me give one to Rita? It'd be nicc for her to play with

[*There is a toot of a taxi horn off left.*]

EDIE (*in panic at once*): Oh, is that the taxi? (*Going up to window at a gallop.*) Yes it is! I must tell Emma! (*As she flies off left.*) Lovely white ribbons on it.

(*Off.*) Emma! The taxi! The taxi's come! Daphne! (*She returns, panting.*) I've told them!

[*Ring at front door bell.*]

(*She exits again, quickly—off.*) They won't be a minute now, driver. (*Then calling.*) Emma!
EMMA (*off*). All right! All right! Have you got rid of. . . ?
EDIE (*off*): No, Emma. She wants to know whether she can ride down to the church with you!

[*Mrs. Lack re-acts to this. Edie returns.*]

Oh dear! I'd better tell Henry. (*She tears off right.*) Henry! The taxi's here. Emma's just going.
HENRY (*off*): Good!
EDIE (*off*): I think you'd better come in, Henry! (*She returns—panting.*) Oh dear! Oh dear!
MRS. LACK (*sorrowfully*): This must be bringing it all back to you, Edie!

[*Edie "gulps, wags and gurgles".*]

Yes, indeed! You must feel as if a knife was piercing your vitals and I should think that must be very unpleasant.

[*Henry enters from right.*]

(*Seeing him.*) Well, Mr. 'Ornett! This must be a sad day for you!
HENRY: Aye, it is. Rosie's just lost one of her youngsters.
EDIE: You mean it's died?
HENRY: Aye, poor little thing. Look! (*And prac-*

tically under Mrs. Lack's nose, he opens his hand and reveals a small bundle of fur—Rosie's property—deceased.)

MRS. LACK (*with a yelp*): Aaah! Take it away!

EDIE (*alarmed*): Henry, you didn't ought to. . . . If Emma saw you with that thing!

[*Emma, now fully dressed, bustles in from left, just in time to hear Edie's last words.*]

EMMA (*as she enters*): With what thing? 'Morning, Florrie! Where's my bag? Ah, here it is! Henry, go and get your hat! I want to see you wearing it before I go. Go on, hurry!

HENRY: Aye! All right.

[*Henry still has the baby ferret in his hand. He does not know what to do with it, and wants to keep it out of Emma's sight. The unfortunate Edie is standing by him. He turns to her, furtively.*]

Edie!

EDIE: Yes, Henry?

HENRY: Get rid of it, will you? (*He puts the ferret in Edie's hand*)

[*Edie looks down at it, she gives a little scream but loyalty to Henry prevents her from dropping it. Shuddering and almost fainting, she dashes off right. Henry exits left.*]

EMMA: What on earth. . . ! (*Looking after Edie.*) She's up the pole! As God's my judge, she's up the pole. (*To Mrs. Lack.*) Now what's this about wanting to ride down to the church with me?

MRS. LACK: Well, if you don't mind, Emma. You see. . . .

EMMA: Yes, I see! Well, I suppose you'll *have* to. Are you ready, 'cos we are?

MRS. LACK: Yes, Emma. I'm all ready.

[*Enters Daphne.*]

DAPHNE (*to Mrs. Lack*): Oh, good morning!
MRS. LACK (*seeing her—looking at dress*): Oh yes! You look very well. You make a nice bridesmaid, don't you? But I wish you could have seen Rita! *She* can wear that colour.
EMMA (*handing posy to Daphne*): Here you are, Daphne.
DAPHNE: Thank you, Aunt Emma. Isn't it lovely!
EMMA: Lovely price, too!

[*Enter Henry with bowler hat on.*]

(*To him.*) Let me look at you (*After the look—doubtfully.*) You'll do!

(*Shirley now enters from left in wedding dress, looking very charming and carrying her bouquet.*)

MRS. LACK (*with genuine delight*): Oh, Shirley love! You look lovely.
SHIRLEY: Thank you, Mrs. Lack
MRS. LACK: Doesn't she look lovely, Emma?
EMMA: Well, though she's my own daughter, I will say. . . .
SHIRLEY: Thank you Mum darling.
EMMA (*to Henry*): 'Aven't *you* got nothing to say?
HENRY: Aye, when I get the chance! (*Going to Shirley.*) You look real bonnie. (*About to kiss her.*)
SHIRLEY (*avoiding him*): Dad, mind my make-up!
HENRY (*disappointed*): Oh, I see. . . . (*Looking at her.*) Well, I will say you'll do Albert credit.
EMMA (*expostulating*): *She'll* do Albert. . . ! Well, I like that!

[*Taxi horn off.*]

Here! We'd better be off. Taxi's waiting. (*This said to Mrs. Lack.*) Now! Are we all set? (*Calling.*) Edie!

EDIE (*off*): Yes, Emma? (*She dashes on, but stops dead as she sees Shirley. This is the last straw, so to speak. Deidre of the Sorrows has nothing on Edie at this moment.*) Oooh!

SHIRLEY: Like it, Aunt Edie?

[*One can only say that Edie does her act and vanishes off right again.*]

EMMA (*looking after her*): I mean to say! What *can* you do about her, except put her in a strait jacket? Right! (*Bustling.*) Now come on, Daphne, Mrs. Lack. . . . Now you'll be all right, won't you, Shirley love? You won't be nervous, will you? You've no need to be. I'm sure you look very nice. (*With surprising emotion—for Emma.*) You won't be my little girl any more, will you? (*She actually sniffs once or twice.*)

MRS. LACK (*sententiously*): Never mind, Emma. You're losing a daughter, but gaining a son!

EMMA (*after a "thank you for nothing" look at Mrs. Lack; to Henry*): Henry! Don't make a fool of yourself during the ceremony! Oh . . . and don't start for the church for five minutes. See you walk down the aisle nicely with Shirley. And while you're waiting, just you think out what you're going to say in your speech at the reception, and for goodness sake, talk about your daughter; not about ferrets!

[*Taxi horn again.*]

(*Calling.*) All right! We're coming! Daphne! Florrie! (*She bustles them out left.*) Got everything, Daphne? Now, Henry!

[*Daphne and Mrs. Lack exit left.*]

(*Bustling over to kitchen door.*) We're off, Edie. And don't forget; you go off to Banfield's when Shirley and Henry go. See that everything's as it should be, and for goodness sake, try to pull yourself together. We don't want you howling the place down and making everyone think they're at a funeral. (*Coming quickly from door and kissing Shirley very carefully.*) Bye-bye, love. Bless you. (*To Henry as she moves to door left.*) You give yourself a good brush down, it won't do any harm! (*She finally departs left.*)

[*Shirley and Henry stand quite still for a moment after Emma's whirlwind speech and exit.*]

HENRY (*at last*): I'm glad we don't 'ave a wedding every day!
SHIRLEY: I'll get you the clothes brush, dad. You *are* a bit dusty. (*She gets brush from drawer in sideboard.*)
HENRY: I've brushed the damn' thing till I've nearly worn all nap off it!
SHIRLEY: Well, if you *will* go messing about with your ferrets!
HENRY: Now don't *you* start! (*He begins brushing his trousers.*)
SHIRLEY (*protesting*): Dad!
HENRY: Now what?
SHIRLEY: Not in here! I don't want dust all over my dress!
HENRY: Well where. . . ?
SHIRLEY: Go into the back yard.

[*Edie enters from right, slowly and apprehensively.*]

HENRY (*grumbling*): 'Ere! I'll be glad when all this is over!

SHIRLEY (*as he goes*). And put your button-hole straight, dad. It's all crooked.

[*With something akin to a snarl, Henry goes off right.*]

You all right, Aunt Edie?

EDIE: I must be brave. I *will* be brave!

SHIRLEY. Of course you will.

EDIE: But you see it brings it all back to me!

SHIRLEY: Don't think about it, Aunt Edie.

EDIE: No, I mustn't, must I?

SHIRLEY: No.

EDIE: But I can't help it!

SHIRLEY: You must try.

EDIE: Yes, I must, mustn't I?

SHIRLEY: 'Course you must.

EDIE: I'd have liked to 'ave come to the church, Shirley love, but you *do* understand, don't you?

SHIRLEY: 'Course I do.

EDIE: I couldn't 'ave stood it. It would 'ave torn my heart out.

SHIRLEY (*she is up at window now—hardly realising what she is saying*): The taxi'll be here in a minute. It won't take them long. . . . You're sure I look all right, Aunt Edie?

EDIE (*whimpering*): You look beautiful. P'raps your veil's a bit crooked.

SHIRLEY (*horrified—rushing to mirror*): *What!* It isn't, is it? Why didn't you tell me before? Is that better? (*She has fiddled with it.*)

EDIE: Let me see. (*She stands looking.*)

SHIRLEY (*impatiently*): Is it?

EDIE (*doubtfully*): I think so.

SHIRLEY: But *is* it? (*Almost in tears as she turns to mirror again.*) Oh, Aunt Edie. . . . (*She puts down bouquet on table.*)

[*Taxi horn off.*]

Oh, there's the taxi! Aunt Edie, is it straight *now?*

EDIE: It's just a little bit. . . . (*She makes a vague gesture.*) I'd better call Henry.

SHIRLEY (*she is now almost demented. She turns to mirror again*): Ooooh!

EDIE (*at kitchen door*): Henry! The taxi's here. Hurry!

SHIRLEY (*turning again*): *Aunt Edie!* Is it all right now?

EDIE: Yes, dear. It's beautiful.

SHIRLEY: You're sure? It would be awful if it. . . .

EDIE: It's as straight as you'll get it.

[*Shirley gives a doubtful whimper and looks in mirror again. Henry enters from right.*]

HENRY: I'm here! Now come on. Let's get it over with! You ready, Shirley?

SHIRLEY: Do I look all right, Dad?

HENRY: Too late to do anything about it *now* if you don't! Come on!

SHIRLEY (*after another doubtful whimper gives a yelp*): *Dad!*

HENRY: What now?

EDIE: Shirley, what's the matter, love!

SHIRLEY (*pointing in horror at Henry's coat*): Your button-hole!

HENRY: What's the matter with it?

SHIRLEY: Well *look* at it! (*Her consternation is fully justified. Henry's button-hole is now a few stalks and ends of fern.*)

HENRY (*taking it out and looking at it*): Well I'm damned! That's Rosie, that is!

SHIRLEY: *What!!!*

HENRY: When I went out just now she was in such a state at losing one of her young 'uns, I 'ad to pick 'er up and comfort 'er, and she must 'ave nibbled all the. . . .

SHIRLEY (*nearly frantic*): For heaven's sake!
EDIE: Never mind, Shirley. There's another one here! Ooh! I must be getting off to Banfield's. (*She takes button-hole to Shirley and hands it to her.*)

[*Taxi horn again.*]

SHIRLEY (*snatching it from Edie*): Come *on*, Dad. I'll have to fasten it in the taxi. We can't keep Albert and everyone waiting. Come and see me off, Aunt Edie.
EDIE: Yes. . . . (*With a sob.*) No, it's no use, I can't! (*She dashes off right.*)
SHIRLEY: Come on, Dad! Give me your arm!
HENRY: What for?
SHIRLEY (*with a howl of exasperation*): Oooh! (*Almost dragging Henry off*). Come on!

[*Exit Shirley and Henry left. The room is empty for a moment, then Edie pokes her head round door right. She enters and takes up her handbag.*]

EDIE (*suddenly seeing bouquet*): Shirley! Your bouquet! (*She dashes to table, picks up bouquet, and with it in one hand and her handbag in the other, dashes off left.*)

[*The front door is heard to slam—and then the taxi driving away. There is a long pause. Then, the door right slowly opens and Albert steps into the room. He stands still for a moment, as if listening to the silence. Then he moves into the room, moves to table, picks up the remaining posy, looks at it and puts it down. He then crosses to wireless, turns it on and moves to easy chair by fireplace, looks at clock and sits lighting cigarette. The wireless slowly warms up, and a female voice is heard faintly singing. The song is " Early One Morning ". The singing increases in volume as the song goes on.*]

WIRELESS: ". . . heard a maiden singing in the valley below,
Oh don't deceive me!
Oh never leave me!
How could you treat a poor maiden so?"

The curtain slowly falls.

ACT THREE

The scene is the same—forty minutes later.

When the curtain rises, Albert is pacing up and down the room, deep in troubled thought. The wireless is playing a popular tune. Albert, after a moment, turns wireless off and resumes pacing. A taxi is heard approaching. He moves quickly up to the window, looks out cautiously then turns with an almost terrified look in his eyes, then, as the front door opens (off stage) he dashes off right.

The moment the front door is heard to open there can also be heard a babble of voices, Emma's predominating.

EMMA (*off*): He'll pay for this! You just see! (*As she comes charging into the room.*) You just see if he doesn't! (*She leans against the sideboard for a moment, panting.*) Oh my God! Oh my. . . ! (*She passes her hand across her brow.*) I can't believe it! I can't believe it! (*She pulls herself together and goes quickly to door left and speaks off.*) Henry! Shut that door! We don't want the whole street poking their noses in to find out what's happened. Not that they don't know already. Daphne, bring Shirley in here. Come in here and lie down a bit, Shirley. (*She moves down and arranges cushions at one end of the settee to serve as pillow.*) Jilted . . . my own daughter! Jilted, and by a common. . . !

[*Shirley, almost supported by Daphne, comes slowly into the room. She is a pathetic sight. Her bouquet hangs limply down from one hand, her bridal veil is just a little askew, and she almost covers her face with her wisp of a handkerchief.*]

(*Seeing them.*) Come in, love. Come and lie down.
SHIRLEY (*in tears*): Oh Mum. . . !

EMMA (*rushing to her and putting her down on settee*). There, there! You mustn't give in, love. Whatever happens, you mustn't give in. (*As she gets her on to settee.*) There we are! Put your feet up. (*She puts them up for her*) That's better, isn't it?

SHIRLEY: Oh Mum. . . !

EMMA: Don't talk, love. Just lie back quiet, and we'll get you a nice cup of tea.

SHIRLEY: I . . I don't want a cup of tea. I just want to die!

EMMA (*not realising quite what she is saying*): But you must have a cup of tea first.

DAPHNE: Shall I make it, Aunt Emma?

EMMA: Yes, you can. You make some for all of us. Lord knows, I can do with one.

SHIRLEY (*wailing*): Oh Daphne, what am I going to do?

DAPHNE (*putting her arm around her*): Try not to think about it for a bit.

SHIRLEY: But . . . but . . . oh! I can't help but think about it. I'll go mad, I know I will!

EMMA: Now lie back, and rest, same as I told you. Here! (*Taking Shirley's veil off.*) Get this off. You'll feel more comfortable.

SHIRLEY (*as veil comes off*): Ooooh! My veil! (*She weeps.*)

EMMA (*after putting veil aside*): And, Daphne, take this away. (*Shirley's bouquet.*) Put it somewhere out of sight. I never want to see it again.

SHIRLEY (*limply*): My bouquet!

[*Henry enters slowly from left looking dejected and apprehensive.*]

DAPHNE (*taking bouquet*): I can't help feeling. . . .

EMMA (*seeing Henry*): Oh, there you are. You've been

a long time coming in, 'aven't you? You been talking to anybody?

HENRY: No, I 'aven't.

EMMA: Well, this is a nice mess, isn't it?

HENRY: Aye, it is.

EMMA: I never thought I'd live to see the day when a daughter of mine would. . . .

SHIRLEY (*in tears*): Oh . . . Mum. . . ! (*Desperately.*) I'm sure we should have waited at the church a bit longer. I'm sure he . . . would have . . . turned up. He might have had an accident. Something *must* have happened! He'd never. . . . (*Sobs.*)

EMMA: Go and make that tea, Daphne.

[*Daphne, after a slight pause, during which she looks helplessly at Shirley and then at the bouquet, goes off right with it.*]

It's no use talking like that, Shirley, and it's no use trying to fool yourself. If you waited from now till Domesday, he wouldn't turn up. As far as marrying your precious Albert Tufnell goes, you've 'ad it!

[*Shirley sobs. Henry is by fireplace removing his collar. Emma painfully sits on edge of settee and painfully removes her own shoes, rubs her feet and gets slippers from near fire during the following.*]

"Waited a bit longer"!! I thought I'd die of shame as it was. Everybody whispering and sniggering. . . .

SHIRLEY: Don't, Mum!

EMMA (*as she eases foot out of shoe*): Ooooh! That's better! (*Then back to the subject in hand.*) *And* poor Mr. Purefoy. . . .

SHIRLEY: I'll never be able to face the Vicar again.

EMMA: . . . standing there trying to look as if he wasn't there at all.

SHIRLEY (*coming from lying to sitting position quickly*): But Mum . . . (*almost wildly.*) . . . what am I going to *do*. . . ? Won't I ever see Albert again?

EMMA (*removing her hat and generally fussing*): You'll see him again, my girl, if there's any justice at all in this world. But you won't see him in church. Where you'll see him is the Police Court!

SHIRLEY (*almost howling*): Oh no, Mum! No, not that. I couldn't bear it.

EMMA: You don't think he's going to be let get away with this, do you?

SHIRLEY: But, Mum, I couldn't. . . . (*Sobbing*) Oooh, it's all dreadful! I don't know what I'm going to do. I'll never live it down. (*Now bordering on hysteria.*) Albert, where are you? I want you I want you.

EMMA: Don't talk about him, love. Don't think about him.

SHIRLEY: What's the use of saying that? How can I help thinking about him? I love him. Ooooh! (*She bursts into a flood of tears.*)

EMMA: Eee! He'll pay for this. I always said he was no good, didn't I?

SHIRLEY: Stoppit, Mum! Stop running him down. I can't bear it. Oh, I wish I could die. Oh, Albert, where are you?

EMMA: I'll tell you where he probably is at this very. . . .

HENRY (*having removed collar, now sitting to undo boots*): Let the lass alone a bit, Emma. What's the use of carrying on at her? You're only making things worse than they are already.

EMMA (*flaring at him*): 'Enry 'Ornett! How you have

the nerve to so much as open your mouth after what you've done. . . .

HENRY: Me? What have I done?

EMMA: What have you. . . !!! You've ruined your daughter's life, that's all.

HENRY (*roused*): What the hell are you talking about?

EMMA: Who brought Albert Tufnell to this house in the first place? You did!

HENRY: But dammit, I didn't tell Shirley to go and fall in love with him, did I?

EMMA: If she'd never 'ave seen 'im, she *wouldn't* 'ave, would she?

HENRY (*wearily*): For Gawd's sake. . . .

EMMA (*with fine scorn*): You and your poor sailor boy that you met at the White Hart . . . your poor sailor boy with no friends . . . and wanted a bed for the night. . . . Must be kind to our Jolly Jack Tars, you said! Well, where's your precious Jolly Jack Tar, *now*? I expect he's being jollier than ever—somewhere the other side of England.

SHIRLEY (*with a loud sob*): Oh! Where's . . . where's Carnoustie? I want to talk to Carnoustie.

EMMA (*with grander scorn*): Carnoustie! There's another of 'em! Let him dare to set foot in this house. . . !

SHIRLEY: But, Mum, I *must* see him. Mum, where is he?

EMMA (*scornfully*): Looking for Albert! But he knows as well as I do that he has as much chance of finding him as a needle in a haystack. I wouldn't be surprised if Carnoustie didn't know all along what Albert was going to do.

[*Daphne enters with tray on which are all the requirements for tea except the teapot.*]

DAPHNE (*overhearing Emma's last remarks*): I'm sure

you're wrong there, Aunt Emma. It's hard enough to believe there's any wickedness in Albert, but I'm *sure* there's none in Carnoustie. If he'd known, he would never have let Shirley be humiliated like this.
EMMA: Oh, my God! Are you telling me that *you've* fallen for a sailor now?
DAPHNE: I'm just telling you what I think, that's all. The tea won't be a minute. The kettle's boiling.

[*Daphne goes into kitchen again.*]

HENRY (*unfortunately*): And I could do with a cup.
EMMA (*rounding on him*): *You* could do with a cup! If you think you're going to just sit sipping cups of tea. . . . (*Seeing Henry has taken off boots and collar.*) That's right! Take your boots off! Take your collar off! In fact, if I were you, I should pop upstairs and get into bed and have a little nap for a couple of hours! I shouldn't let the fact that your daughter's been jilted on her wedding day *and* that you're responsible . . . I shouldn't let that bother you too much! (*With a change of tone—low and almost menacing.*) 'Enry 'Ornett, you'll put your collar and boots on again right away and get yourself down to the police station and tell 'em they've got to find Albert Tufnell if they search all England to do it.
SHIRLEY (*crying*): No, Mum! I won't let you do that. I won't let you go to the police. (*Sobbing.*) The p . . . p . . . police c . . . c . . . can't make him m . . . m . . . marry me if he doesn't want to.
EMMA: It's no use talking that way. 'Enry! Are you going down to the police station, or aren't you?
HENRY: I aren't!
EMMA: *What!!*
HENRY: You 'eard. This is Shirley's concern, not yours. An' if she doesn't want to do nothing about it. . . .

EMMA: Then I'll go myself.
SHIRLEY: Mother, if you do go, I'll . . . I'll drown myself, I swear I will!

[*Daphne enters from kitchen with teapot.*]

EMMA (*baffled*). Oh, well, 'ave a cup of tea, then perhaps you'll see sense.
DAPHNE: Aunt Emma, I just saw Mrs. Lack coming through the. . . .

[*Mrs. Lack's voice, appropriately solemn, is heard off right.*]

MRS. LACK: Are you there, Emma?
EMMA (*under her breath*): If that woman starts. . . . (*To Daphne.*) Give Shirley a cup of tea.
MRS. LACK (*appearing in kitchen doorway*): It's all right, Emma. It's only me. I wouldn't have intruded at a time like this, but I thought I'd just. . . . (*Coming down to Shirley.*) Shirley . . . my 'eart goes out to you!
SHIRLEY: I . . . I. . . .
EMMA: Florrie, I'm sure you mean well, but. . . .
MRS. LACK: I'm not going to stay. I know you want to be alone with your great sorrow, but I just felt I had to. . . .

[*Daphne has poured a cup of tea and is bringing it down to Shirley, but as she is about to hand it to her, Mrs. Lack's hand comes out and takes it.*]

(*Automatically—as she takes tea.*) Oh, thank you, love. I didn't . . . I wasn't . . . but thank you very much. (*She takes a sip of tea.*)

[*In the meantime, Daphne goes into kitchen and returns with another cup and saucer, pours tea and hands it round.*]

Eee! I needed that. I went to Banfield's with all the others, Emma, same as you told us, but could I eat a bite! Not if you'd paid me a thousand pounds! My 'eart was with poor Shirley 'ere. I tried! 'Eaven knows, I tried! I tried to eat a little bun, but it was just as if I'd filled my mouth with sawdust. . . . Banfield's buns always were a bit like that, anyway. . . . So I said to myself, "Florrie, it's no use. Your place isn't here! Where *you* should be is near those who are suffering—and, Gawd, *'ow* you must all be suffering!—in case you're needed. . . . You know—"A friend in need is a friend indeed!"

EMMA: It's very kind of you, Florrie, but. . . .

MRS. LACK: Not at all. You're more than welcome, I'm sure. Besides, I *had* to let poor Rita know. I've just told her. Ooh! She was pleased!

EMMA: What!

MRS. LACK (*hastily*): Pleased she wasn't there, I mean, in her . . . er . . . capacity as bridesmaid. I mean to say, she'd have looked so silly, wouldn't she? Like poor Shirley! All dressed up and nowhere to go, so to speak! (*To Henry, who has been sitting morose and glum.*) Mr. 'Ornett—poor Mr. 'Ornett—you're not saying much, are you? But if we could look into your 'eart, I'm sure we'd find it filled with a black 'atred for the man who's treated your flesh and blood so shamefully.

HENRY (*with meaning*): You'd find it filled with black hatred for *somebody*!

MRS. LACK (*sailing on*): But why should it 'appen to poor Shirley, that's what I keep asking myself. Why? (*With a big heave of the shoulders.*) Ah, well! "The Lord moves in a mysterious way His wonders to perform." Did he leave a note or anything?

EMMA (*shortly*): Who? The Lord?

MRS. LACK: No. The bridegroom.

SHIRLEY (*starting up*): Ooooh! I never thought of that . . . Mum, Daphne, can you see a note anywhere?

EMMA: You'll find no notes—believe me.

MRS. LACK (*heavily*): Perhaps he's thrown himself in the river, sooner than face. . . . (*She looks at Emma.*)

EMMA (*sharply*). Face what?

MRS. LACK: His responsibilities.

EMMA: I'm facing one very big fact at the moment, and that is that. . . .

[*Carnoustie appears at door left.*]

(*Seeing him.*) Oh! It's you.

SHIRLEY (*running to him*): Carnoustie—oh, Carnoustie—have you found him . . . have you heard anything?

CARN (*shaking his head dejectedly*): No, I've no'.

SHIRLEY: Have you looked for him . . . everywhere?

CARN: Aye, I ha'e.

SHIRLEY: Oh, Albert. . . ! (*She collapses, weeping.*)

CARN: I'm awfu' sorry. I've done ma best.

EMMA: *You're* sorry! Well, that's something, I must say.

DAPHNE: Aunt Emma, please. . . .

EMMA (*brushing her aside with a gesture*): I'm going to ask you a question, young man. Did you know about this? Did Albert tell you he was going to do it?

CARN: He did not.

HENRY. 'Course he didn't.

EMMA (*to Henry*): Quiet, you! (*To Carnoustie.*) Do you know *why* he did it?

CARN (*hedging*): Er . . . Shirley would be more likely to know that than me, surely?

EMMA: You *do* know, don't you?

CARN: I know no more than you know yourselves.
EMMA: It wouldn't surprise me if you'd put him up to it.
DAPHNE: That's not fair, Aunt Emma. Why should Carnoustie do that? And why should he know the reason Albert did it any more than you—if as much.
EMMA: I'd like to know just what you're getting at, Daphne. I don't like this sort of talk. If you've got something to say, say it. Don't go throwing out a lot of insinuendos! And as for you, young man, you can be seeing about getting yourself away from here. . . .

[*The front door is heard to open, and close with a slam.*]

Now who. . . ?
SHIRLEY (*leaping up and clutching Daphne*): Oh, Daphne, suppose it's Albert!

[*But it is not! It is Edie who comes quickly into the room, wild-eyed and almost hysterical. She stands inside the door for a minute, panting.*]

Aunt Edie!
DAPHNE (*moving up*): Auntie . . .

[*Edie cannot speak, but, with a howl which increases in volume as she moves, comes down to Shirley and flings herself at her, round her, over her. She almost pushes her on to the settee.*]

SHIRLEY (*before she goes under*): Aunt Edie!

[*Edie is hugging her, kissing her, almost smothering her.*]

EMMA (*sharply, but unavailingly*): Now then, Edie, none of that! (*There is more of it.*) Edie! . . . Do you hear me?

MRS. LACK: You'll 'ave to *do* something, Emma!

EMMA: Stop it, d'y'hear! (*Then, in a fury.*) *Edie 'Ornett*, will you. . . ! (*She tries to drag Edie off Shirley.*) Do you want to . . . (*Struggling.*) smother her? (*Then, as at last she drags Edie to her feet.*) Haven't you a grain of sense?

EDIE (*hysterically*): *It's happened again!* It's happened to poor Shirley—same as it happened to me. I knew it. *I knew it!* Oooooh!

MRS. LACK: Ooh! Isn't she awful!

EMMA (*to Edie*): Shut up, will you! Henry, she's your sister. Can't *you* stop her?

EDIE (*regardless*): I saw it!! I saw it in the teacup! (*Looking wildly round.*) You saw it, too, didn't you, Mrs. Lack?

MRS. LACK: Well . . . I. . . .

EDIE: A bleeding, broken heart! Oh, my poor lamb! (*She hurls herself on Shirley again.*)

EMMA: Will you shut up and leave Shirley alone! (*Again she drags Edie away.*)

EDIE: Ever since I saw it in the teacup I've known! Wherever I've turned I've seen bleedin' broken hearts . . . and they were *all* Shirley's . . . I knew they were Shirley's. Something told me.

EMMA (*shouting*): Will you listen to me while *I* tell you something!

EDIE (*she won't*): Another Great Sorrow in the family! Oh, my poor Shirley! I know . . . I *know* what you're going through . . . I've suffered it, too! The shame! The humiliation!

SHIRLEY (*by now almost in Edie's condition*): Don't, Aunt Edie! Don't!

EDIE: But that it should happen to you . . . just as it happened to me . . . left at the altar rails. . . !

SHIRLEY: Ooooh!

EMMA (*almost dancing with fury*): Edie 'Ornett!

EDIE: Twice in the family. That's twice it's 'appened. It's a curse! That's what it is! It's a *curse*!

MRS. LACK (*horrified*): What!!

EMMA: Will you. . . !

EDIE (*with every ounce of drama she can put into it*): *A curse on the 'ouse of 'Ornett!!!! (She collapses on a chair.)*

MRS. LACK: The Lord save us!

SHIRLEY (*weeping*): Aunt Edie!

CARN (*clearing his throat uncomfortably*): Well, I'll be going—if you'll excuse me.

EMMA: We will.

DAPHNE: If you'll wait a minute while I change, Carnoustie, I'll walk down to the station with you.

CARN: What? Och . . . aye!

EMMA: You'll do as you please, of course, but I *do* think, *and* I shall tell your mother when I write, that you're behaving proper 'eartless, Daphne Pink.

DAPHNE: But why . . . what. . . ?

EMMA: Doesn't it mean anything to you that your own cousin has been deceived and made a fool of?

DAPHNE (*baffled*): Of course it does. I'm as sorry for poor Shirley as any of you.

EMMA: But it doesn't stop your throwing yourself at the best friend of the man who did it . . . does it?

DAPHNE: Aunt Emma, you can't hold Carnoustie responsible for what Albert has done!

EDIE (*with great daring*): And you can't even blame poor Albert!

EMMA (*turning on her*): I thought I told you. . . .

EDIE: Albert isn't to blame. It's *fate*! That's what it is! And fate used Albert for its tool!

MRS. LACK (*to Emma*): She's off again!!

EDIE: "The moving finger writes and having *wrote*, moves on."

EMMA (*now livid*): I've stood just about as much of this as I'm going to! (*To Henry.*) Listen to what I've got to say, 'Enry 'Ornett! I've put up with this crack-pot of a sister of yours. . . .

[*Edie whimpers.*]

SHIRLEY: Mother. . . !

DAPHNE (*rushing to Edie, arms round her*): Oh, poor Aunt Edie! Don't listen.

EMMA (*overlapping*): for nearly twenty years. God knows how I've done it, but I have! But I've finished —do you hear?—finished! I've had all I can stand of her " fates " and " teacups ", her Great Sorrows and bleedin' hearts, and I'm telling you, here and now, that *she* gets out of this house tomorrow morning. And if *she* doesn't, then I *do*!

SHIRLEY: Mother, you can't turn poor Aunt Edie out like that. It isn't fair. She's upset, that's all.

EMMA (*rounding on her*): Now don't you start telling me what I *ought* to do. I should've thought you'd got enough on your plate, without worrying your head about anyone else. You 'aven't managed your *own* affairs so marvellously yourself, 'ave you? Gettin' yourself tied up with a good-for-nothing fly-by-night from God knows where, and letting yourself and all your family be made fools of in front of the whole town.

[*There is an outburst of protestations from everyone at this. Shirley is in tears, Edie has been, and still is.*]

<table>
<tr>
<td>DAPHNE: Aunt Emma!
SHIRLEY: Oh, Mum, you don't realise what you're saying.
HENRY: Now then, Missus!
CARN: Mrs. Hornett, for shame on ye!
MRS. LACK: Far be it from me. . . .</td>
<td>(All this comes together. And more, ad lib.)</td>
</tr>
</table>

[*Everyone on stage is more or less part of the huddled group turned away from kitchen door. The hubbub goes on for a while, and then each person stops (not all together) as they become "aware" that something has happened. As they stop speaking, they turn, almost as if willed to do so, and look towards the door right. Albert is standing there. There is complete and utter silence for a very long time.*]

ALBERT (*at last—and speaking very simply*): 'Ullo!
SHIRLEY (*after another long pause—rushing and flinging her arms around him*): Albert! Oh, Albert!

[*She is sobbing wildly. Albert makes as if to put his arms around her but stops himself. The hubbub breaks out again.*]

CARN: *Albert!* Man! Where have ye been?
EMMA: So you've turned up, have you? Well, let me tell you. . . .
DAPHNE: Oh, thank God! Thank God!
MRS. LACK: Well, far be it from me. . . .
(*Together.*)

[*All the above can be added to ad lib.*]

SHIRLEY (*when the hubbub has ceased*): Oh, Albert, where have you been?

[*Albert appears to be overwhelmed by all the enquiring looks.*]

ALBERT: I . . . I. . . .
SHIRLEY (*desperately*): *Albert*, where *have* you been?
ALBERT: I've been looking at Pop's ferrets.

HENRY (*immediately*): How's Rosie?

[*Emma's glare at Henry almost stuns him.*]

SHIRLEY (*staggered*): You've been. . . ?

[*The others make inarticulate noises of surprise.*]

Albert Tufnell, are you completely *mad*?

ALBERT (*quietly*): No, I'm not. At least, I hope I'm not.

SHIRLEY: But . . . but. . . (*Words fail her.*)

EMMA (*they don't fail her*): Well, I've *tried* to keep quiet, seeing that. . . .

ALBERT (*quietly*): Try a bit harder, Ma.

EMMA: What!!!

HENRY: He said " Try a bit harder ".

SHIRLEY: Albert . . . I don't understand! Don't you realise what you've done? Our wedding. . . .

MRS. LACK: What happened? (*Almost hopefully.*) Did you lose your memory, or something?

ALBERT: No, I didn't lose my memory.

SHIRLEY: Then . . . are you telling me that you did what you did, deliberately?

ALBERT: Yes, I am.

SHIRLEY: You let me go to Church, *knowing* that you weren't going to go yourself?

ALBERT: Yes, I did.

EMMA: You . . . bas . . . no, I won't say it!

ALBERT (*at last—very quietly*): Bastard? (*He pauses.*) My father was a Chief Petty Officer in the Navy, and my mother was a stewardess with the P. & O. Line, and they were married at St. Thomas's Church, Southampton, on April the twenty-seventh, 1931, and I was born on January the thirtieth, 1932. Work that one out!

SHIRLEY (*desperately*). Oh. Albert, I couldn't have believed that you . . . that any man could have done such a cruel thing, but, Albert, that doesn't matter. Nothing matters if only you'll tell me you *still* love me and want to marry me.

ALBERT: I love you, Shirl . . . just as I've always done . . . and I still want to marry you.

SHIRLEY (*brokenly*): Oh thank God! Thank God!

EMMA (*breaking away*): I can't stand it! I can't stand watching my own daughter begging and pleading and cheapening herself . . . asking a man to marry her.

SHIRLEY (*wildly, as she weeps*): I don't care, Mum! I don't care if I am cheapening myself. All that I know is that I want Albert to marry me and he's going to.

ALBERT: I didn't say I was.

SHIRLEY: What?

ALBERT: I said I *wanted* to—not that I was *going* to.

SHIRLEY (*bewildered*): But, Albert. . . .

ALBERT: It isn't always best to do the things we want.

SHIRLEY (*breaking away wretchedly*): I . . . I don't understand you, Albert! You're just standing there, talking in riddles . . . and if it's any satisfaction to you to know it, you're breaking my heart.

EDIE (*coming to her*): Shirley, my poor, poor, Shirley!

SHIRLEY (*sobbing on her shoulder*): Oh, Aunt Edie. . . .

ALBERT (*to Emma*): You don't really want me to marry Shirl, do you, Ma?

EMMA: I never *have*—and you've done nothing today to make me change my mind!

ALBERT: I've always known you didn't. God knows, you've made it plain enough.

EMMA: And if you must know, I'd sooner give her to the first man that'appened to come through that door —even if it was the devil himself!

[*The Reverend Oliver Purefoy appears in doorway left.*]

PUREFOY (*gently as he does so*): May I come in?

[*There is a gasp from Emma, then a truly ghastly pause.*]

(*Aware of their gaping*) The front door was ajar, so I took the liberty. . . .

EDIE: Emma, it's the vicar. It's Mr. Purefoy!	(*Together.*)
SHIRLEY: Oh, Mr. Purefoy. . . .	
EMMA: Oh!	
MRS. LACK: Oh, well *now*, of course. . . !	
CARN (*to Albert*): You're for it the noo!	

[*Mr. Purefoy is a man of about forty. He has an easy manner, a pleasant voice and is a likeable person—not given to "throwing his weight about", but quite capable of using it—and with authority—when needed.*]

EMMA (*faintly*): Come in, Mr. Purefoy.
PUREFOY: Thank you, Mrs. Hornett.
SHIRLEY (*going to Albert and leading him forward a step*): Mr. Purefoy, this is. . . .
PUREFOY (*waving his hand*): No, no, please! Don't let us bother with formal introductions; not at a time like this. I'm sure you're all far too disturbed. (*Looking round.*) Actually, I think I saw you all in church, did I not?
EMMA (*pointing to Albert*): Not *him*, you didn't!
PUREFOY: Oh, perhaps I. . . .
SHIRLEY: Mr. Purefoy, this . . . this is Albert.
PUREFOY (*not understanding*): Albert? (*Holding out his hand.*) How do you do . . . er . . . Albert? (*Then with a start.*) Good heavens! You mean . . . *Albert!* . . . er . . . *The* Albert!!!

SHIRLEY (*nodding her head vigorously*): Ummmps!

PUREFOY (*nonplussed*): Oh . . . er . . . well . . . I . . . The missing bridgroom, eh?

EMMA: Missing bridegroom. If you ask me, there's more missing than. . . .

MRS. LACK: He's turned up, sir. Better late than never.

SHIRLEY: But, Mr. Purefoy, he says he doesn't want to. . . .

ALBERT: I'm sorry I've caused all this trouble, sir. . . .

(*Together.*)

SHIRLEY (*clearly—on her own*): He says he loves me, but he won't marry me.

PUREFOY (*waving his hand*): Forgive me, I. . . . (*He silences them.*) I am a little confused. Perhaps if . . . er . . . *one* person could explain. . . ?

EMMA: *I'll* soon do that!

PUREFOY (*a little dejectedly perhaps*): Oh! I did think perhaps. . . . (*He waves towards Shirley and Albert.*) However! (*He prepares to listen.*) Yes, Mrs. Hornett. . . ?

CARN (*piping up*): If there's any explanation to be given, sir, I should say Albert's the one to do it.

PUREFOY (*heartily*): So should I. I . . . er . . . I mean. . . .

EMMA: *Let* him explain, then, but whatever he says, don't believe him, Mr. Purefoy.

MRS. LACK: I know if my daughter was ever treated the way poor Shirley's been . . .

EDIE: I *still* say, and I'll go on saying it, that Albert's not to blame. It's Fate, and it's no use fighting *Fate*, is it, Mr. Purefoy?

PUREFOY: Er . . . Fate, Miss Hornett?

EDIE: I saw it in the teacup, sir.

EMMA (*to Edie*): If you start. . . .

EDIE (*to Emma*): Ask Mr. Purefoy, he knows, don't you, sir? I saw it in the teacup as plain as daylight, and when you can see it as plain as *that*, there's no use fighting it, is there, sir?
PUREFOY: I'm afraid, Miss Hornett, you are taking me somewhat out of my depth. My . . . er . . . theological studies did not embrace the . . . er . . . mysteries of the . . . er . . . teacup. But . . . please! (*And he now speaks with a suggestion of authority in his voice.*) I came here to offer what comfort I could to . . . er . . . Shirley. . . .
EMMA: And it was very good of you, sir, and. . . .
PUREFOY (*firmly talking her down*): After all, I baptised her, and I prepared her for Confirmation, and I still hope it will be my privilege to marry her.
EMMA: But not to. . . .
PUREFOY (*more firmly, over-riding her*): As I say, I came to offer comfort, but it would appear that I might be able to offer something more concrete . . . er . . . given the opportunity. I should like to have a word with (*Waving hand towards Shirley and Albert.*) these two young people. (*To Emma.*) Don't you think it would be wiser if those who are not primarily concerned were to leave us for a while, Mrs. Hornett?
DAPHNE (*immediately*): Come on, Carnoustie (*She moves to door left.*)
EMMA: If you like, Vicar, though I don't see. . . . (*Turning sharply.*) Edie . . . Henry . . . off you go!

[*Mrs. Lack sits tight hopefully.*]

HENRY: But aren't *you*. . . ? (*Speaking to Emma as he rises.*)
EMMA (*sharply to Mrs. Lack*): *And* you, Florrie!
MRS. LACK (*as she goes reluctantly*): Well, I should have

thought I *was* concerned, seeing Rita was going to be a bridesmaid!

[*She goes left. Edie, Daphne and Henry follow.*]

CARN (*at Albert's side*): Albert. . . ?
ALBERT: What?
CARN: Call oot if ye want me!

[*Carnoustie exits left. Albert is now down right. Purefoy centre. Shirley and Emma left.*]

PUREFOY (*with a bland smile*): I'm afraid I'm treating your house as though it were my own, Mrs. Hornett —driving *you all* out like this.

[*Emma sniffs.*]

But I'm sure that a word or two with these children— alone. . . .
EMMA: No good can come of it. The sooner it's all over, and *him* out of the house, the better.
PUREFOY: But. . . .
EMMA: But as you wish, Mr. Purefoy. *As* you wish! (*She sits.*)
PUREFOY (*still standing*): Thank you. . . . (*He pauses.*) I did . . . er . . . suggest "alone", Mrs. Hornett.
EMMA (*after looking around*): Well, we *are* alone!
PUREFOY (*after coughing discreetly*): I . . . er . . . meant. . . .
EMMA (*aghast*): You mean "alone" without *me*! Is that what you mean?
PUREFOY (*gently*): I'm afraid it is.
EMMA: As Shirley's mother I've a right to be here.
PUREFOY: Only if each of these two wants you to be.
SHIRLEY: You'd better go, Mum.

PUREFOY: Is that your wish, too, Albert?

ALBERT: If Shirl and me can't hear what you've got to say, sir, without her mother being here—then we might as well chuck in our hands straight away.

PUREFOY (*coughing discreetly*): H'm!

EMMA: Well, if I have to go, I go under protest.

PUREFOY: Er . . . quite! . . . Very natural . . . perhaps. . . .

EMMA: And, if you don't mind my saying so, Mr. Purefoy, I can't think why you want *Shirley* here. (*Pointing to Albert.*) *He's* the one that wants the talking to. He's the one that's done wrong—not her. My girl gave a promise to him and was prepared to keep it . . . but not his lordship here! He let her down. He's made her the laughing-stock of the whole town. And not only that! Not content with breaking her heart, he has the nerve to come back here just so we can see him gloating over the misery he's caused.

ALBERT (*quietly*): Are you going, Ma . . . under protest?

EMMA (*snapping at him*): Yes, I am. (*To Shirley.*) And I'm expecting you to come with me.

SHIRLEY: No, Mum. I'm staying.

EMMA: You'll regret it—you see if you don't—as sure as your name is Shirley 'Ornett.

PUREFOY (*with an easy smile*): But I'm hoping we may yet change it to Shirley *Tufnell.*

EMMA (*as she goes angrily out of the room*): Oooh! (*She exits right.*)

[*There is a silence for a moment.*]

PUREFOY (*breaking the silence*): Ahem! A . . . a woman of character, Mrs. Hornett! (*He catches the look on Albert's face and coughs again.*) Well . . . now. . . ! Let us sit down, shall we?

[*Shirley sits on settee. Albert is about to sit beside her but, seeing Shirley's reproachful look, moves to a chair and sits. Purefoy sits easily on edge of table.*]

Now, Albert . . . you said, a moment ago, something about . . . Shirley and you hearing what *I've* got to say. . .

ALBERT: Yes, sir.

PUREFOY: But you're completely wrong there, you know. It isn't what *I* have to say that matters.

ALBERT: Oh?

PUREFOY: Good heavens! Surely you must see that *some* explanation of your extraordinary—and that's putting it mildly, Albert—your extraordinary behaviour is expected?

ALBERT (*muttering*): Yessir.

PUREFOY: Well?

[*Albert is silent and uneasy.*]

(*After waiting.*) Shirley. . . .

SHIRLEY: Yes, Mr. Purefoy?

PUREFOY: You realise, I hope, that there may be a definite and unpleasant explanation for Albert's behaviour?

SHIRLEY (*quietly*): Yes; but I'm sure. . . .

PUREFOY: And the most definite and unpleasant explanation that springs to my mind. . . . (*Slight pause.*) Albert! Is there any legal reason why you shouldn't marry Shirley?

ALBERT (*wonderingly*): Legal reason. . . ?

PUREFOY (*watching him closely*): Yes.

ALBERT (*after a tiny pause—without any trace of "being funny"*): I . . . I haven't got a wife in Honolulu, if that's what you mean, sir.

PUREFOY (*trying not to smile*): Broadly speaking, that *is* what I meant. Nor, we may take it, in the . . . er . . . Home Waters?

ALBERT (*simply*): There's . . . really . . . never been any other girl in my life except (*Looking at Shirley.*) her.

PUREFOY (*impressed by his sincerity*): I'm sure we can accept that, eh, Shirley?

SHIRLEY: I never thought for a moment that there was anything like that, Mr. Purefoy.

PUREFOY: Frankly, neither did I. And you still love Shirley?

ALBERT: Yessir.

PUREFOY: And, Shirley, you love Albert?

SHIRLEY: He knows I do.

PUREFOY: Then . . . Albert . . . Shirley . . . where the devil have we come unstuck? . . . (*After a short pause.*) Albert, I think this is where you begin to talk. Now, come along! . . . (*Another slight pause.*) If it helps you at all to know this, I'm convinced that, in spite of the callous, the cruel thing you have done to Shirley this morning, basically you're . . . all right.

ALBERT: Thank you, sir.

PUREFOY: Of course, I may be wrong; first impressions, you know! But I am waiting for you to *prove* that I am right

ALBERT: I . . . I'm not very good at explaining things . . . thoughts that are in my mind, sir. I *know* how I feel about things, but. . . .

PUREFOY: You find difficulty in putting them into words, eh? Well, there's nothing to worry about there. There's only the three of us. (*Smiling.*) You're not on " Woman's Hour ", Albert.

ALBERT (*half smile*): No, sir. (*Then soberly.*) I didn't turn up at church this morning because . . . well, for one thing I was frightened.

PUREFOY: Frightened? Of what?

ALBERT: The future . . . mine and Shirley's.

PUREFOY (*incredulously*): You. . . ?

ALBERT: I mean . . . whether we'd be able to make a go of it . . . or whether *I* would, I should say.

PUREFOY (*sharply*): My dear Albert, that's nonsense.

ALBERT: It doesn't seem so to me, sir.

PUREFOY: Your offering this particular reason as an excuse for treating Shirley the way you have today *is* the most arrant nonsense! If it's not, then it's the most cowardly, the most blackguardly excuse for wrongdoing I have ever listened to. (*He moves up and down, not hiding his disgust.*)

SHIRLEY (*hating hearing Albert spoken to like this*): Oh, Albert!

PUREFOY (*turning on Albert with something of a Prosecuting Counsel's manner*): You seriously ask us to believe that you gave no thought to the future, and your ability to cope with it, *until this morning* . . . a few hours before your wedding?

ALBERT (*wretchedly*): I thought about it all last night. I never slept a wink.

PUREFOY (*one almost hears the swish of the gown as he turns away*): *Last night!* For heaven's sake, man . . . last night was a hundred years too late to start thinking! You should have thought about it, *and* arrived at a definite conclusion long ago!

ALBERT (*trying to fight back*): How could I, when it didn't happen until last night?

PUREFOY: When *what* didn't happen?

ALBERT (*lamely*): Er . . . what *happened*.

PUREFOY: Albert . . . at this moment I am sorely tempted to kick you hard in the pants!

SHIRLEY (*protesting*): Oh no, Mr. Purefoy, you mustn't. . . !

PUREFOY (*with a grand gesture of hopelessness*): Shirley

(*He speaks patiently.*) you don't seem to understand. (*Pointing at her.*) *You* are on *my* (*Pointing to himself.*) side! (*Then correcting himself.*) I mean, *I* am on yours! If I can't get him to *talk* sense, then I am damn well going to kick it out of him

SHIRLEY: If Albert doesn't want to marry me, sir, I wouldn't want you to force him to—not in any way.

ALBERT: I *do* want to—you know I do.

PUREFOY (*vigorously*): Then why *don't* you?

[*There is a long pause. Albert twiddles his fingers nervously.*]

ALBERT (*after pause*): I don't know whether you know it or not, sir, but I was brought up in an Orphanage.

PUREFOY: Er . . . yes. I remember. Shirley did tell me.

[*Albert's ensuing long speeches do not flow easily. He has to pause frequently to put his thoughts into words.*]

ALBERT: I was in the Orphanage from as far back as I can remember—until I went into the Navy. So . . . I've never had any—what you call—"home life". Whenever I've had a leave I've always stayed at . . . well . . . Y.M.C.A.'s . . . the Union Jack Club . . . the Salvation Army . . . you know, sir.

PUREFOY (*quietly*): Yes, I know.

ALBERT: On board I'd hear other lads talking about . . . their homes; their mums; their dads . . . their families—and it sort-of made me . . . well . . . not sorry for myself—don't think that—but . . . "homesick" for . . . for the home I'd never had—if you follow me, sir.

PUREFOY: I do.

ALBERT: And I made up my mind that as soon as the right girl came along I was going to *have* a home of my own, even if it was only a couple of rooms to start with. . . . (*He pauses.*) Then I met Shirley, and I knew right away that she was the girl I wanted, and, as luck would have it, she felt the same way about me. I told her about . . . what I wanted, and she . . . well, I thought she understood. I've only had two long leaves since we got to know each other, and both times I've . . . I've stayed here at Shirley's. . . . (*He pauses again.*) I've had my first taste of "home life", sir, and . . . (*To Shirley.*) you're not going to like this, Shirl—(*To Purefoy again.*) but if what I've seen in this house is "honest-to-God" home life, then all I can say is, give me "The Salvation Army"!

SHIRLEY (*weeping quietly*): Albert!

[*There is a pause.*]

PUREFOY (*embarrassed*): Albert, I don't know, of course, how justified you are in thinking the way you do, but let me assure you that if, or when, you marry and settle down in a home of your own, that home will be just as happy as you and your wife *make* it.

ALBERT (*quietly—after a look at Shirley*): As we're *allowed* to make it.

PUREFOY: I don't follow you.

ALBERT: What you've just said, sir; that's what I've been telling myself all along. My own sense told me, of course, that *all* homes can't be alike. I'd only to listen to the lads on board to know that, anyway. I've kept telling myself that once we had a place of our own . . . me and Shirl . . . we'd be O.K. . . . we'd have our ups and downs, naturally, and we wouldn't always see eye to eye—but we'd be *on our own* and we'd sort things out ourselves and in our own way.

PUREFOY: And that's how it *will* be. Why not? You're going to work in Badcaster when you leave the Navy, aren't you?

ALBERT: Yes, sir.

PUREFOY: Well, there you are! If you marry Shirley I presume you will find some place, even if it is, as you say it might be, only a couple of rooms. . . .

ALBERT: That would do me.

PUREFOY: I started my married life in *one*. In the luxury of your *two* rooms, Albert, you will lay the foundations of your future happiness.

ALBERT (*looking directly at Shirley—after a pause*): Will we, Shirl?

[*Shirley covers her face with her hands and sobs bitterly.*]

PUREFOY (*surprised*): Shirley! What is it? Why are you. . . ? Don't you want that?

SHIRLEY (*from behind her hands*): Yes . . . yes. . . .

PUREFOY: Then why in heaven's name. . . ! (*He throws up his arms in his bewilderment.*)

[*There is a pause.*]

ALBERT (*quietly to Shirley*): I *know*, Shirl . . . about the house. (*Pause.*) You know that, don't you?

SHIRLEY (*very quietly after another pause*): Yes, Albert.

PUREFOY: You know . . . what? Is there something you two haven't told me?

[*Pause.*]

Something that justifies your conduct this morning, Albert?

ALBERT: Perhaps it doesn't, sir. I dunno. But I think it explains it.

SHIRLEY (*brokenly*): It *does* justify it, Albert. I see that now. I've seen it all along, really.

PUREFOY: Then why have you allowed me to cluck away like a broody hen when all the time. . . ? (*Impatiently.*) What is this, whatever it is, for goodness' sake?

[*Albert looks at Shirley.*]

SHIRLEY (*after a pause*): I . . . I've played a dirty trick on Albert, Mr. Purefoy.

PUREFOY (*after a look, first at Shirley, then at Albert*): Oh?

SHIRLEY: Yes, sir. I . . . I let mother put down the deposit on a house . . . to buy it, I mean . . . for Albert and me. I never said anything to Albert about it. I wasn't going to tell him; not until we were married.

PUREFOY. But why not?

SHIRLEY: Because I knew he'd never agree to it.

PUREFOY: But, surely. . . .

SHIRLEY: You see, sir . . . the house is only three doors away from this one . . . Number twenty-four.

PUREFOY (*very gravely*): Oh!

SHIRLEY: I can't think now why I let mother do it.

PUREFOY: Without consulting Albert . . . it was very wrong of you, Shirley. (*To Albert.*) And that is why you. . . ?

ALBERT: Yes, sir. At first, I was just . . . well, hurt . . . 'cos Shirley hadn't told me. I wouldn't have known if Aunt Edie hadn't let it slip out last night. I felt I was being . . . tricked into something, and what sort of a way is that to start your married life, sir? Then when I'd got over the hurt of it—and I *was* hurt, Shirl, I don't mind telling you. I've always played straight with you ever since I've known you . . . until this morning.

SHIRLEY: I know you have, Albert.

PUREFOY: Go on with what you were saying, Albert —after you had got over the. . . .

ALBERT: Oh, yes. Well, all last night I lay awake thinking about it. And I thought to myself " Suppose we do come to live at Number Twenty-Four . . . what's going to be the result. . . ? " And no matter which way I looked at it, sir, I knew it wouldn't work. I'd seen what life was like in *this* and the thought of the same sort of thing going on in *my* home . . . my dream home; the home I'd longed for; well, it just brought me out in a cold sweat. (*He makes a very definite pause before continuing.*) I've always got on well with people, sir. I'm not patting myself on the back or nothing like that, but I think I can honestly say that most people like me. I never had no trouble on board, never. (*He pauses.*) I don't know what I've done to her to make her hate me as she does. . . .

PUREFOY (*quietly*): Done to whom, Albert?

ALBERT (*slight pause*): Mrs' 'Ornett, sir. Shirley's mother. She *does* hate me, she's let me see that she does. Don't ask me why. I've done my best to get her to think differently, but everything I do only seems to make things worse. I've tried to console myself with the thought that . . well . . . I say to myself " She hates *you*, Albert, but she doesn't seem to like anybody *else* very much, either ". The way she treats Pop and poor Aunt Edie . . . it makes me feel hot and cold. . . . And the thought of her being only three doors away and trotting in and out of *my* home . . . filling it with hatred. . . ! (*His voice rising.*) *No!* (*Covering his face with his hand for a moment.*) My God, no!

[*Purefoy, after a pause, comes to Albert and pats him comfortingly on the back.*)

Well, now you know, sir, why I didn't show up at my wedding . . . what with the trick over the house and knowing what would happen if we. . . .

PUREFOY (*quietly*): What you did was the *wrong* thing, but. . . . (*To Shirley.*) You may not like me saying this, Shirley, (*To Albert again.*) I can almost understand why you didn't do the *right* one.

ALBERT: Thank you, sir; and I'm sorry, Shirl, that I've had to speak of your mother the way I have.

[*Henry pokes his head round door left, then comes quietly into the room and listens.*]

PUREFOY: Albert, there's one thing you haven't explained. Why did you come back . . . here . . . now?

ALBERT: To ask Shirley to marry me, sir.

PUREFOY (*staggered*): To *what*?

ALBERT: On my terms, I mean. I made up my mind last night that I'd got to be firm, sir, about the house and Mrs. Hornett. I'd have talked to Shirley before the wedding, but I wasn't allowed to see her. When I left the house this morning, I was just sick with panic. I walked about the streets, trying to decide what was best to be done. . . . One minute I'd be thinking " You can't let Shirley down like this . . . you can't ", and the next I'd say " You can't go through with it, not as things are now . . . it's the future . . . yours and hers, you've got to think about. Whatever you do today will be forgotten; you'll live that down, but . . . the future. . . ! " And then I decided, sir. I'd skip the wedding, and I'd come back here, and if Shirley saw things as I see them, and if she loved me enough . . . well, we'd get married just as soon as we could.

HENRY: Eee! If only I'd had the courage to do the same!

SHIRLEY (*seeing him*): Dad!

HENRY: If you've got half the sense I think you have, you'll go down on your knees and beg Albert to marry you. *And* you'll tell your mother just what she can do with Number Twenty-Four!

SHIRLEY: But, Dad, she's put a deposit. . . .

HENRY: And she can do the same with the deposit. . . (*To Purefoy.*) Listen, Mr Purefoy, I'm not being . . . er . . . disrespectful about my wife.

PUREFOY (*blankly*) Aren't you?

HENRY: No, sir.

PUREFOY: Good heavens!

HENRY: But I understand 'er Albert doesn't; there's no reason why he should, and understanding 'er wouldn't put things right as far as 'e's concerned.

PUREFOY: If only Mrs. Hornett could learn to like Albert. . . .

HENRY: What good would that do? It wouldn't stop 'er trying to make 'is life a misery.

PUREFOY: But, Mr. Hornett. . . .

HENRY (*almost desperately*): She can't *help* it, sir. It's just *her*, and why should Albert stand for it? With me, it's different. I'm her husband, and . . . and she's done a lot that I have to be thankful for.

ALBERT (*incredulously*): *You* have, Pop?

HENRY: Aye, Albert, *I* have. (*Slight pause.*) Just look round this room. Nothing very wonderful about it, you might say, but it's a home I'd never be ashamed for anyone to see. *She* keeps it this way. If you went into some of the 'ouses in this street. . . . And another thing, I've never yet come 'ome from work to find Emma out at the pictures and a packet of fish and chips waiting for me in the oven. And that's a damn sight more than most husbands in my position can say.

PUREFOY: That is *very* true.

HENRY: And she's been . . . sort of ambitious. Not for 'erself . . . that's the funny part of it. You'd expect with Emma it *would* 'ave been, but no . . . first for me—and then when I didn't turn out much of a success—for Shirley here. And you don't suppose it's been much fun for her saddled with Edie all these years. It isn't every wife that would have stood for it, you know.

PUREFOY: You're very proud of Mrs. Hornett, aren't you?

HENRY (*simply*): Aye, I am. And I'm fond of her. There are times when I could wring her blasted neck if I had the courage. . . .

PUREFOY: Ahem!!

HENRY: You'll excuse me, Mr. Purefoy, but I'm speaking as man to man, now. I *am* fond of her, and I believe she's fond of me, but it doesn't stop her trying to make me miserable—and succeeding. It's a kink she's got. I can put up with it, but what I'm trying to say is, that there's no reason why Albert should.

PUREFOY: Then what you suggest is. . . .

[*Suddenly loud sobbing is heard outside the door left—Emma.*]

(*Looking towards door.*) Good heavens! Who is. . . ?

ALBERT (*overlapping*): What the. . . !

HENRY (*in a voice of panic*): It's *'er*! Has she been listening? My Gawd!

SHIRLEY (*running to door*): Mum!

HENRY (*yelling*): Hey! Let me get out of here while I'm still alive! (*He dashes off right.*)

SHIRLEY (*opening door left*): Mum!

[*Emma steps to just inside the door. She is weeping noisily.*]

PUREFOY: Mrs. Hornett!
SHIRLEY (*amazed*): Mum, what is it?
ALBERT (*shattered*): Well, stone a crow!
EMMA (*coming down wretchedly*): Don't speak to me. I couldn't bear it. I've been listening. I've heard every word that's been said. They say listeners never hear any good of themselves . . . and I've been punished. (*She collapses into a chair.*)
ALBERT: Good Lord!
EMMA: I'm a wicked woman, Mr. Purefoy.
PUREFOY (*soothingly*): No, no, Mrs. Hornett.
EMMA: I am. I must be. All the trouble I've caused. Making Henry's life a 'ell on earth. But I didn't do it with wicked intent, Mr. Purefoy, I swear I didn't.
PUREFOY: I'm sure you didn't, Mrs. Hornett.
EMMA: And hearing him stand up for me like that. . . ! That man's a jewel, Mr. Purefoy . . . and I'm an evil woman! Mr. Purefoy, what can I do to be saved?
PUREFOY (*blinking*): I *beg* your pardon?
EMMA (*with just a trace of "bite" in her voice*): Well, you're a clergyman; you should know.
PUREFOY (*not happy*): Mrs. Hornett, I . . . this is so sudden. (*Realising what he has said.*) Ahem!
EMMA (*still weeping*): I didn't know . . . I didn't realise I was making everyone unhappy! I . . . I . . . just thought I was . . . looking after their interests! (*She finishes in a wail.*)
PUREFOY: Yes, yes, you meant well, Mrs. Hornett, I'm quite sure of that. But you were . . . misguided in your method of approach, shall we say?
EMMA (*obligingly*): Yes, *let's* say that. You see, Mr.

Purefoy, I've always had to manage everybody 'cos they couldn't manage themselves.

PUREFOY: Did you give them the chance to?

EMMA: No, sir. There wasn't any point, Henry . . . doesn't know what he's doing half the time, and Edie . . . well, she doesn't know what she's doing *any* of the time; so you see. . . .

PUREFOY: And Shirley? What about Shirley?

EMMA: Whatever I've done for her, I've done with the best intentions. (*Weeping again.*) I have, Shirley love, I *have*.

SHIRLEY: I'm sure you have, Mum, but. . . .

EMMA: That's why I put the deposit up for Number Twenty-Four. I thought it would be nice for you to have me near . . . a sort of guardian angel. (*To Purefoy.*) After all, sir, I knew she was going to marry a sailor, and . . . well, you know what sailors are!

PUREFOY: I know what *this one* is, Mrs. Hornett. He's a grand fellow who will make Shirley a good husband, and who will make you proud to have him for a son-in-law.

EMMA (*humbly*). Well, if *you* say so, sir. . . .

PUREFOY: I can only say that I wish he were *my* son-in-law!

EMMA (*reflectively, between sobs*): Yes, *your* daughter hasn't made such a good catch, has she?

PUREFOY (*between annoyance and embarrassment*): I . . . I. . . .

EMMA (*bursting into tears*): There I go! Saying things that aren't nice! Ooooh! Making people miserable! Do you think I'm too old to reform, Mr. Purefoy?

PUREFOY: If I may be forgiven a platitude. . . .

[*Emma speaks from now on in almost humble acquiescence, broken by an occasional return to her old style and self.*]

EMMA: I'm sure we'll *all* forgive you. Yes, sir?

PUREFOY: I was merely going to say "It's never too late to mend".

EMMA (*weeping*): Where's Henry? (*Like a small child.*) I want Henry!

ALBERT (*muttering*): My Gawd! She wants Henry!

Shirley has moved up to kitchen door.]

SHIRLEY (*speaking off*): Is Dad there, Aunt Edie?

[*Edie enters from kitchen.*]

EDIE (*as she comes in*): He's out with his ferrets (*Seeing the weeping Emma.*) Why, Emma. . . ?

EMMA (*with all the old "bite"*): Tell him if he doesn't leave them blessed ferrets. . . ! (*Then, realising she is speaking the way she is—dissolving into noisy tears.*) Ooooh! (*Gulping.*) *Ask* him if he'll come in, will you, Edie?

EDIE: !!! *Ask* him?

EMMA: Yes, *please.*

[*Edie gropes for the door right, finds it, and totters through it.*]

ALBERT: Don't overdo it, Ma. Think of our weak 'earts!

EMMA (*still sobbing*): I . . . I don't know what I'm going to do!

PUREFOY: Then I'll tell you, if I may?

EMMA: Do, Mr. Purefoy, please After all, that's your job, isn't it—to be a "very present help in time of trouble"?

PUREFOY (*after wincing*): You are going to dry your tears; collect all your friends and relations; and bring them down to St. Michael's in half an hour.

EMMA: What . . . what for?

PUREFOY: For the wedding of your daughter Shirley to Albert Tufnell, A.B.!

SHIRLEY (*wildly*): Mr. Purefoy! You mean that?

PUREFOY: Certainly, if Albert does!

ALBERT (*excitedly*): Can you *do* that, sir?

PUREFOY. Of course. Why not?

EMMA (*weeping*): Ooooh!

ALBERT: What about it, Shirl?

SHIRLEY: Oh, Albert darling! (*She is in his arms.*)

[*Edie enters right.*]

EDIE (*as she enters*): He's just coming, Emma (*Seeing Albert and Shirley in each other's arms and dissolving into tears.*) Oooooh!

PUREFOY: Good heavens, Miss Hornett, why are *you* crying?

EDIE (*blindly waving a finger at Shirley and Albert*): I . . . I'm so happy! (*She goes off right again.*)

PUREFOY (*coming down, looking at the embracing couple for a moment, then coughing—then, as that has no effect, tapping Albert on the shoulder*): Ahem!

ALBERT (*turning—apologetically*) Oh! Excuse me, sir!

PUREFOY: Not at all, Albert. Shall we say in half an hour?

ALBERT: Thank you, sir. (*Offering his hand.*) And thank you, sir.

PUREFOY: My dear boy, for what?

ALBERT (*lowering his voice*): For being so understanding about Ma and me.

PUREFOY (*lowering his voice still further*): My dear Albert. . . ! (*Almost guiltily.*) I was speaking with the voice of sad experience. You see . . . I . . . I happen to have a mother-in-law, myself!

[*He nods with a melancholy grimace. Albert follows suit.*]

(*Coughing*) . . . Ahem! (*He turns to Emma.*) Well . . . in half an hour, Mrs. Hornett?

EMMA (*rising and dabbing her eyes*): If you say so, sir. In half an hour . . . we'll meet again.

PUREFOY (*in the doorway left*): At Philippi! (*He exits quickly.*)

EMMA (*blinking after him*): At *where*, did he say?

SHIRLEY (*in a panic of joy*): Half an hour! I'll never be ready. Oh! Where's Daphne? Where's my bridesmaid?

ALBERT: With my best man, I expect.

EMMA: We'll have to hurry. Where's Henry?

SHIRLEY (*running to door left, calling*): Daph-ne!! Oh!!

[*There is the sound of a scuffle outside.*]

Oh!!

DAPHNE (*off*): *Oh!!*

[*Daphne enters, followed by Carnoustie, whose mouth is liberally adorned with lipstick.*]

CARN: Och . . . I. . . ! Och!

ALBERT: Dinna stand there "Och-ing" ! Wipe the lipstick off your face.

[*Carnoustie gives a guilty start, and fumbles wildly for his handkerchief.*]

And away out and fetch those taxis back. I'm getting married in half an hour.

CARN: Wha'! . . . *Again?*

ALBERT: I am so.

DAPHNE: Oh, Shirley! How wonderful!

ALBERT (*to Carnoustie*): What are we waiting for? *I'm getting married,* do you hear!

CARN: Aye, I heard. . . . Man, I've an awfu' fear that ma feet are on the same dread, slippery slope as your ain. (*He exits left.*)

EMMA: Now, come along, Shirley. It's time you were seeing about getting yourself made presentable. Go upstairs; and, Daphne, you go with her. Give your face a good wash.

DAPHNE: Why? Have I smeared my lipstick?

EMMA: I was talking to Shirley.

[*Daphne exits left.*]

SHIRLEY (*about to go*): Oh, my veil! (*She crosses and picks it up.*)

ALBERT (*as she is about to go*): Come here, Shirl.

SHIRLEY (*coming to him*): Yes, Albert?

ALBERT: You're sure you *want* to marry me?

SHIRLEY: Oh, Albert! (*She is in his arms at once.*)

[*Henry enters right.*]

HENRY (*as he enters*): Edie says you want me.

EMMA (*bustling*): Yes, I do! You're to go upstairs right away, give yourself a wash, brush your coat, and get yourself ready for the wedding.

HENRY (*blinking*): What! *Another* wedding?

EMMA (*sharply*): No; the same one. Go on! Off you go! Do as I tell you! (*As Henry crosses her to door left.*) Henry! Come back!

HENRY (*returning*): Now, make up your. . . .

[*To his and the astonishment of all assembled, Emma plants a smacking kiss on Henry's cheek.*]

EMMA (*after the kiss*): *There!*

HENRY (*when he has partly recovered*): 'Ave you been drinking? (*He staggers off left.*)

EMMA (*to Albert*): I've started!! (*With a sudden start.*) Oh, my Lord! I've just remembered! (*Going to kitchen door.*) E-die!

[*Edie enters with teapot.*]

EDIE: Yes, Emma? I was just making a cup of tea. I thought you needed it.

EMMA: Never mind about the tea. Go down to Banfield's right away and tell everybody they've got to stop eating.

EDIE. What!

EMMA: They're to go straight back to the church at once—the wedding's in half an hour.

EDIE (*in ecstasy*): No. . . ! Oh, Emma. . . !

EMMA: Go on! Henry!

EDIE: I'll just get my hat. . . .

EMMA (*firmly*): You'll get down there right away. There won't be a thing left if you don't. Lord! I 'ope they 'aven't started on the wedding cake!

EDIE (*planting teapot on sideboard and rushing down to Shirley*): Oh, I'm so happy for you! (*She kisses Shirley, then crosses to Albert.*) Oh, Albert!

ALBERT (*hugging her*): I ought to be marrying you, really!

EDIE (*as she runs up to sideboard*): Oh, Albert! (*She stops dead at sideboard, looking at teapot—in terror.*) Ooooh!

EMMA: What. . . ? (*She sees—rushes up.*) *You. . . !* (*She picks up teapot, holds it for a split second, gulps, then speaks.*) Never mind, love!

EDIE: *What!!*

EMMA: I said, "Never mind". (*And she plants the teapot firmly down on sideboard again.*)

EMMA (*coming down to Albert*): Well, Albert, I don't know whether it's for the best or not, but . . . (*She kisses him.*) I'm sure I *hope* you'll be happy.

ALBERT (*his arm round her*): We will. Don't worry. (*Very confidentially.*) But I'll tell you *one* thing—Ma!

EMMA: What's that—son?

ALBERT (*confidentially whispering it to her out of the corner of his mouth*): We're bloody well not going to live at Number Twenty-Four!

Curtain

THE SHADOW OF DOUBT

by

NORMAN KING

John Clements Plays, Ltd., presented *The Shadow of Doubt* at the Saville Theatre on July 7th, 1955, with the following cast:

ARTHUR	*John Clements*
LAURA	*Jane Baxter*
GLADYS	*Eileen Way*
HUGHIE	*Peter Collingwood*
FRANK	*Patrick Barr*
MANNING	*Raymond Huntley*
CANTRUP	*Henry Hewitt*
LIZ	*Anne Leon*

The play directed by Allan Davis

The set designed by Laurence Irving

CHARACTERS

(in order of appearance)

ARTHUR
LAURA
GLADYS
HUGHIE
FRANK
MANNING
CANTRUP
LIZ

SYNOPSIS OF SCENES

The scene is the living-room of a flat in a city in the North of England.

The action of the play takes place during a Saturday in Spring.

Time: The present.

ACT ONE

Early morning.

ACT TWO

Afternoon, the same day.

ACT THREE

The same evening.

ACT ONE

The living-room of a first-floor flat in a provincial city in the North of England.

This flat is no more and no less comfortable than thousands of others in the old, tired houses of an industrial city. The flat and its furnishings grew out of a utilitarian need; no two pieces of furniture match and the wallpaper is faded. An occupant would have to be very determined to impress his identity on this room, but the indoor plants on the mantelpiece and the spring crocuses which are growing in the window-box outside give pathetic touches of colour to the scene.

A door at the rear opens on to the landing and to the left of this is another door set back to give access to the kitchen which has been built under the stairs. The bedroom door is upstage right and below this is a black marble fireplace. On the left is a large oriel window overlooking the road and the terrace of similar houses opposite. A small table near this window is laid for breakfast.

It is early Saturday morning in Spring. The sun shines strongly on to the table where Arthur Denver is seated, just finishing his breakfast. He is tall, well-built and in his forties. A newspaper is propped up in front of him and, as he reads, he speaks to his wife Laura who is at present in the kitchen.

ARTHUR: They're going to have another shot at rain-making this month.
LAURA (*off*): At what?
ARTHUR: Rain-making. Ice particles on cloud. It releases their moisture content. Rain.
LAURA (*entering*): Why? (*Laura is just over thirty, neatly and quietly dressed.*)

ARTHUR: To regulate humidity, of course. It's very important.

LAURA: Considering we only get about three sunny days a year, it seems a little unnecessary. One day somebody will have a really bright idea and start making sunshine for a change.

ARTHUR: That's quite a thought.

LAURA: If you're going to have thoughts about anything, I wish you'd invent a tap that can be turned off. That one can't.

ARTHUR (*after a moment*): Hughie will see to it. According to the paper this weather's going to last for another two days at least. We ought to get up early to-morrow—catch a bus—get out on the moors and walk—have lunch at a pub. We might go this afternoon—make a week-end of it. Do you realise we haven't been out of this place for months?

LAURA: I realise you'll be late for work if you don't finish your breakfast.

ARTHUR: Laura, I tell you the sun is shining—there is a smell of Spring in the air, or there would be if only we could go anywhere and smell it—and all you can say is—" eat your breakfast ".

LAURA: What's the matter with you this morning?

ARTHUR: I don't know—perhaps it's—seeing the sun rise over those damned chimneys—seeing a lot of things in a different light. I mean that.

LAURA (*gently*): Good.

ARTHUR: Even this job of mine. Oh, I know it's nothing of a job whichever way you look at it, but this morning I realised it won't kill me. At first I thought I shouldn't be able to stand it for a week.

LAURA: I know.

ARTHUR: Well, I'm still there! Three whole months! And this morning I knew suddenly that I can go on for another three months if necessary—and another three after that. There's nothing very terrible about it—all I do is sit, and push ledgers about and add up figures I could have done in my sleep at the age of five—but it's a job! The monotony of it is just what I needed after I came back. And all the time the other business is blowing over—people are forgetting about it. Do you see what I mean? Well, aren't you pleased?

LAURA: I'm very pleased.

ARTHUR: Well, look it then. (*He smiles at her and she returns his smile.*)

LAURA: Arthur, I wish you'd finish your breakfast.

ARTHUR: I can't—I must be off to this damned job.

LAURA Don't be late home for lunch.

ARTHUR: One o'clock. Oh, I did just want to look in at the library for a few minutes.

LAURA: One o'clock—and don't forget your watch again.

[*Arthur goes to bedroom. There is a knock at the door and Gladys enters, lean and forty-five. She carries a coal scuttle.*]

Come in.

GLADYS: Morning, Mrs. Denver.

LAURA: Hullo, Mrs. Gibson.

GLADYS: Where's that Hughie? He's supposed to be in here fixing your tap. All night long it was dripping. The Major's complained. Says he's hardly slept a wink, and running water's supposed to be a cure for insomnia.

LAURA: Hughie's not here, Mrs. Gibson.

GLADYS: Well, where the devil has he got to then? I know he came up. I'll lay ten to one he's nipped in to Mr. Barrett, upstairs. Gossiping! (*Calls.*) Hughie! Hughie!

HUGHIE (*off*): Hello!

GLADYS: I thought you were supposed to be fixing the tap in here.

ARTHUR (*entering*): Let him have his gossip. There's a big match this afternoon.

GLADYS: I'll give him big match. Are you going to it?

ARTHUR: I haven't been to a football match for years.

GLADYS (*abruptly . . it is her manner*): You're looking much better. Isn't he? (*To Laura.*)

LAURA: Much better.

GLADYS: It's all the good nursing your wife's been giving you Better than all your sanitoriums put together. There's nothing to beat home nursing. (*Calls violently.*) Hughie!

HUGHIE (*at door*): What's all the fuss about?

[*Hughie is about fifty, North Country, short and stocky. There is a very close understanding between him and Gladys. Their bickering is just part of this and is deliberate in public.*]

ARTHUR: You're in trouble. That's what.

HUGHIE: I'm always in trouble. Mr. Barrett got a ticket for you for this afternoon.

ARTHUR: For me?

HUGHIE: Aye. He said he'd take a chance. He can always sell it at the gate if he can't talk you into it.

ARTHUR: It's very kind of him, but. . . .

HUGHIE: It'll be a fine match. Be a change for you.

ARTHUR: I'm afraid I can't this afternoon, Hughie.

LAURA: Why don't you go, Arthur?

ARTHUR: You and I are going out this afternoon.

LAURA: But I've got so many things to do. . . .

ARTHUR: Well, you're not doing them to-day.

LAURA: I must, really. Please go. I'd like you to.

HUGHIE: You carry on arguing, Mrs. Denver. Never let 'em think you're eager.

ARTHUR (*to Laura*): Are you sure?

LAURA: Quite sure.

ARTHUR: All right, Hughie. I'll come. Here Hughie. (*Picks up cushion.*) Pass. (*He passes cushion to Hughie, and goes.*)

HUGHIE: This is the third time Frank's bought him a ticket and the first time he's used it. I'll just mention it to Mr. Barrett. (*Moves to door.*)

GLADYS: The tap.

HUGHIE: What's that?

GLADYS: The tap. Drip, drip, drip. They pay you as a fitter at the factory. Start fitting.

HUGHIE: It's Saturday. Anyway, I'm a bench fitter.

GLADYS: To-day you're a tap fitter.

[*Hughie exits to kitchen.*]

GLADYS. And don't be too long, Mrs. Denver wants to get on with the washing-up.

LAURA: I'm in no hurry. I'm off duty until Monday. No tonsils or adenoids for forty-eight hours.

GLADYS. One job's enough for me. How you manage to do the flat as well I don't know.

LAURA: There's not enough here to keep me occupied.

GLADYS: I'd always heard nursing was a hard life. What made you go back to it?

LAURA: After the War? Oh, I don't know. My husband was—ill, and it was the only thing I seemed to know anything about.

GLADYS: My youngest sister always wanted to be a nurse. I've three sisters. How many did you say you had?

LAURA (*smiling*) I don't think I ever said. (*Gladys grins at her.*) I have one.

GLADYS: Any family?
LAURA: She has two—they're twins—a boy and a girl.
GLADYS: That's nice. A woman needs a family. I'll bet you're a good nurse.
LAURA: Why do you say that?
GLADYS: You're always so calm. Never show signs of anything. Your husband's different; up and down like a thermometer. Still, they say opposites make a good match. Hughie!
HUGHIE (*off*): What?
GLADYS: Haven't you finished yet?
HUGHIE (*enters*): Aye. That shook you, didn't it? (*To Laura.*) It didn't need a new washer. I've tightened it up so it doesn't drip any more. It just whistles when you turn it on and off.
LAURA: Thank you, Hughie.

[*Hughie opens the door to go.*]

HUGHIE (*opening door*): Oh, Mr. Barrett. Come in here a minute. We've got a surprise for you.

[*Frank Barrett enters, thirty-five, tall, sturdy.*]

We've got use for that third ticket after all.
FRANK: Who talked him into it? Did you, Laura?
LAURA: Not really.
HUGHIE: He talked himself into it.
GLADYS (*disparagingly*): Soccer!
HUGHIE: Not soccer, woman. Rugby.
GLADYS: Same thing.
HUGHIE: Oh dear, oh dear, oh dear! (*He has given up trying to explain.*)
GLADYS (*taking up washing*): What's this little lot?
LAURA. Oh, just some shirts I'm going to wash.
GLADYS: I'll do them.

LAURA: Oh, no. . . .

GLADYS: Fiddlesticks! You have your week-end off properly. (*She goes off with washing.*)

HUGHIE: Glad's a fine woman. If only she'd learn to speak up for herself. (*To Frank.*) Never get married.

FRANK: I'll remember that.

GLADYS (*off*): Hughie!

HUGHIE: See what I mean. (*He goes.*)

FRANK: They're not such a bad advertisement. Incidentally, good morning.

LAURA: Oh, yes. Good morning, Frank.

FRANK: I was coming down here . . . on the scrounge.

LAURA: Scrounge?

FRANK: I wondered if I might use your telephone.

LAURA: Why yes. Of course.

FRANK: I could walk to the corner, but I'm too idle.

LAURA: I'll be going out in a minute. . . .

FRANK: Oh, it's not private. Nothing I ever do is private. I'm glad Arthur will be able to make it this afternoon.

LAURA: It was very kind of you to think of him.

FRANK (*smiling*): It'll do him good.

LAURA: You've all been very kind to him. (*Played lightly.*) You and the Gibsons and the people at the office. I think he appreciates it.

FRANK: When someone's had a rough passage people rally round.

LAURA: Do they?

FRANK: From what I've seen of him recently I'd say he was over it. What do the doctors say?

LAURA: They say he's almost well again. You don't mind if I go out and leave you to it, do you?

FRANK: Of course not. You go ahead.

LAURA: I'm only going to the corner shop. Can I get you anything?

FRANK: No thank you.

LAURA: If anyone should ring whilst I'm out, would you take the message?

FRANK: I'll see to it.

LAURA (*at door*): I don't think everyone would rally round after a rough passage. People don't, you know. (*It is her way of saying a special thank you.*)

[*Laura goes, leaving door open. Pause. Frank crosses to telephone pad, looks through it, then goes to the window, examines letter, and watches Laura down street. He returns to telephone, sits and dials a number. Manning appears in the doorway. Manning is fifty to sixty, smartly dressed.*]

FRANK (*at telephone*): Hullo, Elsie. Frank here. Nothing for Eric again?

MANNING (*closing door*): Are you calling the office?

FRANK: All right, Elsie. I'll call you back. (*Putting telephone down.*) What on earth are you doing here?

MANNING: Did they have that telephone put in?

FRANK: Yes.

MANNING: Why?

FRANK: She's a nurse. She's got to have one.

MANNING: So this is where they live. I take it they're both out.

FRANK: Yes. Why are you here?

MANNING: I came here to see Mr. and Mrs.—what's the name again—oh yes—Denver. I'm glad I found you here. It'll save you a trip to London.

FRANK: Why London?

MANNING: That's where I work. That's where we keep the carpet.

FRANK: I'm on the carpet, am I?

MANNING: What do you think?

FRANK: There's been nothing to tell you.

MANNING: Haven't you ever heard of nil returns?

FRANK: You've travelled a long way to talk about nil returns.

MANNING: Not really. I came to see Mr. and Mrs. What's-his-name. I've told you.

FRANK: I don't get this. Your coming here blows the lid off everything, doesn't it?

MANNING: The lid is off. Read that. (*Hands him newspaper.*)

[*Frank reads silently for a few moments.*]

FRANK: Is this your bright idea?

MANNING: Why? Don't you like it?

FRANK: Do you know how low this is?

MANNING: I think so.

FRANK: Then don't sit there looking so bloody smug about it. You know what it means, don't you? The whole blasted place will be swarming with reporters in an hour's time. They'll be at the office where he works. Do you know how long it took him to find that job? Ten months. And it wasn't for lack of trying. He walked the soles off his shoes. Now you do this. What do they do now? Change their names again? Move again? And where does that get you? You're back where you started. And how are you going to move someone else in to look after them. . . ?

MANNING: What's the matter, Frank? During the War you seemed to like working for me.

FRANK: During the War it was different. Then there was an enemy. Now there's only an unimportant man and his wife.

MANNING: That same unimportant man did a lot of damage five years ago.

FRANK: What good am I doing here—tell me that? I've been here about twelve months and I'm still no wiser than the day I came.

MANNING. Not yet. You may be—soon.

FRANK: So you're doing it like that. You let him start to find his feet again and then knock him flat on his back. Charming.

MANNING: I'm not doing it like that. Someone's already done it.

FRANK (*indicating newspaper*): That stuff didn't come from you?

MANNING: No.

FRANK. Then how did you get here so early? That's a London paper—this morning's edition.

MANNING: I flew up at the crack of dawn with the ink still wet on the paper. I knew about it late last night. The editor of this—publication—received an anonymous letter, tipping him off about the change of name, address and our friend's new occupation.

FRANK: And they printed it? Just like that? No check on it? No clearance? I don't believe it.

MANNING: Oh, the editor checked—and had a clearance. He telephoned Special Branch and asked them what about it. They referred it to me. I confirmed it. I gave the clearance.

FRANK: Why?

MANNING: It was an anonymous letter—no hope of tracing the man who wrote it. He must have had a reason for writing it. I thought the best thing to do was let the paper print the story and watch developments.

FRANK: You know what this is going to do to him, don't you?

MANNING: No . . . what?

FRANK: Not that you'd care a damn if it finished him off, would you?

MANNING: Don't talk nonsense.

FRANK: I tell you, Manning—I've lived with him for almost a year. He's not at all like your picture of him, or anything you told me about him, or anything you've got on your file.

MANNING: I never saw that view expressed in any of your reports. Why didn't you tell me this before?

FRANK: How the hell could I? Do you expect me to be able to compress the whole of a human being into half-a-dozen sheets of foolscap? You could have blocked that newspaper if you'd wanted.

MANNING: I might have been able to—yes. There's never any guarantee where the Press is concerned.

FRANK: How many more papers have got it?

MANNING: Just this one, so far. This new attitude of yours, Frank—it interests me. I believe you're actually beginning to like the man. You're not as objective as you used to be—not like the old days.

FRANK: I've told you. Things were different then. Look, Manning—I didn't ask for this job. I worked with you for six years during the War.

MANNING: Why? Just out of interest—why?

FRANK: God knows—excitement, I suppose.

MANNING: That's an amateur's reason.

FRANK: I was an amateur. By profession, I'm an engineer I build things. Other people knock them down—not me. When the War was over we shook hands and said good-bye and in no time I'd put the whole thing behind me.

MANNING: Well, I popped up again. All right, lay the blame on me. I've broad shoulders. You weren't forced into living here. There was no coercion. I asked you to do me a favour. You said yes. What are you doing now? Backing out?

FRANK: Talk sense.

MANNING: I am talking sense. This thing's reached a climax. That anonymous letter wasn't the work of an amateur. It was planned with deliberate intent—and it's going to be followed up. And the follow-up will be very interesting and very immediate. Now, either you're still working for me or you're not. (*Pause.*) Which is it? (*Pause.*) I want an answer.

[*Frank is looking out of the window.*]

FRANK: Look out. She's coming back.
MANNING: I want an answer.
FRANK: You know the answer.

[*At telephone—he hasn't dialled. Manning quickly opens door and sits at table.*]

FRANK (*at telephone*): What's that? No, three—three. I told you I might want three. Of course I want them in the stand.

[*Laura enters. She stops—stares at Manning and Frank continues 'phone call.*]

What's wrong with you this morning? Who's going to win? We are, of course. All right, Eric. Thanks very much. (*He replaces the receiver. Turns to Laura.*) There were no calls for you I was just making certain of the tickets for this afternoon. Oh, this gentleman—he's been waiting to see you.
MANNING (*to Laura*): Good morning. It's been a long time since we met. How are you? (*He extends his hand.*)

[*She ignores it by taking off her coat.*]

FRANK (*looking doubtfully towards Laura*): I hope it's all right.
LAURA (*not knowing what to say*): Oh, yes. Yes, it's quite all right.

FRANK: He said he was an old friend.

MANNING: Perhaps that was a little exaggerated. I might have said an old acquaintance. I hope you didn't mind my waiting here, Mrs.—Denver I'd have rung you if I'd known you had a telephone.

FRANK (*to Laura bluntly*): Would you rather not talk to him?

LAURA: I don't know.

FRANK (*to Manning*): What do you want?

MANNING: I want to speak to Mrs. Denver. What I have to say to her is none of your business.

FRANK: I don't see welcome on the mat.

MANNING (*to Laura*): I don't know who this is but you'd be well advised to tell him to go away.

FRANK: I'm nobody. I have the flat upstairs.

MANNING: I'm advising you for your own good, Mrs. Denver.

LAURA: It's all right, Frank.

FRANK: It doesn't look all right.

MANNING: He's very persistent, isn't he?

LAURA. It's nothing really. It was just the surprise of seeing Mr. Manning again. It's some years since we met and just to walk in and see him sitting there. . .

FRANK: I'll be upstairs. (*He goes.*)

MANNING: You seem to have found a Galahad. What is he? A professional chucker-out?

LAURA: What do you want?

MANNING: I want to advise you of something—for your future welfare, and your husband's welfare.

LAURA: Your association with my husband and myself finished several years ago.

MANNING: And there I disagree with you. To all intents and purposes it finished when your husband's trial was over—I say that because that's what I thought at the time, but not now. Should we sit down? I'm not really seeking comfort; just a relaxation of the atmosphere. First your knight-errant; now yourself.

LAURA: What did you tell him? What did you say about us?

MANNING: Tell who? Oh, Galahad. I didn't tell him anything. So far as he's concerned you're just—Mr. and Mrs. Denver. (*Looking around him.*) You seem quite comfortable here. Probably not what you were used to, but comfortable enough. Did you grow those indoor plants yourself? My wife has a mania for indoor plants at the moment.

LAURA: Mr. Manning, I don't know why you've come here or why you want to see me, but it. . . .

MANNING (*cutting in*): But it certainly wasn't to discuss indoor plants. You're perfectly right. Perhaps I'm being clumsy. I'm naturally clumsy.

LAURA: That's why you were selected for the work you do.

MANNING: Sometimes clumsiness produces results where cleverness fails, Mrs. Denver.

LAURA: Whatever it is, it must be something important to bring you all this way—personally.

MANNING: It is important. It's very important. That's why I came myself as you suggest. I might have sent one of my clever people to see you, but you're clever, too, and you'd have seen through them and then you'd never have trusted them.

LAURA: And I'm going to trust you?

MANNING: I think you are. I certainly hope you are. You and your husband

LAURA: You expect my husband to trust you after what you did to him?

MANNING: What did I do to him? I did my job. I gathered certain evidence together; I saw that it was presented in the proper manner. That's all.

LAURA: That's not all.

MANNING: What else did I do?

LAURA (*flatly*): You almost destroyed him.

MANNING: Now, that's being melodramatic.

LAURA. It's not. It's the truth.

MANNING: Professionally, he destroyed himself

LAURA. I don't mean professionally. I mean as a person. Has it never occurred to you what those interviews did to him?

MANNING: Oh, the interrogations? That sounds like the Gestapo, doesn't it? I admit I interrogated your husband; but there was nothing to take exception to; no rubber hose, no arc lamps, no prolonged sessions. He was perfectly comfortable. He smoked, drank tea, we talked and when he'd had enough he said so and was taken back. Or has he told you a different tale?

LAURA· No.

MANNING: Then why the fuss?

LAURA (*savagely*): Did there have to be so many times?

MANNING· Twelve? That's not a lot. I tell you, Mrs.—(*Hesitating on name.*)—Denver—we only talked.

LAURA: And did you enjoy it?

MANNING: No. No, I didn't. But I was doing my job. I was looking for something.

LAURA. The evidence at the trial was crystal-clear.

MANNING: Oh, the evidence was. The facts were clear. But the facts are only one layer of truth—the top layer. It was the second layer that interested me. You see, I wanted to know why. Your husband is only one of several men who have all done the same thing. They've held a position of trust; they've betrayed that trust and in every single case there has been a clear-cut motive—a political motive.

LAURA· I seem to remember you established one in my husband's case.
MANNING: Did I?
LAURA: Regardless of all his denials. Could it be that you're beginning to have doubts, Mr. Manning?
MANNING: In my job there are always doubts.
LAURA (*bitingly*): You used to be so certain.
MANNING: Mrs Denver, the past only interests me because of the present—and your future.
LAURA: Is our future your concern?
MANNING: One never knows. It may be based on certain decisions.
LAURA: There's no question of my husband having to make any decisions—he's no longer that important.
MANNING: You think not? Read that. (*Hands her newspaper.*) I'm here to help you. I'd like you to remember that

[*Laura reads the newspaper*]

LAURA: How did this happen?
MANNING: An anonymous letter to the editor.
LAURA: Who could do a thing like this? We were doing no harm to anyone. My husband was tried and sentenced. It's over and done with.
MANNING: The newspaper claims to have a duty to the public. It's bringing to the notice of the authorities certain facts about your husband. He was once a world-famous scientist, Mrs. Ross, and his particular branch of science always makes sensational news however much people like ourselves may dislike it. So far as the newspaper is concerned it's perfectly fair.
LAURA: Is that what you call it? Fair?
MANNING: From your point of view it's, perhaps, not so fair.

LAURA: Is a thing like this—legal?

MANNING: If you think it isn't, sue the newspaper and find out.

LAURA: Sue the paper? With what?

MANNING: Forgive my being so direct, but haven't you any money?

LAURA: I've been working as a nurse. For almost a year after my husband came back he couldn't find work. Do you think we have any money?

MANNING: Your family. . . ?

LAURA (*hesitates*): I—I have no family.

MANNING: I only wondered.

LAURA: I know what you wondered, Mr. Manning. You wondered if my husband was receiving payment for what he did.

MANNING: I only wondered.

LAURA: The answer is no. We have no money; we have a roof over our heads and three meals a day and in the last couple of months things have started to look a little—brighter. We've begun to make friends.

MANNING: Really?

LAURA: Yes—the people who live here. They believe—that Arthur had been ill—in a sanatorium in Switzerland. Part of it's true—he has been ill. I had to tell them something. When did you last see him?

MANNING: About a month after the trial.

LAURA: I doubt if you'd recognise him now.

MANNING: Someone must have recognised him, or how did that letter come to be written?

LAURA: I don't know. Is it on the streets yet?

MANNING: Here? No, not yet. It will be by noon.

LAURA: Can't you stop it?

MANNING: Don't you think the damage is done already?

LAURA: Yes.

MANNING (*crosses to window*). I suppose I should now say how sorry I am. I would say it too—if I felt it.
LAURA: But you can't feel it?
MANNING: I don't feel it. You see, the letter that started all this wasn't the work of a moment—a casual bit of malice. There's a reason for it.
LAURA: What reason?
MANNING: That's what I want your husband to tell me.
LAURA: But Arthur doesn't know anything about it.
MANNING: If he doesn't he soon will. If I'm not mistaken a great many things are going to happen in the very near future. Don't ask me what—I don't know—but they will happen and when they do your husband will be faced with a decision. He can either co-operate with me or he can go his own sweet way. Whichever choice he makes, I shall learn something
LAURA: You're never on the losing side, are you?

[*Arthur enters and, as Manning is standing in the window recess he doesn't see him*]

ARTHUR (*buoyant and boisterous—acting*): I ought to have my head examined. My opposite number switched with me—this Saturday for next—and I forgot all about it until I got to the office. Well, don't just stand there. Put on your bonnet, let's go somewhere. Anywhere. The sun's shining. Let's make the best of it

[*Laura is looking towards Manning. Arthur turns and sees him. He deflates; the act is over. To Laura:*]

I didn't know. I'm sorry. He's told you. I thought perhaps I could keep you from knowing a little longer. Maybe until Monday. Maybe I could have talked you into a week-end away. This isn't my Saturday off, but we could have afforded it. Look! (*Produces envelope.*) Two months' wages for one month's work. I'm sorry, Laura. Well, what are we going to do about it? No good hanging around with long faces. No problem's insoluble. What's the solution to this one? (*To Manning.*) Do you know? I suppose you know something about all this. That's why you're here, isn't it? I see you've got a paper. I only saw a cutting. Someone kindly dropped it into the Manager's letter-box, with a little note to obviate any question of mistaken identity. The Manager's not a very bright person really, without the note I might have talked myself out of it. No, he's not very bright, but he's respectable and just to add to his problems he's a civic dignitary. I almost felt sorry for him this morning. You could watch his conscience tear apart before your eyes. But he healed the wound—a month's salary in lieu. Cheap at the price. (*He sits suddenly. To Laura.*) Get him out of here.

[*Laura looks at Manning, almost appealingly. He shakes his head.*]

LAURA: Please go. You can see he's in no state to talk to you now.

MANNING: There'll never be a better time. I'm sorry, but I've got to talk to him now. Ross! Ross!

ARTHUR Get out of here.

MANNING: This thing wasn't an accident. It's planned. No interfering busybody would have carried it as far as this so quickly. How do you think that cutting got here from London?

LAURA: Not now—later.

MANNING: You were allowed to find this job; to start finding your feet again, your self-respect. Now the switch has been pulled; deliberately.

ARTHUR (*appeal*): Laura.
LAURA. Mr. Manning; my husband hasn't been well for some time. Please go now. You can come back and talk to him later.
MANNING: I'm going to talk to him now, for his own good, and yours. Doctor Ross, listen to me.
ARTHUR: Stop calling me Ross.
MANNING (*building up*): That's your name. The name you were using when you were sentenced under the Officials Secrets Act. You were found guilty of treason. Of obstructing the development work of your Department and of divulging Official Secrets You changed your name and tried to forget all about that, but you're not being allowed to. I'm not preventing you; someone else has done that. You can forget the name of Denver. In a matter of hours this whole city will know who you really are and where you live. You may not be headline news any longer but I'll lay evens you appear on the front page! (*To Laura.*) I'm sorry, but I'm not certain how much time we have.

[*A pause.*]

ARTHUR (*feeling in his pocket*): I'm out of cigarettes.

[*Manning produces case.*]

MANNING: Here. (*Business—cigarette and lighter*)
ARTHUR: No thank you.

[*He has recovered and there is a complete change in his manner—almost nonchalant.*]

Will you go, please.
MANNING: Not until I've talked to you.

ARTHUR: We've talked before—many times. It never got either of us anywhere.

MANNING: This time's different. I want to help you.

ARTHUR: You said the same thing before.

MANNING: And I meant it.

ARTHUR: Did it help me? I served my time.

MANNING: If you'd listened to me. . . .

ARTHUR: It would have been precisely the same.

MANNING: Now, Ross—

ARTHUR: Either you go or I do. I don't want to talk to you, Manning, now or ever.

MANNING: If you won't talk, listen. Shortly, very shortly, someone is going to approach you.

ARTHUR: Who?

MANNING: I don't know.

ARTHUR: Oh, you mean—the other side—wearing a black cloak, with curled moustache and a smoking bomb in each hand?

MANNING: The approach will be subtle, ambiguous, open to many interpretations because they're learning fast these days, but you'll know where it comes from, and you'll be made an offer.

ARTHUR: What's it going to be this time? Gold, frankincense or myrhh?

MANNING: And you're going to come to me and tell me all about it.

ARTHUR: I doubt that. I doubt it very much indeed What am I supposed to be in all this—ground bait? Do your own dirty work, Manning. I want no part in it. There's nothing you can touch me for now. My hands are clean; my expiation is complete. You've got the fantastic notion that all this is a put-up job and you come crawling to me for my co-operation. You can whistle for it. But if it will set your mind at rest, I'll make a prediction—no-one will approach me. We'll leave the city and start again somewhere else and next time we'll take care no-one finds us. (*By now he is complete master of the situation.*)

MANNING: If you should change your mind and want to talk to me, Doctor Ross, I'm staying at the Queens. You can telephone me there. Good morning, Mrs. Ross. (*He goes.*)

[*The moment he goes we see the change in Arthur. Once again he is lost, bewildered.*]

ARTHUR: My hand's shaking like a leaf.

LAURA: Oh, Arthur. You should have listened to him quietly.

ARTHUR: I couldn't listen to him. I can't bear being in the same room with him. All his fantastic schemes. All this talk about people approaching me. You don't think that, do you, Laura?

LAURA: Of course not.

ARTHUR: I've been through it all once. It's not going to happen again, is it?

LAURA: No, it won't happen again.

ARTHUR: I couldn't stand it all—Manning—everything.

LAURA: You won't have to.

ARTHUR: We'll leave here, won't we, Laura? We'll go away and we'll change our names again. We'll go where no-one will recognise us. Who could have done it, Laura? Who could have written a letter like that?

LAURA: It doesn't matter. We'll do as you say, we'll go away and start again. You sit there quietly. I'll go and make some coffee.

[*She goes to kitchen.*]

ARTHUR (*remains seated, still to Laura, but almost think-*

ing aloud): We were doing so well until this happened I only said . . . earlier this morning. . . . Who could have written a letter like that? Somebody must have recognised me; maybe somebody I used to work with, or one of my old students. It might even have been a newspaper reporter. I don't believe Manning. He makes out the whole thing's deliberate. I don't believe it. . . .

[*There is a knock at the door. They look at each other for a moment in silence.*]

LAURA (*she opens the door*): Oh, it's you, Frank. You'd better come in.

FRANK: I saw your unwelcome visitor disappearing round the corner and I thought I'd. . . . Hallo, Arthur, you're back early.

ARTHUR: I went to work on my morning off, Frank. Bright, wasn't it?

FRANK: I once took the nine-forty to London and it was only when I was getting out of the train that I remembered I was supposed to have gone to Newcastle. (*A pause.*) Hughie tells me you can come to the match.

ARTHUR: What? Oh yes, the match. I don't think I shall be able to, after all.

FRANK: Oh. I'm sorry.

[*Another pause.*]

LAURA. Frank, we've something to tell you. . . .

ARTHUR } *together*: { No, Laura, we don't have to. . .
LAURA } *together*: { He'd better hear it from us. . . .

[*The telephone rings. Laura answers it.*]

LAURA (*at telephone*): Hello. Yes. Who is it, please? No. Doctor Ross is not here.
ARTHUR: Who is it? Who is it?
LAURA (*makes note on pad*): I'm sorry, I didn't catch your name. Yes. Cantrup. What number? Could you possibly tell me what it's about? Could you be a little more explicit? I'll give him your message when I see him. No, I don't know when he'll be back. Good-bye.
ARTHUR: What was his name?
LAURA: Cantrup.
ARTHUR: Cantrup? What did he want?
LAURA: He said a business meeting.
ARTHUR (*reading*): Cantrup. But I've never heard of him.

[*Knock at door. Enter Hughie.*]

HUGHIE: Oh, Mr. Denver, I'm sorry to trouble you. There are two young men downstairs asking for you. They say they're newspaper reporters.
LAURA: Ask them to go away, Hughie, please.
HUGHIE: All right, Mrs. Denver. (*He goes.*)
ARTHUR (*quietly*): Oh, God.

Curtain

ACT TWO

Scene: The same.
Time: Late afternoon.

Arthur is sitting in armchair. It is now raining. There is a knock at the door and Frank enters.

FRANK: Can I come in?

ARTHUR (*turning*): Oh, yes, Frank. Come in. Was it a good match?

FRANK: Hughie says it was a beauty—until the rain spoilt the second half.

ARTHUR: Didn't you go?

FRANK: No.

ARTHUR: Why not?

FRANK: No particular reason. I just didn't feel like it. Where's Laura?

ARTHUR: She went over to the hospital. They telephoned. I don't know what about.

FRANK: It's a mess, isn't it?

ARTHUR: It's just one of those things. Did you want something, Frank?

FRANK: Only to talk to you.

ARTHUR: About my lurid past? Have you come to give me a political lecture?

FRANK: I should have thought you'd had your fill of politics.

ARTHUR: Really? Before I reformed I was a dangerous revolutionary. I've got my press-cuttings to prove it. I'll look them out for you; you can browse through them sometime.

FRANK: I can remember what they said.

ARTHUR: Then that settles it. You've never known the Press be wrong, have you?

FRANK: I've never heard you mention the word politics until today.

ARTHUR: Perhaps that only shows what a subtle and dangerous type I am.

FRANK: Have you thought about what you are going to do now?

ARTHUR: That's what I was doing when you came in.

FRANK: I'll push off if you want. . . .

ARTHUR: No, Frank. Stay and talk. There's no joy in being alone. Oh, I'll find a job somewhere; we'll leave—that's all there is to it.

[*The telephone rings. Arthur answers it.*]

Yes, speaking.

[*He listens for a moment and replaces the receiver.*]

ARTHUR: That's another—a public-spirited citizen. I've had three this afternoon. Isn't it illegal to use offensive language over the telephone? The day after I was arrested Laura had fifteen calls—all like that one.

FRANK: What I can't reconcile is all this and you, as I know you. Two and two just don't make four any longer.

ARTHUR: I'll let you into a secret—unofficial this time; they never did. Two and two can make precisely what you want them to make. I used to know a proof of that when I was at school. We forget all the valuable things

FRANK: I suppose that makes sense to a scientist.

ARTHUR: Not scientist—physicist. Scientist's too vague a term for the specialised world we live in. I'm a specialist—a physicist. I was even a special kind of physicist. The focus gets smaller and smaller.

FRANK: You ranked pretty high at one time, didn't you?

ARTHUR: I hardly need reminding of that.

FRANK: How could you have been such a fool as to throw it all away?

ARTHUR: Fools aren't always such bad things. The old kings found a use for them.

FRANK: You must have been mad. Why on earth did you do it?

ARTHUR: Oh, Frank, how can you understand? You're a practising engineer. You apply the findings of other men. You don't even know what my kind of research means, do you? Do you know the purpose behind it? Do you know why it's carried out? You don't even know the vocabulary.

FRANK: How could I? How could anyone but a specialist? It's all new ground.

ARTHUR: New? Nuclear physics new? Look, Frank, over fifty years ago Becquerel and Röntgen were having strong suspicions; a year after the '14-18 War, Rutherford, only a few miles from where we are now, was beginning to find out what it was all about. By the thirties, Cockcroft and Walton at Cambridge had the whole business taped. There was Otto Hahn in Germany, Niels Bohr in Denmark, Fermi—an Italian, Dunning and Lawrence—Americans, all working along similar lines. And even myself. And how do you think we worked? Each in our own splendid isolation, in our own independent vacuum flasks? Not on your life. We shared, with the exception of a handful, we shared. If a man couldn't share, what did he do? He moved heaven and earth to get out. The thing that mattered was to go on towards a goal that knew no boundaries. Nationality didn't matter a damn. But then the war started and the shutters came down.

FRANK: They had to come down.

ARTHUR: Agreed. For that period of time they had

to come down. So we stopped sharing. We worked behind barbed-wire and armed guards, we carried identity cards and had our finger-prints taken. All right, we put up with it. And then the war was over and we all said, Thank God; now we can get on with the real work; to-morrow the shutters will be lifted and we all can get together again. And were they lifted? Were they Hell! They doubled the barbed-wire and trebled the armed guards. Well, we'd had enough. They were cutting the world's throat.

FRANK: The whole world? Or just one part of it?

ARTHUR: I take it you have one particular part in mind?

FRANK. I was thinking of your press cuttings. They indicated a very specific sector.

ARTHUR: I see. I'm surprised you're still talking to me. Aren't you afraid of contamination? You should be. One of my chief associates, David Haseldine, a man I'd known for nearly twenty years—he hasn't spoken to me since it happened. I can't blame him, I suppose. He had a wife and family. He couldn't afford to take risks.

FRANK: But you could; you only had a wife.

[*There is a knock at the door.*]

ARTHUR: Come in.

[*Gladys and Hughie enter leaving door open.*]

Oh, hullo, Mrs. Gibson.

GLADYS: We'd like to speak to you for a minute, if you can spare the time?

ARTHUR: Yes?

HUGHIE: How are you, Doctor. . . . Mr. . . .

ARTHUR: Stick to Denver, Hughie—that's how you've always known me.

HUGHIE: Aye, until today.
ARTHUR: What do you want?
GLADYS: It's about the newspaper.
HUGHIE: We've been thinking about things.
FRANK: I'll leave you to it.
ARTHUR: No, no, Frank, you stay. Mr. and Mrs. Gibson won't mind saying what they have to say in front of you. You don't, do you?
HUGHIE: You know why we've come up, Mr. Denver.
ARTHUR (*who knows perfectly well*): I have no idea.
HUGHIE: Oh, damn and blast it!
GLADYS: There's nothing spiteful about this. We've got nothing against you—either of you. It's just that—well, people are talking.
HUGHIE: People always talk.
GLADYS: We've been over all that already.
HUGHIE: Aye. For hours.

[*Laura appears in doorway.*]

GLADYS: The people downstairs—they say either you go or they do. You know, he used to be a Major in the Army.
HUGHIE: Aye. Used to be. He's been out nine years and he acts as though he's never been demobbed.
GLADYS: They have a right to their opinions.
ARTHUR: We all have a right to our opinions.
HUGHIE: Aye.
LAURA: And what's your opinion, Mrs. Gibson?
GLADYS: I won't be talked out of it. I've had the devil's own job trying to convince him. But it's no use being sentimental. Business and sentiment don't mix. And so far as we're concerned, this is business. Our savings are in this house, nearly every penny we've got in the world. We can't afford to have

empty rooms There's still hire-purchase to meet on some of the furniture. And they won't wait. So we think you should go. (*This speech is broken and disjointed, Gladys fumbling for excuses.*)

LAURA: I see. I think we're entitled to a week's notice, aren't we?

GLADYS: The Major says if you're not out by Monday, they are.

HUGHIE: Let 'em.

GLADYS: Listen to him. Pig-headed as a mule. We've told 'em a week on Monday. We don't want to be unfair to you. You've always been civil; and . . . pleasant. . . .

HUGHIE: Not like some folks. (*Gesturing downstairs.*)

GLADYS: That's got nothing to do with it. If we get people here we don't like, we have to lump them. That's business.

LAURA: But you can't—lump us?

HUGHIE: Dammit, Gladys, it's not reasonable.

GLADYS: Stop swearing at me, can't you? You've done nothing but swear all day. (*To Laura.*) Well, you'll have to start looking at once. Things are a bit easier now with all these new houses going up.

LAURA: All right.

HUGHIE: This isn't our idea, Mrs. Denver. Gladys doesn't mean to sound hard, do you, Glad? (*Gladys turns and exits and Hughie follows her quietly.*)

ARTHUR: Well, that's that. What did they want at the hospital?

LAURA: They'd seen the papers. Matron was very nice about it. She'd known all the time, of course—but some of the others. . . . I've been given leave until the Board meets again. It's chilly in here. Oh, well, it'll be a change to get away and start somewhere new.

FRANK: I thought you liked nursing.

LAURA: I liked the children.

FRANK (*to Laura*): I'd like to say I'm sorry . . . but sorrows are two a penny, aren't they?

ARTHUR: You've nothing to be sorry about, Frank. We're practically strangers to you. You keep your sorrows for your own troubles.

FRANK (*still to Laura*): If there's anything I can do, Laura. . . .

LAURA: Thank you, Frank. But after we've gone, you won't hear from us again.

FRANK: Why?

LAURA: It's better you shouldn't. We don't bring luck to people. Frank, we've had to lie to you. Over the past year, I mean. We don't enjoy that.

FRANK: Forget it. Regardless of what luck you bring people, I'd still like to hear from you.

LAURA: We'll see.

[*There is a knock at the door which Arthur answers. Cantrup stands on the threshold. Tall, heavy, Irish, white-haired and well over sixty.*]

CANTRUP: I've been doing battle-royal with a female downstairs who insisted I was a reporter. I hope I've found the right flat now; my name's Cantrup.

ARTHUR: Oh, yes. Come in.

CANTRUP: I had a telephone call this afternoon.

ARTHUR: I made the call.

CANTRUP: I see.

FRANK: See you later, Arthur.

[*Frank goes.*]

ARTHUR: Let me have your coat. It can be drying while we talk.

CANTRUP: It's not really wet. I came by taxi.

ARTHUR: By taxi? A Capitalist.

CANTRUP: I beg your pardon.

ARTHUR: I said "a Capitalist". It's a joke. Just ignore it. It's the sort of joke that gets me into trouble. This is my wife.

CANTRUP: How-do-you-do, Mrs. Ross. We spoke on the telephone this morning, didn't we?

LAURA: Good afternoon.

ARTHUR: Won't you sit down?

CANTRUP: Thank you. It was good of you to get in touch with me so quickly, Dr. Ross. I suppose you're wondering who I am?

ARTHUR: It had crossed my mind.

CANTRUP: Perhaps this will explain. (*Hands card to Arthur.*)

ARTHUR: The Dunmallock Cable Company. Well, I'm sorry, but I'm no wiser.

CANTRUP: We make cables. For special purposes only.

ARTHUR: I see.

CANTRUP (*looks around him*): You appear to have come down in the world, Dr. Ross.

LAURA: We are very busy, Mr. Cantrup. If you have a proposal to put to my husband, we'd both be very grateful if you could do it quickly.

CANTRUP: I have no proposal to put before your husband, Mrs. Ross.

ARTHUR: Then why are you here? Is this a sight-seeing trip?

CANTRUP: I said I had no proposal to put to you. My firm has a proposal but I want no part of it.

LAURA: I think it would be as well if you explained the whole situation to us, Mr. Cantrup.

CANTRUP: I was speaking to my senior director on the telephone this morning. He told me that you had turned up again. There are three directors in the Company. I have been out-voted, and as I happened to be in England at the time, I have been given the task of approaching you. My firm wish you to take up employment with them.

ARTHUR: Doing what?

CANTRUP: Research

ARTHUR: Into what?

CANTRUP We manufacture cables for aircraft. You know of insulation failures at high altitudes.

ARTHUR: That's an old story. Mossop & Carruthers found the answer to that in 1942.

CANTRUP: So I've been informed. But look at the cost of their method. The war is over and business is competitive again.

ARTHUR: What you want is someone to take over where they left off. You want an insulation as good as theirs but cheaper to produce. What about the big manufacturers? Surely, you're not the first firm to think of this.

CANTRUP: By no means. Most of the others had a good start. We're not a very big concern as you've probably gathered; but we already have a research team working on this problem. They've been at it for almost two years; so far with no results.

ARTHUR: I don't know that I can help you. My own work became so specialised. . . .

CANTRUP: You are a physicist, aren't you?

ARTHUR: Yes.

CANTRUP: And this problem of insulation—that is a physicist's problem, isn't it?

ARTHUR: Only partly. You'd need a chemist as well.

CANTRUP: That would be arranged, presumably But don't take that as an inducement, Dr. Ross. I'm not attempting to persuade you.

ARTHUR: Why not?

CANTRUP: I think we should be able to succeed in business without having to employ traitors.

LAURA: How dare you come here and insult my

husband? You asked for this appointment . . . until you walked into the room I didn't know that my husband had agreed to see you. . . . Now will you please go at once.

CANTRUP: Thank you. Thank you very much.

[*He rises and goes to the door.*]

ARTHUR: No Laura, no. Wait a minute, Cantrup; you don't like me, do you?

CANTRUP. I don't know you.

ARTHUR: But what you know about me you don't like.

CANTRUP: No.

ARTHUR: And you've been forced to come here, to see me—to make me this offer?

CANTRUP: You might almost say forced.

ARTHUR: How? Why? I think we're entitled to some explanation.

CANTRUP· Yes. Perhaps you are. You see, Mrs. Ross, I'm not really a business man at all. My partners are the business men. They do the money-grubbing. Once my family owned estates in Ireland as large and as prosperous as anything you know in this country. But that was some time ago. (*He shrugs.*) Now I hold a few shares and a passive directorship in this Company. That's all there is to it.

ARTHUR: Not quite all. You still haven't explained why you've come here, against your will.

CANTRUP: Because my—associates wished me to.

ARTHUR: You could have told them to go to hell.

CANTRUP: I could have done—yes.

ARTHUR: It won't do. Your story's no good. There's a piece missing somewhere. What dividend did you pay last year?

CANTRUP· There have been no dividends for several years.

ARTHUR: That's all I wanted to know. Now we can carry on with the conversation

LAURA: I don't understand, Arthur.

ARTHUR: It's only too obvious. (*To Laura.*) They've missed the boat; whilst other firms have been advancing in methods and machinery they've been sitting back milking the concern. You're broke, Cantrup, aren't you? The firm's going under.

CANTRUP: We have had a very difficult period.

ARTHUR (*to Laura*): There! What did I tell you? Come on, man, sit down and we can talk properly, now the air's clear.

CANTRUP: I must apologise, Dr. Ross. I had no right to speak to you like that in your own home. I'm very sorry. I should never have used that word, particularly as it has been applied to me so often.

LAURA: To you?

CANTRUP: There were certain troubles in Ireland at one time. I'm afraid that by nature I'm an—Anglophile.

ARTHUR: Do you still want me to take this job?

CANTRUP: I'm not going to lie to you, Dr. Ross. If you do take up employment with my firm, it will take me some little time to acclimatize myself to the idea.

ARTHUR: What salary can you offer me?

LAURA: Arthur!

CANTRUP: Not very much I'm afraid, Doctor. The most we could offer at the moment would be about eight hundred.

ARTHUR: And when would you want me to start?

CANTRUP: My associates would like you to start immediately, but, of course, that's impossible.

ARTHUR: Why?

CANTRUP: I don't think you read my card very clearly, did you?

ARTHUR (*reading card*): Eire.

CANTRUP: Exactly. There will be so many technicalities; you may not, of course, be able to obtain entry or a permit to work in the country.

ARTHUR: Oh. So the whole thing may fade out—just like that. Disappear in a cloud of smoke. (*To Laura.*) Ah, well! It was a good job whilst it lasted. It was even shorter than my last one.

LAURA (*who hasn't missed a thing*): I think Mr. Cantrup has thought of this. That's so, isn't it?

CANTRUP: My associates believe that if entry to the country were made and residence established, they would have sufficient influence to enable you to remain there.

ARTHUR: What am I supposed to do? Smuggle myself in? You hear that, Laura? That's what he's suggesting. Cantrup, I'm a physicist—that's all I know—physics. I don't belong to any cloak and dagger brigade regardless of what the newspapers may have told you.

CANTRUP: Dr. Ross, from the outset I told you I wanted no part of this.

LAURA: But, Mr. Cantrup. . . .

CANTRUP: Yes.

LAURA: But arrangements have already been made, haven't they?

CANTRUP: Arrangements! Well, I am returning this evening—by air. It would be possible for you to accompany me, Dr. Ross.

ARTHUR: This evening! That's short notice.

CANTRUP: Of course. I told them they were being ridiculous. My associates are both young men. They have—what's the word?—drive. Everything has to be done in five minutes.

ARTHUR: What time would we have to be ready?

LAURA: Arthur, please. . . .

ARTHUR: What time?

CANTRUP: Your wife could accompany you, of course. It might be easier if she followed, say, in a day or so. . . .

ARTHUR: We both go or we both stay.

CANTRUP: As you please. You would have to be ready at—about nine-thirty.

ARTHUR: I want to think about this.

CANTRUP: Naturally. Could you ring me—before, say, eight-thirty? All you need say is yes or no.

ARTHUR: And if I say yes—where would you want us to meet?

CANTRUP (*writing on card*): I hope this will be convenient for both of us.

ARTHUR (*takes card*): Yes. That will be all right.

CANTRUP: You'll let me know then?

ARTHUR: I'll let you know.

CANTRUP: Good-day, Mrs. Ross. (*Opens door.*)

LAURA: Oh, Mr. Cantrup.

CANTRUP (*turns*): Yes?

LAURA: *Slan lath.*

CANTRUP: I beg your pardon?

LAURA: *Agus geniry an boa latt.*

CANTRUP: Oh.

LAURA: That's Gaelic for good-bye.

CANTRUP: You speak Gaelic, Mrs. Ross?

LAURA: I only know a few words.

CANTRUP: Remarkable for an Englishwoman. Good-bye, Mrs. Ross.

LAURA: I take it you don't speak Gaelic, Mr. Cantrup?

CANTRUP: Hardly anyone in Ireland does. But I'm an exception. The correct expression is "*Guh neirey dub vobir lath.*" Slon aguth, Mrs. Ross.

[*He goes, closes the door.*]

ARTHUR: It's manna from heaven; a gift from the

Gods; it's sunshine after rain; I'm still worth something, you see. People still want me to do my own job. I knew; all the time I was in prison I knew there was still a place for me somewhere if only I could find it. And this job they want me to do—I didn't tell him, but Mossop was one of my pupils back in the days when I was lecturing. Eight hundred. Half what we used to get. Twice what I was getting last month. We're rich again. You didn't know I could be mercenary, did you? What's the matter, Laura? I thought you'd be pleased.

LAURA (*quietly*): Oh, my God!

ARTHUR: This is our chance, Laura. We can start again.

LAURA: You've forgotten Manning, haven't you?

ARTHUR: To hell with Manning! We can forget Manning, once and for all.

LAURA: Manning told you this was going to happen.

ARTHUR: To hell with Manning!

LAURA: He told you this offer was going to be made. He told you what was behind it. You shouldn't have telephoned that man—you shouldn't have had anything to do with it.

ARTHUR: Can't you see Manning is obsessed . . . he sees bogey-men at every street corner. All right—that's his job, I suppose . . . but he's been wrong before and he's wrong this time.

LAURA: You don't know that.

ARTHUR: I didn't ask Cantrup here with my eyes shut . . . although I really knew Manning was talking nonsense I couldn't be sure—at first . . . but Cantrup . . . didn't want me to have the job! Couldn't you see that? He'd have been delighted if I'd turned him down flat at the start. He's been made to do this.

LAURA: But, Arthur. . . .

ARTHUR: I tell you this offer's genuine. I know the type. Damn-it-all; I'm not a child.
LAURA: No?
ARTHUR: All right, then, maybe Manning is right. Perhaps there will be other offers and there may be a fake one amongst them, but this isn't it. He didn't talk me into it—I talked him into it.
LAURA: You've made up your mind already, haven't you?
ARTHUR: I'm trying to convince you, Laura. Now's our chance to make a break once and for all. A clean start, a new country. A new life, a new home, friends, respect—all the things you want, Laura.
LAURA: But not this way, can't you see?
ARTHUR: There's no other way.
LAURA: There has to be another way. Telephone the Queens now. Ask Manning about these people.
ARTHUR: Laura.

[*There is a knock on the door. The door opens and Liz, Laura's sister, comes in. She is expensively dressed.*]

LIZ: May I come in?
LAURA: Liz!
LIZ: Here's a surprise for you.

[*She holds out her arms and Laura runs to her.*]

LAURA: Oh, Liz! (*She throws her arms round her and holds her tight.*)
LIZ: Darling, what a welcome! It's worth sixty miles of Roger's driving for this! Did you ever know anything more idiotic? Only sixty miles away—all this time—and we never knew. Oh, how wonderful to see you again! Hallo, Arthur.
ARTHUR: Hallo, Liz.

LIZ: A fine sister you are to shut yourselves away like this . . . so near . . . and never a word out of either of you. (*She puts her arm round Laura's shoulder.*) It's all right, it's only Liz. (*Gently.*) Let's sit down, darling, shall we?

LAURA: Yes—yes, of course.

LIZ: How are you, Arthur?

ARTHUR: I'm all right, Liz. How are you?

LIZ: Roger says I've got to see a doctor.

LAURA: Oh, Liz! Why?

LIZ: Because I'm putting on weight and I'm slimming like mad . . . and Roger says it's bad for me.

ARTHUR: He's right.

LIZ: Now don't you start! I asked him what he would do if I got fat . . . and the brute promptly said he'd go off with the nearest chorus girl . . . he wouldn't, I know . . . but I flatly refuse to get myself into a shape when I wouldn't blame him if he did . . . even if he actually didn't . . . if you see what I mean.

ARTHUR: Would you mind saying that again—slowly?

LIZ: Well, what I was trying to say was . . . Roger said . . . you're making fun of me!

ARTHUR: Heaven forbid!

LIZ: You always did—both of you! The trouble is I never expect intellectuals to have any sense of humour . . . it's all wrong somehow . . . I know it isn't, but it seems it, if you see what I mean . . . no, I don't suppose you do . . . never mind. Anyway, I do know when my leg's being pulled! (*She puts her arm round Laura.*) Don't I, my sweet? Do you know—I was absolutely delighted when you two got married—I said to myself " She's met her match at last! As Arthur's even brainier than she is, she'll get *her* leg pulled for a change ". . . Actually, I cried like an idiot when you drove her away in that terrible old car. I'm talking too much, as usual, aren't I? Darling Laura!

LAURA (*laughing*): Oh, Liz!

LIZ: Do we still look like sisters, Arthur? Everybody always said we did . . . which always made both of us absolutely livid . . . but I suppose we did really . . . do we still? I should rather like it now, if you said yes—I suppose that's what you and Roger would call typically feminine. Oh, Laura, I *am* so glad to see you! I think you might say you're glad to see me. . . . I'm only here for two shakes—Roger's waiting in the car and although the poor lamb's got many virtues, patience isn't one of them.

LAURA: Why don't you ask him up?

LIZ (*hedging*): Well, it's—it's not worth it really. We've got to dash back to have dinner with some terribly hearty Canadians. It couldn't be a more infuriating moment to have to cope with hands across the sea and all that. You're not going, Arthur?

ARTHUR: Only to the corner shop. I'm out of cigarettes.

LIZ: I can't help, I'm afraid. I stopped smoking last month. I'm feeling terribly virtuous and saving money at a tremendous rate.

ARTHUR: And eating chocolates at a tremendous rate instead . . . no wonder you're putting on weight!

LIZ: Arthur, you're a beast . . . you're perfectly right. I hadn't thought of that. I don't count chocolates in my slimming schedule! Oh, dear! I suppose I'm quite mad!

ARTHUR: Stay mad, Liz.

[*He goes out.*]

LIZ: Doesn't that just go to show how wrong you

can be! I've always thought of Arthur as the serious, brainy one, and Roger as the . . . well, no-one could call dear Roger a serious type, could they . . . and yet here is Arthur telling me to stay mad and Roger always trying to make me sane! It's all very confusing.

[*She looks at herself in the mirror over the mantelpiece.*]

My God! Do I really look like that?
LAURA: Not really, darling—it's that mirror. It sort of gives you jaundice.
LIZ: It sort of gives me mumps, too.
LAURA: I ought to have warned you—but I've got used to it. It's surprising what you can get used to.
LIZ: You can't have got used to that vase! Nobody could!
LAURA (*laughing*): Put it down, Liz, before you drop it.
LIZ (*threatening to drop the vase*): I could do you a great favour during this fleeting visit.
LAURA: It was a present from our landlady.
LIZ (*putting it back on the mantelpiece*): It's the sort of thing Roger always wins at hoop-la.

[*Laura goes on laughing (a little hysterically). Liz goes to her and puts her arm round her.*]

It wasn't as funny as all that, my sweet.
LAURA: I'm sorry—it's just seeing you again. (*She pulls herself together.*) How is everyone?
LIZ: Very well.
LAURA: The children?
LIZ: Very well. (*Pause.*) Father's very well, too.
LAURA: Oh, good. Does he still keep the house going?
LIZ: Wonderfully. I wish you could see the garden—it was lovelier than ever last year.

LAURA: I miss the garden. I have some wonderful crocuses.

LIZ: Where?

LAURA: In the window box.

LIZ: Oh.

LAURA: Tell me all the news?

LIZ: Well, Roger's positively blooming. Next month he's off to Montreal—he's going to study productivity methods, whatever that may mean

LAURA: Are you going too?

LIZ: I wish I could—but the children have to be coped with—oh, and talking about them. . . . The presents you sent each Christmas; one year the postmark said Glasgow; another year, Leeds. Then there was somewhere in Cumberland. What have you been doing—riding round in a charabanc?

LAURA: I had other nurses post them for me when they went home on leave.

LIZ: You went to so much trouble, didn't you? But you were wrong, you know. Each year there was something for the twins. (*Mischievously*)—but what about poor Robin?

LAURA: Robin? But I didn't know. . . .

LIZ: And Elspeth?

LAURA: Elspeth? Four of them. (*Delighted.*) Oh, no!

LIZ: That's right. Four. Don't worry, dear. That's the lot.

LAURA: You must be very happy, Liz.

LIZ: The house is like Barnardo's. Robin's three and Elspeth's two. Jennifer's taking after you—can't stop her reading. Roger says Paul's going to be very good at cricket. You'd love to see them all together.

LAURA: Yes. How did you find out where we lived?

LIZ (*hedging*): Why, from the paper.

LAURA: When? You must have travelled very quickly.

LIZ: Why, to-day, of course. Somebody just mentioned it. (*Pause.*) Oh, it's no good, Laura. I never could tell a decent lie, could I? Father telephoned. One of his friends had rung him from London first thing this morning.

LAURA: I see.

LIZ: He wanted me to come and see you.

LAURA: Yes?

LIZ (*quietly*): He wants you to come home.

LAURA: Oh!

LIZ: You mustn't worry about the things he said before. His bark was always worse than his bite.

LAURA: And Arthur? When last time I was at home —just after the trial—Father insisted that I should get a divorce. He wrote to Arthur and told him it was his duty to give me one. What did he have to say about Arthur?

LIZ: You mustn't pay any attention to all that. He was a bit upset at the time, of course . . . everyone was . . . but. . . .

LAURA: When I told father that I wouldn't divorce Arthur he said he never wanted to speak to me again

LIZ: Well, he's changed his mind; and not a minute too soon. You're his favourite daughter, Laura darling . . . you always were.

LAURA: You still haven't answered my question. Was Arthur included in this invitation?

LIZ. Oh, Laura, you do make things difficult.

LAURA: Was he?

LIZ: No.

LAURA: Then will you thank father from me and tell him I must stay with Arthur.

LIZ: I knew from the start that I was wasting my time. In your position I'd say exactly the same. You don't mind my trying?

LAURA: Of course not. (*Pause.*)

LIZ (*suddenly*): Laura, I've a wonderful idea! I know I only have about one a year but—look—I told you Roger was going to Canada. Or didn't I? Anyway, he is, and he'll be away three or four weeks. Come and stay with me—just for a holiday . . . we'll have a wonderful time . . . really relax and let our hair down, and talk our heads off . . . and all the children will be there at Easter . . . the house will be like a bear garden . . . you'll love it, I know you will. . . .

LAURA: And Arthur?

LIZ: I'm talking about a holiday, darling . . . just you and me and the children . . . just a holiday.

LAURA: Don't go on about it, Liz, please. . . .

LIZ: It's not that Roger's narrow or mean or even particularly strait-laced, or anything. . . .

LAURA: I know.

[*A car horn is heard from the street below.*]

LIZ: That's Roger.

LAURA: I expect he's getting impatient.

LIZ: Well, he'll have to wait a bit longer.

LAURA: No, Liz, you must go.

LIZ: But you still haven't told me if you'll come. You do want to come, don't you?

LAURA: More than I can tell you.

LIZ: Then you'll talk to Arthur, and you'll telephone me in the morning.

LAURA: All right.

LIZ: We'll have such a wonderful time.

[*She turns and looks at Laura.*]

LIZ: Oh, Lau-Lau darling, I don't want to leave you here! I want to gather you up in my arms and take you with me now—this very moment.

[*Liz crosses to Laura, a quick embrace and she goes. Laura alone, is obviously distressed. Only the most rigid self-control prevents her weeping. There is a knock at the door, Frank enters carrying books. She turns, sees who it is, and again turns her back to him.*]

FRANK. These books are yours. I thought I'd better let you have them back.
LAURA (*without turning*): Put them down somewhere, please.
FRANK: Where do you want them? On the table?
LAURA: Anywhere!

[*Frank places the books on the table and quietly closes the door, but remains standing in the room. She thinks he has gone and sobs. As she turns, she sees he is still standing there. She starts.*]

LAURA: I thought you'd gone.
FRANK: Why don't you tell me? I know so much already, a little more won't hurt.
LAURA: You don't know anything about it.
FRANK: Laura; you've got to talk to someone. You can't batten down your emotions for ever. I know why you've had to. I know you're Arthur's sheet-anchor.
LAURA (*recovering during this*): You're very observant, Frank.
FRANK: Yes, I am. Where you're concerned.
LAURA: And what does that mean?
FRANK: Whatever you want it to mean.
LAURA: I don't know what I want, Frank. Yes, I do, that's not true. I want—above all things—Arthur to be what he was before you ever knew him and that could only happen if he got back to his own kind of work again. But he must do it the right way and not the wrong.

FRANK: Is he doing it the wrong way?

LAURA: I don't know. I think so. I don't know.

FRANK: Won't you tell me?

LAURA: If I do, you're involved. Do you want to be involved—with us?

FRANK: Tell me.

LAURA: Arthur has been offered a job in Eire. Manning . . . the man you met this morning . . . thinks it's prearranged—that it's all linked with that anonymous letter to the paper. He asked Arthur to tell him the moment anything like this happened.

FRANK: And has he?

LAURA: No.

FRANK: Why?

LAURA: It must be because he wants to go. That's one reason.

FRANK: And the other?

LAURA: Maybe there isn't another.

FRANK: What is the other reason? Don't hold back now.

LAURA: He doesn't like Manning. He doesn't trust him. He's afraid of him.

FRANK: Afraid! What has Manning done to make Arthur afraid?

LAURA: He was responsible for Arthur's conviction. He's not to blame. He had his job to do.

FRANK: I see. You said—just now—that what you wanted most in the world was for Arthur to get back to what he was. You mean before he ever came up against Manning?

LAURA: Yes. Oh, Frank, I wish you had known him then! Have you ever met a really . . . dedicated person?

FRANK: Yes. Yes, I think so. Particularly one during the War. He was a doctor. . . .

LAURA: Then perhaps you can understand. I don't

know how to describe Arthur as he was then . . . he was . . . aglow. He made me feel . . . oh, I don't know . . . proud and humble at the same time. I know that's difficult for you to understand . . . you've only seen him as he is now. . . .

FRANK: Yes, but Laura . . . the man I mentioned just now . . . the doctor . . . hadn't got a wife, or any kind of home. He could live for nothing but his work

LAURA: I wouldn't have Arthur live for anything else, but it wasn't only his work, it was everything he did . . . the way he walked, the way he talked, even the way he opened a door; he was quite brilliant. Of course, there were lots of things—quite ordinary things—to you and me—which Arthur simply knew nothing about—things like dancing, playing tennis, and talking nonsense at parties, and reading silly books; they just didn't come into his world. I don't think, until he met me, he'd ever been to a theatre or concert or even a cinema. I used to tease him about them and tell him that all he ever did when I took him was to formulate a theory of acoustics, or think up some equation on the velocity of light. It was partly true, too. He used to try so hard not to . . . more for my sake than his own . . . and concentrate on the music or the play-or whatever it was . . . and then something, probably some quite little unimportant thing would start an idea in his head, and he would be back in his own world, oblivious of the music . . . the play . . . me . . . everything. When we got home I would ask him about it and sometimes he would talk on and on far into the night . . . it might be anything; why petrol engines would soon be things of the past . . . exactly how we should all soon be flying to the moon. It wasn't what he said . . . I doubt if I really understood a quarter of it . . . it was the way he said it. He could make you see further than you'd ever seen before . . . it was all so alive and confident . . . so unlike the Arthur you know now.

FRANK: Laura—I know this is brutal . . . but you're clinging to the past. You have to face Arthur as he is now, not as he was. You can't live on memories.

LAURA: You can if you have to. . . .

FRANK: No, Laura . . . no. Can't you see he's destroyed himself and now he's destroying you? Oh, God! Do you expect me to stand by and watch and say nothing?

LAURA: There's nothing to say. . . .

FRANK. This job that Arthur's been offered—you think it's a fake? Why do you think that?

LAURA: If he takes it, we have to leave tonight.

FRANK: Tonight!

LAURA: Arthur has an address. We are to be there at nine-thirty.

FRANK: What address?

LAURA: I don't know. He didn't tell me.

FRANK (*thinking aloud*): If this job's a fake, the firm's probably a fake also. Do you want me to find out?

LAURA: But how can you find out?

FRANK: I have a friend. He may be at home now. He's a stock-broker. They have records, directories and so on, of all registered companies.

LAURA: But it's Saturday afternoon and this firm isn't even in the country.

FRANK: He can find out. Do you want me to try?

LAURA: Yes. It's called—I only heard it once.—Dunmallock Cables, Limited. It's in Eire.

[*Frank crosses to 'phone, dials a number.*]

FRANK (*at telephone*): Dunmallock Cables? Elsie? Frank here. Is Eric at home? Good. (*Pause.*) Hullo,

Eric. I want you to do me a favour. Find out everything you can about a company called Dunmallock Cables Limited. Somewhere in Eire. What? (*Turns to Laura.*) How do you spell it? O-C-K, or O-C-H?

LAURA: I've no idea.

FRANK (*back to telephone*). I don't know. It doesn't matter. I want to know if they're sound, who runs them, how long they've been going—the whole works. You've got two hours. That's the limit. Oh, and look, Eric, this is confidential. One hundred per cent. Just you and me. Nothing goes on file until to-morrow. I don't give a damn about that. (*Half-joke.*) Refer the boss to me if you like, but not until to-morrow. I'll call back later. (*He hangs up.*) (*Turns to Laura.*) You'll know the colour of the office cleaner's eyes by the time he's finished.

LAURA: Thank you very much.

[*The door opens and Arthur enters.*]

ARTHUR: Hullo, Frank.

LAURA: Frank was just returning some books he'd borrowed.

ARTHUR: Oh, yes, books. (*He picks one up.*) Did you like this, Frank?

FRANK: Very much.

ARTHUR: Here. It's yours, a keepsake. I see I've written my most recent name on the fly-leaf. In years to come it'll be worth a fortune. Like Crippen's spectacles.

FRANK: I don't find that funny.

ARTHUR: Nor do I. I don't know why I say these things. It's what's called a twisted sense of humour, isn't it? Do you think I'm twisted, Frank?

FRANK: Do you want me to answer that?

LAURA: Frank. . . .

ARTHUR: I thought you'd been discussing me. It hangs in the air, afterwards. I seem to be the favourite topic of conversation at the moment.

FRANK: Arthur, we've never quarrelled yet.

LAURA: Frank, please. . . .

ARTHUR: Don't pay any attention to me. I've been thinking—making decisions. It's so long since I had to make a decision the strain's telling on me.

LAURA: Did you see Roger? He was sitting in the car.

ARTHUR: Oh, yes. I saw Roger. He didn't see me. He had something in his eye as I passed. Here, Frank—have a cigar?

LAURA: Cigar? Where did you get that?

ARTHUR: I bought it. I've got three cigars. It's years and years since I smoked a cigar. I just felt like one tonight. Here, Frank—have one. I'll be hurt if you don't. This is for old time's sake

LAURA. I'll let you know when your telephone-call comes through.

[*Frank goes.*]

ARTHUR: Liz didn't stay long.

LAURA: No.

ARTHUR: What did she want?

LAURA: She just came to see us.

ARTHUR: One good thing about newspapers. They put you on the map. People know where to find you. She's looking very well.

LAURA: Very well.

ARTHUR: It was just a social call, I suppose?

LAURA: Why?

ARTHUR: I only wondered. I thought she might have come here for a purpose. Is your father well?

LAURA: He wants me to go home again.

ARTHUR. That's what I wondered. Roger's moustache is even bigger than it used to be. Are you going to?

LAURA: Am I going to what?

ARTHUR: Go home again?

LAURA: Liz has four children now. (*Evading a reply.*)

ARTHUR: This going home again—was I included in the invitation? (*No reply.*) I see. Ah, well—it doesn't really matter. It wouldn't have made any difference.

LAURA. What are you saying?

ARTHUR: I'm saying that it wouldn't have made any difference—now.

LAURA: You've telephoned that man, haven't you?

ARTHUR: Not yet.

LAURA: You've decided to go with him.

ARTHUR: I've got to, Laura. I may never get another chance like this again. What do you expect me to do? Ignore it?

LAURA: No. I expect you to think about it quietly; to examine it and find out whether or not it's genuine.

ARTHUR: And whilst I'm doing that, what happens? They wait for me for ever? And Cantrup goes back and tells them I'm not really interested. He doesn't want me. Once let him get back there and my chances are finished! I've waited too long to start work, Laura. Three—four times a week I go to the Public Library to read the new scientific journals. I sit among the misfits, the unemployed. I can't go on like that. I'm a trained physicist. Do you know what that means?

LAURA: Of course I know.

ARTHUR: You don't. Close as we've been, and close as we are now, you've never understood. Laura, until I met you nothing mattered but my work. There had been no time for anything else. Up here (*touches his head*) a man can carry only so much, and all I carried was vital. Success wasn't handed to me on a plate. I drove myself through every scholarship and bursary I could find until half the world knew my name. I did it by work. Do you understand that—work! For over twenty years I thought of nothing but my work.

LAURA: Arthur, you must listen to me.

ARTHUR: No; let me finish. All the time I was locked away I wasn't allowed to work, but they allowed me books—do you know what that means? They fed my imagination but denied me any means of applying it. I thought, when I came out, things will be difficult for a little while; but someone will want me. I'll be able to use all my experience and knowledge again. Apart from application, I'm up to date, Laura. I'm more than up to date. I'm years ahead of most of them. And what happened? For twelve months I tramped the streets looking for work. I'm not so young. I can't learn new tricks. But turn me loose in a lab. again—I'll solve their blasted insulation problems for them—I don't give a damn about them, but I'll solve them. I'll earn my money, they'll get a square deal. But in my own time, Laura—look what I can do in my own time. Why, there's no limit to what I can do. But I must have facilities. Whatever they've got—a corrugated shed in a back-yard or the finest lab. in the country—it will be somewhere to start again.

LAURA: Arthur, you don't have to convince me of these things. I understand them.

ARTHUR: You don't understand them. How can you? You know I don't sleep well. You think it's because of what I did. It's not because of that. It's because of ideas; all these ideas I have pounding around inside my head. I didn't tell you—three months ago I sent one of these ideas to Research. I thought if only I could get another view on it, another opinion—that was vital to me, Laura, you don't know how vital—if only they can do the lab. work and let me know the answer. It was a small thing, it would have been easy for them to do it. They returned it—without comment. A week later I took my courage in both hands, I 'phoned Haseldine—he hung up on me. I have to take this job. What else can I do, Laura, tell me, what else can I do?

LAURA: You can tell Manning about it.

ARTHUR: No.

LAURA: Why?

ARTHUR: He'd stop me going.

LAURA: Why should he stop you going? If the offer is a genuine one as you say, why should he stop you?

ARTHUR: Laura, don't you realise he's not concerned with whether it's genuine or not? Manning would never let me leave the country. He's convinced I'm not to be trusted. He'd never let me out of his reach.

LAURA: You believe only what you want to believe. You want to get aboard that plane and fly away and not care where you land so long as one of your beloved labs. is handy.

ARTHUR: I want to work.

LAURA: Yes. Anywhere . . for anyone.

ARTHUR: I want to work again.

LAURA: Last time I could forgive you. This time it's treason.

ARTHUR: Laura!

LAURA: This time it's treason.

ARTHUR: In all these years you've never said that to me.

LAURA: That's why I'm saying it now. You want to sneak out of the country like a criminal. You want to go away with a man you know nothing about. He might take you anywhere in the world, and it wouldn't matter to you—so long as you could work again. All right, then, go. But this time you'll go alone.

ARTHUR: Alone? I can't go alone. You've got to come with me.

LAURA: No. I'm not coming.

ARTHUR: I don't believe you. You're only saying that because you think it will stop me going. You do think that, don't you?

LAURA: I've stopped thinking. All I do now is stand on one side and watch things happen around me.

ARTHUR: But you must come with me.

LAURA: No.

ARTHUR: Laura. . . .

LAURA: No. I can't argue any more. You must make up your own mind. You must decide for yourself.

ARTHUR: I'm no good alone. I'm no good without you. (*Simply.*) I love you, Laura. I love you with all my heart. But this way, the way I am now, I'm no good to you—I'm no good to anyone. (*Violent outburst.*) But some day I will be. Some day I'll blind the world.

[*He goes, slamming door. Laura breaks down.*]

The curtain falls

ACT THREE

Scene: The same.

Time: Later the same evening.

Curtains drawn—no lights. The door opens and Gladys shows in Manning

GLADYS: There; you can see for yourself. I told you there was nobody in.
MANNING: I'll wait until they come back.
GLADYS: Here?
MANNING: Why not?
GLADYS: I'm not sure it's right. That's why not

[*Frank has walked downstairs behind them.*]

FRANK: Hello, Mrs. Gibson. Something wrong?
MANNING: Good evening, Mr. Barrett.
GLADYS: Do you two know each other?
FRANK: We met here this morning.
GLADYS: Here?
MANNING: The front door was open then. I walked straight up.
GLADYS: Well, you found it locked tonight.
FRANK. I'm going to wait down here for a 'phone call if that solves the problem.
GLADYS: All right then. (*To Manning.*) If you let me know when you're going I'll show you out.

[*She goes.*]

MANNING: Thank you, Frank. I'd have managed on my own, but you made it easier. Maybe I can repay the debt by saving you a long wait. (*Produces flimsy.*) Eric asked me to give you this.
FRANK: Eric did?

MANNING: I was with him when you telephoned. Don't blame Eric. There was nothing else he could do. You shouldn't put people into the position of having to short-circuit me. They don't like it and I don't like it either. Read what he's got to say. Go on —read it.

[*Frank reads flimsy.*]

I didn't know you'd come into money, Frank. Personally, I'd put it in War Savings. They mightn't pay such a good dividend as that firm, but they're safe. Well?

FRANK: It's obvious, isn't it?

MANNING: The note's obvious, but why are you so interested in this firm? That's the first thing to explain. The second thing is—why did you ask Eric to keep this under cover until to-morrow?

FRANK: I'll tell you about it later.

MANNING: I don't think so. I think you'll tell me about it now. If I didn't know you so well, Frank, I'd have grave doubts about you. For some time I've been wondering whether you were fed up with this job—whether you'd lost interest.

FRANK: And what do you think now?

MANNING: I don't know. Perhaps I'm beginning to wonder about something else.

FRANK: About what?

MANNING: Let's say your—loyalty. It's an old-fashioned word, but you and I have a personal definition of it.

FRANK: Who's on trial in this house, me or Ross?

MANNING: We're all on trial, Frank. But just at the moment—you are.

FRANK: I see.

MANNING: You were sent here to keep Ross out of any further mischief. I believe you've succeeded.

FRANK: No, Ross has succeeded. He's never put a foot wrong.
MANNING: Maybe he's had no opportunity?
FRANK: He could have made opportunities—if he'd wanted to. Instead he's been sitting on an office stool, sweating it out at a job he loathed.
MANNING: Maybe he's clever.
FRANK: I don't think he's clever—outside his old job—I think he's honest.
MANNING: In face of all the facts you think he's honest?
FRANK: Facts!
MANNING: Yes, facts, Frank. The things I trained you on. You can't get away from the fact that here was a man who held a position of immense responsibility and then suddenly threw it to the wind to follow some mad-headed line of research of his own. Instead of working to orders he held up vital development work for almost a year.
FRANK: We know why he did that.
MANNING: Do we? We know why he said he did it. Stick to the facts, Frank. After someone rumbled what Ross was up to—when he knew he'd had it—he deliberately went to this man, Bernard Fletcher, this ex-student of his, and told him everything—every secret detail, past, present and future—it took him all night. And the fact that Fletcher held peculiar political beliefs never occurred to him. He never knew, he said. Come, come, Frank!
FRANK: All right, all right . . . but there's one fact you've left out.
MANNING: What is it?
FRANK: The one that I know and you don't. The fact of the man himself. I've lived with him—for a year——
MANNING: Then give me the answers to the questions

I sent you here to find. Is Ross a dyed-in-the-wool political with a front we can't break down?

FRANK: I don't think so but I can't prove it.

MANNING: You can't prove it. Then does he really believe in all this guff he put up at the trial about science having no boundaries?

FRANK: I'm not sure.

MANNING: You're not sure. Or is there something else, something we all missed at the trial? Do you know the answers?

FRANK. No—but I believe . . .

MANNING: I'm not asking what you believe. Do you know?

FRANK: No.

MANNING: No. So we're back exactly where we started—with a traitor on our hands; and not just an ordinary traitor, either. Do you know how much damage Ross is capable of doing if he chooses to play ball with the other people?

FRANK: I can guess.

MANNING: And what can we do to stop him? A knife in the back, prussic acid, a street accident? That's the only one hundred per cent method to stop a man talking—off with his head! But the price is too high for people like us, so what do we do? Do you know the answer to *that*?

FRANK: I don't know any answers.

MANNING: Earlier to-day I told Ross that he d shortly be faced with a choice. I was right, wasn't I? He's been offered a job. That's why you asked Eric to check up on this firm—all right, you needn't answer. I gave him the opportunity of getting in touch with me if the offer was made. He hasn't done so.

FRANK: Did you expect him to? If he turns down this job do you know anyone who'd offer him another?

MANNING: I'm holding out no stick of rock to him. Inducement would ruin everything.

FRANK: But is there a stick?

MANNING: Ross must decide. No inducements.

FRANK: Heads you win, tails he loses. Poor Laura.

MANNING (*repeating*): Poor Laura? A minute ago it was poor Arthur. Tell me, Frank, if, for the sake of argument—Ross were to do something stupid again, do you think his wife would leave him this time?

FRANK: She might.

MANNING: And then she'd be all alone. She might even need someone to look after her.

FRANK: You've got a rotten mind, Manning.

MANNING: Well, didn't that point ever occur to you?

FRANK: So far as I'm concerned you can leave her out of this.

MANNING: You're sure?

FRANK: I'm quite sure.

[*He says this very deliberately and Manning appears to accept it.*]

MANNING: All right. When is Ross supposed to start this new job?

FRANK: They're to leave tonight—at nine-thirty.

MANNING: From?

FRANK: I don't know. Only Ross knows the address.

MANNING: I see. The back door. Another disappearing act.

FRANK: How can you possibly say that? You've nothing to go on—or have you? If you know something that I don't, tell me. I run round in blinkers on this job.

MANNING: What's worrying you?

FRANK: Look, Ross goes to prison, he comes out, he starts looking for work and you do nothing about him. Then one day—out of the blue—you say, "Frank, I've got another job for you. I want you to keep an eye on him." Why?

MANNING: The thing was routine.

FRANK: Come off it. Something happened. Some new development, some new fact turned up. What was it, Manning? What did you find that decided you to put me in here?

MANNING: I don't stand for this sort of thing. Not from you or anyone else who works for me. You do as you're told in this job and that's all there is to it. I run these shows the way I want them to go and I don't take back-chat from anyone!

FRANK (*grinning*): All right, Manning. All right. That's all I wanted to know. Something new did turn up.

MANNING: It's possible to be too clever, Frank. What exactly is it you want?

FRANK: I want to handle it alone.

[*Hughie's voice off.*]

HUGHIE: Don't natter, Gladys. Leave it to me. I'll do it.

FRANK: It's all right. It's only Hughie.

MANNING: And who the hell's Hughie? Nobody tells me anything.

[*The door opens and Hughie enters; he has had a few drinks, is flushed, but not drunk. He carries a bundle of laundry.*]

FRANK: Come in.

HUGHIE: I'm not going to disturb you. I've just brought the washing back. What with one thing and another, Gladys hasn't managed to get it done. (*To Manning.*) Are you a friend of theirs?

MANNING: Yes. In a way.

HUGHIE: What do you mean—in a way? You're either a friend of someone or you're not a friend of someone. There's no "in a way" about it.

MANNING: In that case, I'm their friend.

HUGHIE: Good. So am I. You've heard all about this rumpus to-day, have you?

MANNING: Yes.

HUGHIE: And what do you think about it? For I'll tell you what I think about it. It's a bloody shame. That's what I think about it. And I know what you're thinking—you're thinking I've had a couple. You're dead right, I 'ave. And it makes me see red.

FRANK: In that case you shouldn't have a couple.

HUGHIE: It's not the couple makes me see red; it's what's going on. That's why I had the couple But it's all because of him. (*Gesturing downstairs.*)—Him. You know?

MANNING: No.

HUGHIE: The flaming galloping Major—on the ground floor. He says either they go or he goes. What would you do?

MANNING: You're asking me?

HUGHIE: Of course I'm asking you. You're a friend of theirs, aren't you?

MANNING: I think you've got to make up your own mind.

HUGHIE: It always comes back to that, doesn't it? When all the talking's done—it always comes back to making up your own mind. Like backing horses. (*He goes.*)

MANNING: And what's all that about?

FRANK: Nothing. Well, do I handle this alone?

MANNING: For how long?

FRANK: An hour—half-an-hour.

MANNING (*smiling*): You can have your hour, Frank.

FRANK: Thanks.

[*The telephone rings.*]

MANNING: Hallo. Speaking. All right. (*He rings off.*) Mrs. Ross has just passed the telephone box on the corner.
FRANK: Are you going out, or do you want to wait in my room upstairs?
MANNING: You get on with your hour Frank—never mind about my trouble.
FRANK: Some day, Manning, you're going to slip up. You're going to let your left hand know what your right hand's doing.

[*Manning goes. Frank goes to telephone. (Quickly). Laura enters.*]

FRANK: I've just made that telephone call.
LAURA: Have you seen Arthur?
FRANK: No.
LAURA: Frank, what am I going to do? I can't find him!
FRANK: What's happened, have you quarrelled with him?
LAURA: I told him that if he goes to Eire tonight he goes alone. He may have gone!
FRANK: He can't have gone yet. There's plenty of time.
LAURA (*she calms down a little*): Yes. Yes, I suppose so.

[*She takes off her coat. Frank takes it from her and hangs it up.*]

If only I knew where he was!
FRANK: He'll come back, Laura. He won't go without you.
LAURA: I think he will—I'm not sure. I suppose there's nothing we can do but wait.

FRANK: You'd give anything to stop him going, wouldn't you?
LAURA: I love him.
FRANK: You make it sound so simple and easy.
LAURA: It is simple and easy to love someone.
FRANK: Laura—listen—suppose I could stop him.
LAURA: You? How?
FRANK: It doesn't matter how.
LAURA: Oh Frank, what would you do? You couldn't stop him.
FRANK: I'm afraid I could.
LAURA: What do you mean by that?

[*Pause.*]

FRANK: Do you want me to say it straight out so you'll never look me in the face again?
LAURA: What are you trying to tell me?
FRANK: It's what I'm trying not to tell you that matters. Laura, what is this loyalty thing, anyway? Where does it begin and end? There's no sharp line to tell you when you're on your own side of the road. Before to-day I always thought there was.
LAURA: Why don't you say what you really mean? You said I'd never look you in the face again. You don't lose respect and—affection—for people so easily as that.
FRANK (*fumbling*): The treachery that Arthur was tried for was to his country; your loyalty's to Arthur. . . .
LAURA: And yours? Where does your loyalty lie?
FRANK: A man can tear himself in two . . . I work for Manning.

[*Pause.*]

Did you hear what I said? I work for Manning. I've worked for him for years. He sent me here as a spy. It was part of my job to pretend friendship for you and Arthur.—Can't you even tell me to get out?

LAURA: Do you want to get out?

FRANK: I want to know what you're thinking.

LAURA: Is that important to you?

FRANK: What are you thinking, Laura?

LAURA: I'm not thinking at all. Perhaps if I was, I'd be thinking about all the lies and pretence of friendship you've just talked about. But, I don't believe that all that's happened since we met has been planned and calculated . . . I don't believe you.

FRANK: I've told you the facts.

LAURA: Why did you tell me?

FRANK: Because now I can talk to you openly. There's no longer any need for lies and pretence. Because I want to help you—I want to help you both. But before that, there's a question you must answer. Will you?

LAURA (*pauses*). If I can.

FRANK: Why did Arthur talk?

LAURA: Don't you know? I thought you said you worked for Manning?

FRANK: I know the reason he gave at the trial. About science has no boundaries.

LAURA: That's not it . . . not all of it.

FRANK: Because of political convictions?

LAURA (*smiling*): Arthur and politics . . . (*she shakes her head.*)

FRANK: Then what?

LAURA: There was a change in Arthur. It wasn't the trial that did it, or his sentence . . . it wasn't Manning . . . it happened before he ever met Manning.

FRANK: Could it have been anything to do with Fletcher? Do you think he knew Fletcher was going to betray him?

LAURA: No. He didn't know. When it happened he

couldn't believe it. I know that. It may not have been anything to do with Fletcher at all. I don't know what it was. I've never known.

FRANK: Tell me about Fletcher? You say he was Arthur's friend.

LAURA: I think he was the only person Arthur has ever thought of as a friend . . . except you.

FRANK: Me?

LAURA: Didn't you know that?

FRANK: No.

LAURA: It's true. Fletcher was his friend, yes, in a way . . . but he was really more his . . . sort of . . . disciple. He was much the younger man but they had the same background, the same single-mindedness. He came to the house occasionally,—small, untidy, tremendous nervous energy. His work was industrial research and whenever he got stuck he used to bring his problems to Arthur. He always acted as if he were his God. Arthur thought a great deal of him, too.

FRANK: Fletcher came out of prison last month.

LAURA: We saw it in the paper. He hasn't tried to get in touch with Arthur, if that's what you're thinking.

FRANK: Not unless he's tied up with Cantrup in any way.

LAURA: You've no evidence of that, have you?

FRANK: No.

LAURA: When you said just now that you could stop Arthur I suppose you meant you could have him arrested.

FRANK: No Laura, I couldn't. It wasn't true. He's a free agent. He can go to any country he wishes, as long as they've got no objection.

LAURA: Have you heard from your friend yet about Cantrup?

FRANK: Yes, just before you came in. The firm was founded in 1916. They have a capital of forty thousand; the directors are a J. L. Knight, R. H. O'Brien and A. G. A. Cantrup.

LAURA: It's genuine?

FRANK: The firm's genuine enough, but this doesn't tell us everything.

LAURA: Oh, well, it seems Arthur was right about Cantrup. You should have seen him browbeating that poor old man, as if he hadn't been browbeaten enough by his partners.

FRANK: Why was he browbeaten by his partners?

LAURA: He didn't want Arthur to have the job. They forced him into coming here to make the offer.

FRANK: Say that again.

LAURA: Say what again?

FRANK: By partners, you mean co-directors, don't you?

LAURA: I suppose so.

FRANK: And they forced Cantrup into doing something he didn't want to do?

LAURA: That's what he told us.

FRANK: Then this is it! This is what we've been waiting for. Look at the holdings, Knight and O'Brien twenty per cent, Cantrup eighty per cent. Cantrup owns the Company virtually. The other holdings are damn-near nominal. How the hell can they force him to do anything?

LAURA: But he led us to believe he was only a junior partner. . . .

FRANK: Oh, it's slim. It's damn slim and I can't see the point of it. But it's got a point; it's got to have.

[*The door opens and Arthur enters.*]

LAURA (*excitedly*): Arthur, come in quickly. Frank

has something to tell you. This man Cantrup, didn't he say he was being forced to offer you a job?

ARTHUR: So you told Frank about it?

LAURA: I said I was going to. I asked him to find out something about the firm.

ARTHUR: You'd no right to tell anyone. I told you this was our affair. It's nothing to do with Frank or anyone else.

FRANK: You'd better hear what I've got to say, Arthur

ARTHUR. I don't want to hear it.

FRANK: But you're going to all the same. You've got plenty of time to get to the 'plane.

ARTHUR (*to Laura*): He knows about that, too?

LAURA: Yes. But listen to what he has to say.

FRANK: The man who talked you into this job. Laura tells me he was forced into doing it by his co-directors.

ARTHUR (*desperately*): He didn't talk me into it. I talked him into it.

FRANK: Oh! For God's sake Arthur. Read that. (*Gives him paper.*) Look at the shareholdings—look who's boss.

ARTHUR: It doesn't matter. There could be a hundred reasons we know nothing about. Perhaps the shares have changed hands; perhaps he's afraid of his partners.

FRANK: There could be a hundred and one reasons; but they wouldn't make any difference. The important thing is that something stinks.

ARTHUR (*as before*): Laura will tell you. . . .

FRANK (*savagely*): Laura will tell me nothing. There's no Laura this time. You cut your own throat when you said you were going without her.

ARTHUR: I wasn't going without her.

LAURA: Arthur!

FRANK: She told you she wasn't going.

ARTHUR: She'd have changed her mind, wouldn't you, Laura? At the last moment you'd have changed your mind.

FRANK: Why should she? What did you ever do for her? Two years of marriage, then years of loneliness and then what? More years hearing you whine your belly out about your bad luck.

ARTHUR: I don't understand you, Frank. I thought we were friends.

FRANK: You have no friends. You cut yourself off from friends years ago.

LAURA: Arthur, there's something I must tell you about Frank.

FRANK: All right. Tell him.

LAURA: I want to say it gently. . .

FRANK: There's no time to be gentle. (*To Arthur.*) I work for Manning.

ARTHUR: What?

FRANK: Don't you see the initials branded on my forehead. M.I.5. Can I make it any clearer?

ARTHUR: Oh, my God! (*To Laura.*) And you've told him—about Cantrup . . . to stop me going.

FRANK: She didn't know then, but you're not going anywhere, Ross. You're going to sit there and you're going to talk. I'm going to ask you questions and you're going to tell me the answers.

ARTHUR (*violently*): No! No! It's all finished. It was finished years ago.

FRANK: It will never be finished. Can't you see that? Why did you talk to Bernard Fletcher? You had a position most men would have given their right hand for and you threw it away. Why?

ARTHUR: You know. Everybody knows.

FRANK: Everybody knows what you said and nobody believes it.

ARTHUR: I can't help that. It was true.

FRANK: Tell me—the whole story.

ARTHUR: No! Not again!

FRANK: Yes.

ARTHUR: I can't—not all over again.

LAURA: Stop it, Frank.

FRANK: Keep out of this, Laura (*Waves her aside.*)

ARTHUR: What God-damned right have you to give her orders.

FRANK: She's had too much of you already. As a scientist you may be brilliant, Ross,—as a man, you're nothing.

LAURA: Don't listen, Arthur. . . .

FRANK: He's got to listen. She's given up everything in life for you—her home, her family, the children she's never had. As if that wasn't enough, now you have to take everything else from her, every last shred of respect. This is your chance, Ross,—not that fake job you're thinking of—but this. No, don't look at me—look at her.

[*Arthur returns and sits, deeply moved.*]

ARTHUR: I—I can only tell you the truth; the same story I've always told. For years I've fought to push it into the back of my mind and now you want me to live it all again. (*He breaks down.*)

LAURA (*crossing to him*): Arthur, darling. (*As with a child.*)

FRANK: Ross, listen to me. This man, Fletcher, you talked to that night—he used to be one of your students?

ARTHUR: Yes.

FRANK: You used to meet him regularly.

ARTHUR: No. Only occasionally. He worked in industrial research. He came to me for help.

FRANK: Did you give it to him?

ARTHUR: Yes. But his problems had nothing to do with the work I was engaged on.

FRANK: You discussed politics with him?

ARTHUR: No.

FRANK: But you knew what his politics were?

ARTHUR: No.

FRANK: He gave you no indication? You never suspected him in any way?

ARTHUR: No.

FRANK: Why were you in London that day?

ARTHUR: We used to have meetings each month; the Heads of Departments met to discuss progress.

FRANK: And this was just a normal monthly meeting you attended?

ARTHUR: How can I talk to you? How can I talk to anyone? How can you hope to understand I'd lived so long in a world shut away from people like you—a world of specialists who invent their own language and their own vocabulary until they can't communicate with anyone outside it any longer.

FRANK: But you communicated all right—to Fletcher?

ARTHUR: That's the whole point. He was in my world. He was a fellow scientist.

FRANK: That's what you said at the trial, but was it necessary to communicate quite so much?

ARTHUR: I had to.

FRANK: Why?

ARTHUR: Because . . . because, he could understand.

FRANK: It's not enough, Ross. Can't you see it's not enough?

ARTHUR: I'm telling the truth. What more do you want?

FRANK: I want it all—the whole truth . . . every

bit of it . . . can't you see I'm trying to help you? Go back—right back. What started it, Arthur? Tell me.

ARTHUR: I found something.

FRANK: What was it?

ARTHUR: A little thing—such a little thing. I was in the laboratory—about a year after Laura and I were married. It was late at night. I was alone. I was sitting at a bench watching a confirmatory test-run of a piece of apparatus. I was drinking coffee from a thermos flask and noting down the results as the test went on. The figures ran in a pattern, a basic conventional pattern as they had done for weeks and months and ever since the apparatus was devised. I was doing the job of a junior—I should have been at home, but I wanted to do the final run myself—just for my own satisfaction. Satisfaction! As I sat and watched and noted down the results—the pattern changed, the basic conventional form disappeared and a new form was set up. And I realised I was seeing it happen for the first time in the history of nuclear physics, and at that moment, sitting in that quiet room with only the singing of the dynamos and the humming of the transformers for company, I knew with absolute certainty what the breakdown of the pattern meant.

FRANK: What did it mean?

ARTHUR: Once or twice in a lifetime of research a man may stumble on something new. Only once in a thousand life-times does he find anything of magnitude; and when he does it becomes the justification of every working hour he has ever spent. What I had seen might have been the beginning of an entirely new conception of power—a power as vast and unlimited as anything yet known, but infinitely simpler. It could have had a million uses. . . .

FRANK: Go on.

ARTHUR: For several minutes I recorded that new pattern with my mind full of all the images and implications of what I was doing. And then, suddenly, it changed back into the old form. I spent the rest of the night trying to set it up again, but there were too many variables. (*Shakes his head as if to get rid of the memory.*) Always, always, too many variables.

FRANK: And the next day you reported what you'd seen?

ARTHUR: No.

FRANK: Why?

ARTHUR: Because what I had was too flimsy. Eight or nine sequences of figures in a lab. book an entirely new conception. Ideas like that belonged to the realm of long-term planning. (*Bitterly.*) We were working at full pressure on vital top secret development. So I made my own decision. I transferred men from development work to research—the same test—over and over again. I wanted a re-appearance of that pattern under control conditions.

FRANK: And you never reported this transfer?

ARTHUR: No. It would never have been allowed. Our programme was more than full then. We searched desperately but the pattern never returned. A few months later I was called before the Board to explain lack of progress.

FRANK: You told them what you'd seen and what you believed it meant?

ARTHUR: Yes, they set up a Committee to enquire into it and examine my interpretation. They instructed me to return all the men to development and abandon the research.

FRANK: And did you?

ARTHUR: No. I stalled. I carried on whilst the Committee sat, because I believed so implicitly in what I was doing. Eventually their report was ready. The decision was against me. The men of that Committee were some of the greatest physicists in the country. They had destroyed all my arguments, all my theories. I was wrong . . . I'd been wrong all along the line. What I had seen . . . I hadn't seen. What had been there, couldn't have been there. They had proved it, beyond doubt. A week later I went to London to hear the report of the Committee read to the Board and as I left the meeting I knew that soon I would be asked to resign. I walked through the streets for hours and hours. Then I went to my hotel. Bernard Fletcher was sitting in the entrance-hall waiting to see me. He wanted my advice on some problem of his own. We went up to my room and instead of talking about his problem—I talked about mine.

FRANK: Why? Don't hold anything back now. *Why did you talk to Fletcher?*

ARTHUR: Because—in spite of the report—in spite of all its cold logic staring me in the face, I couldn't believe it. I had to talk to someone who could understand—someone who might find a flaw in the report that I couldn't see for myself. Don't you understand that if that report was true I could no longer trust myself in a laboratory—I could no longer trust myself anywhere—I was finished. I'd trained Fletcher since he was a youth . . . he worked as I worked . . . thought as I thought . . . he was my last hope.

FRANK: Why didn't you say this at the trial?

ARTHUR: What difference would it have made? I talked when I shouldn't have talked. Nothing could alter that. Was I to blazon to the world on top of everything else that I was a failure at my work—worse than a failure—a man who could no longer believe what his eyes saw and his senses told him? Do you suppose anyone would have cared?

[*He breaks down.*]

LAURA: Oh! Arthur, why didn't you tell me?

ARTHUR: Don't you see I couldn't? Whatever you thought of me at least you still had faith in my work. Was I to lose that too? Can't you see I couldn't bear to?

LAURA: Oh, my dearest!

ARTHUR: *Now* do you understand why I must have the chance to prove to myself—to Laura—that everything I worked and sweated for so long wasn't all based on a fallacy—miscalculations—mistakes. Can't you see why—I must get back to my own kind of work. I must take this job. For God's sake, Frank, don't stop me now.

LAURA: He can't stop you.

ARTHUR: What?

LAURA: He told me so—before you came in.

ARTHUR: I'm free—to go?

FRANK: Oh yes . . . you're quite free.

ARTHUR: Laura, you understand, don't you . . . I must go.

LAURA: Yes Arthur.

ARTHUR: And you. . . ?

FRANK: Arthur! How can you. . . ?

LAURA (*cutting in*): It's no use, Frank. I must.

ARTHUR: Laura!

LAURA: I don't know whether he should or shouldn't go . . . but I don't care any more . . . I only know that wherever Arthur goes . . . whatever you or Manning or anyone suspects . . . I must go too. I'd better start to pack.

[*She moves towards the bedroom. The main door opens and Manning comes in and stops her.*]

MANNING: Don't be in too great a hurry, Mrs. Ross.
ARTHUR (*to Frank*): You were lying. (*To Manning.*) He said we were free to go. . . .
MANNING: So you are, Dr. Ross, I assure you—but I should like a few words with you first. . . .
ARTHUR: No—I won't listen to you—either of you—not any more.
MANNING: Sit down, Dr. Ross. . . .
ARTHUR: No!
MANNING: Sit down, Dr. Ross . . . please.

[*Laura goes to Arthur. She takes his hand in hers. Slowly, holding on to Laura's hand, Arthur sits.*]

MANNING: Thank you.

[*There is a knock at the door and Hughie opens it.*]

HUGHIE: Is your name Manning?
MANNING: Yes.
HUGHIE: There's a chap at the door says he's got something for you. He won't give it me and I won't let him in. I've put the chain up.
MANNING: Frank, will you?

[*Manning nods to Frank, who goes.*]

HUGHIE. Are you all right, Mr. . . ? (*He is looking at Arthur.*)
LAURA: Yes, yes, of course, Hughie.
HUGHIE: I've been watching him. He was standing outside on the landing.
LAURA: There's nothing to worry about.
HUGHIE: I dare say . . . but I've been hearing a bit of shouting from up here. I just wanted to make it clear that I can be up these stairs in a minute if I'm wanted. (*To Manning.*) Just you remember that.

[*He exits.*]

MANNING: You seem to have made a friend, Dr. Ross.

[*Frank returns, carrying an envelope which he gives to Manning.*]

FRANK: Eric. He said it was urgent.

[*Manning looks at the contents of the envelope, then puts it in his pocket.*]

MANNING: Yes. Now, Dr. Ross, tell me . . . the night you talked to Fletcher . . . the night you had to talk to someone who could understand . . . what exactly did Fletcher say?

ARTHUR: I . . . I . . . don't know . . . I can't remember.

MANNING: That's not true, Ross.

ARTHUR: What do you want me to say? I tell you I can't remember what he said . . . only what he did. I'm not likely to forget that.

MANNING: What was it?

ARTHUR: He laughed. . . .

MANNING: I see. And yet you went on . . . telling him everything . . . describing all your recent development work . . . in every detail?

ARTHUR: I tried at first to tell him just enough to grasp the fundamentals of the problem but it was no use. Once I'd started I couldn't stop . . . it was like opening a sluice and letting the waters pour out. When you've carried so many secrets in your head for so long you have only to let one go . . . no matter how small, and the crack is there, and then the others pour out and there is nothing you can do to hold them back.

MANNING: And when you'd finished, Fletcher only laughed?

ARTHUR: Yes.

MANNING: Then why did he bother to betray . . . in every detail . . . all you had told him?

ARTHUR: Even failure has its value. It can teach a lot. Haven't you learnt that? Fletcher knew, from the depths of his scientific training that even my failure might be of some use to someone—somewhere.

MANNING: It wasn't a question of *someone—somewhere*—Ross.

ARTHUR: Oh, I know you're convinced that Fletcher had the whole thing planned to the last inch, that I was in league with him, and all the rest of it, but you're wrong. You were wrong about me and you're wrong about him. What he did must have been the outcome of a sudden wild impulse. If he'd realised what he was doing he would never have done it—above all, he would never have done anything to hurt me. I tell you I've known him since he was a boy. Someone must have filled him up with a lot of political rubbish and he just lost his head.

MANNING: Did he? For the past year I've had a copy of his report in my office. It's a remarkably comprehensive document. I wish all my men could lose their heads to such accurate purpose. Fletcher was no amateur with crazy ideals—he'd been trained to perfection. He sold you out once and you know it.

ARTHUR: All right, Manning. All right. He sold me out. Well, since then he's learnt his lesson.

MANNING: I wonder. In a few moments I'm going to ask for your final decision, but before that there's just one question.

ARTHUR: No! No more questions. I've answered enough. You have no right to question me.

MANNING: I have every right in the world. You are the man without rights. You are the traitor, Ross.

You betrayed everyone in this room . . . this city . . . this country . . . and you did it deliberately.

ARTHUR: That's a lie. . . .

MANNING: You did it deliberately! For what? I was standing outside on that landing and heard you tell your tale of misery. I heard a man who once held a position of trust wallowing in an orgy of self-pity because one of his miserable little experiments was a failure.

ARTHUR (*rushes at Manning but is held back by Frank*): What do you know of failure? What do you know of the way it stares you in the face? Day and night until you can't escape. Until it eats down inside you and tears you to pieces. Get him out of here, for God's sake! I can't stand any more.

LAURA: Go. Please go at once.

[*Frank holds door open.*]

MANNING: Mrs. Ross, you would not ask me to go if you realised the importance of what your husband has just said.

LAURA: I don't understand you.

MANNING: Of course you don't. Shut the door. (*Frank closes it.*) I had to goad him beyond reason and calculated effect. There had to be a moment of unmistakable truth. I believe there has been.

LAURA: What do you mean?

MANNING: I mean, Mrs. Ross, that had your husband been working for the other people he would have known beyond any shadow of doubt that his discovery was not a failure.

FRANK: *What?*

MANNING: I had to be sure that he did not know.

FRANK: That was it! That was the thing that turned up! That was why I was sent here!

MANNING: Exactly.

FRANK: Arthur was right, don't you see? He was right all the time, and they knew it!

LAURA: Arthur was *right*?

MANNING: I don't know what salary Cantrup offered your husband, Mrs. Ross, but you can take it from me they would consider him cheap at—say—£50,000.

ARTHUR: I was—right?

MANNING: The people to whom Fletcher made his report are capable of producing that same strange pattern of yours whenever they wish.

LAURA: Oh, my God!

ARTHUR: What did you say? Whenever they wish?

MANNING: Thanks to Fletcher. To your face he laughed; in his report he said yours might well be the most brilliant conception of our time. He sold you out once and now he's doing it again. He's the man who sent that letter to the Press. He's the man they've been waiting for to come out of prison and approach you direct—the personal touch—the repentant disciple. But the moment he came out I put the pressure on. The plan went wrong so they had to improvise. This photograph was taken since I arrived here less than an hour ago. It shows two men at a street corner in the centre of this city. One of them has just given the other a light for his cigarette. A casual encounter lasting less than ten seconds. Now, look. Is the man on the left Cantrup?

ARTHUR: Yes.

MANNING: Tell me if you recognise the other man?

ARTHUR: Fletcher. The other man is Bernard Fletcher.

MANNING: Now are you convinced? If you join Cantrup you join Fletcher and all he stands for—for them you can resume work on your old project . . . at any price you care to name.

FRANK: And if not?

MANNING: I can't answer that. Well, Doctor, I've laid all my cards on the table. Now make your choice. Go or stay, exactly as you wish.
LAURA: Arthur.
MANNING: No, Mrs. Ross. The choice must be his alone.

[*Arthur goes to the telephone and dials.*]

ARTHUR: Cantrup? Ross. The answer is yes, at nine-thirty.

[*Arthur replaces receiver. Manning moves to door.*]

Manning, the appointment is at nine-thirty. Take my place.

[*He throws Cantrup's card on table.*]

MANNING: Thank you, Doctor. I am sorry I had to drive you so far. It had to be done, but I should like you to believe that I found no joy in doing it. Good-night.
FRANK: Manning! There's something more to tell, isn't there? Tell it!
MANNING (*smiling*): Are you threatening me, Frank?
FRANK: No. I'm asking for the inducement—the stick of rock you couldn't hold out before. I'm asking you to be indiscreet for once. I'm asking you to have a heart! Have I got to wring it out of you?
MANNING (*he is looking at Arthur*): It will surprise you to know it has already been wrung. (*A pause. He makes up his mind.*) You're right, Frank. There are exceptions to all rules—even mine. (*He comes down to Arthur.*) Dr. Ross, I have seen your pattern.
ARTHUR: Seen it? Where?

MANNING: In your old laboratory. We couldn't let Fletcher's friends have it all their own way, you know. When the news of their success came a year ago, there was no hesitation then in setting up a special department to continue your work. Your old colleague, Dr. Haseldine, is in charge. And as I have gone so far I may as well go further. Telephone Haseldine on Monday, Doctor. I am going to recommend he doesn't hang up on you this time. Good-night, Mrs. Ross. Good-night, Doctor. Coming, Frank?
FRANK: Yes. (*Manning and Frank go.*)

[*Laura goes to Arthur. He looks up at her, incredulous of the implications of Manning's last remark. She smiles at him and he knows he is not mistaken. He is struggling hard to return her smile as*

The curtain falls]

www.ingramcontent.com/pod-product-compliance
Lightning Source LLC
LaVergne TN
LVHW021224040526
837984LV00016B/1793